THE HISTORY OF
THE ROMEWARD MOVEMENT
IN THE
CHURCH OF ENGLAND

THE HISTORY
OF THE
ROMEWARD MOVEMENT
IN THE
CHURCH OF ENGLAND
1833–1864

BY

WALTER WALSH

AUTHOR OF
"THE SECRET HISTORY OF THE OXFORD MOVEMENT," ETC.

LONDON
JAMES NISBET & CO., LIMITED
21 BERNERS STREET
1900

PREFACE

MANY books have been written on the Oxford Movement, but this is, so far as I am aware, the first attempt to write its History from the standpoint of an Evangelical Churchman. It will be admitted by all that there is room for a distinctly Protestant, just as much as for a Ritualistic or High Church, record of events which have transformed the outward appearance of a considerable portion of the Church of England during the past sixty-seven years. I have not undertaken this task unasked, nor without a sense of the difficulty to deal with such an important subject in anything like an adequate manner. But I have honestly tried to do my best, and no man can do more than that. As to how far I have succeeded, or failed, others are better able to judge than I am. Although an Evangelical Churchman, I have certainly tried to deal with my theme in no narrow-minded manner. I claim to be as broad as the Church of England, nor would I banish from her ranks any of her loyal sons, though they may disagree with me on minor matters. I believe that I have written nothing but that which will meet with the approbation of old-fashioned High Churchmen and Broad Churchmen, as well as of those who glory in being termed Evangelical Churchmen. And certainly I have set down nothing in malice. I would not willingly misrepresent my opponents; my desire is only to tell the truth about them. It is human to err, yet I have done my best to be accurate. Full references are given for every statement in this work, and nothing is brought forward without ample proof. I am not afraid to have my assertions tested by the original documents. I claim that not more than one alleged fact has been refuted in my last book, *The Secret History of the Oxford Movement*, though the Ritualists in every part of the British Empire have attacked it fiercely again and again during the past three years. Whether I shall be as fortunate this time remains to be seen.

And I have tried to write in moderate language, even about very immoderate and highly censurable conduct. There is much recorded in the following pages which would justify stronger language than I have applied to it; but I prefer that my readers shall judge the Romeward Movement in the Church of England by *facts* rather than by adjectives of abuse and insult. I cannot, of course, expect to please the Ritualists; indeed, I think it possible that they will be even more angry with this book than with its predecessor, for, in some respects, the facts here recorded are more damaging to their cause than those revealed in the *Secret History*. The exposures, herein contained, of the conduct of not a few of the leaders of the Oxford Movement will be unpleasant reading for their followers, as well as for those loyal Churchmen who love honest, straightforward conduct, and hate all crooked ways and double-dealing. It is a sad, though true, story I have to relate. Yet these are days when the truth, however unpleasant, needs to be told without fear or favour, and in the plainest terms.

No candid person who reads this book can fail to see that the destination of the Oxford Movement from its very birth has been Rome. The evidence is too abundant and clear to leave room for doubt. For Corporate Reunion with Rome Newman (in his Anglican days), Froude, Keble, and, above all, Dr. Pusey, laboured and prayed. They did not wish to go to Rome as individuals. They wished to take the whole Church of England, with all her Cathedrals and Parish Churches, and her vast wealth, with them—a present worthy of the Pope's acceptance, and on conditions easy for him to accept. Nothing less than this would satisfy them, and nothing less than this will satisfy the leaders of the Ritualists of the present day. But before they can succeed the Protestantism of the Church must be destroyed, and the work God did for us in the sixteenth century, through the Protestant Martyrs and Reformers, must be undone. How they hope to accomplish this, and the tactics necessary for such a cause, are revealed in these pages. It is an attack not merely on the

Protestantism of the Church of England, but of the whole nation also, with which we have to deal. What affects the National Church must, indirectly at least, affect Free Churchmen also. They have cause to dread the Romeward Movement; while the Church of Rome has cause to view it with unbounded joy. It is *her* work that the Ritualists are doing, and if it is allowed to go on unhindered we may expect ere long that the forces of Rome and of the Romanisers will join hands, with a view to destroying our National Protestantism by political weapons. And, therefore, it is that I rejoice to see the formation of an organisation like the Imperial Protestant Federation, in which some twenty-seven organisations have united, on strictly Evangelical lines, to defend Reformation principles against the attacks of Romanists and Romanisers, quite apart from ordinary views of Church polity and party politics. I believe that, with God's blessing, this Federation has a great future before it, in the Colonies as well as in the mother country. While Ritualists are looking to the Church of Rome for unity, let true Protestants seek unity with their brethren who hold the Evangelical faith. It was so at the time of the Reformation. Cranmer, Ridley, Latimer, Jewel, and all the learned English Reformers sought brotherly sympathy and help from their Protestant brethren on the Continent, even though they did not accept an Episcopal form of Church government. Their brotherly letters one to another may be read in the publications of the Parker Society, and in the historical works of Burnet and Strype.

I have only been able to bring this History down to the year 1864. If God shall spare my life I may complete it at a future date. It is not a repetition of my *Secret History*, but an entirely distinct work, covering different ground, though here and there I have been compelled, in a few instances only, to touch upon subjects already referred to. The book is issued with thankfulness to God for the wide circulation throughout the British Empire of my former work, and with an earnest prayer that He may graciously use this volume to open still more widely the eyes of the British nation to the many dangers which surround it from the labours of a gigantic army within the gates, whose dearest ambition it is to bring us back to the spiritual darkness of the Dark Ages, to the rule of priestcraft, and to the intolerable bondage of the Papacy. But, "We are not of the night, nor of the darkness. Therefore let us not sleep, as do others; but let us watch and be sober" (1 Thess. v. 5, 6).

W. W.

LONDON, *October* 30, 1900.

CONTENTS

CHAPTER I

The Reformation and Justification by Faith—The Evangelical Party represents the Reformers — Evangelicals and Puritans — The Evangelical Revival—What It did for the Church and Nation—Testimony of Canon Liddon, Mr. Gladstone, Dean Church, Lord Selborne, and Mr. Lecky—The Oxford Movement not a supplement to the Evangelical Revival—The two Movements were antagonistic — The Rule of Faith—The Founder of the Oxford Movement — Its real object — Was Newman ever an Evangelical?—Newman's early life—Blanco White's warning—What Newman thought of the Reformation in 1833 . . . 1

CHAPTER II

The Birth of the Oxford Movement—Newman and Froude's Interview with Wiseman at Rome—Its deep impression on Wiseman's mind — His bright expectations from it — Was the Tractarian Movement born in Oxford or Rome?—Keble's sermon on *National Apostasy*—He denounces the State and exalts the Church—Archbishop Sumner on Foreign Protestant Non-Episcopal Pastors—The Tractarians on Church and State—Generally favourable to entire separation—Dr. Arnold's *Principles of Church Reform*—Its good and objectionable features—Newman wants to "make a row in the world"—The Conference at Hadleigh—The Association of Friends of the Church—Its plans of work—Efforts to win Evangelical Churchmen—"The seeds of revolution planted"—They wished to bring back the principles of Laud—Clerical and Lay addresses to the Archbishop of Canterbury—The *Tracts for the Times*—Their Romeward tendency—Newman called a "Papist"—Names of the writers of the *Tracts for the Times* — Dr. Pusey joins the Movement—Fasting—Roman Catholic opinion of the *Tracts*—Exalting the priesthood—Dr. Arnold's faithful warning . . 18

CHAPTER III

The first "outbreak of Tractism"—Dr. Hampden's case—Newman on Subscription to the Articles—He was "not a great friend to them"—Hampden appointed Regius Professor of Divinity—

Agitation against his appointment—Lord Melbourne's letter to Pusey—Newman's *Elucidations*—Stanley's opinion of them—Dr. Wilberforce and Hampden—Lord Selborne and Dean Church's testimony as to Hampden's views—The real cause of opposition was Hampden's Protestantism—Proof of his Protestantism—Extracts from his writings—Vote of want of confidence by Convocation—Hampden's Letter to the Archbishop of Canterbury—Mr. Macmullen's case—Hampden appointed Bishop of Hereford—Protest of thirteen Bishops—Lord John Russell's reply—Archdeacon Hare defends Hampden—A Prosecution commenced—Organised by Pusey, Keble, Marriott, and Mozley—Wilberforce's eleven questions for Hampden—His answer—The Bishop withdraws his Letters of Request—Pusey's bitter disappointment—Tractarian anxiety to prosecute their opponents—Bishop Phillpotts denounces the Episcopal Veto—Protests by the Dean of Hereford—Hampden elected Bishop by the Chapter of Hereford—Protest in Bow Church—An exciting scene—Consecration of Dr. Hampden—The new Bishop's sympathisers—Addresses of confidence . . . 46

CHAPTER IV

Dr. Pusey's early Protestantism—Extracts from his *Historical Enquiry*—His Theological Society—"The young Monks"—The *Library of the Fathers*—Mr. Bickersteth approves of the *Library*—Lord Selborne on the Fathers—Richard Hurrell Froude—His influence on Newman—His admiration of Rome, and dislike of the Reformation—Newman's early love of Rome—His mind "essentially Jesuitical"—Froude's *Remains*—Extracts from the *Remains*, showing his Romanising principles—Professor Faussett's University sermon against the Tractarians—The Rev. Peter Maurice's *Popery in Oxford*—Dr. Pusey insults Mr. Maurice—Newman's reply to Faussett—Dr. Hook's *Call to Union*—Bishop of Oxford's Visitation Charge—The Oxford Martyrs' Memorial—Pusey thinks it "unkind to the Church of Rome"—Keble thinks Cranmer a Heretic—"Cranmer burnt well"—Tractarian opposition to the Memorial—The inscription on the Oxford Martyrs' Memorial 86

CHAPTER V

Newman in 1839—Influenced by an article in the *Dublin Review*—Remarkable acknowledgments—Corporate Reunion with Rome—Preparing the way for Rome—The Pastor of Antwerp—Breakfasts with Newman and his friends—Startling and treasonable advice given him—Pusey writes on *Tendencies to Romanism*—He pleads for peace in the Church—Dr. M'Crie on the cry for peace—Prayers for the Dead—Breeks v. Woolfrey—West v. Shuttleworth—Egerton v. All of Rode—Moresby Faculty Case—Dr. Pusey begins to hear Confessions in 1838—In 1846 he goes to Confession for the first time—His Protestant notes in the Works of Tertullian—Wiseman hopes the Tractarians will "succeed in their work"—He realises the Roman tendency of their teaching—Extracts from the *Tracts for the Times*—Margaret Chapel as a centre of Tractarianism—Mr. Serjeant Bellasis—Oakeley claims the right to "hold all Roman doctrine"—He is prosecuted by the Bishop of London His licence revoked—Pusey defends Oakeley—Says the judgment against him has no moral force—Pusey says he believes in Purgatory and Invocation of Saints—Thinks England and Rome "not irreconcilably at variance"—Oakeley secedes to Rome 114

CHAPTER VI

Tract XC.—List of Pamphlets on *Tract XC.*—Newman's object in writing the *Tract*—Extracts from it—Rejoicings at Oscott—The letter of the Four Tutors—Dr. Arnold's opinion of the *Tract*—Declaration by the Heads of Houses—Interesting letter from one of the Four Tutors—Newman's *Letter to Dr. Jelf*—Wiseman's attitude towards the advanced Tractarians—Ward's traitorous letter to the *Univers*—An English Catholic's letter to Newman—Wiseman's reply to Newman—Mr. Ambrose Lisle Phillipps' letter—The Bishop of Oxford's difficulties—His correspondence with Pusey and Newman—The *Tracts for the Times* discontinued—Newman's *Letter to the Bishop of Oxford*—Newman withdraws his "dirty words" against Rome—His reasons for doing so—The Rev. William George Ward—Thinks the Reformers guilty of rebellion and perjury—Mr. Percival's defence of the *Tracts for the Times*—Keble's defence of *Tract XC.*—His opinion on Canonical Obedience to the Bishops—Pusey's defence of *Tract XC.*—Manning's dislike for *Tract XC.*—Bricknell's *Judgment of the Bishops upon Tractarian Theology*—What the Bishops said against *Tract XC.* 147

CHAPTER VII

Mr. Golightly's letters to the *Standard*—His serious charges against Ward and Bloxam—Palmer of Magdalen anathematises Protestantism—Startling revelations—Mr. Ambrose Phillipps de Lisle—A secret Papal emissary to the Oxford Romanisers—De Lisle intimate with and trusted by the Oxford leaders—Newman's Correspondence with De Lisle—De Lisle hopes to introduce some foreign Theologians to his Oxford friends—He promises to be "prudent and reserved"—Bloxam's fear of publicity—De Lisle's extraordinary letter to his wife—The Oxford men wish "to come to an understanding with the Pope at once"—Their proposals to be sent to the Pope—The Fathers of Charity—A startling suggestion—Cordial meetings at Oxford between the Tractarians and Romanists—Negotiations with Wiseman and Rome—Wiseman visits Oxford—Has an interview with Newman—Wiseman writes to Rome for secret instruction and guidance—He desires to become "the organ of intercourse" between Rome and Oxford—A secret conspiracy—De Lisle's letter to Lord Shrewsbury—It is necessary "to blind" the Low Church party—"Throwing dust in the eyes of Low Churchmen"—"Unpleasant disclosures" in the papers—"A holy reserve"—Ward's double-dealing—Remains in the Church of England "to bring many towards Rome"—The ultimate aim "submission to Rome" 180

CHAPTER VIII

The Jerusalem Bishopric—Chevalier Bunsen's mission to England—Puseyite opposition—Hope-Scott's objections—Dr. Hook supports the Bishopric—His description of the Romanisers—Pusey's *Letter to the Archbishop of Canterbury*—Lord Ashley's letter to Pusey—Mr. Gladstone supports the Bishopric—Newman and the Jerusalem Bishopric—He thinks it "atrocious" and "hideous"—His Protest—Contest for Professorship of Poetry—Isaac Williams and *Reserve in Communicating Religious Knowledge*—Extracts from his writings—Mr. Garbett, the Protestant candidate—Samuel Wilberforce on the contest—He denounces the Romanisers—Success of the Protestant candidate—Secessions to Rome—The Rev. F. W. Faber—His visit to the Continent—His *Sights and Thoughts in Foreign Churches*—How he deceived the public—The Rev. William Goode—His Protestant works—His *Case as It Is*—His *Divine Rule of Faith and Practice*—Bishop Bagot's Visitation Charge—Mr. Goode answers it—The Parker Society 201

CHAPTER IX

Dr. Pusey's sermon on *The Holy Eucharist*—Denounced to the Vice-Chancellor—The Six Doctors—Their opinion of the sermon—Private negotiations with Pusey—Pusey suspended for two years—His protest—Dr. Hawkins' explanatory letter—Proposed friendly prosecution—Lord Camoys on Pusey's sermon—Curious Clerical Libel Case—An extraordinary Clerical Brawling Case—Protests against Puseyism—The *English Churchman* started by the Puseyites—Newman's progress

Romeward—He resigns St. Mary's and retires to Littlemore—Archdeacon Wilberforce on "the insane love for Rome"—Palmer's *Narrative of Events*—Pusey issues "adapted" Roman Catholic books of devotion—Newman tells him they will "promote the cause of the Church of Rome"—Hook thinks "they will make men Infidels"—Extracts from these books—What Pius IX. said about Dr. Pusey—Bishop Blomfield on the effect of adapted Roman books—Puseyites advocate Ecclesiastical Prosecutions of Protestant clergy—The Bishop of Exeter and the Surplice in the Pulpit—Legality of the Black Gown in the Pulpit—Ward's *Ideal of a Christian Church*—Puseyite attack on Dr. Symons—Defeated—Attempt to prosecute the Rev. James Garbett—Failure—Stone Altars and Credence Tables—*Faulkener* v. *Litchfield*—Judgment of the Court of Arches—The Cambridge Camden Society—Denounced by the Rev. F. Close . 226

CHAPTER X

Pusey thinks that God is "drawing" Newman to Rome—Pusey refuses to write against the Church of Rome—Newman secedes to Rome—Father Dominic's narrative of Newman's reception—Pusey on the secession—Newman goes to see the Pope—When and where was Newman ordained a Roman Catholic? Some noteworthy circumstances—St. Saviour's, Leeds—Founded by Dr. Pusey—He insists on an Altar—The distinction between an Altar and a Table—Dr. Hook's anxiety—Dr. Wilberforce appointed Bishop of Oxford—Pusey tries to secure his goodwill for Puseyism—He fails—Pusey's desire for Union with Rome—His subtle tactics with his penitents—Hook believes Pusey is under the influence of the Jesuits—The Exeter Surplice Riots—Debate in the House of Lords—More Puseyite exhortations to prosecute Evangelical clergy—An extraordinary case in Salisbury Diocese—*Extempore* prayers in a Schoolroom "a gross scandal"—The case of the Rev. James Shore—Pusey's Sermon on *The Entire Absolution of the Penitent*—Extracts from the Sermon—Pusey goes to Confession for the first time—The effect of Pusey's Confessional work on his penitents—Testimony of Dean Boyle—Clerical Retreats 256

CHAPTER XI

Trouble at St. Saviour's, Leeds — Secessions to Rome — Hook's vigorous attack on Pusey—"It is mere Jesuitism"—"A semi-Papal colony"—Hook hopes all the Romanisers will go to Rome—Bishop Phillpotts prosecutes a Puseyite clergyman—The Cross on a Communion Table—The present state of the law on this point—Reducing the distance to Rome—Sackville College, East Grinstead—The Rev. J. M. Neale inhibited—*Freeland* v. *Neale*—The Gorham Case—Judgment of the Court of Arches—Judgment of the Judicial Committee of Privy Council—Puseyite Protest against the judgment—Dr. Pusey and Keble wish to prosecute Gorham for heresy—Bishop Phillpotts threatens to excommunicate the Archbishop of Canterbury—The Exeter Synod—The case of the Rev. T. W. Allies—His extraordinary and disloyal conduct—His visit to Rome—The Pope tells him that Pusey has "prepared the way for Catholicism"—What Mr. Allies told the Pope—Allies secedes to Rome—Correspondence with Pusey on Auricular Confession—Startling charges against Pusey—"In fear and trembling on their knees before you"—"The rules of the Church of Rome are your rules"—How the Oxford Movement helped Rome—Wilberforce calls Pusey "a decoy bird" for the Papal net—He says that he is "doing the work of a Roman Confessor"—The Papal Aggression—Lord John Russell's Durham Letter—Bishop Blomfield on the Romeward Movement—St. Paul's, Knightsbridge—St. Barnabas', Pimlico—Riots in St. Barnabas' Church—Resignation of the Rev. W. J. E. Bennett—St. Saviour's, Leeds—Traitorous resolutions of twelve clergymen—A Confessional inquiry by the Bishop—The Clergy defend questioning women on the Seventh Commandment 284

CHAPTER XII

The Bristol Church Union—Pusey objects to a protest against Rome—Archbishop Tait on the Church Discipline Act—The Judicial Committee of Privy Council—Lay Address to the Queen—Her Majesty's action in response—Lay Address to the Archbishop of Canterbury—The appeal to the Bishops—An Episcopal Manifesto—A Clerical and Lay Declaration in support of the Gorham judgment—The Confessional at Plymouth—Revival and reform of Convocation—Prosecution of Archdeacon Denison—The power and privileges of examining chaplains—The Archbishop's Commission of Inquiry—The Archbishop's judgment at Bath—How the Archdeacon evaded punishment—Pusey hoists the flag of rebellion—The protest against the Bath judgment—The Society of the Holy Cross—The Association for the Promotion of the Unity of Christendom—Startling revelations as to its early history—Secret negotiations with Rome—De Lisle's secret letter to Cardinal Barnabo—The Cardinal's answer—Newman consulted by De Lisle—The conspirators meet in London—Their secret, traitorous, and treacherous message to the Pope—The case of *Westerton* v. *Liddell*—Judgment—A Ritualistic rebel 326

CHAPTER XIII

The Convent Case at Lewes—Charges against the Rev. J. M. Neale—Riot at Lewes at the burial of a Sister of Mercy—Bishop of Chichester's letters to Mr. Scobell and the Mother Superior—The Bishop withdraws his patronage from St. Margaret's, East Grinstead—Threatening the Bishop—Mr. Neale's pamphlet—His underhand conduct—Confession on the sly—The Case of the Rev. Alfred Poole—His licence withdrawn—His admissions—Remarkable assertions at a Communicants' Meeting—Mr. Poole appeals to the Archbishop of Canterbury—His judgment The Lavington Case—Romanising books—Theological Colleges—Attack upon Cuddesdon College—Mr. Golightly's *Facts and Documents Showing the Alarming State of the Diocese of Oxford*—An exciting controversy 363

CHAPTER XIV

The St. George's in the East Riots—The Rev. Bryan King—The Rev. Hugh Allen—The attitude of the Bishop of London—The Rector resigns—Church of England Protection Society—Formation of the English Church Union—Its early delight in Ecclesiastical Prosecutions—Opposes Prayer Book Revision "at present"—Dr. Littledale advocates "Catholic Revision"—He is "bowed down" with grief, shame, and indignation—Expulsion of Protestant clergymen aimed at—Preaching in Theatres "a profane and degrading practice"—The Union attempts to prosecute Evangelical clergymen — The Union praises the Bishop of Salisbury for prosecuting Dr. Williams—The Union demands the prosecution and deprivation of the Evangelical Bishop Waldegrave—The E.C.U. demands a cheap and easy way to prosecute Archbishops, Bishops, and clergy—Tries to prosecute foreign Protestant Pastors—The *Church Review* says the Union was established to "enforce the law"—It declares that "to silence the teaching of heresy is the plain duty of the Church's Governors"—Dr. Pusey prosecutes Professor Jowett—Pusey says that "prosecution is not persecution"—The *Church Review* praises prosecutors as men of "moral courage"—The President of the E.C.U. promises obedience to the Courts of Judicature 405

INDEX 421

THE HISTORY OF THE ROMEWARD MOVEMENT IN THE CHURCH OF ENGLAND

1833–1864

CHAPTER I

The Reformation and Justification by Faith—The Evangelical Party represents the Reformers — Evangelicals and Puritans—The Evangelical Revival—What It did for the Church and Nation—Testimony of Canon Liddon, Mr. Gladstone, Dean Church, Lord Selborne, and Mr. Lecky—The Oxford Movement not a supplement to the Evangelical Revival — The two Movements were antagonistic—The Rule of Faith—The Founder of the Oxford Movement—Its real object—Was Newman ever an Evangelical?—Newman's early life—Blanco White's warning—What Newman thought of the Reformation in 1833.

At the Protestant Reformation there was one truth which, perhaps, more than any other, came before the world with all the freshness and power of a new revelation from God. It had been revealed to man fifteen hundred years before in the New Testament, but there it had remained buried during the Dark Ages, unheard of and unknown to those to whom the Bible was a closed book. Men learnt, in the sixteenth century, with joyful surprise, that it was possible to obtain absolution of their sins, and an entrance to Heaven, without the assistance of any Sacrificing Priest, and without the aid of a Father Confessor. They learnt that it was the blessed privilege of even the vilest and most sinful to go for pardon direct to the Saviour of mankind, to approach direct to the Mercy Seat, without money and without price, and without any priestly intervention or aid. "At the very root of the Reformation changes," said the Bishop of Winchester, in his Visitation Charge, in 1899, "lay the principle of the direct access of the individual soul to God, without human intervention of any kind, a principle which destroys the whole theory upon which the Roman Confessional had built its power."[1] This doctrine was embodied by our Reformers in the *Book of Homilies*, in which we are taught, as to the application of the merits of Christ to our souls :—" Herein thou needest no other man's help, no other sacrifice or Oblation, no Sacrificing Priest, no Mass, no means established by man's invention."[2]

The acceptance of this grand and glorious truth made our Reformers free men. It was the death-knell of priest-craft, and the grave of Sacerdotalism. The cry of "No priest between the sinner and his Saviour," soon led to the further cry of "No Pope between the Englishman and his Sovereign." The rule of the priest was intolerable for men who were no longer spiritual slaves, and submission to Papal Supremacy became an impossibility for free-born Englishmen. Round this great truth, this doctrine of Justification by Faith only, centred the whole battle of the Reformation. Everything else, however important in itself, was of comparatively little moment. Here we have the real heart and soul of the Reformation Movement; this is the centre from which its pulsations vibrate, and from which its life-blood flows. Those who preach it are alone the true descendants of those to whom, under God, we owe the English Reformation of the sixteenth century. It is quite a mistake to suppose that the Evangelical party is new in the Reformed Church of England. The Reformers, with scarcely a solitary exception, held Evangelical doctrines, while their Protestantism was far more extreme than anything heard from Protestant platforms in the present day. A study of their writings, as reprinted by the Parker Society nearly sixty years since, affords ample evidence of their hatred of Sacerdotalism. Evangelical Churchmen do not represent

[1] *The Times*, October 2, 1899.
[2] *Homily Concerning the Sacrament*, Part I.

now the Puritan party of the reign of Elizabeth, who were bitterly opposed to the Episcopal form of Church government, while Evangelical Churchmen were its warm friends. The Churchmen who fought against the Elizabethan Puritans held Evangelical views. All other parties within the Church date their birth from long after the Reformation.

Canon Overton, a member of the English Church Union, proves conclusively how great was the difference between Evangelical Churchmen and Puritans.

"The typical Puritan," he says, "was gloomy and austere; the typical Evangelical was bright and genial. The Puritan would not be kept within the pale of the National Church; the Evangelical would not be kept out of it. The Puritan was dissatisfied with our Liturgy, our ceremonies, our vestments, and our hierarchy; the Evangelical was perfectly contented with them. If Puritanism was the more fruitful in theological literature, Evangelicalism was infinitely more fruitful in works of piety and benevolence; there was hardly a single missionary or philanthropic scheme of the day which was not either originated or warmly taken up by the Evangelical party. The Puritans were frequently in antagonism with 'the powers that be,' the Evangelicals never; no amount of ill-treatment could put them out of love with our constitution in both Church and State."[1]

The Evangelical Movement of the latter half of the eighteenth and the early part of the nineteenth centuries was a *Revival* and not a *Birth*. It did great things for England and England's Church, as even those who have been its keenest critics have admitted. The testimony of Canon Liddon, the intimate friend and biographer of Dr. Pusey is, on this subject, important. He writes:—

"In its earlier days the Evangelical Movement was mainly if not exclusively interested in maintaining a certain body of positive truth. The great doctrines which alone make 'repentance towards God and faith towards our Lord Jesus Christ' seriously possible were its constant theme. The world to come, with its boundless issues of life and death, the infinite value of the one Atonement, the regenerating, purifying, guiding action of God the Holy Spirit in respect of

---

[1] Overton's *English Church in the Eighteenth Century*, chap. iii.

the Christian soul, were preached to our grandfathers with a force and earnestness which are beyond controversy. The deepest and most fervid religion in England during the first three decades of this century was that of the Evangelicals; and, to the last day of his life, Pusey retained that 'love of the Evangelicals' to which he often adverted, and which was roused by their efforts to make religion a living power in a cold and gloomy age."[1]

We thus learn that the Evangelicals were chiefly engaged on the most important subjects affecting the glory of God and the salvation of human souls, and that, under God, to them it is mainly due that true religion was revived as "a living power in a cold and gloomy age." What higher praise could be offered to any Church party than this, which comes from one of the warmest friends of the Oxford Movement? I may now be permitted to cite the opinion of Mr. Gladstone, who, in his essay on "The Evangelical Movement," which first appeared in the *British Quarterly Review* for July 1879, pointed out what he conceived to be many serious defects in its system. Yet even he was constrained to admit that, "though Evangelicalism as a system may have been eminently narrow and inconsequent, it was born to do a noble work, and that the men to whom the work was committed, were men worthy of this high election."[2] Mr. H. O. Wakeman, an active supporter of the Ritualists, admits that, "During the latter part of the eighteenth century the Evangelical party were the salt of the Church of England."[3]

Two more High Churchmen I will quote before I pass on. The testimony of the first of these proves that the Evangelical Revival was powerful in the interests of philanthropy, and did not forget the interests of the body while engaged chiefly in looking after the eternal welfare of immortal souls. The late Dean Church had many supposed faults to point out in the Evangelical Movement when he wrote his historical sketch of *The Oxford Movement;* but he acknowledged that

"Evangelical religion had not been unfruitful, especially in

---

[1] Liddon's *Life of Dr. Pusey*, vol. i. p. 255.
[2] Gladstone's *Gleanings of Past Years*, vol. vii. p. 236.
[3] Wakeman's *History of the Church of England*, p. 452, 6th edition.

public results. It had led Howard and Elizabeth Fry to assail the brutalities of the prisons. It led Clarkson and Wilberforce to overthrow the slave trade, and ultimately slavery itself. It had created great Missionary Societies. It had given motive and impetus to countless philanthropic schemes."[1]

In this Dean Church was of one mind with the Evangelical Lord Shaftesbury, who with truth declared:—"I am satisfied that most of the great philanthropic movements of the century have sprung from" the Evangelicals.[2]

The testimony of the late Earl of Selborne, at one time Lord Chancellor of England, a decided High Churchman, though not a Ritualist, is important. He says:—

"Next to the home influence which surrounded me, none contributed more to preserve the balance of my mind than that of the excellent representatives of 'Evangelical' opinion, with whom I had been brought into contact. There were many things in that system, particularly the Calvinistic tenets held by the most powerful of its teachers, with which I never agreed; and it always seemed to me defective, as leaving too much out of sight the organic side of Christianity. But in its spirituality, in its constant presentation of Christ and His work as the foundation of faith and practice, and in its reverence for the Scriptures, I thought it set an example which all might have done well to follow."[3]

One of the most bitter writers against the Evangelical party whom I have ever met with is the Rev. W. H. B. Proby, an enthusiastic supporter of the Ritualistic party. Yet even he, writing in 1888, was compelled to acknowledge its services both to the Church of England and to the cause of practical godliness.

"And what, with all this dignity and influence," he asks, "had the Low Church party effected? They had effected a true conversion to God in Christ in the cases of numberless individuals, and they had effected certain reforms and improvements in the English Church at large, tending to the edification of individuals. Then

---

[1] *The Oxford Movement.* By Dean Church, p. 13, 1st edition.
[2] *Life and Work of the Seventh Earl of Shaftesbury*, popular edition, p. 519.
[3] *Memorials Family and Personal*, 1766-1865. By the Earl of Selborne, vol. i. p. 211.

they had been the means of improving the psalmody, by the singing of hymns, the psalmody having previously been confined almost entirely to the performance of metrical versions of Psalms. They had caused the public service of the Church to be gone through generally in a more becoming manner than had too often been customary; doubtless through practising the same rule which in later times was formulated by Charles Simeon, of Cambridge, 'Do not *read* the prayers, but *pray* them.' . . . There was, besides, an improvement of the outward face of society at large. There was less drunkenness in the upper classes, less indecent language, and less profane swearing. Shops were not so frequently opened on Good Friday. And of course there was an improvement in the general efficiency of the clergy; that is to say, owing to the Low Church movement there were more religious clergymen than there had ever been before. There was an increased care about Divine Service: the Prayer Book (so far, that is, as Low Churchmen chose, or had learnt to use it) was used more devoutly; several parts of the system of religion inculcated by the Church of England began to be made of more account than they had been; people learned to come to church in time for the commencement of the prayers; people were induced to join in the *Amens* and responses aloud."[1]

Many of my readers will, I doubt not, be influenced on this subject by the opinion of an historian, who would pay but little attention to the opinion of divines. I may therefore appeal to the testimony of Mr. Lecky, who also criticises the Evangelical party, but is constrained to acknowledge their valuable services to the country.

"Great, however," he remarks, "as was the importance of the Evangelical Revival in stimulating these [philanthropic] efforts, it had other consequences of perhaps a wider and more enduring influence. Before the close of the century in which it appeared, a spirit had begun to circulate in Europe threatening the very foundations of society and belief. The revolt against the supernatural theory of Christianity which had been conducted by Voltaire and the Encyclopædists . . . had produced in France a revolutionary spirit, which in its intensity and its proselytising fervour was unequalled since the days of the Reformation. . . . Religion, property, civil authority, and domestic life were all assailed, and doctrines incompatible with the very existence of government were embraced by multitudes with the

---

[1] *Annals of the Low Church Party.* By the Rev. W. H. B. Proby, vol. i. pp. 350–352.

fervour of a religion. England, on the whole, escaped the contagion. Many causes conspired to save her, but among them a prominent place must, I believe, be given to the new and vehement religious enthusiasm which was at that very time passing through the middle and lower classes of the people, which had enlisted in its service a large proportion of the wilder and more impetuous reformers, and which recoiled with horror from the anti-Christian tenets that were associated with the Revolution in France." [1]

To have contributed thus powerfully towards preserving England from Atheism and the horrors of the French Revolution constitutes, I venture to suggest, a strong claim on the gratitude of all patriots to the Evangelical party. Referring to the Evangelical leaders of the latter part of the eighteenth and the commencement of the nineteenth centuries, Mr. Lecky affirms that:—

"All these possessed, in an eminent degree, the qualities of heart and mind that influence great masses of men; and they and their colleagues gradually changed the whole spirit of the English Church. They infused into it a new fire and passion of devotion, kindled a spirit of fervent philanthropy, raised the standard of clerical duty, and completely altered the whole tone and tendency of the preaching of its ministers. Before the close of the [eighteenth] century the Evangelical Movement had become the almost undisputed centre of religious activity in England, and it continued to be so till the rise of the Tractarian Movement of 1833." [2]

The Tractarian Movement has been to the Evangelical Movement what the Jesuit Order was to the Reformation. It has paralysed the energies of every Evangelical who has yielded to its influence. It has been frequently asserted that the new Sacerdotal Revival in the Church of England is only supplementary to the Evangelical Movement and is not opposed to it. "The High Church Revival," writes Canon Overton, "was not the antagonist but the supplement of the Evangelical Revival which preceded it." [3] And Canon Liddon asserts that "the Oxford Movement was a completion of the earlier Revival of religion

---

[1] Lecky's *History of England*, vol. iii. pp. 145, 146, edition 1892.
[2] *Ibid.* p. 134.
[3] *The Anglican Revival.* By J. H. Overton, D.D., p. 15.

known as Evangelical."[1] Mr. H. O. Wakeman asserts that the Oxford Movement "did not so much supersede the Caroline, Latitudinarian, and Evangelical Movements as *supplement* them."[2] To all this, so far at least as it applies to the Evangelicals, I reply by denying that the Oxford Movement was either the "supplement" to or the "completion" of the Evangelical Revival; and by asserting most emphatically that its attitude was distinctly antagonistic. If in any sense it was a "supplement" it was in the sense that poison is a supplement to wholesome food. The chief characteristics of Evangelical religion can never be reconciled with the Sacerdotal system. The Evangelical theory that Divine grace with pardon of sins is conveyed *directly* to each individual soul by God Himself, through Jesus Christ, our only Mediator, and not by Sacramental elements or priestly absolution, can never be reconciled with the general teaching of the early Tractarians and their successors of the present day. That well-known champion of Ritualism, the late Rev. Dr. Littledale, perceived and acknowledged this thirty years since. He said: "And first, it ought to be said that they [the 'Catholic and Protestant'] are logically two distinct religions, and not merely differing aspects of the same religion. They are quite as diverse from each other as Judaism is from Islam; though like these two creeds, they have a common stock of books, sacred names, and ideas." And, again: "But the real fact, that these two systems are rival religions, can easily be discovered by considering what we mean by Religion."[3] Another characteristic of Evangelical teaching is the doctrine that the Bible is the sole and only Rule of Faith, and a claim to the right of Private Judgment; while that of the Tractarians and Ritualists is that Tradition also forms a part of the Christian's Rule of Faith, and that Private Judgment is a thing to be condemned. The ingenuity of man can never reconcile these opposing theories together, or prove

[1] *Life of Dr. Pusey*, vol. i. p. 254.
[2] Wakeman's *History of the Church of England*, p. 491.
[3] *The Two Religions.* By Richard F. Littledale, LL.D., pp. 2, 3. London: G. J. Palmer. 1870.

that the one is but the supplement to the other. In this connection it is worthy of note that one of the first blows struck by the leaders of the Oxford Movement was aimed against direct access to God for pardon of sins, and with the object of riveting once more on English Churchmen the intolerable chains of priestcraft. Writing to the Hon. and Rev. A. P. Percival, on August 14, 1833, the Rev. Richard Hurrell Froude announced:—

"Since I have been back to Oxford, Keble has been here, and he, and Palmer, and Newman, have come to an agreement, that the points which ought to be put forward by us are the following:—

"'(1) The doctrine of Apostolic Succession as a rule of practice, *i.e.* that the participation of the body and blood of Christ is essential to the maintenance of Christian life and hope in each individual.

"'(2) That it is conveyed to individual Christians *only* by the hands of the successors of the Apostles, and their delegates.'"[1]

Here it is implied that something which "is essential to the maintenance of Christian life," can "only" be "conveyed to individual Christians," not direct by the Saviour Himself, but by "the successors of the Apostles," a term which, in the estimation of the Tractarians, excluded all ministers who did not possess Episcopal ordination. Here we have the essence of Sacerdotalism, taught by the founders of the Oxford Movement within a month from its birth. In 1835 Newman declared, in his "Advertisement" to the second volume of the *Tracts for the Times*, that "the essence of Sectarian Doctrine" was found in those who "consider faith, and not the Sacraments, as the instrument of justification":—

"We have," he exclaimed, "almost embraced the doctrine, that God conveys grace only through the instrumentality of the mental energies, that is, *through faith*, prayer, active spiritual contemplations, or (what is called) *communion with God*, in contradiction to the primitive view, according to which the Church and her Sacraments are the ordained and direct *visible means of conveying to the soul* what is in itself supernatural and unseen."[2]

---

[1] Percival's *Collection of Papers connected with the Theological Movement of 1833*, p. 12. "*James Skinner*," p. 2.
[2] *Tracts for the Times*, vol. ii. p. vi.

This doctrine, that "visible" things, viz., priests and Sacramental elements, "convey to the soul" Divine grace, instead of its being conveyed "through faith" and by "communion with God," has been the general teaching of the Tractarians and their successors from 1833 to the present time. In recent years, however, it has been expressed in clearer and more daring language. The so-called "Cowley Fathers" teach that :—

"They (priests) are peacemakers under Him who carry on this work for Him, applying the precious Blood to the souls of men by the Sacraments for the remission of sins."[1]

The Rev. Edward Stuart, formerly Vicar of St. Mary Magdalene, Munster Square, London, actually had the daring to write :—

"God alone is the Giver of all spiritual life and grace and favour, and yet we are not bid to *go direct to God* for these gifts (*for that right we forfeited at the Fall*), but we are to go to the Church which stands *between us and God* in its appointed sphere."[2]

On the subject of the Bible as the only Rule of Faith, and the right and duty of Private Judgment in its interpretation, the teaching of Evangelical Churchmen is, as I have just asserted, irreconcilably opposed to that of Tractarians and Ritualists. As early as the month of September 1833—only two months after the birth of the Oxford Movement—Mr. Newman published his views on these gravely important questions. No amount of sophistry could persuade a Protestant Churchman to accept his teaching :—

"Surely," wrote Mr. Newman, "the Sacred Volume was never intended, and is not adapted, to teach us our creed; however certain it is that we can prove our creed from it, when it has once been taught us, and in spite of individual producible exceptions to the general rule. From the very first, that rule has been, as a matter of fact, that the Church should teach the truth, and then should appeal to Scripture in vindication of its own teaching. And from the first, it has been the error of heretics to neglect the information thus pro-

---

[1] *The Evangelist Library: Exposition of the Beatitudes*, p. 31.
[2] *The Mediation of the Church.* By the Rev. Edward Stuart, p. 9.

vided for them, and to attempt of themselves a work to which they are unequal, the eliciting a systematic doctrine from the scattered notices of the truth which Scripture contains. . . . The insufficiency of the mere private study of Holy Scripture for arriving at the exact and entire truth which Scripture really contains, is shown by the fact, that creeds and teachers have ever been divinely provided."[1]

When, in 1837, Mr. Newman published his *Lectures on Popular Protestantism*, he expressed himself more clearly and strongly:—

"Accordingly," he said, "acute men among them [Protestants] see that the very elementary notion which they have adopted, of the Bible without note or comment being the sole authoritative Judge in controversies of faith, is a self-destructive principle."[2]

"For though we consider Scripture a satisfactory, we do not consider it our sole informant in divine truths. We have another source of information in reserve, as I shall presently show. . . . We rely on Antiquity to strengthen such intimations of doctrine as are but faintly, though really, given in Scripture."[3]

"I would not deny as an abstract proposition that a Christian may gain the whole truth from the Scriptures, but would maintain that the chances are very seriously against a given individual. I would not deny, rather I maintain that a religious, wise, and intellectually gifted man will succeed: but who answers to this description but the collective Church?"[4]

Of the Rev. Richard Hurrell Froude, one of the principal founders of the Tractarian Movement, Cardinal Newman states that:—"He felt scorn of the maxim, 'The Bible and the Bible only is the religion of Protestants'; and he gloried in accepting Tradition as a main instrument of religious teaching."[5]

A refutation of the assertions in these extracts would take up several chapters of this work, and would be generally considered out of place here. But I am happy to state that they have all been ably and amply discussed and refuted in Dean Goode's *Divine Rule of Faith and*

---

[1] *The Arians in the Fourth Century.* By the Rev. J. H. Newman, p. 50, 7th edition.
[2] Newman's *Via Media*, vol. i. p. 27, edition 1891.
[3] *Ibid.* pp. 28, 29.
[4] *Ibid.* p. 158.
[5] Newman's *Apologia Pro Vita Sua*, 1st edition, p. 85.

Practice,[1] one of the most valuable works on the subject ever produced by an Evangelical Churchman. It seems a pity that it has never yet been issued in a condensed form in one volume. I need only remark here that once a Christian man gives up the theory that the Bible and the Bible alone contains a perfect Rule of Faith, and at the same time discards the use of Private Judgment, he is open to believe any false doctrine, however preposterous it may be. The ridiculous superstitions now advocated by the Ritualists may be appealed to in proof of this assertion.

Who was the founder of the Oxford Movement? Cardinal Newman asserts that "the true and primary author of it" was the Rev. John Keble.[2] No doubt Newman was better qualified than any other man to express an opinion on this question, yet no one who has carefully studied the early history of the Movement can fail to see that the principal worker and the most prominent figure was Newman himself. The ostensible cause of its birth was the alleged encroachments of the State on the province of the Church, more especially as manifested in the proposal of the Irish Church Temporalities Bill to suppress a large number of the Bishoprics of the Church of Ireland, and the demands of men like Dr. Arnold to enlarge the borders of the Establishment so as to embrace Dissenters. The real reason was the desire to exalt the clergy into a sacerdotal caste, and to bring the laity under the rule of the priesthood, with a view to the Reunion of Christendom. The way for the movement had been prepared by the publication of Keble's *Christian Year* in 1827, and many of the chief actors had themselves been prepared by study and conversations with each other, for the part they were about to take in the work before them. It is quite a mistake to suppose that the founders commenced the Oxford Movement while sound Protestants. I know that Newman is said to have been originally an Evangelical.

[1] *The Divine Rule of Faith and Practice*, 2nd edition. By William Goode, M.A. Three vols. London: J. H. Jackson. 1853.
[2] Newman's *Apologia*, p. 75.

It is true that he was brought up under Evangelical influence, but I do not believe that he ever accepted the system in its entirety. A true Evangelical is one in heart as well as in name, whose soul and life are moved by its Gospel teaching, and not merely his intellect. Much ado is made about his "conversion" in his young days, yet after all it is evident that what *he* meant by it was something different from what Evangelicals themselves mean by the term "conversion." In his "Autobiographical Memoir," written in 1874, he speaks of himself in the third person. In it he affirms:—

"And, in truth, much as he [Newman] owed to the Evangelical teaching, so it was *he never had been a genuine Evangelical.* That teaching had been a great blessing for England; . . . but, after all, the Evangelical teaching, considered as a system and in what was peculiar to itself, *had from the first failed to find a response in his own religious experience*, as afterwards in his parochial. He had indeed been converted by it to a spiritual life, and so far his experience bore witness to its truth; but he had not been converted in that special way which it laid down as imperative, but so plainly against rule, *as to make it very doubtful in the eyes of normal Evangelicals whether he had really been converted at all.* Indeed, at various times of his life, as, for instance, after the publication of his *Apologia*, letters, kindly intended, were addressed to him by strangers or anonymous writers, assuring him that he did not yet know what conversion meant, and that the all-important change had still to be wrought in him if he was to be saved. . . . He [Newman] was sensible that he had ever been wanting in those special Evangelical experiences which, like the grip of the hand or other prescribed signs of a secret society, are the sure token of a member."[1]

It is interesting to note the various steps by which Newman at length reached the position he held at the birth of the Oxford Movement. He tells us that when he was not quite ten years old he drew, in a "verse book" in his possession, "the figure of a solid cross upright, and next to it is, what may indeed be meant for a necklace, but what I cannot make out to be anything else than a set of beads suspended, with a little

[1] *Letters and Correspondence of J. H. Newman*, 1st edition, vol. i. pp. 122, 123.

cross attached."[1] Newman tells us that when he was fifteen years old he "was very superstitious, and for some time previous to my conversion used constantly to cross myself on going into the dark."[2] In 1823 he began to believe in the doctrine of Apostolic Succession.[3] His first sermon after his ordination—which event took place on June 13, 1824—implied in its tone a denial of Baptismal Regeneration; but it was not long afterwards when he accepted that doctrine, having been persuaded into believing it from reading Archbishop Sumner's *Treatise on Apostolic Preaching*. This book, he asserts, "was successful beyond anything else in rooting out Evangelical doctrines" from his creed.[4] In 1824 his brother, F. W. Newman, was shocked, while arranging the furniture in some new rooms he was about to occupy, to find a beautiful engraving of the Blessed Virgin Mary fixed up, and that it was a present from his brother, John Henry.[5] About a year later Dr. Hawkins taught him to believe in the doctrine of Tradition, and that "the sacred text [of the Bible] was never intended to teach doctrine, but only to prove it, and that if we would learn doctrine we must have recourse to the formularies of the Church."[6] In 1832 Newman had gone so far wrong on this gravely important subject as to write to Dr. Pusey: "As to Scripture being practically sufficient for making the Christian, it seems to me a mere dream."[7]

As early as his fifteenth year Newman "became most firmly convinced that the Pope was the Antichrist predicted by Daniel, St. Paul, and St. John," and he states that his "imagination was stained by the effects of this doctrine up to the year 1843; it had been obliterated from my reason and judgment at an earlier date."[8] It is, indeed, marvellous how any one who ever held such views as to the Pope could go over to Rome. With this view of Antichrist Newman also believed that Rome was

---

[1] *Apologia Pro Vita Sua*, p. 57.   [2] *Ibid.* p. 56.   [3] *Ibid.* p. 67.
[4] Newman's *Letters and Correspondence*, vol. i. p. 120.
[5] *The Early History of Cardinal Newman.* By his Brother, F. W. Newman, p. 18.
[6] *Apologia*, p. 66.   [7] *Life of Dr. Pusey*, vol. i. p. 233.   [8] *Apologia*, p. 63.

the Babylon of the Revelation; but while at Naples, early in 1833, he adopted the view held by many Roman Catholic writers, and in substance sanctioned in the notes to the Rheims New Testament, that Babylon was the *city* of Rome, but not the *Church* of Rome. He communicated his views on this question to his friend, the Rev. S. Rickards:—

"A notion has struck me," he wrote, "on reading the Revelation again and again, that the Rome there mentioned is Rome considered as a city or a *place*, without any reference to the question whether it be Christian or Pagan. As a seat of government, it was the first cruel persecutor of the Church, and as such condemned to suffer God's judgments, which had not yet been fully poured out upon it, from the plain fact that it still exists. Babylon is gone. Rome is a city still, and judgments await her therefore."[1]

By adopting this theory, one of the greatest barriers against reunion with the Church of Rome is removed in the mind of any one who accepts it. The command of God, as to Babylon the Great, is "Come out of her, my people, that ye be not partakers of her sins, and that ye receive not of her plagues."[2] If the Church of Rome be identical with Babylon, this divine command, "Come out of her," settles the whole question as to union with her, either on the part of individuals or Churches. And that she is Babylon has been most ably and learnedly proved by the late Bishop Christopher Wordsworth, of Lincoln (an old-fashioned High Churchman), in his little book, entitled *Union with Rome*, which has never yet been refuted.

Sometime before 1828, when Dr. Copleston resigned the office of Provost of Oriel College, Oxford, Mr. Newman's conduct seems to have alarmed one, at least, of his intimate friends. His brother writes:—

"The Provost of Oriel (Dr., afterwards Bishop, Copleston), admired him [Blanco White], and invited him to join the Fellows'

---

[1] Newman's *Letters*, vol. i. p. 388.
[2] Rev. xviii. 4.

table; but breakfast and tea he shared with us. He and my brother [John Henry Newman], enjoyed the violin together. I gradually heard their theological talk, which was apt to end by Blanco's sharp warning: 'Ah! Newman! if you follow that clue it will draw you into Catholic error.' But I believe he meant into self-flagellation, maceration of the body."[1]

Mr. Blanco White was a converted Roman Catholic priest of great learning, and, no doubt, he could see more clearly than others around him in what direction Newman was at that time moving. On this occasion White was a true prophet. In 1829 Newman sent his mother and sisters two sermons which he had published. In acknowledging their receipt his sister remarked: "We have long since read your two sermons; they are very High Church."[2] By the year 1831 Newman appears to have become dissatisfied with the present Book of Common Prayer, and wished to restore one which had in it a considerable amount of Romanism. "You may assure Rickards from me," he wrote to his sister, on Oct. 16, 1831, "that I am a reformer as much as he can be. I should like (as far as I can understand the matter), to substitute the First Prayer Book of King Edward for the present one."[3] His ideas at that time of what a reformer should accomplish were set forth very clearly in his *Apologia Pro Vita Sua*:—

"I saw," wrote Newman, "that Reformation principles were powerless to rescue her [the Church of England]. As to leaving her, the thought never crossed my imagination; still, I ever kept before me that there was something greater than the Established Church, and that was the Church Catholic and Apostolic, set up from the beginning, of which she was but the local presence and organ. She was nothing, unless she was this. She must be dealt with strongly, or she would be lost. There was need of a second Reformation."[4]

Writing from Rome, March 19, 1833, Newman told Dr. Pusey what he even then thought of the Protestant

---

[1] *Early History of Cardinal Newman*, p. 13.
[2] Newman's *Letters*, vol. i. p. 215.
[3] *Ibid.* vol. i. p. 250.
[4] *Apologia*, p. 95.

Reformation. "I wish," he wrote, "I could make up my mind whether the 1260 years of Captivity begin with Constantine—it seems a remarkable coincidence that its termination should fall about on the Reformation—(I speak from memory)—which, amid good, has been the source of all the infidelity, the second woe, which is now overspreading the earth."[1]

At about the same time Newman defined more clearly what he then meant by "a second Reformation." "It would be," he said, "in fact a second Reformation: a better Reformation, for it would be a return, not to the sixteenth century, but to the seventeenth."[2] Unfortunately, as we shall see later on, Newman's "second Reformation" developed into a return, not merely to the seventeenth century, but to a period anterior to the sixteenth century Reformation.

e of Dr. Pusey, vol. i. p. 249.
wman's *Apologia*, p. 113.

CHAPTER II

The Birth of the Oxford Movement—Newman and Froude's Interview with Wiseman at Rome—Its deep impression on Wiseman's mind—His bright expectations from it—Was the Tractarian Movement born in Oxford or Rome?—Keble's sermon on *National Apostasy*—He denounces the State and exalts the Church—Archbishop Sumner on Foreign Protestant Non-Episcopal Pastors—The Tractarians on Church and State—Generally favourable to entire separation—Dr. Arnold's *Principles of Church Reform*—Its good and objectionable features—Newman wants to "make a row in the world"—The Conference at Hadleigh—The Association of Friends of the Church—Its plans of work — Efforts to win Evangelical Churchmen — "The seeds of revolution planted"—They wished to bring back the principles of Laud—Clerical and Lay addresses to the Archbishop of Canterbury—The *Tracts for the Times*—Their Romeward tendency—Newman called a "Papist"—Names of the writers of the *Tracts for the Times*—Dr. Pusey joins the Movement—Fasting—Roman Catholic opinion of the *Tracts* — Exalting the priesthood — Dr. Arnold's faithful warning.

ON Tuesday, July 9, 1833, Mr. Newman returned to Oxford from a prolonged visit to Italy. The Rev. R. H. Froude, who had been his companion during a portion of his journey, had returned some time before. "The following Sunday," writes Mr. Newman, "July 14th, Mr. Keble preached the Assize sermon in the University pulpit. It was published under the title of *National Apostasy*. I have ever considered and kept the day as the start of the religious movement of 1833."[1] During their travels in Italy, Newman and Froude had two interviews with Monsignor Wiseman at Rome, to which the latter gentleman ever afterwards attached the highest importance, and apparently considered as the real birth date of the Oxford Movement. I have already, in the ninth chapter of my *Secret History of the Oxford Movement*, referred to this interview, which seems to have been kept

---

[1] Newman's *Apologia*, p. 100.

from the knowledge of the other leaders of the Tractarian Movement for some years after. These two gentlemen discussed with the Monsignor the conditions upon which they could be taken into the Church of Rome, and, according to the testimony of one of their friends, the Rev. William Palmer, they seem to have thought it possible to obtain from the Papal authorities " some dispensation" which " would enable them to communicate with Rome without violation of conscience"—apparently thinking that they could thus " communicate with Rome" while remaining as clergymen of the Church of England. The impression produced on the mind of Wiseman by these visits was deep and lasting. He evidently was led to understand that a Movement towards Corporate Reunion was about to be started at Oxford, by men whom he considered as of a " truly Catholic turn of mind ;" and so much impressed was he by the interviews that he determined to abandon his favourite studies and devote himself to " the new era" which would soon dawn upon England. Cardinal Wiseman's Roman Catholic biographer relates of one of these meetings at Rome:—

"The interview left Wiseman with two vivid impressions—sparks which the course of the Oxford Movement fanned later into a flame. He was struck by the truly Catholic temper of mind of the two men, and by their utter sincerity. Both these impressions were contrary to the views current among his co-religionists alike in Rome and in England, who thought that Catholic sympathies in the Anglican Church were, for the most part, purely superficial and æsthetic. Where they were deeper, adherence to the Church of England—then beyond question predominantly Protestant in its religious tone—was supposed to be incompatible with sincerity. Wiseman judged differently from this brief visit, and, with characteristic hopefulness, made up his mind that if these men represented the rising generation at Oxford, the centre of English religious life, great changes were in store for the country. The existence of such opinions in Oxford itself was not, indeed, a justification of Father Spencer's chimerical hopes. But it promised no longer the accession of units only in a people of millions. A movement which was in its degree corporate was apparently beginning among leading minds within the Anglican Church. Such a movement must have peculiar elements of power, resulting from its claim to be national as well as Catholic. It appealed to English Churchmen as the work of their friends, while the hereditary supporters of the Roman See necessarily appeared in a measure to assail them as foes. From this year dates the rise of a new hopefulness in Wiseman. 'From the day of Newman and Froude's visit to me,' he wrote in 1847, 'never for an instant did I waver in my conviction that a new era had commenced in England . . . to this grand object I devoted myself . . . the favourite studies of former years were abandoned for the pursuit of this aim alone.'"[1]

There can be no doubt that Wiseman's biographer accurately describes his attitude towards the Oxford Movement from the moment that he had the interview with Newman and Froude in Rome, three months before the avowed birth of the Movement. The biographer's statements are confirmed by the writings of Wiseman himself. In the preface to the second volume of his *Essays*, Wiseman writes :—

"I have already alluded, in the preface to the first volume, as well as in the body of this, to the first circumstance which turned my attention to the wonderful movement then commenced in England —the visit which is recorded in Froude's *Remains*. FROM THAT MOMENT *it took the uppermost place in my thoughts*, and became the object of their intensest interest."[2]

In a footnote to the reprint of his review of Froude's *Remains*, and written fourteen years after its appearance in the *Dublin Review*, Wiseman remarks :—

"In p. 307 of the *Remains*, will be found an account of what remains marked, with gratitude in my mind, as *an epoch in my life* —the visit which Mr. Froude unexpectedly paid me, in company with one [Newman] who never afterwards departed from my thoughts, and whose eloquent pleadings for the faith have endeared him to every Catholic heart. For many years it had been a promise of my affection to St. Philip, that I would endeavour, should opportunity be afforded me, to introduce his beautiful Institute into England. But little could I foresee, that when I received *that most welcome visit*, I was in company with its future founder. FROM THAT

---

[1] *Life and Times of Cardinal Wiseman*. By Wilfrid Ward, vol i. pp. 118, 119.
[2] Wiseman's *Essays on Various Subjects*, vol. ii. p. vi.

HOUR, however, I watched with intense interest *and love* the Movement of which I THEN caught the first glimpse. My studies changed their course, the bent of my mind was altered, in the strong desire to co-operate with the new mercies of Providence." [1]

We may here well ask, in amazement, What could Newman and Froude have told Monsignor Wiseman, at this secret interview, which led him to alter greatly the course of his life, to form apparently extravagant hopes for the future, and such blessings for the Church of Rome, as the result of their forthcoming labours in the Church of England? A really adequate report of their interview will, I fear, never be given to the public. But it is evident that these founders of the Oxford Movement consulted with this Roman prelate as to their plans for the future, and gave him clearly to understand that their work would be on "Catholic" lines. Nothing less than information of this kind would ever have led Wiseman to look upon their call on him as a "most welcome visit," or made him ever afterwards to think of it as "an epoch" in his life. "From THAT HOUR," he declares, "I watched with intense interest and love the Movement of which *I* THEN *caught the first* glimpse." From that memorable day, he assures us, he was certain that "a new era had commenced in England," and he determined to give up his "favourite studies," and instead of following them he gave "the uppermost place in his thoughts," and his most zealous labours to help on "with intense interest and love the Movement" of which he "*then* caught the first glimpse," revealed to him, there can be no reasonable doubt, by Newman and Froude. These founders of the Romeward Movement do not appear to have, at first, consulted the Archbishops of the Church of England. They thought, no doubt, that their schemes would have a better chance of success if they first consulted a prelate of that Church which has ever been the bitterest enemy of the Church of England. No doubt, from their own standpoint, they acted wisely. But their most shameful conduct naturally suggests the important

[1] Wiseman's *Essays on Various Subjects*, vol. ii. pp. 94, 95, *note.*

question, Was the Oxford Movement really born in *Oxford*, or had it its birth in *Rome?*

Keble's sermon on *National Apostasy*, with which Newman considered that the Tractarian campaign commenced, was in reality a denunciation of the State, and an exaltation of the Church. He mourned over the "impatience under pastoral control," which he considered was one of the characteristics of the day, and "a never-failing symptom of an unchristian temper."[1] He was particularly indignant at any want of respect shown to the "Successors of the Apostles," meaning, of course, the Episcopally ordained clergy only. "Disrespect to the Successors of the Apostles, *as such*," he exclaimed, "is an unquestionable symptom of enmity to Him, who gave them their commission at first, and has pledged Himself to be with them for ever. Suppose such disrespect general and national . . . that nation, how highly soever she may think of her own religion and morality, stands convicted in His sight of a direct disavowal of His sovereignty."[2] And all this respect he claimed for the clergy, quite apart from their personal character. Apparently, no one, in the opinion of Mr. Keble, should show any "disrespect" to a "Successor of the Apostles," no matter what his character might be. On this occasion Mr. Keble took the gloomiest view of the condition of the country, affirming that it "is fast becoming hostile to the Church, and cannot therefore long be the friend of God"[3] — an assertion which implies that no Dissenter, who is hostile to the Church of England, can be "the friend of God." He defined the "Church," in this sermon, as "the laity, as well as the clergy in their three orders—the whole body of Christians united, according to the will of Jesus Christ, under the Successors of the Apostles."[4] From this it manifestly follows that the "*whole* body of Christians" are united only under those "Successors of the Apostles" who are divided into "*three* orders;" and therefore no non-

---

[1] *National Apostasy Considered.* By John Keble, M.A., p. 18. Oxford: Parker. 1833.
[2] *Ibid.* p. 18.   [3] *Ibid.* p. 20.   [4] *Ibid.* p. 21.

Episcopalian body can possibly be any part of the visible Church of God at all. This sermon stamps the Tractarian Movement from its commencement as narrow-minded and bigoted, and void of true Catholicity. The whole sermon was a glorification of the clerical order at the expense of the State.

It is refreshing to turn from such assertions as those of Keble to the broad-minded and Christian charity of Dr. J. B. Sumner, Archbishop of Canterbury, who, replying to the Brighton Protestant Defence Committee, on October 13, 1851, said:—

"It would as little represent my sentiments, as it would ill become my station, if I should be suspected of undervaluing the perfect constitution of the Church of England. It is our great privilege to enjoy apostolical discipline, together with apostolical doctrine. But we do not disparage these advantages when we acknowledge our conviction that foreign Protestants who teach apostolical doctrine though not under apostolical discipline, may yet be owned of God as faithful Ministers of His Word and Sacraments, and enjoy His blessing on their labours."[1]

And there was surely much wisdom in what the late Duke of Argyll (a Presbyterian) said at a meeting in London in May 1851:—"Remember too," he said, "that in after times, when influences come to operate upon the character of the English Church, similar to those which you are dreading now, in the latter end of the reign of Elizabeth, and of the succeeding Stuarts, then was the time when there was a withdrawal of sympathy from the other non-episcopal communions. You will find as an historical fact that the feeling of sympathy with other Protestant communions, non-episcopal, was coincident with the best and most Protestant times of the Church of England, whilst the withdrawal of that sympathy was coincident with times when Romish tendencies and Romish influences began to invade that Church."[2]

It seems to have been forgotten in the present day, that many of the leaders of the Tractarian party were

---

[1] *Guardian*, October 29, 1851, p. 761.
[2] *Guardian*, May 14, 1851, p. 348.

from its very birth favourable to the entire separation of the Church of England from State control. Mr. F. W. Newman tells us that, on one occasion, when he visited his brother, Dr. Newman, at Birmingham, soon after the Colenso Case was ended, the future Cardinal said to him:—

"'When in 1833 we met to start the *Tracts for the Times*, we thought it only prudent to be frank to one another, and we all submitted to free questioning on every important subject: among them, the Union of Church and State. To our astonishment we found that, one and all, we desired entire separation. The book on Scotch Episcopalianism (ascribed to Archbishop Whately) had converted us.' 'Is this a secret?' asked I. 'Not at all,' was his reply, 'tell it as widely as you choose.'"[1]

I do not wonder that Mr. F. W. Newman adds, in relating this anecdote:—" I am amused to find, that while the clergy were looking to the Puseyites as their defence against the formidable Dissenters, those very Puseyites were on the side of the foe." In his *Apologia*, Newman admits that Whately fixed in his mind "those anti-Erastian views of Church polity which were one of the most prominent features of the Tractarian Movement," and that his work on Scotch Episcopalianism "had a gradual but a deep effect" upon his mind.[2] And yet, on August 14, 1833, Mr. R. H. Froude was able to announce that Newman had agreed to a declaration containing the following clauses:—" IV. We protest against all efforts directed to the subversion of existing institutions, or to the separation of Church and State; V. We think it a duty steadily to contemplate and provide for the contingency of such a separation." Mr. Froude added:—"Keble demurs to these, because he thinks the union of Church and State, as it is now understood, actually sinful."[3] The Rev. William Palmer, of Worcester College, Oxford, who was for several years a leader of the Tractarian party until its rapid

[1] *The Early History of Cardinal Newman*, p. 37.
[2] *Apologia*, pp. 69, 71.
[3] *A Collection of Papers Connected with the Theological Movement of* 1833. By the Hon. and Rev. A. P. Percival, 2nd edition, p. 12.

progress towards Romanism alarmed him, states that at the commencement of the movement "there was some difference of opinion on the question of the union of Church and State, which some of our friends seemed inclined to regard as an evil; while I (and perhaps another), was desirous to maintain this union."[1] This statement shows that only one or perhaps two of the party were in favour of the union of Church and State. Mr. Froude himself seems to have anticipated a separation, and to have looked forward to it with hope. Writing from Rome, March 16, 1833, he remarks:—"To be sure it would be a great thing to have a true Church in Germany; in Scotland it seems to be thriving, and if the State will but kick us off we may yet do in England."[2] In the following August Froude wrote to another friend mentioning that a sermon which he had written had met with strong approbation from an unnamed gentleman, and adding:—

"My subject is the duty of contemplating the contingency of a separation between Church and State, and of providing against it, *i.e.* by studying the principles of ecclesiastical subordination, so that when the law of the land ceases to enforce this, we may have a law within ourselves to supply its place."[3]

Although, as we have seen, early in August, Newman had agreed to a protest against efforts being put forth for "the separation of Church and State," yet, on the 31st of the same month, he wrote a letter to an intimate friend, Mr. J. W. Bowden, in which, by contrast, his double-dealing is clearly revealed:—

"Not," wrote Newman, "that I would advocate a separation of Church and State unless the nation does more tyrannical things against us; but I do feel I should be glad if it were done and over, much as the nation would lose by it, for I fear the Church is being corrupted by the union."[4]

---

[1] *Narrative of Events Connected with the Tracts for the Times.* By William Palmer, edition 1883, p. 103.
[2] Froude's *Remains*, vol. i. p. 302.
[3] *Ibid.* p. 323.
[4] Newman's *Letters*, vol. i. p. 449.

What the Tractarian party, as a whole, seemed to desire in the relations of Church and State was, perhaps, accurately expressed in No. 59 of the *Tracts for the Times*, dated April 25, 1835, and written by Mr. R. H. Froude. It pleads for "State Protection" for the Church, and protests against "State Interference" with its concerns. The early Tractarians were alarmed at what seemed to them the increasing encroachments of the State on the province of the Church. They believed that the Government of the day were in favour of a Revision of the Liturgy with a view to a comprehension of Dissenters within the pale of the Established Church; and they were certainly made extremely angry by the publication of Dr. Arnold's pamphlet on *Principles of Church Reform*, which was issued from the press early in 1833, and obtained a very large circulation.[1] It created a great sensation by its daring proposal to "extinguish Dissent" "by comprehension." Apart from the main object of the pamphlet, it contained several expressions which must have been peculiarly distasteful to the rising party of Sacerdotalists. In it Dr. Arnold declared that Christianity "has provided in the strongest manner against superstition and priestcraft";[2] and he expressed himself as "ashamed" of "the petty tyranny of Laud";[3] affirming that "the mischievous confusion of the Christian ministry with a priesthood, that anything can be lawful for a Christian layman which is unlawful for a Christian minister," was "a most groundless superstition."[4]

"I may be allowed to express an earnest hope," wrote Dr. Arnold, "that if ever an union with Dissenters be attempted, and it should thus become necessary to alter our present terms of communion, the determining on the alterations to be made should never be committed to a Convocation, or to any commission consisting of clergymen alone. . . . Laymen have no right to shift from their own shoulders an important part of Christian responsibility; and as no educated layman individually is justified in taking his own faith upon

---

[1] *Principles of Church Reform.* By Thomas Arnold, D.D., Head Master of Rugby School. London: B. Fellowes. 1833.
[2] *Ibid.* 2nd edition, p. 11. [3] *Ibid.* p. 20. [4] *Ibid.* p. 62.

trust from a clergyman, so neither are the laity, as a body, warranted in taking the national faith in the same way. If ever it should be thought right to appoint commissioners to revise the Articles, it is of paramount importance, in order to save the plan from utter failure, that a sufficient number of laymen, distinguished for their piety and enlarged views, should be added to the ecclesiastical members of the commission."[1]

I do not wonder that such assertions, and such proposals, made the Tractarians furious with Dr. Arnold. It must be admitted that there were valid objections against certain portions of his scheme of Church Reform. What he really aimed at was to turn the Church of England into a kind of ecclesiastical Noah's Ark, in which its inmates, however, would remain untamed. A plan for including the orthodox Nonconformists only in the Establishment would no doubt have secured the support of many members of the Church of England. In the reign of William III. a scheme of comprehension was drawn up by a Royal Commission, consisting of the Archbishop of York, the Bishops of London, Winchester, St. Asaph, Rochester, Carlisle, Exeter, Salisbury, Bangor, and Chester, and a large number of lesser Dignitaries and Divines; but unfortunately it was eventually defeated. Dr. Arnold's scheme was far more Latitudinarian than that which was proposed in the reign of William III.; for it aimed at including Unitarians and Romanists also; and treated Christian doctrine as a matter of little or no importance.

"Might it not be possible," asked Dr. Arnold, "to constitute a Church thoroughly national, thoroughly united, thoroughly Christian, which should allow great varieties of opinion, and of ceremonies, and forms of worship, according to the various knowledge, and habits, and tempers of its members, while it truly held one common faith, and trusted in one common Saviour, and worshipped one common God?"[2]

As to Quakers, Roman Catholics, and Unitarians, Dr. Arnold admitted that their "differences appear to offer greater difficulty" than those amongst ordinary Dis-

[1] Arnold's *Principles of Church Reform*, pp. 80, 81.
[2] *Ibid.* p. 28.

senters; and that so long as these three particular sects " preserve exactly their present character, it would seem impracticable to comprehend them in any national Christian Church." But, nevertheless, he was full of hope that these difficulties would be removed. " Is it," he asked, " beyond hope, that many who are now Roman Catholics, would ere long unite themselves religiously as well as politically with the rest of their countrymen? Lastly, with regard to the Unitarians, it seems to me that in their case an alteration of our present terms of communion would be especially useful," provided they (the Unitarians) would, as to our Saviour, " call him Lord and God."[1] In a comprehensive Church of this kind, Dr. Arnold, however, insisted on the necessity of an Episcopal form of government, though not as a matter of divine right. " It will be observed," he wrote, " that the whole of this scheme supposes an Episcopal government, and requires that all ministers should receive Episcopal ordination."[2]

Dr. Arnold's scheme of Church Reform was attacked from all quarters. His biographer, Dean Stanley, states that: " Dissenters objected to its attacks upon what he considered their sectarian narrowness; the clergy of the Establishment to its supposed Latitudinarianism; its advocacy of large reforms repelled the sympathy of many Conservatives; its advocacy of the importance of religious institutions repelled the sympathy of many Liberals."[3] It is remarkable that, notwithstanding so much violent opposition from so many quarters, nearly all the plans of Church Reform laid down in Dr. Arnold's pamphlet, excepting that for Church comprehension, have since been adopted, many of them with the hearty approbation of the Ritualists. He pleaded for an increased number of Bishops, but without seats in the House of Lords; the " institution of diocesan general assemblies " now realised in Diocesan Conferences; for the ordination of Clergymen too poor to pay for a University education; for parochial

---

[1] Arnold's *Principles of Church Reform*, pp. 36, 37.
[2] *Ibid.* p. 56.
[3] Stanley's *Life of Dr. Arnold.* Ward, Lock, & Co.'s edition, p. 190.

councils; the removal of sinecures and pluralities ; the opening of our Universities to Dissenters ; and that " the people should have a more direct check than they have at present on the nomination of their ministers," which yet, unfortunately, remains to be realised.

And so, nominally to oppose the Latitudinarian spirit of the age, but in reality to build up a High Church Movement opposed to Protestantism, Keble, Newman, Froude, Percival, and their disciples banded themselves together into a party. Meeting the Rev. Isaac Williams one day soon after their work began, Newman said to him, " Isaac, we must make a row in the world ! "[1] No one can now deny that the Oxford Movement has made " a row in the world." It has torn the Church of England asunder, broken up its peace, and filled it with quarrels and dissensions. Those who begin a " row " are to be held primarily responsible for it. How the work began is related by the Rev. William Palmer :—

"I had not," he writes, "been very intimately acquainted with Mr. Newman and Mr. Froude, and was scarcely known to Mr. Keble or Mr. Percival, when our deep sense of the wrongs sustained by the Church in the suppression of Bishoprics, and our feeling of the necessity of doing whatever was in our power to arrest the tide of evil, brought us together in the summer of 1833. It was at the beginning of long vacation (when, Mr. Froude being almost the only occupant of Oriel College, we frequently met in the common room) that the resolution to unite and associate in defence of the Church, of her violated liberties, and neglected principles, arose. This resolution was immediately acted on; and while I corresponded with Mr. Rose, Mr. Froude communicated our design to Mr. Keble. Mr. Newman soon took part in our deliberations, on his return from the Continent. The particular course which we were to adopt became the subject of much and anxious thought; and as it was deemed advisable to confer with Mr. Rose on so important a subject, Mr. Froude and myself, after some correspondence, visited him at Hadleigh, in July, where I also had the pleasure of becoming personally acquainted with Mr. Percival, who had been invited to take part in our deliberations. The conference at Hadleigh, which continued for nearly a week,

---

[1] *Autobiography of Isaac Williams*, p. 63.

concluded without any specific arrangements being entered into, though we all concurred as to the necessity of some mode of combined action, and the expediency of circulating tracts or publications on ecclesiastical subjects, intended to inculcate sound and enlightened principles of attachment to the Church. On our return to Oxford, frequent conferences took place at Oriel College, between Mr. Froude, Mr. Newman, Mr. Keble, and the writer, in which various plans were discussed, and in which especial attention was given to the preparation of some formulary of agreement as a basis for our Association."[1]

Hadleigh was, indeed, a strange place for holding such a conference. "The town of Hadleigh," says Foxe, "was one of the first that received the Word of God in all England, at the preaching of Master Thomas Bilney, by whose industry the Gospel of Christ had such gracious success, and took such root there, that a great number of that parish became exceeding well learned in the Holy Scriptures, as well women as men . . . that the whole town seemed rather a university of the learned, than a town of cloth-making or labouring people; and, what most is to be commended, they were for the most part faithful followers of God's Word in their living."[2] At this period Rowland Taylor was rector of Hadleigh, a holy and godly man in life and doctrine, and a very decided Protestant. Soon after Queen Mary came to the throne, hearing his church bells ringing one day, he went into the building to ascertain the cause. There, to his utter astonishment, he found that his honest communion table had been changed for a Popish altar, and a priest was actually saying Mass there at the moment, surrounded by armed men. Thereupon Dr. Taylor said to the priest, in the forcible language common in those days, "Thou devil! Who made thee so bold to enter into this Church of Christ to profane and defile it with this abominable idolatry? I command thee, thou Popish wolf, in the name of God to avoid hence, and not to presume here, with such Popish idolatry, to poison Christ's flock."[3] For

---

[1] Palmer's *Narrative of Events*, pp. 101, 102.
[2] Foxe's *Acts and Monuments*, vol. vi. p. 676, edition 1859.
[3] *Ibid.* p. 679.

faithful conduct like this Dr. Taylor was committed to prison, and put upon his trial. The principal charges against him were his denial of the doctrines of the Real Presence and the Sacrifice of the Mass, both of which doctrines are now commonly taught by the men who are the successors of those who, by a strange coincidence, met in Hadleigh Rectory in the month of July 1833. And was it not strange indeed, remembering what has passed since then, that in the course of a special sermon preached in Hadleigh church during this High Church conference, the preacher should have said: "I stand where the Martyr, Rowland Taylor, stood [*i.e.* in the self-same pulpit from which Taylor preached the Protestant religion]. May God in His mercy give grace to the clergy of this day to follow his example, and, if need be, to testify for the truth, even unto the death."[1] In the very spot where the Protestant Reformation began in that part of the country, the anti-Reformation Movement first erected its head. What the nature of the work done at the Hadleigh Conference was we learn from a statement of Mr. Newman made late in his life. He remarks that:—

"Between July 25 and 29 a meeting was held at Mr. Rose's Rectory at Hadleigh, at which were present Mr. Palmer, Mr. Froude, Mr. Percival, and Mr. Rose. Mr. Keble was to have been there, but there is evidence that he was not. Mr. Newman was not there. There appears to have been some division of opinion at the meeting, but two points were agreed on: to fight for the doctrine of the Apostolical Succession, and for the integrity of the Prayer Book. And two things followed from it—the plan of associating for the defence of the Church, and the *Tracts for the Times*. Mr. Newman was not at the meeting, but he had already suggested the plan of the Association to Froude and Keble, with whom he was in close correspondence; and, as soon as the determination was taken to move, he, with Mr. Palmer, took the labouring oars in the effort which followed."[2]

There was another work undertaken at this Hadleigh

[1] Percival's *Collection of Papers*, p. 43.
[2] Newman's *Letters*, vol. i. pp. 431, 432.

Conference. It was that of revising a new Catechism for the laity, which was subsequently published under the title of *The Churchman's Manual.* Mr. Percival, in his *Collection of Papers,* reprints the whole of this noteworthy document, in which the chief feature is the doctrine of Apostolical Succession. The attitude of the new party towards Dissenters is indicated by the following uncharitable statement :—

"In what respect do all the Protestant Dissenters differ from the Church?

"*A.* Each sect has some point of difference peculiar to itself; but they all differ in this, namely, that their teachers can produce no commission from Christ to exercise the office of Ministers of the Gospel. These have departed from the Apostles' fellowship."

From the commencement of the Oxford Movement its proceedings were conducted with a considerable amount of secrecy. Ample evidence in proof of this assertion is given in the first chapter of my *Secret History of the Oxford Movement,* to which I must refer my readers, since I am anxious, as far as possible, to avoid travelling over the same ground a second time.

After the Hadleigh Conference the friends of the cause held several private meetings at Oriel College, Oxford, for the purpose of maturing their plans. Eventually it was decided to form "The Association of Friends of the Church." The founders of this Association pledged themselves to inculcate on all committed to their charge "the inestimable privilege of communion with our Lord through the successors of the Apostles"; to "provide and circulate books and tracts which may tend to familiarise the imaginations of men to the idea of an Apostolical Commission"; to revive "among Churchmen the practice of daily Common Prayer, and more frequent participation of the Lord's Supper"; and "to resist any attempt that may be made to alter the Liturgy on insufficient authority, *i.e.* without the exercise of the free and deliberate judgment of the Church on the alterations proposed." It will thus be seen that the party did not object in itself to any alterations, or Revision of the Liturgy, but only to such as were made on "insufficient authority."[1]

The intention of the founders of the new Society was to form an organisation which should extend through the whole of England. For this purpose they issued a series of "Suggestions for the Formation of an Association of Friends of the Church," to be composed of both clergy and laity. In these Suggestions they asserted that, "The privilege possessed by parties hostile to her [the Church of England] doctrine, ritual, and polity, of legislating for her, their avowed and increasing efforts against her, their close alliance with such as openly reject the Christian faith, and the lax and unsound principles of many who profess and even think themselves her friends," were "calculated to inspire the true members and friends of the Church with the deepest uneasiness." The question of keeping up the Establishment was pushed on one side as of comparatively little importance. "The most obvious dangers," said the Suggestions, "are those which impend over the Church as an Establishment; but to these it is not here proposed to direct attention. However necessary it may be on the proper occasion to resist all measures which threaten the security of Ecclesiastical property and privileges, still it is felt that there are perils of a character more serious than those which beset the political rights and temporalities of the clergy." A brief statement of "The Objects of the Association" followed the Suggestions. They were as follows:—

"1. To maintain pure and inviolate the doctrines, the services, and the discipline of the Church; that is, to withstand all change which involves the denial and suppression of doctrine, a departure from primitive practice in religious offices, or innovation upon the Apostolical prerogatives, order, and commission of bishops, priests, and deacons.

"2. To afford Churchmen an opportunity of exchanging their sentiments, and co-operating together on a large scale."[2]

It will be observed that these were "objects" which

[1] Percival's *Collection of Letters*, pp. 13, 14.
[2] Palmer's *Narrative of Events*, pp. 104, 105.

might well receive the countenance and aid of Evangelical Churchmen. The real objects of the wire-pullers were, in it, kept carefully out of sight, in accordance, no doubt, with that doctrine of "Reserve in Communicating Religious Knowledge," which was so widely adopted by the Tractarians from the commencement of their Movement. On September 18, 1833, Newman informed Froude: "Palmer is about to make a journey to Hook and others, and has sounded the Evangelicals of Liverpool."[1] On November 14, 1833, one of the leaders of the party wrote to a Member of Parliament, with reference to the Association: —"We want to unite all the Church, orthodox and Evangelical, clergy, nobility, and people in maintenance of our doctrine and polity."[2] A little over two months before this letter was written, the Rev. J. B. Mozley wrote to his sister (September 3, 1833) a confidential letter, in which he revealed the *real* object of what he termed a "Society established for the dissemination of High Church principles."[3] With his letter Mr. Mozley enclosed some of the Tracts, which he described as "the first production of the Society," and added this significant opinion:—"The fact is, we must not be very scrupulous as to views or particular as to sentiments in the distribution of these things."

The promoters of the Association at once set to work to push it with all the energy of young and enthusiastic men. They visited various parts of the country, taking with them copies of an address to the Archbishop of Canterbury, to be signed by the clergy. "There was indeed," says Mr. Palmer, "much misapprehension abroad as to our motives, and we had no means of explaining those motives, without the danger of giving publicity to our proceedings, which, in the then state of the public mind on Church matters, might have led to dangerous results."[4] Meetings of Churchmen in support of the work of the Association were held in various towns, including York, Liverpool, Nottingham,

---

[1] Newman's *Letters*, vol. i. p. 458.
[2] Palmer's *Narrative of Events*, p. 212.
[3] Mozley's *Letters*, p. 33.
[4] Palmer's *Narrative of Events*, p. 108.

Cheltenham, Northampton, Derby, Plymouth, Dorchester, Poole, Norwich, Newcastle, Hull, Bristol, Bath, and Gloucester. But, says Mr. Palmer, "so great was the apprehension at this time, that they did not venture at first to assemble openly, for the purpose of recording their attachment to the Established Church; admission was in general restricted to those friends who were provided with tickets."[1] Enthusiastic friends rapidly joined the Association, but some of them had their doubts about portions of the policy adopted. The Rev. S. Rickards, for instance, wrote to Newman, on September 6, 1833:—"As far as my opinion goes for anything, I disapprove of the concealment of names."[2] Two days later Newman boasted to a friend of the cause:—

"We have set up Church Societies all over the kingdom, or at least mean to do so. Already the seeds of revolution are planted in Oxfordshire, Berkshire, Devonshire, Gloucestershire, Kent, and Suffolk. Our object is to maintain the doctrine of the Apostolical Succession and save the Liturgy from illegal alterations. Hitherto we have had great success. . . . It is no slight thing to be made the instrument of handing down the principles of Laud till the time comes. . . ."[3]

There is here a provoking omission in Newman's letter, as printed in his *Letters and Correspondence*. What "time" did he refer to, when he wrote "till the time come"? And what further would happen when the "time" came? Newman's object was evidently that of propagating a system which had ever been hateful to Protestants, whether they were Evangelicals or not. And yet, with the cunning worthy of a Jesuit, he could boast to his friend Froude, two months after, that his real ambition was to bring back Laudianism:—

"Evangelicals, as I anticipated, are struck with the 'Law of Liberty' and the 'Sin of the Church' [referring, no doubt, to expressions in the eighth of the *Tracts for the Times*, issued a few days previously]. The subject of Discipline, too (I cannot doubt), will take them. Surely my game lies among them."[4]

---

[1] Palmer's *Narrative of Events*, p. 113. [2] *Newman's Letters*, vol. i. p. 453.
[3] *Ibid.* p. 454. [4] *Ibid.* p. 479.

The men who were sent out into various parts of the country to push the new Association received "instructions" for their guidance, written by Newman, headed "Objects of your Journey." They included the following:—"To form local Associations. To instruct the corresponding member. To sound men on certain questions." These emissaries were termed by Newman "Propagandists," and with the subtlety which characterised him all his life, he advised them thus:—"If men are afraid of Apostolical ground [*i.e.* the ground of Apostolical Succession], then be cautious of saying much about it. If desirous, then recommend prudence and silence upon it at present."[1]

The Clerical Address to the Archbishop of Canterbury promoted by the Association was extensively signed, and when it was presented to his Grace, on February 5, 1834, it had received no fewer than 6530 signatures. It was presented by a deputation, which included the Deans of Lincoln, Carlisle, and Chichester; the Archdeacons of Canterbury, London, Middlesex, Stowe, Bedford, Sarum, Brecon, Taunton, Rochester, and St. Albans. Archdeacon Froude, father of Rev. R. H. Froude, termed the address a "milk and water production";[2] but as it played such an important part in the early history of the Oxford Movement, I think it well to reproduce it here. It was as follows:—

"We, the undersigned Clergy of England and Wales, are desirous of approaching your Grace with the expression of our veneration for the sacred office, to which by Divine Providence you have been called, of our respect and affection for your personal character and virtues, and of our gratitude for the firmness and discretion which you have evinced in a season of peculiar difficulty and danger.

"At a time, when events are daily passing before us which mark the growth of Latitudinarian sentiments, and the ignorance which prevails concerning the spiritual claims of the Church, we are especially anxious to lay before your Grace the assurance of our devoted adherence to the Apostolical doctrine and polity of the Church over which you preside, and of which we are ministers; and our deep

---

[1] Newman's *Letters*, vol. ii. p. 4.   [2] *Ibid.* vol. i. p. 492.

rooted attachment to that venerable Liturgy, in which she has embodied, in the language of ancient piety, the Orthodox and Primitive Faith.

"And while we most earnestly deprecate that restless desire of change which would rashly innovate in spiritual matters, we are not less solicitous to declare our firm conviction, that should anything, from the lapse of years or altered circumstances, require renewal or correction, your Grace, and our other spiritual rulers, may rely upon the cheerful co-operation and dutiful support of the Clergy in carrying into effect any measures that may tend to revive the discipline of ancient times, to strengthen the connection between the Bishops, Clergy and people, and to promote the purity, the efficiency, and the unity of the Church."

This Clerical Address to the Archbishop was followed by one from the laity of the Church of England, which was written by Mr. Joshua Watson and signed by the immense number of 230,000 heads of families. In this Address occurred an expression of approval of the alliance between the Church and State, which was conspicuous by its absence from that which emanated from the clergy.

"In the preservation, therefore," said the Lay Address, " of this our National Church in the integrity of her rights and privileges, and in her alliance with the State, we feel that we have an interest no less real and no less direct than her immediate ministers; and we accordingly avow our firm determination to do all that in us lies, in our several stations, to uphold unimpaired in its security and efficiency that Establishment which we have received as the richest legacy of our forefathers."[1]

Although Newman became one of the earliest members of the "Association of Friends of the Church," his heart was never in it. He felt himself in fetters while connected with it. His imperious will would brook no control. "We shall," he wrote to the Rev. C. Girdlestone, "be truly glad of your co-operation, as of one who really fears God and wishes to serve Him; but if you will not, *we will march past you.*"[2] And so he "marched past" the chief friends of the Association, who were anxious to move forward at a slower pace than suited his impetuous temper. He

---

[1] Churton's *Memoir of Joshua Watson*, p. 208, 2nd edition.
[2] *The Early History of Cardinal Newman*, p. 77.

finally broke away from the Association, which soon after came to an end.

The first great work undertaken by Newman after the Hadleigh Conference was the commencing of the now well-known *Tracts for the Times*. The first of the series was issued on September 9, 1833, and the last on January 25, 1841. Of these, twenty were issued before the close of 1833, thirty in the year 1834, twenty in 1835, seven in 1836, five in 1837, three in 1838, one in 1839, two in 1840, and two in 1841. Several of the series were not really "Tracts" at all, but large volumes; *Tract LXXXI.* ran into 424 pages. At first they were not offered for sale to the public. They were, says Mr. Palmer, "privately printed and dispersed amongst friends and correspondents in the country."[1] "Probably," writes Cardinal Newman's sister, "they never got into circulation through ordinary trade machinery. They were read by thinkers and talkers, they were widely distributed, and universally discussed; but at a vast expense of money, trouble, and worry to the writers, and with real difficulty to the readers, who could rarely procure them through the ordinary channels."[2] It was not long before they produced a spirit of well-founded suspicion. One clergyman wrote about them:—"They have been the cause of more injury to the *united* operations of the Church than can well be calculated"; while another uttered the much needed warning:—"We must take care how we aid the cause of Popery."[3] Even the earliest of the *Tracts* fully justified the fears of the enlightened friends of the Church of England. In *Tract I.* the Non-Episcopal Churches were declared to have no validly ordained Ministers, and the doctrine of "Apostolical Succession" was taught in unmistakable terms. The *Tract* was addressed to the clergy, to whom Newman said:—"We must necessarily consider none to be *really* ordained who have not *thus* been ordained"—*i.e.* by Bishops. While Non-Episcopal Ministers were thus to be brought down to the level of

---

[1] Palmer's *Narrative of Events*, p. 120.   [2] Newman's *Letters*, vol. ii. p. 44.
[3] Palmer's *Narrative of Events*, pp. 226, 227.

ordinary laymen, the Bishops and the priests were to exalt themselves as far above ordinary mortals. "Exalt," he exclaimed to the clergy, "our Holy Fathers the Bishops, as the Representatives of the Apostles, and the Angels of the Churches; and magnify your office, as being ordained by them to take part in their Ministry."[1] In the third *Tract* Newman objected to "Alterations in the Liturgy," not, however, on the ground that revision was evil in itself, but because of the dangers which at that time would have attended it. In a note to the fourth *Tract* Mr. Keble discussed the question, "Where is the competent authority for making alterations" in the Liturgy? And he answered it negatively only:—"It does not lie in the British Legislature."[2] In the tenth *Tract* the Bishops were raised almost to an equality with the Apostles. "In one sense they [the Apostles] are still alive; I mean, they did not leave the world without appointing persons to take their place; and these persons ['the Bishops'] represent them, and may be considered with reference to us, as if they were the Apostles."[3] With the Bishops the clergy must be exalted also. "Then you [the laity] will honour us [the clergy]," says this *Tract*, "as those (if I may say so) who are intrusted with the keys of heaven and hell, . . . as intrusted with the awful and mysterious privilege of dispensing Christ's Body and Blood."[4] This last sentence was, I believe, the first in which the Tractarians taught the Real Presence. I do not wonder that directly after this *Tract* was issued, the Tractarians "were called heretics, Papists," as Newman admits in a letter which he wrote on December 15, 1833,[5] and it is not astonishing even to learn that some persons called Newman "a Papist" to his face.[6] To a friend, who remonstrated with him for his language in *Tract X.*, he candidly acknowledged:—"In confidence to a friend, I can only admit it was *imprudent*, for I do think we have most of us dreadfully low notions of the Blessed Sacra-

---

[1] *Tracts for the Times*, No. I. pp. 3, 4.
[2] *Ibid.* No. IV. p. 8.   [3] *Ibid.* No. X. p. 2.   [4] *Ibid.* pp. 5, 6.
[5] Newman's *Letters*, vol. ii. p. 8.   [6] *Ibid.* p. 10.

ment. I expect to be called a Papist when my opinions are known."[1] Startling, then, as Newman's opinion was, as expressed in *Tract X.*, that publication only revealed a portion of what he really believed. His full faith was held in reserve, to be revealed on some more auspicious occasion.

It may be useful to mention here the names of the writers of the *Tracts for the Times*, and the *Tracts* for which each was responsible. My authority for this list is the Appendix to the third volume of the *Life of Dr. Pusey*. The Rev. J. H. Newman wrote Nos. 1, 2, 3, 6, 7, 8, 10, 11, 19, 20, 21, 31, 33, 34, 38, 41, 45, 47, 71, 73, 74, 75, 76, 79, 82, 83, 85, 88, and 90. The Rev. J. Keble wrote Nos. 4, 13, 40, 52, 54, 57, 60, and 89. The Rev. Thomas Keble, Nos. 12, 22, 43, and part of 84, the other part being written by the Rev. G. Prevost. The Rev. R. H. Froude wrote Nos. 9, 59, and 63. Mr. J. W. Bowden (a layman) wrote Nos. 5, 29, 30, 56, and 58. The Rev. Dr. Pusey wrote Nos. 18, 66, 67, 68, 69, 77, and 81. Mr. Alfred Menzies, No. 14. The Rev. B. Harrison, Nos. 16, 17, 24, and 49. The Rev. R. F. Wilson, No. 51. The Rev. A. Buller, No. 61. The Rev. C. P. Eden, No. 32. The Rev. H. E. Manning (afterwards Cardinal Manning), part of No. 78, the other part being by the Rev. C. Marriott. The Rev. Isaac Williams, Nos. 80, 86, and 87. The Rev. A. P. Percival, Nos. 23, 35, and 36. Nos. 25, 26, 27, 28, 37, 39, 42, 44, 46, 48, 50, 53, 55, 62, 64, 65, 70, and 72, were reprints from old authors.

Next to Newman and Keble the most noteworthy of all the *Tract* writers was Dr. Pusey. He did not join the Movement at its commencement, and, when he did join, the fact was for a time kept a secret from the public. As early as November 7, 1833, Newman was able to announce to Froude that "Pusey circulates *Tracts*."[2] On November 13th he was able to tell another friend of the cause that Pusey had joined them, but that his name "must not be mentioned as of our party";[3] while on

---

[1] Newman's *Letters*, vol. i. p. 490.
[2] *Ibid.* p. 476.   [3] *Ibid.* p. 482.

December 19th he was able to communicate the good news to Mr. F. Rogers (afterwards Lord Blackford):—
"I have a most admirable *Tract* from Pusey, but his name must not yet be mentioned."[1] At length, however, Pusey was drawn into the net, and became publicly known as connected with the Tractarians, and this is how it seems to have come about, as related by the Rev. Isaac Williams:—

"I had," writes Williams, "up to this time no acquaintance with Pusey, but he would (now that we had lost Froude from Oxford) join Newman and myself in our walks. They had been Fellows of Oriel together, and Newman was the senior. But Pusey's presence always checked his lighter and unrestrained mood; and I was myself silenced by so awful a person. Yet I always found in him something most congenial to myself—a nameless something which was wanting even in Newman, and, I might almost add, even in Keble. But Pusey at this time was not one of us, and I have some recollection of a conversation which was the occasion of his joining us. He said, smiling to Newman and wrapping his gown around him, as he used to do, 'I think you are too hard upon the "Peculiars," as you call them (*i.e.* the Low Church party); you should conciliate them. I am thinking of writing a letter myself with that purpose,' or rather I think it was of printing a letter which had been the result of private correspondence. 'Well,' said Newman, 'suppose you let us have it for one of the *Tracts?*' 'Oh, no,' said Pusey, 'I will not be one of you.' This was said in a playful manner, and before we parted Newman said, 'Suppose you let us have that letter of yours, which you intend writing, and attach your own name or signature to it? You would then not be mixed up with us, or be in any way responsible for the *Tracts*.' 'Well,' Pusey said at last, 'if you will let me do that, I will.' It was this circumstance of Pusey attaching his initials to that *Tract* that furnished the *Record* and the Low Church party with his name, which they at once attached to us all."[2]

Mr. Williams seems to think that it was Pusey's *Tract on Baptism* which was the subject of conversation on this occasion, but in this his memory must have been at fault, for Pusey's initials were placed on *Tract XVIII.* (the first he wrote), which was issued on December 21, 1833,

[1] Newman's *Letters*, vol. ii. p. 9.
[2] *Autobiography of Isaac Williams*, pp. 70-72.

while the first of those he wrote on Baptism was not published until August 24, 1835 — one year and eight months after. This first of the *Tracts* written by Pusey, was entitled "Thoughts on the Benefits of the System of Fasting, Enjoined by Our Church." In urging upon his readers the observance of Fasting Dr. Pusey was, to a considerable extent, on common ground with Evangelical Churchmen, and even with Puritans, though he attached greater value to the practice than they have done. He quoted the Church's *Homily of Fasting* in support of his views, but omitted from his extracts some cautions which are, perhaps, as necessary for these times as when they were first put forth, such, for instance, as the following :—

"To fast then, with this persuasion of mind, that our fasting and other good works can make us good, perfect, and just men, and finally bring us to heaven, is a devilish persuasion ; and that fast is so far off from pleasing of God, that it refuseth His mercy, and is altogether derogatory to the merits of Christ's death and His precious blood shedding. This doth the parable of the Pharisee and the Publican teach."[1]

It was not quite fair either, on the part of Dr. Pusey, to omit any mention of the real reason why so many Fast Days are mentioned in the Prayer-Book Calendar. Any one who consults Cardwell's *Doctrinal Annals of the Reformed Church of England* will learn that they were appointed, not in the interests of religion, but in the interests of the fishermen of the time, who, but for these Fast Days, in which fish and not flesh was eaten, would have been utterly ruined. They were the days mentioned by the *Homily on Fasting*, as "appointed by public order and laws made by Princes, and by the authority of the magistrates, upon policy, *not respecting any religion at all in the same*."[2] In 1576 Queen Elizabeth's Council sent a letter to the Archbishop of Canterbury, requiring him to enforce the observance of these Fast Days, and requesting him to "give order" to the Ministers in his province that

---

[1] *Homily of Fasting*, Part I.
[2] *Ibid*. Part II.

they, in their sermons, should teach the people that the observance of these days "is not required for any liking of Popish ceremonies heretofore used (which utterly are detested), but *only* to maintain the mariners and navy in this land, by setting men a fishing."[1]

In January, 1834, the new *Tracts for the Times* came under the notice of Mr. Ambrose Phillipps De Lisle, a wealthy Leicestershire squire, and a pervert to Romanism. On reading *Tract IV.* he returned it to the gentleman who had lent it to him, with this remarkakle assertion: "Mark my words, these *Tracts* are the beginning of a Catholic Movement which will one day end in the return of her Church to Catholic unity and the See of Peter."[2] Having formed such a hopeful view of the work of the Tractarians it is not wonderful to learn that De Lisle spent the best years of a prolonged life in supporting the Oxford Movement in the interests of the Pope. The *Tract* which thus impressed this young Roman Catholic squire was an argument in favour of Apostolic Succession, and it asserted that, "Except, therefore, we can show such a warrant [that is, of 'commissioned persons'], we [the clergy] cannot be sure that *our hands convey the sacrifice;* we cannot be sure that souls worthily prepared, receiving the bread which we break, and the cup of blessing which we bless, are partakers of the Body and Blood of Christ." The writer further asserted of the Church of England that she is "the only Church in this realm which has a right to be quite sure that she has the Lord's Body to give to His people."[3] In *Tract X.*, which had been published before De Lisle wrote his opinion, Newman urged that the clergy should be considered "as if they were the Apostles"; and as saying to the laity:—

"Then you will honour us, with a purer honour than many men do now, namely, as those (if I may say so) who are intrusted with the keys of heaven and hell, as the heralds of mercy, as the denouncers of woe to wicked men, as intrusted with the awful and

---

[1] Cardwell's *Documentary Annals*, vol. i. p. 427.
[2] *Life and Letters of Ambrose Phillipps De Lisle*, vol. i. p. 199.
[3] *Tract No. IV.* pp. 2-5.

mysterious privilege of dispensing Christ's Body and Blood, as far greater than the most powerful and wealthiest of men in our unseen strength and our heavenly riches." [1]

Thus did Priestcraft rear once more its proud head in the Reformed Church of England and demand of the laity that they should meekly bow their necks to its arrogant sway.

Mr. Francis Lyne, a highly respected layman, when in his seventy-ninth year, wrote to me on January 11, 1879, from 5 Seagrave Place, Cheltenham:—"The state we, as Protestants, are now in was foretold by the Roman Catholic party many years ago. My relation, the late Mr. John Adolphus, a notable Q.C., one day on leaving the Temple—just when the *Tracts for the Times* appeared— was joined by a Roman Catholic, and he said:—'Ah! Adolphus, this is the grandest move for our Church there has been since the Reformation.'"

It was not long before voices of warning were heard. Dr. Pusey sent his Tract on Fasting to Dr. Arnold, the famous Head Master of Rugby, who was not long in finding out what way the Tractarians were going. In acknowledging, on February 18, 1834, the receipt of the *Tract*, Arnold told Pusey a few plain truths, the wisdom of which can be seen now after many days. "By the form in which your *Tract* appears, I fear you are lending your co-operation to a party second to none in the tendency of their principles to overthrow the truth of the Gospel. . . . I stand amazed at some apparent efforts in this Protestant Church to set up the idol of Tradition; that is, to render Gibbon's conclusion against Christianity valid, by taking, like him, the Fathers and the second and subsequent periods of the Christian History as a fair specimen of the Apostles and of the true doctrines of Christ. But Ignatius will far sooner sink the authority of St. Paul and St. John than they communicate any portion of theirs to him. The system

---

[1] *Tract No. X.* pp. 2-5.
[2] Palmer's *Narrative of Events*, pp. 226, 227.

pursued in Oxford seems to be leading to a revival of the Nonjurors, a party far too mischievous and too foolish ever to be revived with success. But it may be revived enough to do harm, *to cause the ruin of the Church of England* first, and, so far as human folly can, to obstruct the progress of the Church of Christ."[1]

[1] *Life of Pusey*, vol. i. pp. 282, 283.

CHAPTER III

The first "outbreak of Tractism"—Dr. Hampden's case—Newman on Subscription to the Articles—He was "not a great friend to them"—Hampden appointed Regius Professor of Divinity—Agitation against his appointment—Lord Melbourne's letter to Pusey—Newman's *Elucidations*—Stanley's opinion of them—Dr. Wilberforce and Hampden—Lord Selborne and Dean Church's testimony as to Hampden's views—The real cause of opposition was Hampden's Protestantism—Proof of his Protestantism—Extracts from his writings—Vote of want of confidence by Convocation—Hampden's Letter to the Archbishop of Canterbury—Mr. Macmullen's case—Hampden apppointed Bishop of Hereford—Protest of thirteen Bishops—Lord John Russell's reply—Archdeacon Hare defends Hampden—A Prosecution commenced—Organised by Pusey, Keble, Marriott, and Mozley—Wilberforce's eleven questions for Hampden—His answer—The Bishop withdraws his Letters of Request—Pusey's bitter disappointment—Tractarian anxiety to prosecute their opponents—Bishop Phillpotts denounces the Episcopal Veto—Protests by the Dean of Hereford—Hampden elected Bishop by the Chapter of Hereford—Protest in Bow Church—An exciting scene—Consecration of Dr. Hampden—The new Bishop's sympathisers—Addresses of confidence.

WHAT Archbishop Whately termed "the first outbreak of Tractism" was directed against the Rev. Dr. R. D. Hampden. In 1832 Dr. Hampden had been selected to preach the Bampton Lectures at Oxford, which were subsequently published under the title of *The Scholastic Philosophy Considered in its Relation to Christian Theology*. These lectures were delivered to large congregations; but do not appear to have excited any remarkable attention after their publication, until their author was appointed, in 1836, Regius Professor of Divinity in the University of Oxford, when they became the centre round which a fierce contest raged, a contest which was renewed with even greater violence in 1847, when Dr. Hampden was appointed Bishop of Hereford. A pamphlet which he issued in

1834 added greatly to the flame of Tractarian wrath, and was used against its author again and again during the succeeding thirteen years. It bore the title of *Observations on Religious Dissent. With Particular Reference to the Use of Religious Tests in the University*. It was, in brief, a plea for the admission of Dissenters into the University of Oxford, on certain conditions. He wished to abolish Subscription to the Thirty-Nine Articles on the part of those entering the University, as had already been done in the University of Cambridge, and therefore there was nothing new in his proposal in itself, though no doubt it seemed revolutionary to the authorities of the University of Oxford, and was particularly distasteful to those Tractarians who wished to keep Dissenters out of the University. Newman led the attack on Hampden's pamphlet, a copy of which the author had sent to him on its publication. In thanking him for his courtesy, Newman wrote:—" While I respect the tone of piety in which the pamphlet is written, I feel an aversion to the principles it professes, as (in my opinion), legitimately tending to formal Socinianism."[1] Newman's real opinion as to Subscription to the Thirty-Nine Articles was given on January 11, 1836, in a letter which he addressed to Mr. Percival, in the course of which his hatred for the study of Christian Evidences, and his wish that young men should believe "prior to reason"; and should, without reason, accept what their instructors taught them, is clearly manifested. "Shut your eyes, and open your mouths, and take what the priests may give you, without examination," is a policy which is ever dear to a proud Sacerdotal priesthood; but is quite inconsistent with the Scriptural injunction:—" Believe not every spirit, but try the spirits whether they are of God; because many false prophets are gone out in the world " (1 John iv. 1).

"The advantage of subscription (to my mind) is," Newman wrote, "its witnessing to the principle that religion is to be approached with a submission of the understanding. Nothing is so

---

[1] Newman's *Letters*, vol. ii. p. 77.

common, as you must know, as for young men to approach serious subjects as judges, to study them as mere sciences. Aristotle and Butler are treated as teachers of *a* system, not as if there was more truth in them than in Jeremy Bentham. *The study of the 'Evidences,' now popular (such as Paley's), encourages this evil frame of mind.* The learner is supposed *external* to the system ... and to have to choose it by an act of reason before he submits to it; whereas, the great lesson of the Gospel is faith, *an obeying prior to reasoning*, and *proving* its reasonableness by making experiment of it—a casting of heart and mind into the system and investigating the truth by practice. I should say the same of a person in a Mahometan country or under any system which was not plainly and purely diabolical[1] ... In an age, then, when this great principle is scouted, Subscription to the Articles is a memento and a protest, and again actually does, I believe, impress upon the minds of young men the teachable and subdued temper expected of them. THEY ARE NOT TO REASON, BUT TO OBEY, and this quite independently of the degree of accuracy, the wisdom, &c., of the Articles themselves. *I am no great friend of them, and should rejoice to substitute the Creeds for them*, were it not for the Romanists, who might be excluded by the plan you suggest of demanding certificates of baptism and confirmation."[2]

This is, I think, the first recorded instance in which Tractarian dislike to the Thirty-Nine Articles was clearly expressed. In later years members of the party spoke out more emphatically. A collection of extracts from their utterances on this subject will be found in the Appendix to my *Secret History of the Oxford Movement*. Newman's exhortation to young men "NOT TO REASON, BUT TO OBEY," reminds me of the advice of a priestly member of the English Church Union. "It was not," said the Rev. Luke Rivington, at a meeting of the Union, January 14, 1868, "that he undervalued the office of *the laity, whose high and noble prerogative it was to listen and obey;* but it was for the ministers of the Church to magnify their office."[3] A Ritualistic newspaper recently put the matter thus: "In the Catholic Church it is for the clergy

---

[1] In other words, this is equivalent to advising a young man to swallow any spiritual poison offered to him first, and after it has done its deadly work he will be able to refuse to take any more of it. Such advice would justify a belief in any lying legend taught by a Roman Catholic priest.

[2] *Life of Dr. Pusey*, vol. i. p. 301.

[3] *English Church Union Monthly Circular*, vol. for 1868, p. 65.

to teach and govern, for the people to obey."[1] This kind of teaching tends to make slaves of the laity, and enables the clergy to assume the position of "being lords over God's heritage" (1 Peter v. 3).

There was a Latitudinarian spirit throughout Dr. Hampden's pamphlet which I, for one, deeply regret, especially in his remarks on Unitarians. He avowed himself as "favourable to a removal of all tests, so far as they are employed as securities of orthodoxy among our members at large."[2] As to the Unitarians, he specially applied to them the following statement: "In religion, properly so called, few Christians, if any (I speak, of course, of pious minds) really differ"; and he further declared, "When I look at the reception by the Unitarians, both of the Old and New Testament, I cannot, for my part, strongly as I dislike their theology, deny to those, who acknowledge this basis of divine facts, the name of Christians."[3] He was no great friend to articles of faith: "Articles of religious communion," he declared, "from their reference to the fixed objects of our faith, assume an immovable character fatally adverse to all theological improvement."[4] Though in favour of admitting Dissenters to the University without subscribing to the Articles, Dr. Hampden insisted that when they entered they should receive religious instruction from clergymen of the Church of England. "I see," he wrote, "no objection at the same time to the admission of Dissenters into the University, *because* they are Dissenters. I should be glad indeed to see them appearing among us, as on a neutral ground, on which we may forget war, and learn together the arts of peace and charity. If persons of different communions are willing to conform to our discipline, and receive instruction from us, knowing that we are members of the Church of England, and sincere teachers of its theological system, where can be the real objection in such a case?"[5]

---

[1] *Church Review*, August 23, 1900, p. 583.
[2] Hampden's *Observations on Religious Dissent*, 2nd edition, p. 35.
[3] *Ibid.* p. 20.   [4] *Ibid.* p. 22.   [5] *Ibid.* p. 34.

The Tractarian party took the lead in resisting every attempt to admit Dissenters into the University of Oxford, and with such success that it was not until 1854 that Subscription to the Thirty-Nine Articles was made no longer compulsory as a condition of matriculation.

Towards the end of 1835, the Rev. Dr. Burton, Regius Professor of Divinity at Oxford, died. At that time Lord Melbourne was Prime Minister. The Archbishop of Canterbury (Dr. Howley), whose sympathies were to a considerable extent with the new Oxford Movement, sent to his lordship a list of persons whom he conceived to be best qualified to succeed Dr. Burton. Eight names were mentioned by his Grace, the first being Dr. Pusey; the fourth, the Rev. J. H. Newman; and the fifth, the Rev. John Keble. Lord Melbourne consulted Archbishop Whately as to the merits of these gentlemen. "It will be observed," writes Canon Liddon, "that each of the three leaders of the Movement, as they subsequently became, was named by the Archbishop for the vacant Chair of Divinity. What might not have been the result on the future of the English Church had any one of them been chosen!"[1] Whatever may be said against the gentleman who succeeded Dr. Burton, there can be no doubt that his appointment was a serious blow to the hopes of the sacerdotalists. A rumour of Dr. Hampden's appointment reached Oxford on February 8, 1836. No time was lost in getting up an agitation against it. That very evening Pusey brought his friends together at a dinner party, at which the case was fully discussed. There was still a hope that an agitation would prevent the dreaded appointment being made. Two days later another meeting was held in Corpus Common Room, at which a petition to the King was agreed to, and by the next evening it was sent off to the Archbishop of Canterbury for presentation to his Majesty, signed by seventy-three resident Masters. It seems to have produced a considerable effect upon the King, who at once communicated with Lord Melbourne,

[1] *Life of Dr. Pusey*, vol. i. p. 370.

The Prime Minister, however, remained firm, and on February 15th, wrote to William IV.:—

"To what do the charges against Dr. Hampden amount? That Dr. Hampden is known to have expressed himself in printed publications in such a manner as to produce on the minds of many an impression that he maintains doctrines and principles fundamentally opposed to the integrity of the Christian faith. Is this sufficient? Is his faith to be denied on such grounds as these— 'an impression on the minds of many,' without even stating whether in the opinion of those who signed the paper the impression is just? There are innumerable impressions upon the minds of many, but who ever considered such impressions as any proof against the person whom they affected?"[1]

Archbishop Whately lost no time in informing the Prime Minister what was, in his opinion, the real secret of the opposition to Hampden's appointment. "Hampden," he wrote, "is not a Tory. And he was for the relaxation of the subscription to the Articles at Matriculation. *Hence it is* that men now bring a charge of heresy against him which, if they had been sincere and honest, they would have brought before the regular tribunal three or four years ago, when he was delivering before the University of Oxford and printing at the University Press the sermons which they charge with Socinianism."[2]

No stone was left unturned to prevent the appointment. Pusey hoped that he could reach the heart or move the will of Lord Melbourne, and therefore he lost no time in writing to him what Newman has termed "one of his most earnest, weightiest, crushing letters"; but all in vain, for Newman adds that Lord Melbourne "answered him cleverly and sharply, and did not conceal the great antipathy he felt in consequence towards Pusey."[3] The answer is printed in full in *Lord Melbourne's Papers*. It was dated February 24, and contains a hint that Pusey

[1] *Lord Melbourne's Papers*, p. 499.
[2] *Ibid.* p. 501.
[3] Newman's *Letters*, vol. ii. p. 158.

would do well to clean out his own stables before he attempted to clean those of other persons :—

"Your principle," he wrote, "would make the opinions of the present Professors the standard of every future appointment. Before persons are chosen on account of the consonance of their tenets with those of the individuals who at present fill the theological chairs, you must admit that we must a little consider what are the tenets of those gentlemen ; and you are very well aware that great alarm has been excited in the minds of many whose authority I respect by certain tenets, which have, I believe, been published anonymously, but with which you are supposed to have had some connection, and which are represented to me to be of a novel character and inconsistent with the hitherto received doctrines of the Church of England. I have not seen the *Tracts* I refer to, and I should be glad to obtain them; I only speak from what I hear. I therefore mean to pronounce no opinion upon them."[1]

Meanwhile the Committee for resisting Dr. Hampden continued its sittings in Corpus Christi College. They brought before the Heads of Houses a petition asking them to bring before Convocation a censure of the alleged errors of Dr. Hampden. That gentleman, however, heard of the proposal in time, went to the special meeting of the Heads of Houses, and defeated, for the time being, the plot against himself. Writing to his friend, Archbishop Whately, on February 17th, he tells him what occurred. "At a special meeting" of the Board of Heads of Houses, he wrote, "on Thursday last, it was the subject of deliberation whether any step should be taken by the Board in consequence of the rumour that it was the intention of Ministers to place me in the Divinity Chair. Numbers were canvassed beforehand in order to get a majority for the hostile measure designed, and they tried, out of mock kindness, to prevent my attendance. I did attend, however, to confront their folly and intolerance, and with the kind and skilful support of the Provost of Oriel succeeded in disappointing their attempt."[2]

Mr. Henry George Liddell, afterwards well known as

[1] *Lord Melbourne's Papers*, p. 504.
[2] *Memorials of Bishop Hampden*, p. 54.

Dean of Christ Church, Oxford, was in Oxford at the time of the Hampden controversy, and wrote an interesting description of the meeting of the Heads of Houses, at which Dr. Hampden was present:—

"On Wednesday," wrote Mr. Liddell, "the Heads of Houses, roused by the energy of the Movement party, called a meeting. To the horror and surprise of the Doctors, the Principal of St. Mary Hall (Dr. Hampden) himself appeared. 'Strange,' said the Dean of Christ Church, 'very strange that *you* should be here, Mr. Principal: we have met to talk of you. Do you mean to stay?' 'I do,' was the reply. 'And to vote?' interposed Shuttleworth (Warden of New College). 'I have not made up my mind,' said Hampden. A very angry discussion followed, after which certain propositions (I know not what) were put to the vote. On the first two Hampden was left in a minority, himself taking no part. On the third the division was equal, whereupon Dr. Hampden interposed, and by his vote turned the decision of the august body in his own favour."[1]

Newman was quick in perceiving that attacks like these needed supplementing by material of a more formidable kind. He therefore at once set to work to write a pamphlet containing extracts from Hampden's published works, adding to them such comments as he thought necessary. It was published on February 13th, only five days after the rumour of the appointment had reached Oxford. He had to sit up all through one night writing, so as to get it out as quickly as possible. It bore the title of *Elucidations of Dr. Hampden's Theological Statements*, and formed a pamphlet of forty-seven pages. It was certainly the most influential document ever produced against Dr. Hampden; and yet, by friends and foes alike, it was censured for unfairness. Mr. Arthur Penrhyn Stanley, subsequently known as Dean Stanley, was at that time in residence at Oxford, and took the deepest interest in the Hampden controversy. He did not approve of the new appointment to the Divinity Chair, but when the *Elucidations* appeared, he attacked the pamphlet in the most vigorous style.

---

[1] *Henry George Liddell, D.D.: A Memoir*, p. 33.

"No one," he remarked, "who has not compared Newman and Pusey's[1] extracts with the original writings of Hampden, and who has not had experience, in himself or others, of the fearfully erroneous impression that those extracts convey, can duly appreciate the appearance that must have presented itself to Arnold's mind of shameless and wilful fabrication. If they (the extracts) had been made by any one else than Newman and Pusey, I should not have hesitated to attribute them to wilful dishonesty; as it is, I must call it culpable carelessness, blindness, and recklessness, in matters of the most vital importance to the Church and nation, and to the peace of a good man. They have applied to doctrines what Hampden says of phraseology, to the Atonement what he said of Penance, to denial of Sacramental Grace, and original sin, and regeneration, and Trinitarianism, what he has said in confirmation and approval of all these truths. They have, till they were compelled by counter-pamphlets to notice that there were such books, kept out of sight his *Parochial Sermons* and *Philosophical Evidences*, which contain the very essence of orthodoxy; they have attacked him because he has impugned their own peculiar theory of Church authority, and the submission of human reason, and have enlisted in their ranks persons who differ as entirely from that theory as does Hampden himself; and all this while they themselves hold tenets barely compatible with their remaining in the English Church."[2]

Newman's *Elucidations* had a most powerful effect on the public mind. People were entirely guided by the pamphlet who had never read a word of Hampden's writings in his published books. The Rev. T. Mozley, one of the opponents of Hampden, and all his life through a friend of the Oxford Movement, frankly tells us that when Hampden was condemned by the Oxford Convocation:—

"The great mass of the multitude that inflicted this penalty were very, if not entirely, ignorant of the book which was the *corpus delicti*. They might have seen it on a counter, or on a table; they might have opened it, turned over a leaf or two, and might even have had their attention directed to a few passages. The very hurry in which the thing was done, and the fact that the book was and is compara-

---

[1] *Dr. Hampden's Past and Present Statements Compared.* By Dr. Pusey. Oxford: Parker. 1836.
[2] *Life of Dean Stanley*, vol. i. p. 163. London. 1893.

tively rare, forbid the supposition that there could have been much, or even an adequate, acquaintance with its contents."[1]

One of those who took a leading part in opposing Dr. Hampden's appointment was the Rev. Samuel Wilberforce, who based his opposition on the extracts from his Bampton Lectures given in Newman's *Elucidations*. It was not until Hampden's appointment to the Bishopric of Hereford, in 1847, that Wilberforce carefully read the book for himself, and then he at once changed his opinions on the question. How this change of opinion came about is told, in an interesting narrative, by Newman's brother, Mr. F. W. Newman:—

"My old friend, the late Bonamy Price, well known in recent Oxford, had been a Rugby Master, and with Grenfell and the rest had voted against disabling Hampden. Happening to be in Oxford just after the *Bubble* burst [*i.e.* in 1847], he called upon Dr. Hawkins, who had been gracious to him in old days; and inevitably the two began mutual congratulation on the event [*i.e.* Bishop Wilberforce's decision to veto the proposed prosecution of Hampden]. Hawkins was delighted and boiling over, and soon poured out ample details of what passed between him and the Bishop [Samuel Wilberforce].

"After the Bishop perceived that his old tutor looked grave on the open war against Crown Patronage, and on the rumour that the Dean of Hereford would risk a Præmunire, the Bishop said that to listen to Keble was not a new or active deed: that in fact he was constrained to it [that is, to grant permission to prosecute Hampden] by consistency; for he had voted against Hampden's becoming Regius Professor of Divinity, and he could not possibly make light of unsoundness concerning such a doctrine as the Trinity. (These two points were the *fulcra* of the talk.) On the former, the Provost said, 'You voted in 1836, true; but then you were a Curate; then you were one out of four hundred; now you are a Lord Bishop: then your responsibility was *nil;* now, you will bring on yourself the chief responsibility. An error here may affect all your future life.' When the Bishop made some remark that for sacred truth we must encounter great risk, he so expressed himself that Hawkins exclaimed: 'Bless me! why, you cannot have read Hampden's lectures; you can only have read Newman's *Elucidations* of

---

[1] Mozley's *Reminiscences of the Oxford Movement*, vol. i. pp. 366, 367.

them.' The Bishop replied: 'Well, I must confess I could not for a moment distrust Newman.' 'Ah! my Lord, I do not blame you; four hundred trusted him, and I have no right to say, believe me rather than him. But since you have not read Hampden yourself, and must now, as Bishop, seem to judge his book, and to oppose his appointment by the Crown, I do say, that if you are a wise Bishop you will read his book *at once*. And I will tell you what! We ought this evening to sit side by side, and read the book together.'

"The Bishop freely confessed the wisdom of the advice, and acted on it. The two sat together, with feet on fender, and read the lectures through from end to end.

"Then the Bishop said, 'My kind old tutor, you are right. I have no right to open my lips against Hampden.'

"What actual words the Bishop next day used to Keble I am not sure that I learned from Bonamy, but either from him or from some other quarter I heard them to be: '*I have now read Hampden myself*, and cannot presume to blame him.'"[1]

This interview between Bishop Wilberforce and Dr. Hawkins took place, as Mr. F. W. Newman informs us, in December 1847, and the substantial accuracy of the story of what took place is corroborated by a letter of Wilberforce himself to Hampden, dated December 28, 1847, as published in his biography. In this he wrote:—

"Unless I was satisfied that there was matter for a criminal suit, I could not think myself justified in sending an accusation against you to be tried in the Arches Court. Whether there was such matter could be determined by me only after a careful study of the works in question, with all your explanations in my mind.

"Regarding, then, the *Observations on Dissent* as virtually withdrawn, I accordingly applied myself to a thorough and impartial examination of the 'Bampton Lectures.' I have now carefully studied them throughout, with the aid of those explanations of their meaning which you have furnished to the public since their first publication, and now in your private communications. The result of this examination, I am bound plainly to declare, is my own conviction that they do not justly warrant those suspicions of unsoundness to which they have given rise, and which, *so long as I trusted to selected extracts*, I myself shared."[2]

---

[1] *Contributions Chiefly to the Early History of the late Cardinal Newman.* By his Brother, F. W. Newman. 1891, pp. 85-88.
[2] *Life of Bishop Wilberforce*, vol. i. pp. 486, 487.

Not only was Bishop Wilberforce misled by Newman's *Elucidations:* many Evangelical Churchmen also joined in the hue and cry against Hampden, under the impression that he was heretical in his teaching as to the Trinity and the Incarnation. But, after all, the question here arises, was there sufficient ground for these charges? As early as February 27, 1836, Hampden wrote to the Archbishop of Canterbury:—"I may be indulged on this occasion with saying, that a belief in the great revealed truths of the Trinity and the Incarnation has been my stay through life; and I utterly disclaim the imputation of inculcating any doctrines at variance with these foundations of Christian hope."[1] Though not holding heretical views on these points himself, Hampden was, apparently, willing to oppose the use of strong abuse against those who really were heretical. It was true that he held very liberal views as to the value of Confessions of Faith and Articles of Religion; but, as Bishop Wilberforce cleverly showed in the letter just cited, Newman himself, at about the very time when Hampden's accused publications had first appeared, was himself guilty of a very similar offence.

"I read in them [Hampden's Bampton Lectures]," wrote Wilberforce, "a thoughtful and able history of the formation of dogmatic terminology, not a studied depreciation of authorised dogmatic language, still less any conscious denial of admitted dogmatic truth. *I see in them, in fact, so far, little more than what has already been expressed in the words* (never, I believe, considered liable to censure) *of one of your ablest opponents* [Newman] in 1834, who says: 'If I avow my belief that freedom from symbols and Articles is abstractedly the highest state of Church communion and the peculiar knowledge of the Primitive Church, it is . . . first, because technicality and formality are, in their degree, inevitable results of public Confessions of Faith.' And again: 'Her rulers were loth to confess that the Church had grown too old to enjoy the free unsuspicious teaching with which her childhood was blest, and that her disciples must for the future calculate and reason before they acted' (Newman's *Arians,* pp. 41, 42)."[2]

---

[1] *Memorials of Bishop Hampden,* p. 55.
[2] *Life of Bishop Wilberforce,* vol. i. p. 487.

The fact is that it is now admitted by prominent High Churchmen that Hampden was not, strictly speaking, heretical at all. That well-known High Churchman, Lord Selborne, admits that:—" Dr. Hampden, as a Bishop, was neither better nor worse than many others; he did nothing to confirm any suspicion of his orthodoxy."[1] Archdeacon Clark testifies, " after twenty years' intimacy" with Dr. Hampden, that:—" He was as loyal and sound a member of the Church of England as any of her sons; as orthodox in his views and teaching on the doctrines of the faith as it is held by our Reformed Church, and expressed in her Articles and formularies, as any who belong to the ranks of her ministering clergy; as clear and as sound in his views and teaching on the subject of the Church's two Sacraments, nay, much more so than many who thought it their duty to attack him."[2] The testimony of the late Dean Church will, no doubt, carry great weight with many High Churchmen. And this is what he says:—" Dr. Hampden was in fact unexceptionably, even rigidly orthodox in his acceptance of Church doctrine and Church Creeds. He had published a volume of sermons containing, among other things, an able statement of the Scriptural argument for the doctrine of the Trinity, and an equally able defence of the Athanasian Creed."[3]

Why, then, it may be asked, was such an ado made about the appointment of such a man to the office of Regius Professor of Divinity in 1836; and, again, to his appointment as Bishop of Hereford in 1847? The real fact is, I believe, that the outcry against Hampden for heresy was but the ostensible and not the real cause of the furious opposition of the Tractarian party. They simply used this cry for the purpose of blinding the eyes of Evangelical Churchmen, and induce them to join in the hue and cry against him. The real head and front of Dr. Hampden's offence was his Protestantism, and his

[1] *Memorials Family and Personal*, 1766-1865. By the Earl of Selborne, vol. ii. p. 10.
[2] *Memorials of Bishop Hampden*, p. 259.
[3] *The Oxford Movement*. By Dean Church, 1st edition, p. 144.

well-known opposition to the sacerdotal doctrines of the rising Tractarian party, whom he thoroughly distrusted. The Rev. William Sinclair, who knew him well, tells us that (apparently soon after the commencement of the Tractarian Movement):—"I well remember seeing the Doctor come into his study, flushed with excitement and with a little tract in his hand. It was one of the well-known *Tracts for the Times*. His remark upon it was: These gentlemen, without even knowing it, have passed the Rubicon; they do not see that they are already Romanists.'"[1]

Hampden's Protestantism was seen in his *Observations on Religious Dissent*, in which he placed the Holy Scriptures above every human composition, and avowed himself an opponent of the theory that Tradition is of equal value with the Bible. He wished to "guard the depository of sacred doctrine, the Scripture itself, against the inroads of *Tradition*, or any human authority"; and he urged his readers "to go to Scripture for every matter of religious debate. If the alleged point cannot be proved out of Scripture, it is no truth of revelation."[2] In his Bampton Lectures Hampden's opposition to the Sacerdotalism which had been adopted by the Tractarian leaders, was revealed in a most unmistakable manner. He attributed the "theory of Sacramental influence," advocated in the Scholastic philosophy, not to Holy Scripture, but to "the general belief in Magic in the early ages of the Church."[3]

"The relative importance of the Eucharist," said Dr. Hampden, "in comparison with the other Sacraments, and, indeed, with the whole doctrine and ritual of Christianity, in the system of the Church of Rome, may be drawn from this primary notion of Sacramental efficiency. It may well be asked, why this sacred rite should stand so pre-eminent in the scheme of Christianity. I do not say, that it ought not to hold a principal station among the observances of a holy life. But it is the doctrinal supremacy given to it, to which I refer. View it, as it exists in the Roman Church, and it is there found absorbing into it the whole, it may be said,

---

[1] *Memorials of Bishop Hampden*, p. 32.
[2] *Observations on Religious Dissent*, 2nd edition, p. 9.
[3] Hampden's *Scholastic Philosophy Considered*, 1st edition, p. 315.

of Christian worship. There, the ministers of religion seem to be set apart chiefly for this sacred celebration: it is the spiritual power of their office—the essence of their priesthood. If we ask then, why this particular Sacrament should have attained this superiority over all other rites of Christianity, we may find an answer in the Scholastic theory. Whilst the other Sacraments, recognised by that theory, *participate* of the virtue of Christ's passion, this is the *passion itself* of Christ—the *whole virtue* of His priesthood mystically represented and conveyed. . . . It was freely admitted that Christ was once offered for all on the Cross; that henceforth He is seated at the right hand of the Divine Majesty, to die no more. But the sacrifice performed by the priest was still a real offering of Christ; as being the appointed channel through which the expiatory virtue of the Great Sacrifice descends in vital efflux from the person of the Saviour.[1]

"The history of the Sacraments, in the Scholastic system, is God working by the instrumentality of man. The theory is of the Divine causation, but the practical power displayed is the sacerdotal; the necessary instrument for the conveyance of Divine grace becoming in effect the principal cause.

"Surely it requires no research into ecclesiastical history or philosophy, to see that so operose a system is utterly repugnant to the spirit of Christianity. Contemplate our Saviour at the Last Supper, breaking bread, and giving thanks, and distributing to His disciples; and how great is the transition from the institution itself to the splendid ceremonial of the Latin Church? Hear Him, or His Apostles, exhorting to repentance; and can we suppose the casuistical system, to which the name of Penance has been given, to be the true sacrifice of the broken and contrite spirit? . . .

"Thanks to the Christian resolution of our Reformers, they broke that charm which this mystical number of the Sacraments carried with it, and dispelled the theurgic system which it supported. We are not, perhaps, sufficiently sensible of the advantages which we enjoy through their exertions in this respect—exertions which cost them so many painful struggles, even to the bitterness of death. They have taken our souls out of the hand of man, to let them repose in the bosom of our Saviour and our God. We have been enabled thus to fulfil the instruction of Scripture, to 'come boldly to the throne of Grace,' and ask of Him who gives liberally and denies to none. The perplexities and distress of heart, of which we have been relieved, none perhaps can now adequately conceive.

---

[1] Hampden's *Scholastic Philosophy Considered*, pp. 321, 322.

We must ask of those who have experienced the false comfort of that officious intercession of the Sacramental system of the Latin Church. They will tell us that, under that system, they knew not the liberty of the Gospel. They were unhappy without resource. Their wounds were opened, but there was none to heal."[1]

In statements such as these we find, I believe, the real cause of the Tractarian attack on Dr. Hampden. Latitudinarian views as to Holy Scripture are now very common and widespread amongst a certain section of the Ritualistic party. Their zeal now, as was that of their predecessors in 1836, is mainly directed to building up that sacerdotal system against which our Reformers testified with their blood. Hampden protested against the same evil system; hence the hatred of Pusey, Newman, Keble, and others, who made the life of their opponent unhappy for many years. In saying this I wish to guard myself against being supposed to be a friend to Hampden's Latitudinarian views. I have no sympathy with them whatever, and I think that Lord Melbourne in 1836, and Lord John Russell in 1847, would have acted more wisely had they selected some one else who valued Christian doctrines more highly than did Dr. Hampden.

We now return to the history of the case. The appointment of Hampden as Regius Professor of Divinity was published in the *London Gazette* on February 17, 1836, and after that it was felt by his opponents that there was no chance of upsetting it. But it was possible to move the University to express its disapproval of the appointment. The first attempt in this direction proved, as I have already stated, a decided failure owing to the firm action of Hampden himself. But the effort could be renewed, and it was renewed. At last the Heads of Houses decided, though with not a little hesitation, that they would bring before Convocation a new statute, providing that Dr. Hampden should not (like his predecessors in office) be placed on the Board which nominated select preachers before the University; and

[1] Hampden's *Scholastic Philosophy Considered*, pp. 341-343.

that he should not be consulted when a sermon was called in question before the Vice-Chancellor. The Convocation was to meet to decide this important matter on March 22nd, and in preparation for it Pusey issued a pamphlet entitled: *Dr. Hampden's Theological Statements and the Thirty-Nine Articles Compared*. It contained extracts from Hampden's writings. Every effort was made to bring up voters from the country, and with the result that on the eventful day about 450 members were present. But they came up in vain, for no sooner had the Vice-Chancellor put the question of the proposed new statute, than the Proctors interposed with their veto, which at once put an end to the proceedings. The Tractarians were, of course, very much vexed, but they certainly had subsequently an ample revenge, when, in 1844, a proposal to censure *Tract XC.* was, in the interests of the Tractarians, vetoed by the then Proctors, Mr. Church and Mr. Guillemard. The names of the Proctors who vetoed the proposed statute against Dr. Hampden should here be mentioned. They were the Rev. E. G. Bayly, Fellow of Pembroke College; and the Rev. Henry Reynolds, Fellow and Tutor of Jesus College. Though defeated on this occasion the opponents of Hampden did not lose hope. They knew that new Proctors would soon be appointed. This was done on April 13th. In that month appeared Dr. Arnold's famous article in the *Edinburgh Review*, on "The Oxford Malignants and Dr. Hampden," which, by the strength of its denunciations of the Tractarians fanned the flame to fiercer heat than ever. The Convocation met again on May 5th: the vetoed statute was again introduced. Its adoption was moved by Dr. Cardwell, Principal of S. Albans Hall; and seconded by Dr. Symons, Warden of Wadham; the latter being an opponent of Tractarianism. It was carried by 474 votes for, and 94 against, being a majority of 380. The statute was in the following terms

"Since it is committed by the University to the Regius Professor of Sacred Theology that he shall be one of the number of those whom the select preachers are appointed, and, moreover, that his advice shall be had if any preacher shall be called in question before the Chancellor; but since he, who is now the Professor, in certain of his published works has so treated theological questions, that in this behalf the University has no confidence in him; it is enacted that the Regius Professor shall be deprived of the aforesaid functions until the pleasure of the University be otherwise, &c."[1]

This statute was a sting for Dr. Hampden, but it did not lead to his removal from office, and therefore in the contest he became the substantial victor. Three eminent lawyers were consulted as to its legality. Their decision was given in these terms:—" We think the statute of 1836 is illegal, as violating the restrictions imposed by the Laudian Code, and as passed by the assumption and exercise of a power which has not been conceded to the University."[2] There were, even amongst the leading opponents of Hampden, some who thought the statute illegal. The Rev. Thomas Mozley was one of these. He denounced it as an " audacious act," and declared that:— "Any reasonable person, too, may doubt the validity of an act depriving the Regius Professor of Divinity of privileges appertaining to the very essence of the office. If he is not to have a vote in the selection of University preachers, or upon a charge of heresy, where is he?"[3]

On December 21, 1837, the case of Dr. Hampden was debated in the House of Lords, in the course of a discussion on University Reform. The Earl of Radnor warmly defended the Professor, and said that he had no doubt that all the hostility to him arose from his advocating the admission of Dissenters into the University. Lord Melbourne said:—" I certainly do not think that there is anything to be condemned in the writings of Dr. Hampden." The Archbishop of Canterbury attacked Dr. Hampden in such a very marked manner that he felt it necessary to defend himself in a lengthy letter to his Grace, in which he demanded to know what were the actual charges brought against him by his accusers, and also that he should not be judged by mere clamour and shouting, but by proper

---

[1] *Life of Bishop Wilberforce*, vol. i. p. 425.
[2] *Memorials of Bishop Hampden*, p. 65.
[3] Mozley's *Reminiscences of the Oxford Movement*, vol. i. p. 364.

ecclesiastical judges; and he concluded by a fearless exposure of the real motives of his chief opponents.

"I implore your Grace," he wrote, "effectually to put an end to this unnatural warfare. I ask, as I have said, for specific charges if such exist. I ask to be called to account before a legal ecclesiastical tribunal, if there be real matter of accusation against me. ... It is also well known, that among the prime movers of the disturbance were the leaders and disciples of a new theological school, which is now attracting notice by its extraordinary publications, and exciting considerable alarm in the Church. Am I to satisfy this party? Am I to purchase exemption from censure by folding my arms, and suffering myself to be led away captive by a band whom I regard as making inroads on the constitution of the Church of England? You would not, my Lord, have me to consent to such terms of peace. . . . If, indeed, the price of quiet is to be a surrender of the name and principles of Protestantism—if I am to admit the authority of Tradition on a parity with Scripture—if the profession of Justification by Faith only is no longer to be the sign of a standing Church, but a doctrine of Episcopal Grace and Sacramental Justification is to overlay God's free pardon through Christ to sinful men—if private judgment is to be restrained, not by appeal to Scripture and argument, but by intimidation—if self-constituted associations and the names of men are to rule questions of theology —if Dissent is to be called sin; and taking of oaths, piety; and mysticism, religion; and superstition, faith; and Antichrist, Christ— then there is no alternative but that I must be objected against by those who hold what, if I read the Gospel aright, are the most serious perversions of its truth and its spirit."[1]

In 1842 the Heads of Houses at Oxford formed a new Theological Board of Examiners, and actually appointed Dr. Hampden as its Chairman. This was, of course, *practically* a withdrawal of the censure passed upon him in 1836, and, curiously enough, the appointment did not evoke any public opposition; but when the Heads of Houses decided to go further, and, at the next meeting of Convocation, to formally remove the statute of 1836, the Tractarians took alarm at once, and again set to work to whip up their friends to vote against the proposal. This time, however, they had to lament the coldness of

[1] *Memorials of Bishop Hampden*, pp. 110, 111.

those Evangelicals who had helped them in 1836. A few days before the question came on for decision, Dr. Pusey wrote despondingly to Keble:—" I fear there is increasing ground for anxiety; the Low Church keeps aloof; the *Standard* has begun the Anti-Newman cry."[1] Archdeacon Samuel Wilberforce, who had voted for the statute of 1836, was strongly inclined to vote against rescinding it; but he had his doubts on the point, which seem to have prevented him from voting either for or against it. " My principal doubt," he said, " is this—by an *unopposed* statute Hampden was made Chairman of the new Theological Board; now, how can we refuse him one voice amongst five in nominating select preachers on the disqualification of heresy, and yet allow him to be Chairman of this Theological Board? It is not so much the absolute contradiction of this, as the look of party which it wears, that moves me."[2] On June 7th, the proposition of the Heads of Houses was discussed in Convocation, and rejected by 334 to 219, a majority for Hampden's opponents of 115. The voting showed unmistakably that the opposition to Hampden was considerably less than in 1836, when the statute of censure was passed by a majority of 380. " The Convocation of the University," in Canon Liddon's opinion, " saved its consistency; but the diminished majority showed that recent alarms, and perhaps Dr. Hampden's appeals to the popular Protestantism, had not been without effect."[3]

In 1842 a considerable amount of public interest centred round a case with which Dr. Hampden had to deal as Regius Professor of Divinity. The Rev. Richard Gell Macmullen, Fellow of Corpus Christi College, was required by the statutes of his College to take his B.D. degree, if he wished to retain his Fellowship. It appears to have been the custom, under such circumstances, for the applicant to defend two theses given to him by the Regius Professor of Divinity. Accordingly, Mr. Macmullen

---

[1] *Life of Dr. Pusey*, vol. ii. p. 289.
[2] *Life of Bishop Wilberforce*, vol. i. p. 218.
[3] *Life of Dr. Pusey*, vol. ii. p. 290.

applied to Dr. Hampden to give him two theses to defend. It was very well known to the Professor and in the University that Mr. Macmullen was a Tractarian of a very pronounced type. Probably as a test of his soundness in the faith, Dr. Hampden gave him the following theses to defend:—

"1. The Church of England does not teach, nor can it be proved from Scripture that any change takes place in the Elements at Consecration in the Lord's Supper."

"2. It is a mode of expression calculated to give erroneous views of Divine Revelation to speak of Scripture and Catholic Tradition as joint authorities in the matter of Christian Doctrine."

Mr. Macmullen refused to defend these theses, and demanded, as of right, that he should select his own instead. Dr. Hampden refused to grant the demand, and with the result that Mr. Macmullen appealed to the law, which ultimately led to his defeat, with costs. Dr. Hampden having thus gained the victory, Mr. Macmullen gave way, and consented to read his exercises for the B.D. degree from the original theses submitted to him about two years before. He read them on April 18 and 19, 1844, in the Divinity School.[1] They were afterwards published in pamphlet form;[2] but instead of *defending* the theses, he really did his best to *upset* them by a series of Jesuitical arguments. He said: "It will therefore be my object to endeavour to establish in the first place, That the Church of England does teach or imply that some change takes place in the Elements at Consecration"; and he actually declared that "The very order and rite of Consecration itself in our Book of Common Prayer is a presumption in favour of the view that the Church of England does teach that the Sacramental Elements are themselves *changed* into the Body and Blood of Christ."[3] In his exercise on the second thesis Mr. Macmullen attacked the Protestant doctrine of Private Judgment in vigorous language.

[1] Browne's *Annals of the Tractarian Movement*, 3rd edition, pp. 570, 571.
[2] *Two Exercises for the Degree of B.D.* By Richard Gell Macmullen, M.A. Oxford: Parker. 1844.
[3] *Ibid.* pp. 6, 7.

"The statement of our Church," he said, "That 'Holy Scripture containeth all things necessary to salvation,' does not mean that it can possibly be the duty, much less, as is often proudly and profanely said, the *right* of every man to go to Scripture to gather out his own system of opinion for himself, to receive no doctrine, to believe no truth, but what *he* sees to be declared therein."[1] Dr. Hampden expressed himself as dissatisfied with the exercises, but, as Dean Church expresses it, "Somehow or other, Mr. Macmullen at last got his degree." Within about two years from doing so he seceded to the Church of Rome.

Towards the end of 1847, Lord John Russell startled the country by nominating Dr. Hampden to the Bishopric of Hereford. It was a most injudicious measure, since it could not be said that there was no other suitable man for the post in the country, whose appointment would not have caused such a violent agitation as now arose. The opposition was fiercer and more widespread than in 1836. Even the Bishops took alarm, and thirteen of them signed a united remonstrance to Lord John Russell, which, because of its importance, I print here entire:—

"My Lord,—We, the undersigned Bishops of the Church of England, feel it our duty to represent to your lordship, as head of her Majesty's Government, the apprehension and alarm which have been excited in the minds of the clergy by the rumoured nomination to the See of Hereford of Dr. Hampden, in the soundness of whose doctrine the University of Oxford has affirmed, by a solemn decree, its want of confidence.

"We are persuaded that your lordship does not know how deep and general a feeling prevails on this subject, and we consider ourselves to be acting only in the discharge of our bounden duty both to the Crown and the Church, when we respectfully but earnestly express to your lordship our conviction that, if this appointment be completed, there is the greatest danger both of the interruption of the peace of the Church, and of the disturbance of that confidence which it is most desirable that the clergy and laity of the Church should feel in every exercise of the Royal Supremacy, especially as regards that very delicate and important particular, the nomination to vacant

---

[1] Macmullen's *Two Exercises for the Degree of B.D.*, p. 58.

sees. We have the honour to be, my Lord, with sincere respect, your lordship's obedient and faithful servants, &c., &c."

It was the first time since the Reformation that such a protest against an Episcopal appointment had been made by so large a number of Bishops, and there were high hopes held by some that it would be effectual in preventing the consecration of Dr. Hampden. But such hopes were doomed to disappointment. On November 26, the Archbishop of Canterbury wrote to the Prime Minister to apprise him "of the extent and intensity of the feeling" against the appointment; to whom Lord John Russell replied on the following day, attributing the opposition mainly to Mr. Newman's disciples, and giving them a well-merited censure:—

"I am sorry," he wrote, "to find from your Grace's letter that the outcry has been greater than you expected. I must attribute it chiefly to that portion of the clergy who share Mr. Newman's opinions, but have not had the honesty to follow Mr. Newman in his change of profession.

"I confess I am not surprised that such persons should dread to see a man on the Bench who will actively maintain Protestant doctrines. So long as a Bishop is silent and winks at their attempts to give a Roman Catholic character to the Church of England, they are not alarmed; but when they see a man promoted who has learning to detect and energy to denounce their errors, they begin to fear that Confessions, and Rosaries, and Articles taken in a non-natural sense, and Monkish Legends of Saints, will be discouraged and exposed."[1]

In reply to the remonstrance of the thirteen Bishops, the Prime Minister wrote:—

"I observe that your lordships do not state any want of confidence on your part in the soundness of Dr. Hampden's doctrines. Your lordships refer me to a decree of the University of Oxford, passed eleven years ago, and founded on lectures delivered fifteen years ago.

"Since the date of that decree, Dr. Hampden has acted as Regius Professor of Divinity in the University of Oxford, and many

---

[1] *Life of Lord John Russell.* By Spencer Walpole, edition 1891, vol. i. p. 495.

Bishops, as I am told, have required certificates of attendance on his lectures before they have proceeded to ordain candidates who had received their education at Oxford. He has likewise preached sermons, for which he has been honoured with the approbation of several prelates of our Church. Several months before I named Dr. Hampden to the Queen for the See of Hereford, I signified my intention to the Archbishop of Canterbury, and did not receive from him any discouragement.

"In these circumstances, it appears to me that, should I withdraw my recommendation from Dr. Hampden, which has been sanctioned by the Queen, I should virtually assent to the doctrine that a decree of the University of Oxford is a perpetual bar of exclusion against a clergyman of eminent learning and unimpeachable life; and that, in fact, the supremacy which is now vested in the Crown, is to be transferred to a majority of the members of one of our Universities.

"Nor should it be forgotten that many of the most prominent among that majority have since joined the communion of the See of Rome.

"I deeply regret the feeling which is said to be common among the clergy on this subject. But I cannot sacrifice the reputation of Dr. Hampden, the rights of the Crown, and what I believe to be the true interests of the Church, to a feeling which I believe to be founded on misapprehension and fomented by prejudice."

Meetings of the clergy to protest against the appointment of Dr. Hampden were organised in various parts of the country. At these gatherings many strong protests against the agitation were heard. The Venerable Julius Charles Hare, Archdeacon of Lewes, was asked to convene a meeting of the clergy of his Archdeaconry to protest against the appointment. This request led him, for the first time, to make a careful examination of Hampden's writings, and with the result that he not only refused to call such a meeting, but also published a pamphlet on the subject, in which he gave his reasons for believing that Hampden was not a teacher of heresy. In this pamphlet the Archdeacon stated that on first hearing of the appointment he had at once condemned it as "an act of folly almost amounting to madness."[1]

---

[1] *A Letter to the Dean of Chichester on the Agitation Excited by the Appointment of Dr. Hampden.* By Julius Charles Hare, Archdeacon of Lewes, p. 6. London: Parker. 1848.

Of "Dr. Hampden personally," he added, "I know nothing, and ten days ago had never read a word of his writings,"[1] but that, having now read them, he believed that "Clamour on the part of the accusers, Ignorance on that of their hearers—in which it is to be hoped that the accusers themselves have no small share—these are the powers relied on to bar his way to the Episcopate, the two uncouth, unwieldy giants that throw their clubs across his path."[2] In 1836 Hampden's opponents circulated privately a pamphlet of fifteen pages, without any title on the outside. On page 7 commenced a section headed, "Propositions Maintained in Dr. Hampden's Works," followed by a classified set of extracts, far more unfair than those given by Newman in his notorious *Elucidations*. They were reprinted in 1842, and circulated privately for a third time in 1847, with no author's name attached. Archdeacon Hare reprinted the whole of these extracts, and then tested them by the original documents, proving their dishonest character thoroughly, and concluding thus :—

"Here at length we may pass out of this valley of death. There are still three or four Propositions that I have not noticed ; but they seem to be merely stuck in to swell out the list, and, after what has already been said, need no examination. Such a collection of fraudulent misrepresentations has hardly ever come under my notice, though I have had much sad experience in this way; and it has been a painful task to expose them. But, as I have had to say on a former occasion, a lying spirit is stalking through our Church, and even taking possession of some minds that would otherwise be among its pillars and noblest ornaments : and this spirit we must endeavour to cast out at whatsoever cost. Who the collector of this series of Propositions may be, I know not. Most probably he will be found among those whose love of truth has sought a congenial resting-place in the Romish schism ; and his natural end seems to be, unless some higher spirit arrest him, to become a Familiar of the Inquisition."[3]

There were but very few of the clergy who took the trouble of imitating the excellent example of Archdeacon

---

[1] Hare's *Letter to the Dean of Chichester*, p. 61.
[2] *Ibid.* p. 23.   [3] *Ibid.* pp. 58, 59.

Hare and studying Hampden's writings for themselves. Almost in every instance they formed their opinions of the merits of the case from Newman's *Elucidations*, and that set of "Propositions" which raised the just indignation of Archdeacon Hare. Stanley, who was by no means favourably disposed towards Hampden, "was," his biographer states, "especially struck by the injustice of condemning a man for writings which his accusers had probably not read, and certainly had not studied." While the excitement about the Hereford Bishopric case was at its height, Stanley wrote: "The Dean of Norwich told me to-day that Murray had told him that not one copy of Hampden's *Bampton Lectures* had been sold since these disturbances had begun. 'Not one copy!' I exclaimed, perfectly boiling with indignation. 'What! not one amongst the thousands of the clergy, who are petitioning or clamouring against his appointment, has had the conscience to buy his book? I never heard anything so disgraceful.'"[1]

It cannot be doubted that a large number of the clergy who had no sympathy with Tractarianism, or, as it was then termed, Puseyism, took part in the agitation against Hampden; but the real wire-pullers and chief organisers of the opposition, from first to last, were the Tractarians. On the very day that Hampden's appointment was announced Pusey wrote to the Rev. B. Harrison, suggesting that "his elevation to the Episcopate might be hindered at Bow Church,"[2] that is, by a formal protest at his confirmation. Eight days later, on November 23rd, he announced to Archdeacon Churton: "He will be opposed at Bow Church, if by no others, by J. Keble."[3] Hampden, by virtue of his office as Regius Professor of Divinity, was also Rector of Ewelme, in the Diocese of Oxford, a living attached officially to the Professorship. Here was a further opening for attack on the part of his opponents. It was seen that while it would be very difficult to prosecute Hampden for heresy *as a Professor*, it

---

[1] *Life of Dean Stanley*, vol. i. p. 349.
[2] *Life of Dr. Pusey*, vol. iii. p. 159.
[3] *Ibid.* p. 160.

would be comparatively easy to do so, *as a Rector*. "Thereupon," says Canon Liddon, "Pusey and Keble set to work to draw up articles for the 'oppositores' in Bow Church, and, following the advice of Dr. Addams and Dr. Harding, and of Keble's proctor, Mr. Townsend, they endeavoured to institute a suit against Hampden in the Ecclesiastical Courts. . . . Mr. Townsend visited Oxford in order to talk over the matter with Pusey, Marriott, and J. B. Mozley. Mr. Marriott then applied to the Bishop of Oxford for Letters of Request, by which the case would be transferred to the Court of Arches."[1] The four chief workers in the protest at Bow Church, and especially in the organising of the proposed prosecution, were Keble, Pusey, Marriott, and J. B. Mozley, all leaders of the Tractarian party, by whom they were in every respect thoroughly trusted. But these gentlemen, though the real wire-pullers of the prosecution, do not appear to have actually given their names as formal prosecutors, and it was not until Dr. Hampden had demanded from the Bishop of Oxford the names of his accusers that he received them from the Bishop. They were the Revs. W. H. Ridley, E. Dean, and H. J. Young.[2] Canon Liddon informs us that "Keble characteristically made himself responsible for the legal expenses, which Badeley estimated at £2000. There is no doubt that Pusey did not allow the burden to fall on him alone. 'Keble,' wrote Badeley to Pusey on January 21, 1848, 'has sent me the guaranty for the costs signed by himself only; do you know of any others who would be willing to join with him?' The object was that 'the expenses should not fall on *those who were put forward as the nominal objectors.*'"[3] It thus appears *who* the real prosecutors were. What the theological opinions of the nominal prosecutors were I have no means of knowing. I cannot tell whether they were High Churchmen or Evangelicals.

Bishop Samuel Wilberforce lost no time in dealing

---

[1] *Life of Dr. Pusey*, vol. iii. p. 161.
[2] *Life of Bishop Wilberforce*, vol. i. p. 466.
[3] *Life of Dr. Pusey*, vol. iii. p. 161, *note*.

with the request of the Tractarian leaders to send the case on for trial before the Court of Arches. At first he was in favour of the prosecution, and on December 16th he actually signed the Letters of Request to the Court of Arches, which, however, he subsequently withdrew. But, before withdrawing them, he induced the promoters of the suit—I quote the language of Bishop Wilberforce's biographer—"to consent to the withdrawal of the 'Letters' if he could induce Dr. Hampden to give satisfactory assurances as to some of the points on which the language of the Bampton Lectures and the *Observations on Religious Dissent* was most disquieting."[1] Accordingly the Bishop wrote to Hampden, on December 17th, asking him to give to the Church "such a distinct avowal on your part of sound doctrine, and such a withdrawal of suspected *language*, as may terminate all opposition to your consecration"; and adding that he (the Bishop) believed him "to hold the true faith."[2] At the same time Dr. Wilberforce asked Dr. Hampden certain important questions:—

"I will," he wrote, "take *seriatim* the truths concerning your supposed denial of which articles are now prepared in reference to the Court of Arches, and ask you: 1st, To avow your unhesitating reception of them. They are these:—

"1. That you believe that certain doctrines may be required to be believed, as necessary to salvation, on the ground that they may be proved by Holy Scripture.

"2. That you believe that the doctrine of the Holy Trinity, as it is taught by the Church, is the expression of that which is from all eternity in the Divine nature.

"3. That you fully believe that 'The Son was begotten before all worlds, being of one substance with the Father,' and that it is 'necessary to salvation that a man believe rightly the Incarnation of our Lord Jesus Christ.'

"4. That you believe that the offering of Christ upon the Cross was not only a means of reconciling us to God, but was also 'a satisfaction for the sins of the whole world.'

"5. That you believe, in the plain sense of the words, 'all men to be by nature born in sin and the children of wrath,' and that such

---

[1] *Life of Bishop Wilberforce*, vol. i. p. 455.
[2] *Ibid.* p. 455.

terms may be properly applied to infants before they may have committed actual sin; and that 'original or birth sin is the fault and corruption of the nature of every man that naturally is engendered of the offspring of Adam.'

"6. That you believe, in the plain sense of the words, 'that the souls of the faithful, after they are delivered from the burden of the flesh, are in joy and felicity.'

"7. That you believe, in the plain sense of the words, that in Baptism we are made 'members of Christ,' and that they who 'with a true penitent heart and lively faith receive' 'the Holy Communion' do 'spiritually eat the flesh of Christ and drink His blood,' —'are one with Christ and Christ with them.'

"8. That you admit, as containing true doctrine, the words, 'the mystical union between Christ and His Church.'

"9. That you admit, as a true and wholesome doctrine, that 'we have no power to do good works without the grace of Christ preventing us, that we may have a good will, and working with us when we have that good will.'

"10. That you receive as true the words, 'Pour Thy grace into our hearts.'

"11. That you believe the Sacraments of the Church to be 'effectual signs of grace, by the which God doth work invisibly in us,' and are 'means whereby we receive the same inward grace.'"[1]

Bishop Wilberforce also asked Dr. Hampden to withdraw his Bampton Lectures and his *Observations on Dissent* from circulation. To Lord John Russell the Bishop sent a copy of his letter to Dr. Hampden. The Prime Minister in his reply showed himself far from satisfied with the Bishop's action:—

"Dr. Hampden has," wrote Lord John Russell on December 18th, "for eleven years taught divinity as Regius Professor. Candidates for Orders were required by the Bishops, with the exception of five or six, to bring certificates that they had received from Dr. Hampden instruction in theology. The Bishops of Manchester and Salisbury, as I am told, sent away candidates who were not provided with Dr. Hampden's certificates. How is such a man to be interrogated upon articles framed, not by the Church, but by one of its Bishops, as if he were himself a young student in divinity?

"This remark applies to two of the three articles drawn up by your lordship, to which I should not otherwise object. But the

---

[1] *Life of Bishop Wilberforce*, vol. i. pp. 456, 457.

eleventh, asking Dr. Hampden to withdraw his Bampton Lectures and his *Principles of Dissent*, appears to me to require that Dr. Hampden should degrade himself in the eyes of all men for the sake of a mitre. He has repeatedly declared that in these works he has not intended to profess any doctrine at variance with the doctrines of the Church. Dr. Arnold could see nothing unsound in them, nor can the Bishop of Durham, or the Bishop of Chester, or the Bishop of Norwich, or the Bishop of Llandaff. Indeed I believe that Dr. Pusey himself, who must be considered as the leader and the oracle of Dr. Hampden's opponents, has written that he does not consider the opinions of Dr. Hampden unsound, but that they lead to unsoundness, and are, therefore, dangerous in a teacher of divinity."[1]

On the same day that Lord John Russell wrote thus to the Bishop of Oxford, Dr. Hampden wrote also to that prelate, in reply to his queries. He might easily have assumed the dignity of his position as a reason for declining to answer the questions put to him. He might reasonably have refused to be interrogated, to quote Lord Russell's words, "as if he were himself a young student of divinity." But instead of assuming this position he assumed one which was greatly to his credit.

"If," wrote Dr. Hampden to the Bishop, "the queries which this letter contains had come from any other source, or been addressed to me under other circumstances, I think I should have been justified in considering that an insult was not only conveyed but intended to be conveyed to me, by having such elementary tests applied to one who holds the position I do. But, my Lord, I am sure your intention is to be a messenger and instrument of peace; and I know too well what even Christian warfare is, not to meet such a proceeding on your part in the like kindly spirit. On this ground, therefore, and in perfect respect to you as the Bishop of the diocese, and for your personal satisfaction, I unhesitatingly reply in the affirmative. I say 'Yes' to all your queries on my belief—in that sense in which they are the plain natural sense of the statements of our Articles and Formularies. I need not discuss them, for I have repeatedly affirmed every position in them drawn from those authoritative sources, commencing with my Catechism as a child, in the daily use of the Liturgy, in my subscription and adherence to the Articles, and in the constant use of my ministerial office. I have affirmed

---

[1] *Life of Bishop Wilberforce*, vol. i. p. 459.

them in public and in private, in the pulpit, in my works, from the Chair of Divinity, and in the other offices I have held in the University, and in the very works which have attracted so much notice, and have been subjected to so much misrepresentation."[1]

Such a letter as this ought to have satisfied Dr. Hampden's prosecutors. It was sufficient to prove to any candid mind that, as Bishop of Hereford, there was no reason to fear that he would teach heretical doctrine. What had happened would have been quite enough to make him careful as to the language he employed in teaching Christian doctrine, however careless he might have been in this respect in the past. But his prosecutors were not satisfied. Nothing would suffice for them but a public apology, and a withdrawal of his Bampton Lectures. His *Observations on Dissent* had not been issued with Dr. Hampden's consent since the second edition was sold out some years previously. When Bishop Wilberforce learnt that the pamphlet was no longer in circulation with the consent of Dr. Hampden, and after he had received a letter from the Archbishop of Canterbury, stating that in his opinion the Letters of Request should be withdrawn, he felt that it was no longer desirable that the prosecution should proceed, and, therefore, he withdrew the Letters of Request accordingly. The Tractarians, of course, at once directed their fury against the unfortunate Bishop of Oxford, who had now given them mortal offence. Dr. Pusey declared that the Bishop's conduct " was far more injurious to the Church than Dr. Hampden's appointment. An act of tyranny hurts not the Church; the betrayal by her own guardians does;" and he went on to express the opinion that his lordship's withdrawal of the Letters of Request was "the greatest blow the Church has had since Newman's secession."[2] At that time the Tractarians were bitterly opposed to the exercise of the Episcopal Veto on the prosecutions which *they* had initiated. When the High Church Bishop of Exeter (Dr. Phillpotts) heard that Bishop Wilberforce had vetoed

[1] *Life of Bishop Wilberforce*, vol. i. pp. 461, 462.
[2] *Life of Dr. Pusey*, vol. iii. pp. 162, 163.

the prosecution of Hampden he was greatly annoyed and disappointed. He thought the Church Discipline Act of 1840 did not permit of the exercise of the Episcopal Veto, which he considered "a very invidious" and "dangerous" power to be placed in the hands of the Bishops.

"I may," he wrote the Bishop of Oxford, "be mistaken in my construction of the Statute. It may give you the power to do what you have done—to determine absolutely, of your own mere will or on your own mere opinion, that the suit shall not be prosecuted. If this be the proper construction of the Statute, *I shall deeply lament it*, for it will give to us Bishops a much greater amount of power, and, in consequence, of responsibility, than I think safe for ourselves, much less wise in the law to entrust to any men.

"Still, even so, I should myself deem it at once my wisdom and my duty to forbear from acting on *so very invidious and dangerous a power* in any case whatever which I can contemplate, certainly in any way which should have the slightest semblance of affinity to the one in which you have exercised it."[1]

One can almost afford to smile at the anxiety of the early Tractarians to prosecute their opponents. Had they been successful in their efforts we should never have heard any Ritualistic complaints against the existing Ecclesiastical Courts. It was only when they discovered that the Courts were against them that they turned against the Courts. When Hampden's opponents found the doors of the Court of Arches closed against them by the Bishop of Oxford, they determined to oppose him by publicly protesting in Hereford Cathedral against his election by the Dean and Chapter. On the receipt of the *Congé d'élire* addressed to the Dean and Chapter of Hereford, the Dean of Hereford addressed a Memorial to the Queen, dated December 17, 1847, containing the following petition: —"We most humbly pray your Majesty to name and recommend some other person whom your Majesty shall think meet to be elected by us for our Bishop, or that your Majesty will graciously relieve us from the necessity of proceeding to the election till you shall have been pleased

[1] *Life of Bishop Wilberforce*, vol. i. p. 490.

to submit Dr. Renn Dickson Hampden's published writing (so judged as aforesaid by the Convocation of the University of Oxford), to the judgment either of the two Houses of Convocation of Clergy of the Province of Canterbury which is now sitting, or of the Provincial Council of Bishops of the same Province, assisted by such divines as your Majesty or the said Provincial Council shall be pleased to call, or of some other competent tribunal which your Majesty shall be graciously pleased to appoint."[1] Unfortunately for the Dean, his Memorial received a very chilling reception. He received from Sir G. Grey a reply, stating that it had been laid before the Queen, but that " Her Majesty has not been pleased to issue any commands thereupon." Nothing daunted, the militant Dean once more addressed a letter of protest to Lord John Russell, dated December 22nd, and concluding with the announcement :—" I say, my Lord, having fully counted the cost, having weighed the sense of bounden duty in the one scale against the consequences in the other, I have come to the deliberate resolve, that on Tuesday next no earthly consideration shall induce me to give my vote in the Chapter of Hereford Cathedral for Dr. Hampden's elevation to the See of Hereford."[2] The Dean's letter to the Prime Minister was in vain. His lordship coldly replied as follows :—" SIR,—I have had the honour to receive your letter of the 22nd inst., in which you intimate to me your intention of violating the law.—I have, &c., J. RUSSELL."

At length the day of Election arrived. People were everywhere full of curiosity to know what the Dean and Chapter of Hereford would do. The Chapter assembled in the Cathedral Library on Tuesday, December 28th. Seventeen members (including the Dean, who presided) were present. After the *Congé d'élire* and the Queen's Letter Missive had been read, the Chapter proceeded to the election. Fifteen voted for Dr. Hampden, and two against, viz., Canon Huntingford and the Dean. These

[1] The full text of the Memorial was published in the *English Churchman*, Dec. 23, 1847, pp. 920, 921.
[2] *Ibid.* Dec. 30, 1847, p. 934.

gentlemen each read a separate protest, explaining their reasons for the course they took. Canon Huntingford said:—"With the utmost respect for the Royal Prerogative, and with a full conviction that it is for the peace and safety of the Church, that the Crown should nominate to vacant Sees, yet in this particular instance I feel obliged to defer complying with the recommendation which has been sent down to us, until a competent tribunal shall have pronounced to have been well founded or not the sentiments expressed by so many Bishops of our Church, and by so many members of one of our Universities."[1] The Dean of Hereford gave similar reasons for his vote, and concluded with this statement:—"I, therefore, John Merewether, D.D., Dean of the Cathedral Church of Hereford, am dissentient. I cannot vote for Dr. Renn Dickson Hampden as a Bishop and Pastor of the Cathedral Church where I am Dean. And I further protest."[2] It must, I think, be admitted that both the Dean and Canon Huntingford deserved credit for the courage which led them thus to act according to the dictates of their consciences, however mistaken their judgments may have been. But all their efforts were in vain. Dr. Hampden was declared elected as Bishop of Hereford. Certificates of his election were at once forwarded to the Queen, the Archbishop of Canterbury, and to the Bishop Elect, in which nothing whatever was said about the alleged unsound teaching of the divine elected; but the Dean succeeded in having a formal protest of his own appended to each of the three certificates. In *this* protest the Dean did not object to Dr. Hampden on account of his supposed heresy, but because "certain persons have voted, who (I have reason to believe, being merely Honorary Prebendaries, and not having conformed to the provisions of the statutes of this Church, which I have sworn to observe), are not qualified to vote in Chapter, and also because the majority so constituted has not, according to the said statutes, the

---

[1] *The Case of Dr. Hampden.* By Richard Jebb, Barrister-at-Law, p. 6. London: 1849.
[2] *Ibid.* p. 11.

Dean and three Residentiaries at the least voting therein."[1] No official notice, so far as I am able to ascertain, appears to have been taken of this protest.

And now, all efforts at preventing the Election of Dr. Hampden having utterly failed, the efforts of his enemies were next directed to preparation for opposition to his forthcoming Confirmation in Bow Church. Pusey and Keble were particularly zealous in this direction. "Pusey and Keble," writes Canon Liddon, "were busily engaged in preparing theological matter for the use of Counsel at Bow Church. 'I found things,' writes Pusey to Marriott, on January 2, 1848, 'in Godliman Street, in most utter confusion. Our articles of indictment just in the state in which they were sent in. The heads of K.'s [Keble's] articles (that is, his preamble) not fitted in into the sequel (the allegations). I spent five and a half hours there on Friday, and put them to rights; at least ready to be copied out.'"[2] The Confirmation of the Election of Dr. Hampden took place in Bow Church on Tuesday, January 11, 1848. No fewer than ten legal gentlemen appeared in the Church, three representing the Dean and Chapter of Hereford, one for Dr. Hampden, and six for the opposers of the Confirmation. When opposers were publicly called by the Apparitor-General to the Archbishop of Canterbury, several of the learned Counsel rose one after the other and asked to be heard; but the Court refused to hear their objections, after allowing them at some length to argue in favour of being heard. The arguments used on this occasion are printed verbatim in *The Case of Dr. Hampden*, edited by Mr. Richard Jebb, Barrister-at-Law, pp. 30–50. Dr. Hampden's accusers were again unsuccessful, and his Confirmation was therefore completed. An interesting account of the scene is given by Archdeacon Clark in his "Recollections," printed in the *Memorials of Bishop Hampden*.

"I was present," he writes, "at Bow Church when his [Dr. Hampden's] Confirmation as Bishop was opposed by the Dean of

---

[1] Jebb's *The Case of Dr. Hampden*, p. 13.
[2] *Life of Dr. Pusey*, vol. iii. p. 163.

Hereford. The ceremony took place on a week day, at a busy hour, when Cheapside is usually most densely crowded. On this occasion, as we approached the Church, the stream of human beings usually in motion was arrested, Cheapside was in a state of congestion, and it was with difficulty that the Bishop's carriage reached the Church. It was evident that all other business was suspended, and that the one object of interest to the excited crowd was the new Bishop. There could be no doubt that the popular feeling was on his side. Again and again, as he passed to and from the Church, he was loudly cheered, not a single sound of dissent or disapproval being heard. On entering the Church the scene was still more striking and memorable. The whole area of the Church and the galleries were crowded, spectators were standing on the seats and backs of pews. . . . When at length the ceremony was over, and we succeeded in forcing our way through the vestry and the crowded porch into the street, the enthusiasm of the people could not be restrained. It was really a service of danger for those who accompanied the Bishop. Everybody pressed forward to see and congratulate him; and if we had not turned ourselves into his body-guard, and almost covered him as he passed through the crowd, he was in some danger of being crushed by his admirers. When we were seated in the carriage, Cheapside rang again with repeated cheers, which followed us until we were fairly out of sight. Some of the crowd pursued the carriage for some distance through St. Paul's Churchyard, to see and congratulate the persecuted Bishop."[1]

But the Bishop-Elect of Hereford was not yet out of his troubles. Only three days later, viz. on January 14th, Sir Fitzroy Kelly applied to the Court of Queen's Bench for a rule to show cause why a *mandamus* should not issue directed to the Archbishop of Canterbury, and his Vicar-General, commanding them, or one of them, to hold a Court at which they should permit and admit to appear in due form of law, the Rev. R. W. Huntley, Vicar of Alderbury; the Rev. John Jebb, Rector of Peterstow; and the Rev. W. F. Powell, Vicar of Cirencester, "to oppose the said Confirmation of the said Election of the said Dr. Renn Dickson Hampden, and to hear and determine upon such opposition, and upon the articles, matters, and proof thereof."[2] The application was really

[1] *Memorials of Bishop Hampden*, pp. 251-253.
[2] *The Case of Dr. Hampden*, p. 92.

made for the purpose of setting aside the decision of the Vicar-General at Bow Church refusing to hear objectors. The Court granted the Rule, and on January 24th the case came on for hearing before Lord Denman, and Justices Coleridge, Pattison, and Erle. After hearing Counsel on both sides the Court reserved judgment until February 1st, when Mr. Justice Coleridge and Mr. Justice Pattison gave judgment in favour of granting the Rule, while Lord Denman and Mr. Justice Erle gave judgment against the Rule. The result was that, the Court being equally divided, the application of Dr. Hampden's opponents fell to the ground.

On the 4th of February the three clergymen whose application to the Court of Queen's Bench fell through, petitioned the Archbishop of Canterbury (Dr. Howley) as their "remaining and best resource," to grant "a competent ecclesiastical inquiry into our objections, and into the whole of the works we have mentioned," before the consecration of Dr. Hampden.[1] But, unfortunately for their hopes, the Archbishop was then on his death-bed, and died only seven days later. His successor (Dr. Sumner) sent a formal acknowledgment of the receipt of the Memorial, but he did not think it wise to grant its request. And so, on March 26, 1848, Dr. Hampden was at last consecrated in the Chapel of Lambeth Palace as Bishop of Hereford. The consecrating prelate was the Archbishop of Canterbury (Dr. Sumner), who was assisted by the Bishop of Llandaff (Dr. Copleston), the Bishop of Norwich (Dr. Stanley), and the Bishop of Worcester (Dr. Pepys).

It must not be supposed that throughout this heated controversy Dr. Hampden was without friends and supporters. On the contrary, he received the sympathy and help of many influential personages in Church and State. The Prime Minister was throughout one of his firmest friends, and when the news of his election reached Woburn Abbey, Lord John Russell's residence, it created quite an

[1] *The Case of Dr. Hampden*, p. 500.

excitement. Baron Bunsen was on a visit there at the time, and in a letter to his wife described what took place on the reception of the news:—

"Yesterday," he wrote, "was a day of satisfaction for the house of Russell, the news having arrived of Dr. Hampden's election. Lord John had been much vexed in the latter days by the unreasonableness of the people he had to deal with—but yesterday at three o'clock, when we were collected in expectation, and talking against time, in came little Johnny [Viscount Amberley], escorted by his aunt-like sister, and stationed himself at the entrance of the library, distinctly proclaiming, like a herald, 'Dr. Hampden,—a Bishop!' We cheered him, and some one asked him whether he liked Dr. H——. 'I don't mind (was his answer) for I don't know him.' His father came in afterwards, radiant with satisfaction. After dinner, I suggested as a toast, 'The Chapter of Hereford,' adding *sotto voce* to Lord John, 'and he who has managed them.' Milnes and Stafford gave 'The Dean,' in opposition, and we were just divided, like the Chapter, two against fifteen. Lord John took all very kindly."[1]

Dr. Hampden received many addresses of sympathy from both clergy and laity. His fellow-citizens in Oxford presented him with a public address, expressing confidence in him as one who had set forth and enforced "the great cardinal doctrines of a religion based on the Word of God." He received also a general address from friends throughout the country, chiefly signed by the clergy, but including the names of members of both Houses of Parliament; and other addresses from members of Oxford Convocation, and the Chapters of York and Gloucester. His daughter states that, in connection with these addresses, "the point to which he attached the greatest importance was, that this support was offered to him on account of his teaching and defence of the principles of the Church of England as established by the Reformation."[2] Of these addresses perhaps the most important and significant was that which was signed by no fewer than

[1] *Memoirs of Baron Bunsen*, vol. ii. p. 155.
[2] *Memorials of Bishop Hampden*, p. 153.

fifteen out of the twenty-two Heads of Houses. It was as follows:—

"To the Rev. Dr. Hampden, Regius Professor of Divinity, &c.

"We, the undersigned Heads of Houses in the University of Oxford, have seen with great concern the report of proceedings in various parts of the country upon your proposed appointment to the See of Hereford, tending to injure your reputation, impede your future usefulness, and even create a general distrust of the soundness of your faith in our Blessed Lord. Under such circumstances, although we only declare the sentiments which many of us have expressed before, and particularly upon the enactment in 1842 of the new statute concerning theological instruction, we desire to assure you, that having for years enjoyed ample opportunities of learning the tenor of your public teaching, and hearing your discourses from the pulpit of the University, we are not only satisfied that your religious belief is sound, but we look forward with confidence to your endeavours to preach the Gospel of Christ in its integrity.

"B. P. Symons, Warden of Wadham, and Vice-Chancellor.
Edward Hawkins, Provost of Oriel.
James Ingram, President of Trinity.
Philip Wynter, President of St. John's.
John Radford, Rector of Lincoln.
Henry Foulkes, Principal of Jesus College.
Thomas Gaisford, Dean of Christ Church.
John David Macbride, Principal of Magdalene Hall.
David Williams, Warden of New College.
Frederick Charles Plumptre, Master of University College.
Henry Wellesley, Principal of New Inn Hall.
R. Bullock Marsham, Warden of Merton.
William Thompson, Principal of St. Edmund Hall.
James Norris, President of Christ Church College.
Francis Jeune, Master of Pembroke."[1]

The history of the Hampden Case throws a great deal of light on the early tactics of the Tractarian party. In reality, as I have already said, I believe, Dr. Hampden's latitudinarian views were only the ostensible cause of the furious attacks made upon him. The real cause of

[1] *English Churchman*, January 6, 1848, p. 6.

offence was his outspoken Protestantism, though it must be admitted that the early Tractarians were sincerely opposed to his latitudinarian tendencies. But they could not bear that the "Traditions" of the Church, her decrees and Creeds, should be thought of less importance than the written Word of God. Dr. Hampden's vigorous attacks upon the sacerdotal teaching, ever so dear to the hearts of the enemies of the Gospel and the friends of priestcraft, made the Tractarians almost wild with rage. But, as far as possible, they carefully concealed from the public gaze the real cause of offence, and in this way they gained the support of many Evangelicals, who were at least quite as zealous for the Orthodox Faith, as any of the Tractarians. And is it not a remarkable fact that Rationalistic views as to the inspiration and truth of the Bible, far more objectionable than were ever taught by Dr. Hampden, are now openly avowed by many leading members of the Ritualistic party, the successors of the Tractarians? The Hampden Crusade was conducted by the real wire-pullers as a part of a deeply laid scheme to banish Ultra-Protestantism, as held by the Reformers in the sixteenth century, out of the Church of England. All opponents were to be removed out of the way, and Dr. Hampden, as Regius Professor, and afterwards as a Bishop, was very much in the way of the success of their schemes. They tried to get rid of him, and failed. And in their prosecution of their Crusade they did not despise the strong arm of the law. The existing Courts of Law, now so much reviled and abused, were then thought good enough to decide the law as to the highest Christian doctrines. The chief leaders of the party, Dr. Pusey and Keble, were, as we have seen, the most zealous, and the leading workers in the proposed prosecution of Dr. Hampden, thirty years before the Church Association came into existence. Ecclesiastical prosecutions were not abused then by the leaders of the Oxford Movement. On the contrary, they were in high favour, and if they had only succeeded in their hands all our present troubles about Ecclesiastical Courts would have been unknown.

CHAPTER IV

Dr. Pusey's early Protestantism—Extracts from his *Historical Enquiry* —His Theological Society—"The young Monks"—The *Library of the Fathers*—Mr. Bickersteth approves of the *Library*—Lord Selborne on the Fathers—Richard Hurrell Froude—His influence on Newman—His admiration of Rome, and dislike of the Reformation —Newman's early love of Rome—His mind "essentially Jesuitical" —Froude's *Remains*—Extracts from the *Remains*, showing his Romanising principles—Professor Faussett's University sermon against the Tractarians—The Rev. Peter Maurice's *Popery in Oxford* —Dr. Pusey insults Mr. Maurice—Newman's reply to Faussett— Dr. Hook's *Call to Union*—Bishop of Oxford's Visitation Charge— The Oxford Martyrs' Memorial—Pusey thinks it "unkind to the Church of Rome"—Keble thinks Cranmer a Heretic—"Cranmer burnt well"—Tractarian opposition to the Memorial—The inscription on the Oxford Martyrs' Memorial.

THE leaders of the Oxford Movement were wise in their day and generation. They realised the vast importance of influencing those who were destined to be the teachers and leaders of the rising generation. At first, the movement was mainly confined to the educated classes, the poor were only thought of afterwards. I do not say they were wise in making, even for a time, the poor a secondary consideration; but they certainly realised from the commencement, in a way the Evangelicals never have done yet (to anything like a sufficient extent), that if the laity are to be instructed and influenced, their clergy must first of all have been educated sufficiently in their faith.

The formation by Dr. Pusey of a Theological Society, in 1835, greatly assisted the Tractarians in this direction. Dr. Pusey was much slower in imbibing Roman doctrine than Newman. As recently as 1828 he had published the first part of *An Historical Enquiry into the Rationalist Character of the Theology of Germany*, the second part of which appeared in 1830, containing many opinions which in after life he ceased to hold. Its strong praise of Martin Luther, and its declaration that Scripture is its own interpreter, instead of being interpreted by the Church, show that at that early period Pusey was in full sympathy with much that is held dear by Lutheran Protestants.

"The fruitless attempts," wrote Pusey, "to satisfy an uneasy and active conscience by the meritorious performances of a Romish Convent had opened his [Luther's] eyes to the right understanding of Scripture, in whose doctrines alone it could find rest; and the clear and discerning faith which this correspondence of Scripture with his own experience strengthened in him, gave him that intuitive insight into the nature of Christianity, which enabled him for the most part unfailingly to discriminate between essentials and non-essentials, and raised him not only above the assumed authority of the Church and above the might of Tradition, but above the influence of hereditary scholastic opinions, the power of prejudices, and the dominion of the letter. Unfortunately, however, the further expansion of his views necessarily yielded to the then yet more important practical employments, to which *this Great Apostle of Evangelical Truth* dedicated the most of his exertions."[1]

The following statement of Pusey as to the right method of interpreting the Bible, would certainly not be accepted by his followers of the present day:—

"The Reformers, in consistency with their great tenet, that Scripture is the only authoritative source of Christian knowledge, had laid the study of the sacred volume as the foundation of all Theological science. In the pursuance of this principle they had established as the rule of interpretation one which, when correctly developed, contains all the elements of right exposition, which have since been gradually vindicated by the combination of several partial efforts. *Their, or rather the Biblical, rule* that 'Scripture is its own interpreter,' includes in itself the religious, historical, grammatical elements which were imperfectly, because separately, brought forward by Spener, Semler, and Ernesti. For it is obvious that if Scripture is to be understood from itself, those only can rightly and fully understand it who have a mind kindred to that of its author; and as any human production, upon which the mind of its author is impressed,

---

[1] *An Historical Enquiry into the Probable Causes of the Rationalist Character of the Theology of Germany.* By E. B. Pusey, M.A. Part I. p. 8. London: 1882.

will be best understood by him whose intellectual and moral character is most allied to the original which it expresses. ... In religious writings it is plain that the spirit required is a religious spirit; that none can truly understand St. Paul or St. John, whose mind has not been brought into harmony with theirs, has not been elevated and purified by the same Spirit with which they were filled; and this, unquestionably, is what the pious Spener meant by his much disputed assertion, that *none but the regenerate could understand Holy Scripture.*"[1]

Pusey withdrew both parts of his book from circulation, and Canon Liddon informs us that "he never referred to them without regret and self-condemnation";[2] and that "to the last he felt anxious as to the untoward influence," as he called it, "of these books." In his will, dated November 19, 1875, he desired that "the two books on the Theology of Germany should not be republished."[3] At the period when this work was issued, Pusey's views as to Episcopacy were Protestant. "Pusey," says Canon Liddon, "had not quite realised, as Rose had in fact implicitly asserted, that the Episcopate is an organic feature of the Church of Christ, the absence of which could not but be attended by spiritual disorder."[4] Even in 1836 Pusey believed that priestly absolution was not a judicial act. Writing to the Rev. J. F. Russell on December 10, 1836, he remarked:—"In Absolution, the contrast is not between 'declaratory' and 'ministerial,' but between 'ministerial' and 'judicial.' It is this last which the Church of Rome holds *and we do not.*"[5] In the preface to his *Scriptural Views of Baptism*, written in 1836, Pusey declared that, in his opinion, "the Romanist, by the *Sacrament* of Penance," "would forestall the sentence of his Judge."[6] Later on in life, Pusey accepted the doctrine that the priest acts as "judge" when bestowing Absolution—the doctrine of the Church of Rome.

But even when, in 1835, Pusey founded the Theological Society at Oxford, he had gone far away from

---

[1] Pusey's *Historical Enquiry*, Part I. pp. 26, 27.
[2] *Life of Dr. Pusey*, vol. i. p. 173.
[3] *Ibid.* p. 176.   [4] *Ibid.* p. 171.   [5] *Ibid.* p. 401.
[6] *Tracts for the Times.* Preface to Nos. 67, 68, 69, p. xiv.

Protestantism in many respects, and the consequence was that, while in theory the new Society was open to every party in the Church, it became practically a propaganda for Tractarianism. This is frankly acknowledged by Canon Liddon, who tells us that :—"There can be no question of the influence of this Society on the Oxford Movement. It stimulated theological thought and work more than any other agency in Oxford at the time. . . . Above all, it fed both the *British Magazine* and the *Tracts for the Times*, especially the latter, with a series of essays upon subjects of which little was known or thought in those days."[1] Canon Overton tells us that this Theological Society "was at first intended to be confined to no party in the Church. Men were invited to join who had no sympathy with the founder's views; but these either declined or soon withdrew; and the Society became as much a part of the Movement as the *Tracts* themselves."[2]

At about the time when the Theological Society was founded, Pusey took into his house at Oxford three or four Bachelors of Arts, and kept them there at his own expense, in order that they might give themselves more fully to the study of Divinity. Of course, those selected were men likely to prove serviceable to the Oxford Movement. This plan was continued until the summer of 1838, when Newman took a house for the young men in St. Aldate's, Oxford, and for about two years it seems to have been under his control. It was to be used, Mr. J. B. Mozley (who was its first inmate) informed his sister, on April 27, 1838, as "a reading and collating establishment, to help in editing the Fathers."[3] Newman seems to have looked upon this house as a home for "young Monks," and desired that his plans concerning it should be kept as secret as possible. His friend, Mr. J. W. Bowden, made a contribution towards the expenses of the house, and to him Newman wrote, on January 17, 1838:—"Your offering

---

[1] *Life of Dr. Pusey*, vol. i. p. 334.
[2] *The Anglican Revival.* By J. H. Overton, D.D., p. 67. London: 1897.
[3] Mozley's *Letters*, p. 78.

towards the young Monks was just like yourself, and I cannot pay it a better compliment. It will be most welcome. As you may suppose, we have nothing settled, but are feeling our way. We should begin next Term; but since, *however secret one may wish to keep it*, things get out, we do not yet wish to commit young men to anything which may hurt their chance of success at any College, in standing for a fellowship." [1]

The first volume of the now well-known *Library of the Fathers* was published on August 24, 1838, and the last in November 1885. The series comprised forty-eight volumes, and included the writings of thirteen Fathers, translated into English. It is remarkable that when, nearly two years before the first volume was issued, that well-known Evangelical and thoroughly Protestant clergyman, the Rev. E. Bickersteth, heard of the projected *Library* he wrote enthusiastically about it to Pusey, promising to become a subscriber, and adding:—

"Though personally unacquainted with you, and differing in some respects from views which, judging from the volumes of the Oxford *Tracts*, I suppose you hold, I cannot but write a few lines to express the sincere pleasure with which I view your design, in connection with Mr. Keble and Mr. Newman, of publishing a select *Library of Fathers*. Few things could be more seasonable, or more beneficial to the Church of England." [2]

When Mr. Bickersteth wrote this letter he probably expected that the *Library* would include all the Fathers of the first three centuries at least. If so, he must have been disappointed. Of the thirteen Fathers, whose writings were translated, only three wrote in the first three centuries, the remaining ten flourished in the fourth, fifth, sixth, and seventh centuries. It is well known that during the latter periods many false doctrines crept into the Church, and the tendency of the early Tractarians, as of their successors, the Ritualists, was to rely chiefly on the later Fathers, rather than on those who lived near Apostolic times. In 1845 Bishop (afterwards Cardinal) Wiseman remarked, on

---

[1] Newman's *Letters*, vol. ii. p. 249.
[2] *Life of Dr. Pusey*, vol. i. p. 435.

the authority of Newman, that "in Pusey's celebrated Sermon on the Eucharist, out of 140 texts of Fathers only four are from the first three centuries."[1]

There is a very interesting passage on this subject in the late Lord Selborne's *Memorials*. His lordship, I may here mention, was a friend of the early Tractarians, and a sympathiser with their religious views; but he afterwards became an opponent of the advanced section of the party:—

"My father," writes Lord Selborne, "once said to my brother William—repeating, unless I am mistaken, some words of Bishop Horsley, who knew the Fathers well—that 'the Fathers must be read with caution.' When Isaac Taylor, in his *Ancient Christianity*, collected out of the Fathers many things tending to disturb the ideal conception of a golden primitive age of pure faith and practice; and when William Goode, afterwards Dean of Ripon, in his *Divine Rule of Faith and Practice*, called the Fathers themselves as witnesses in favour of the direct use of Scripture for the decision of controversies, some of those who placed confidence in the Oxford Divines, but were themselves ignorant of the Fathers, waited anxiously for answers which never came. I remember a reply once made to myself, when I asked whether anybody was going to answer Isaac Taylor, whose work I perceived to be producing in some quarters a considerable effect. I was told that in a little time he would answer himself, which he never did. It seemed plain that, although the advocates of Patristic authority might be powerful in attack, they were weak in defence."[2]

The Oxford Movement suffered a great loss by the death, on February 28, 1836, of the Rev. Richard Hurrell Froude, at the early age of 33. Young as he was, his influence on the Oxford Movement was next only to that of Keble and Newman. At the time of his death he had done more than either of these to move the Tractarians in a Romeward direction. The Rev. Thomas Mozley, who was personally acquainted with Froude, tells us that:—"He was a High Churchman of the uncompromising school, very early taking part with Anselm, Becket, Laud, and the

[1] *Life and Times of Cardinal Wiseman*, vol. i. p. 434.
[2] *Memorials Family and Personal*, 1766-1865. By the Earl of Selborne, vol. i. p. 210.

Nonjurors. Woe to any one who dropped in his hearing such phrases as the Dark Ages, Superstition, Bigotry, Right of Private Judgment, enlightenment, march of mind, or progress."[1] His influence on Newman, leading him to adopt many Roman Catholic doctrines and practices, was very great. Of Froude, Newman writes:—

"His opinions arrested and influenced me, even when they did not gain my assent. He professed openly his admiration of the Church of Rome, and his hatred of the Reformers. He delighted in the notion of an hierarchical system, of sacerdotal power, and of full ecclesiastical liberty. He felt scorn of the maxim, 'The Bible and the Bible only is the religion of Protestants'; and he gloried in accepting Tradition as a main instrument of religious teaching. He had a high severe idea of the intrinsic excellence of Virginity; and he considered the Blessed Virgin its great pattern. He delighted in thinking of the Saints; he had a keen appreciation of the idea of sanctity, its possibility and its heights; and he was more than inclined to believe a large amount of miraculous interference as occurring in the early and Middle Ages. He embraced the principle of penance and mortification. He had a deep devotion to the Real Presence, in which he had a firm faith. He was powerfully drawn to the Mediæval Church, but not to the Primitive. . . . It is difficult to enumerate the precise additions to my theological creed which I derived from a friend to whom I owe so much. He made me look with admiration towards the Church of Rome, and in the same degree to dislike the Reformation. He fixed deep in me the idea of devotion to the Blessed Virgin, and he led me gradually to believe in the Real Presence."[2]

We thus learn that, for ten years at least before Newman announced his secession to the Papacy, he had "looked with *admiration* towards the Church of Rome," and "disliked" that Protestant Reformation which, while a clergyman in the Church of England, he did his best to destroy. It is evident that Newman's heart was with Rome many years before he left the Church of England. First of all, at the very commencement of the Oxford Movement, as he tells us:—"I learned to have *tender feelings* towards her [Church of Rome]; but still my reason

[1] Mozley's *Reminiscences of the Oxford Movement*, vol. i. p. 226.
[2] Newman's *Apologia Pro Vita Sua*, 1st edition, pp. 85-87.

was not affected at all. My judgment was against her, when viewed as an institution, as truly as it had ever been. This conflict between *reason* and *affection* I expressed in one of the early *Tracts*, published July 1834 ... As a matter, then, of simple conscience, *though it went against my feelings*, I felt it to be a duty to protest against the Church of Rome ... *I did not at all like the work.* Hurrell Froude attacked me for doing it; and besides, I felt that my language had a vulgar and rhetorical look about it. I believed, and really measured my words when I used them; but I knew that I had a temptation, on the other hand, to say against Rome as much as ever I could, *in order to protect myself against the charge of Popery.*"[1]

It is very easy to persuade ourselves that those whom we love are in the right, and most unpleasant to say anything against them. Newman's affections and "feelings" went out to Rome first, and after a time his reason followed them. There are many in a similar position at the present time: they are guided by feelings instead of reason; by what they like rather than by what God requires in His Holy Word. We know that Newman kept his love of Rome a secret from the public for several years after Froude's death, and that his denunciations of Romanism were largely the result of a selfish desire to "protect himself from the charge of Popery" which was justly brought against him. How could any man be suspected of a leaning towards, and a love for, Rome, who wrote against her as Newman did? One of his intimate friends, and a former curate of his, the Rev. Isaac Williams, says:—" I have lately heard it stated from one of Newman's oldest friends, Dr. Jelf, that *his mind was always essentially Jesuitical.*"[2] Before the public, at that time, Newman appeared as the *enemy* of Rome, while at heart and in secret he was her *lover*.

Froude had written three of the *Tracts for the Times*. He was the author of *Tract IX.*, on "Shortening the Church Service," in which he expressed the opinion

[1] Newman's *Apologia Pro Vita Sua*, 1st edition, pp. 127, 128.
[2] *Autobiography of Isaac Williams*, p. 54.

that the Church services were already short enough; and affirmed that our Reformers "added to the Matin Service what had hitherto been wholly distinct from it, the Mass Service or Communion"—thus implying that the "Mass" and "Communion" were identical. He also held up the Church of Rome to the admiration of his readers because she had retained the "primitive mode of worship," in that she uses the Seven Canonical Hours of Prayer daily. This was but a small compliment to the Church of Rome, but it was a compliment nevertheless, and was published to the world as early as October 31, 1833, but a little over three months from the birth of the Oxford Movement. *Tract LIX.*, "On the Position of the Church of Christ in England Relatively to the State and Nation," was also written by Froude. In it he tried to prove that the Church of England is suffering from greater tyranny from the State than in the Dark Ages. "It cannot," he asserts, "be denied that at present it [Church of England] is treated far more arbitrarily, and is more completely at the mercy of the chance Government of the day, than ever our forefathers were under the worst tyranny of the worst times."[1] The author argues in favour of what he terms "State Protection" and against "State Interference" with the Church. Under the first of these heads, however (to his credit be it recorded), he objects to "the law *De Excommunicato Capiendo*, by which the State engages that on receiving due notice of the excommunication of any given person, he shall be arrested and put in prison until he is absolved." This he justly terms "a bad, useless law, which cannot be done away with too soon."[2] In this *Tract* Froude was careful not to let his readers know all that he believed about the connection of Church and State. He did say in it that he thought "State Interference" with the Church was an evil, but he did not tell them what Newman revealed nearly twenty-eight years after Froude's death, in his *Apologia*, "With Froude, Erastianism—that is, the union (so he

---

[1] *Tract LIX.*, p. 6.   [2] *Ibid.* p. 3.

viewed it) of Church and State—was the parent, or if not the parent, the serviceable and sufficient tool, of Liberalism. Till that union was snapped, Christian doctrine could never be safe."[1] The last of Froude's contributions to the *Tracts for the Times* was *Tract LXIII.*, on "The Antiquity of the Existing Liturgies," in which he declared of those ancient documents, that "next to the Holy Scriptures, they possess the greatest claim on our veneration and study,[2] thus placing them above the present Liturgy of the Reformed Church of England in her Book of Common Prayer. He was careful also to point out that all of those Ancient Liturgies, which have such a high claim on our "veneration," contain a prayer "for the rest and peace of all those who have departed this life in God's faith and fear"; also "A sacrificial oblation of the Eucharistic bread and wine"; and "A prayer of consecration, that God will 'make the bread and wine the Body and Blood of Christ.'"[3] The tendency of this *Tract* is to produce the impression that the present Liturgy of the Church of England, because it does not contain either of the features just mentioned, is not of equal value with those extant Ancient Liturgies, "which possess the *greatest* claims on our veneration and study." It must be sorrowfully admitted that Froude's exhortation to "study" these ancient documents has not been in vain, and that the studies of his successors have not been confined to the portions to which he called attention. The Ritualists of the present day do study the Liturgies of the past, but they prefer to imitate those which were in use in the Church of Rome during the darkest period of the Dark Ages of Christianity.

The opinions expressed by Froude in the *Tracts for the Times* were extremely moderate, when compared with others which he held, but which were not made known to the public until after his death, when his writings were published in four volumes, edited by Keble and Newman. The first two volumes were issued in 1838, the others

[1] *Apologia Pro Vita Sua*, p. 107.
[2] *Tract LXIII.*, p. 16.
[3] *Ibid.* p. 7.

later on, under the general title of *Remains of tne late Reverend Richard Hurrell Froude, M.A.* The public interest in these volumes mainly centred round the first, which produced a profound sensation throughout the country, owing to the startling statements in favour of Roman doctrines which it contained. Until then no one—outside the Tractarian party—seems to have even dreamt that it was possible that one of the chief and trusted leaders of the Oxford Movement could possibly have gone so far towards Rome, and yet retain his position as a clergyman of the Reformed Church of England. I subjoin some extracts from his "Letters to Friends" in the order in which they were published. The italics are mine. On August 31, 1833, Froude wrote:—

"It has lately come into my head that the present state of things in England makes *an opening for revising the Monastic System.* I think of putting the view forward under the title of 'Project for reviving Religion in great towns.' . . . I must go about the country to look for the stray sheep of the true fold; there are many about I am sure; only *that odious Protestantism* sticks in people's gizzard. I see Hammond takes that view of the *infallibility of the Church*, which P. says was the old one. *We must revive it*" (vol. i. p. 322).

August, 1833.—"Since I have been at home, I have been doing what I can to *proselytise in an underhand way*" (p. 322).

September 16, 1833.—"I should like to know why you flinch from saying that the power of making the Body and Blood of Christ is vested in the Successors of the Apostles" (p. 326).

November 17, 1833.—"Is it expedient to put forth any paper on 'the doctrine necessary to Salvation'? I am led to question whether Justification by Faith is an integral part of this doctrine. I have not breathed this to a soul but you, and *express* myself offhand. . . . I wish you could get to know something of S. and W., and un-ise, *un-Protestantise*, un-Miltonise them" (p. 331).

January 9, 1834.—"You will be shocked at my avowal, that I am every day becoming a less and less loyal son of the Reformation. It appears to me plain that in all matters that seem to us indifferent or even doubtful, we should conform our practices to those of the Church which has preserved its traditionary practices unbroken. We cannot know about any seemingly indifferent practice of the Church of Rome, that it is not a development of the Apostolic *ethos;* and it is to no purpose to say that we can find no proof of it in the writings of the six first centuries" (p. 336).

August 22, 1834.—"If you are determined to have a pulpit in your Church, *which I would much rather be without*, do put it at the west end of the Church, or leave it where it is; every one can hear you perfectly, and what can they want more? *But whatever you do, pray don't let it stand in the light of the Altar, which,* if there is any truth in my notions of Ordination, *is more sacred than the Holy of Holies* was in the Jewish Temple" (p. 372).

October, 1834.—"As to the Reformers, *I think worse and worse of them.* Jewell was what you would in these days term an irreverent Dissenter. His *Defence of the Apology* disgusted me more than almost any work I ever read" (p. 379).

December 26, 1834.—"When I get your letter I expect a rowing for *my Roman Catholic sentiments.* Really *I hate the Reformation and the Reformers more and more*" (p. 389).

January 1835.—"I am more and more indignant at the Protestant doctrine on the subject of the Eucharist, and think that the principle on which it is founded is as proud, irreverent, and foolish as that of any heresy, even Socinianism" (p. 391).

January 1835.—"I shall never call the Holy Eucharist 'The Lord's Supper,' nor God's Priests 'Ministers of the Word,' or the Altar 'The Lord's Table,' &c., &c.; innocent as such phrases are in themselves, they have been dirtied; a fact of which you seem oblivious on many occasions. *Nor shall I even abuse Roman Catholics as a Church* for anything except excommunicating us" (p. 395).

February 25, 1835.—"The Rural Dean and the Clergy 'went a whoring' after the Wesleyans, Moravians, and the whole kit besides, to concoct a joint plan of general education" (p. 400).

February 25, 1835.—"I can see no other claim which the Prayer Book has on a Layman's deference, as the teaching of the Church, which the Breviary and Missal have not *in a far higher degree*" (p. 402).

In the first volume of Froude's *Remains* there is a chapter headed, "Sayings and Doings." Unfortunately, with only two exceptions, no dates are mentioned when these sayings were uttered. There are two or three which are against Rome to a certain extent. He declared:— "I never could be a Romanist; I never could think all those things in Pope Pius' Creed necessary to salvation. But I do not see what harm an ordinary Romanist gets

G

from thinking so."[1] On another occasion he termed the Romanists, "wretched Tridentines everywhere."[2] But, inasmuch as, only one year before his death, he, as we have seen, declared that he would never "abuse Roman Catholics as a Church for anything, except excommunicating us," I am inclined to think that his anti-Roman sayings must have been uttered some considerable time before his death. Two more of Froude's sayings may be cited here:—"I wonder a thoughtful fellow like H. does not get to hate the Reformers faster." "The Reformation was a limb badly set—it must be broken again in order to be righted."[3]

These extracts will serve to make my readers understand why the publication of Froude's *Remains* created such a stir throughout the country. Moderate High Churchmen, like Samuel Wilberforce, deplored their publication, as likely to do "irreparable injury."[4] Archdeacon Edward Churton said that one result of the *Remains* was to "give deep offence to many minds, and to unsettle the principles of many more."[5] They were edited by Keble and Newman, but in their preface to the first volume not one word of censure of Froude's disloyal utterances is to be found. On the contrary, the editors appear therein as his apologists, contenting themselves, by way of caution, with saying in the mildest possible manner:—"It can hardly be necessary for them to add, what the name of editor implies, that while they of course concur in his [Froude's] sentiments as a whole, they are not to be understood as rendering themselves responsible for every *shade* of opinion or expression."[6] Pusey hailed the publication with pleasure. "For myself," he said, "I am very glad of the publication of the *Remains*; they may very likely be a check, but that in itself may be the very best thing for us, and prevent a too rapid and weakening growth."[7]

But the Rev. Dr. Faussett, Lady Margaret's Professor

[1] Froude's *Remains*, vol. i. p. 434.   [2] *Ibid.* p. 434.   [3] *Ibid.* pp. 434, 433.
[4] *Life of Bishop Wilberforce*, vol. i. p. 112.
[5] *Life of Joshua Watson*, p. 270, 2nd edition.
[6] Froude's *Remains*, vol. i. p. xxii.   [7] *Life of Dr. Pusey*, vol. ii. p. 45.

of Divinity in the University of Oxford, was not at all pleased with the publication of Froude's *Remains*. He felt, and rightly felt, that the work was calculated, on the whole, to glorify the Church of Rome, and to disparage the Church of England, and to hold up to public contempt that Protestantism of which Englishmen were justly proud. Accordingly, he determined to raise his voice in the University pulpit, not only against the *Remains*, but also against certain statements of the *Tracts for the Times*, and of the *British Critic*, of which at that time Newman was editor. On Sunday, May 20, 1838, Dr. Faussett preached before the University of Oxford a sermon on *The Revival of Popery*, which became a bombshell in the enemies' camp. It was subsequently published as a pamphlet. The text selected by the preacher was:—" Come out of her, my people, that ye be not partakers of her sins, and that ye receive not of her plagues" (Rev. xviii. 4). He first of all directed attention to the revival of genuine Popery in the country, and then proceeded to show how the cause of Rome was being assisted by certain trusted leaders of the Tractarians. He admitted that "a few unguarded statements, the result probably of individual haste and indiscretion," might easily have been passed over without "any severity of censure."

"But," he added, "when they assume more and more unequivocally the marks of deliberation and design, the evidence of numbers and of combination; when the most plausible palliations of Romish corruption, and the most insidious cavils against the wisdom, and even in some measure the necessity, of the Reformation, find their way into the periodical and popular and most widely disseminated literature of the day;—when the wild and visionary sentiments of an enthusiastic mind [Froude's], involving in their unguarded expression and undisguised preference for a portion at least of Papal superstition, and occasionally even a wanton outrage on the cherished feelings of the sincere Protestant—his pious affection for those venerated names which he habitually associates with the inestimable blessings of the Reformation—are dragged forth from the sanctuary of confidential intercourse, and recommended to the public as a 'witness of Catholic views,' and 'to speak a word in season for the Church of God'; as 'likely to suggest thoughts on doctrine, on Church policy, and on individual conduct, most true and most necessary for these times,' and as 'a bold and comprehensive sketch of a new position' for the Church of England; and this, too, under circumstances which imply the concurrence and approval, and responsibility too, of an indefinite and apparently numerous body of friends and correspondents and editors and reviewers;—who shall any longer deny the imperative necessity which exists for the most decisive language of warning and caution, lest these rash projectors of a new position for our Church should be unwarily permitted to undermine and impair her old and approved defences."[1]

"To affirm," said the preacher, "that these persons are strictly Papists, or that within certain limits of their own devising they are not actually opposed to the corruptions and the Communion of Rome, would, I believe, be as uncharitable as it is untrue. But who shall venture to pronounce them safe and consistent members of the Church of England? and who shall question the obvious tendency of their views to Popery itself? For if by some happy consistency they are themselves, and for the present, saved from the natural consequences of their own reasoning, what shall we hope for the people at large, should these delusive speculations (which God in His infinite mercy forbid) extend their influence beyond the circle (and it is hoped not yet a very extensive circle) of educated men, to which they are at present limited? If such should become the ordinary instruction of the unwary pastor to his credulous flock, what shall preserve them from all the fascinations and idolatries of the Mass, or from welcoming with open arms those crafty emissaries who have already succeeded to such a fearful extent in reimposing the yoke of spiritual bondage on the neck of our deluded countrymen?"[2]

Dr. Faussett rendered an important service to the Church of England by his faithful and outspoken sermon. Its warnings were greatly needed, and seem to us now almost prophetic. All that he foretold, and more than all, has come true in our own day, and to an extent which Dr. Faussett never could have anticipated. He proved his case by numerous quotations from the writings of the men whose conduct he so justly denounced. Of course they did not like it. Those who do wrong never love the

[1] *The Revival of Popery.* By Godfrey Faussett, D.D., 1st edition, pp. 13-15. Oxford: Parker. 1838.
[2] *Ibid.* p. 24.

man who has given them a richly deserved castigation. Dr. Faussett's was not the first public attack on the teaching of the Tractarians, but it was, I believe, the first which they had condescended to reply to publicly. Of these, perhaps, the most noteworthy was that written by the Rev. Peter Maurice, Chaplain of New and All Souls' College, Oxford, and published by him with the title of *Popery in Oxford*, in 1837. He declared that "an attack is made by this newly organised system [Tractarianism] upon the very vitals of our religion, as embodied in the Book of Common Prayer,"[1] and he brought against the party a charge of secrecy, just sixty years before the publication of the first edition of my *Secret History of the Oxford Movement*:—

"We find," he said, "a party, *whom nobody knows*, though everybody seems to pay deference to, entering into a combination, and issuing *Tracts* in the capacity of 'Members of the University of Oxford,' containing the most absurd statements that ever issued from any body of educated men, addressed to the clergy as well as to the laity as if they were vested with supernatural powers; and moreover (who would credit it?) *suppressing their names.*"[2]

"What are the names of these our Members [of the University of Oxford]. Let them be announced, that we may know them, at least by name. Had I not found Dr. Pusey there, by name, I should have scorned to put my name alongside of his. I fight in the daylight, neither with small nor great, but with those only who are not ashamed of their doings."[3]

The Islington Evangelical clergy censured the Tractarians. Writing on January 6, 1837, Mr. Dodsworth (one of the Tractarians) said: "I hear that there was a most violent and abusive attack on us at a meeting of clergy at Islington yesterday, and great alarm expressed at the spread of High Church principles, which they did not scruple to denounce as heretical."[4] Later on in the same year Archdeacon Spooner, of Coventry, in charging the clergy of his Archdeaconry, denounced the *Tracts for*

---

[1] *Popery in Oxford.* By Peter Maurice, M.A., p. 4. London: 1837.
[2] *Ibid.* p. 4.   [3] *Ibid.* p. 11.
[4] *Life of Dr. Pusey*, vol. ii. p. 12.

the Times in vigorous terms. To him belongs the honour of giving utterance to the first official condemnation of the Oxford Movement. Pusey wrote to the Archdeacon a private letter of remonstrance, which brought back a reply, in the course of which the Archdeacon disclaimed any intention of imputing any intentional dishonesty to the writers of the *Tracts*, but adding that he believed that "the respectable and learned authors of those *Tracts* were, unawares to themselves, injuring the pure and Scriptural doctrines of the Protestant faith."[1] At about this time the Bishop of Oxford received so many letters of complaint against the Tractarians that he felt it necessary to write to Dr. Pusey on the subject, asking him for an explanation. This Dr. Pusey gave in a long letter, dated September 26, 1837, in which he specially dealt with the charges brought against his friends by Mr. Peter Maurice, whose book on *Popery in Oxford* had by this time caused a great stir throughout the country, and had been quoted by Canon G. Stanley Faber, of Durham, in a Charge which he delivered to the clergy. The charges brought against Mr. Newman and his friends by Mr. Maurice were: (1) Needless bowings; (2) turning to the East while reading certain prayers; (3) the use of a Credence Table; and (4) the use of a stole with embroidered crosses. Dr. Pusey did not deny the truth of either of these charges, excepting the first, stating that there had been "no bowings, except at the name of our Lord"; as to the other charges he endeavoured to prove that they were directed against lawful practices. But, inasmuch as he was writing a private letter to his Bishop, Dr. Pusey was not ashamed to unjustly slander an opponent in his letter:—

"The reports," against his friends, he informs his lordship, "began with a Mr. Maurice, a Chaplain of New College, who seems a very excited and vain and half-bewildered person, who seems to think that he is called by God to oppose what he calls the Popery of Oxford. He published a heavy pamphlet, which would have

---

[1] *Life of Dr. Pusey*, vol. ii. p. 14.

died a natural death had not the *Christian Observer* wished to have a blow at Mr. Newman and the 'High Church,' and so taken it up though with a sort of protest against identifying itself with Mr. Maurice's language; and thence, I am sorry to say, Mr. Townsend, Prebendary of Durham, has repeated it in a 'Charge to the Clergy of the Peculiar of N. Allerton and Allertonshire.'"[1]

After all, this "very excited and vain and half-bewildered person," as Pusey insultingly termed Mr. Maurice, had only told the truth. I had the pleasure of Mr. Maurice's personal acquaintance many years later, and found in him no trace of being either a "vain" or a "half-bewildered person." Down to his death, at an advanced age, he was ever foremost in exposing the misdeeds of the Romanisers. His two volumes on *The Ritualists or Non-Natural Catholics*, now long since out of print, contain a considerable quantity of useful—though badly-arranged—information concerning the history of the Oxford Movement, to be found nowhere else.[2]

Though the Tractarians were much annoyed at these criticisms, they were careful to abstain as far as possible from taking public notice of anything said against them. But when Dr. Faussett publicly denounced them in such vigorous terms from the University pulpit, and held them up to the reprobation of all loyal Churchmen, they could keep silence no longer. His sermon was not published until June 21st, and yet before the next day was over Newman had written a reply of 104 pages. It was a calmly written and clever document, in which all the subtlety for which he was famous seems to have been called into action. He complains much of Dr. Faussett that, in his sermon, he had not proved that the opinions and practices he condemned were "inconsistent with the doctrines of our Church."[3] Newman here very conveniently chose to forget that Dr. Faussett was addressing men whom he knew to be already (with but few excep-

---

[1] *Life of Dr. Pusey*, vol. ii. pp. 14, 15.
[2] *The Ritualists or Non-Natural Catholics.* By the Rev. Peter Maurice, D.D. London: J. F. Shaw & Co., pp. xxiv. and 191. *Sequel to the Ritualists.* By the Rev. Peter Maurice, D.D., p. 188. Yarnton: 1875.
[3] *A Letter to the Rev. Godfrey Faussett, D.D., on Certain Points of Faith and Practice.* By the Rev. J. H. Newman, B.D., 2nd edition, 1838, p. 6.

tions) convinced that the doctrines and practices censured were inconsistent with the doctrines of the Church of England. He had no need to stop and argue the case with men who were already convinced. His object was to *expose* a subtle attempt to revive Popery in the Church of England, and in proof of the existence of such an attempt he gave ample extracts from Froude's *Remains*, the *Tracts for the Times*, and the *British Critic*. It was simply impossible, in the course of the sermon, to give the proof demanded. Newman certainly had a point against his opponent when he complained that he had not cited what Froude had written against the Church of Rome. Not that Newman had much to gain from those passages, which had been specially cited by the editors of the *Remains* in their preface. Bishop (afterwards Cardinal) Wiseman, in the *Dublin Review*, commenting on the argument sought to be built on these anti-Roman utterances of Froude, justly remarks:—

"We think we are justified in saying that proofs of Mr. Froude's disinclination to Catholicity must have been very scarce, for the editors to have been induced to bring together these superficial observations, made during a brief residence in a Catholic city, not generally reputed one of the most edifying. These, however, will not bear comparison with the growing and expanding tendency of his mind towards everything Catholic; and we cannot help feeling, as we peruse his later declarations, that the passages brought so prominently forward by his editors, would have been among those which, dying, he would have wished to blot."[1]

There is an interesting statement by Newman at page 25 of his pamphlet, in which he declares that:—"It is idolatry to bow down to any emblem or symbol as divine which God Himself has not appointed; and since He has not appointed the worship of images, such worship is idolatrous; though how far it is so, whether in itself or in given individuals, we may be unable to determine." He then proceeds to argue at considerable length in favour of the doctrine of the Real Presence, though he repudiates

---

[1] Cardinal Wiseman's *Essays on Various Subjects*, vol. ii. p. 80.

Transubstantiation. He denies that the Church of Rome is "the mother of harlots," but terms her "our ancient Mother."[1] As to "the rite of the Roman Church, or St. Peter's Liturgy," he terms it a "sacred and most precious monument,"[2] and adds:—

"Well was it for us that they [the Reformers] did not discard it, that they did not touch any vital part; for through God's good providence, though they broke it up and cut away portions, they did not touch life; and thus we have it at this day, a violently treated, but a holy and dear possession, more dear perhaps and precious than if it were in its full vigour and beauty, as sickness or infirmity endear us to our friends and relatives."[3]

This was, of course, equivalent to asserting that the Communion Service of the Church of England is not in a state of spiritual "vigour and beauty"; but rather in a state of "sickness or infirmity"—thus showing clearly how much Newman admired the Church of Rome's Mass Book. Of course he repudiated Dr. Faussett's assertion that the work of himself and his friends tended to a "Revival of Popery," and was calculated to lead men to Rome. Yet within little more than seven years he practically proved the charge by seceding to Rome himself; and it is the biographer of Dr. Pusey who tells us that "to Newman himself, when a Roman Catholic, the Movement seemed to have been a steady impulse towards Rome."[4] In his *Letter to Dr. Faussett* Newman did not censure any of Froude's extravagant statements.

Dr. Hook was at that time Vicar of Leeds, where he was busily engaged in promoting High Church principles. It was his boast that he had learned and accepted Tractarian doctrines before the commencement of the Tractarian Movement. Later on in life he came into direct conflict with the advanced party, whom he boldly charged with Romanising; indeed, the first indication of disagreement came out in connection with the publication of Froude's *Remains*. In August 1838 Hook was selected by the Bishop of Ripon (Dr. C. T. Longley) to preach the

[1] Newman's *Letter to Dr. Faussett*, p. 33. [2] *Ibid.* p. 46.
[3] *Ibid.* p. 47. [4] *Life of Dr. Pusey*, vol. ii. p. 80.

sermon at his Primary Visitation, and soon afterwards he published it. He availed himself of the opportunity to add some lengthy notes to it, in which he dealt with the *Tracts for the Times*, Froude's *Remains*, and Dr. Faussett's sermon on *The Revival of Popery*. For the two former he had a mixture of praise and blame; but for the latter nothing but unmixed censure and vulgar personal insult and abuse. As to the *Tracts for the Times*, he said:—

"Against some of the pious opinions supported in these *Tracts* objections may occasionally be raised, for perfect coincidence of opinion is not to be expected. I do not, myself, accord with *all* the opinions expressed in them, or always admit the deduction attempted to be drawn from the principles on which we are agreed. I think, too, that while manfully vindicating the principles of the English Reformation, in their fear lest they should appear to respect persons too highly, the writers of the *Tracts* do not appreciate highly enough the character of some of our leading Reformers, or make due allowance for the difficulties in which they were placed. . . . I am *not* one of those who would say, 'Read the Oxford *Tracts*, and take for granted every opinion there expressed,' but I *am* one of those who would say, 'Read and digest those *Tracts* well, and you will have imbibed principles which will enable you to judge of opinions.'"[1]

As to Froude's *Remains*, and Dr. Faussett's sermon, Dr. Hook gave his opinion in one lengthy paragraph:—

"The present discourse," he said, "is sufficient to show that I am not, any more than Dr. Faussett, inclined to approve of Mr. Froude's *Remains*. I deeply, indeed, regret the publication of that work without a protest, on the part of the editor, against some of the author's paradoxical positions. With a kind heart and glowing sensibilities, Mr. Froude united a mind of wonderful power, saturated with learning, and, from its very luxuriance, productive of weeds, together with many flowers . . . from many of his opinions the majority of his readers will, like myself, dissent. But if, in contemplating the evils inseparable from a great movement, he does not sufficiently appreciate, and I think he does not, the wisdom of our Reformation, or the virtues of many of our Reformers; if while condemning the *Romish* he censures the *English* Church; still, while we think him to be in error in these particulars, we may do

---

[1] *A Call to Union on the Principles of the English Reformation.* By Walter Farquhar Hook, D.D., 2nd edition, pp. 108-110. London: 1838.

so without condemning him by wholesale;—still less ought those persons to condemn him for not fully appreciating our Reformation, who, like Mr. Scott, consider the work of the Reformers, in retaining our present Baptismal Service, 'a burden hard to bear,' 'an absurdity which they did not believe in their hearts.' Had Dr. Faussett contented himself with having written a pamphlet or a review, while we might have considered him incompetent to sit in judgment on such a mind as Mr. Froude's, we should have had no cause of complaint. But cause of complaint the Church has when he makes one work a pretext for attacking certain of his clerical brethren, whose learning he may be unable to appreciate, but whose piety and zeal he would do well to imitate; when he uses the pulpit to compel that attention to himself which he could not secure from the press."[1]

Hook's sermon pleased nobody altogether. His Oxford friends were bitterly disappointed. On receiving a copy of it Pusey wrote to Newman in sorrowful tones:—
"I send you Hook's sermon, which Parker brought me to-day, to read in your way back; it shows me that my letters have been wasted upon him, for he will neither say one thing nor the other; not say wherein he disagrees, and yet say that he does disagree. However, what he does say will do good, and perhaps keep some young ones quiet. What he says about Froude is as much as you could expect."[2]

In the month of July 1838, the Bishop of Oxford (Dr. Bagot) delivered his third Visitation Charge, which greatly disturbed Newman, when he read a report of it in an Oxford paper. Indeed he was so upset that he determined to give up publishing any more *Tracts for the Times*, under the impression, as he told Pusey, that "an indefinite censure was cast over the *Tracts*" by the Bishop's Charge. Pusey also was troubled:—"It is," he wrote to Newman, "not simply disheartening; it seems like a blow from which I shall never live to see things recover."[3] Pusey entered into a correspondence with the Bishop on the subject. His lordship said that he hoped the *Tracts* would not be given up, and he felt sure that when Pusey

[1] Hook's *Call to Union*, pp. 167, 168.   [2] *Life of Dr. Pusey*, vol. ii. p. 66.
[3] *Ibid.* pp. 53, 54.

read what he had said in his published Charge, he would form a different judgment. When the Charge did appear in print, Pusey was surprised, and wrote to the Bishop:— "What your lordship says about our *Tracts* looks different from what it did when extracted and put forth by the *Oxford Journal* and the like. I need hardly say to your lordship that I am, for myself, perfectly satisfied, grateful for your lordship's advice, and for the warning to those who are more or less our pupils."[1] I have not been able to see the report of the Bishop's Charge as it appeared in the *Oxford Journal;* but certainly as it appeared in pamphlet form, and as issued by the Bishop himself, Newman and Pusey had little or nothing to complain of, but, on the contrary, a great deal to be thankful for. The fact is that Dr. Bagot was, at this time, a great admirer of the *Tracts for the Times*, and, so far as I can ascertain, he was the first Bishop in England who publicly said a good word in their favour. These were the Bishop's words as issued by himself:—

"With reference to errors *in doctrine*, which have been imputed to the series of publications called the *Tracts for the Times*, it can hardly be expected that, on an occasion like the present, I should enter into, or give a handle to anything which might hereafter tend to controversial discussions. Into controversy I will not enter. But, generally speaking, I may say that in these days of lax and spurious liberality, anything which tends to recall forgotten truths is *valuable:* and where these publications have directed men's minds to such important subjects as the union, discipline, and the authority of the Church, I think *they have done good service;* but there may be some points in which, perhaps, from ambiguity of expression, or similar causes, it is not impossible, but that evil rather than the intended good may be produced on minds of a peculiar temperament. I have more fear of the Disciples than of the Teachers. In speaking therefore of the authors of the *Tracts* in question, I would say that I think their desire to restore the ancient discipline of the Church *most praiseworthy;* I rejoice in their attempts to secure a stricter attention to the Rubrical directions in the Book of Common Prayer; and I heartily approve the spirit which would restore a due observance of the Fasts and Festivals of the Church: *but* I would

---

[1] *Life of Dr. Pusey*, vol. ii. p. 62.

implore them, by the purity of their intentions, to be cautious, both in their writings and actions, to take heed lest their good be evil spoken of; lest in their exertions to re-establish unity, they unhappily create fresh schism; lest in their admiration of antiquity, they revert to practices which heretofore have ended in superstition."[1]

It will be observed that in this statement the Bishop did not censure the writers of the *Tracts for the Times* for anything they *had* written; he only expressed his fears lest in the *future* they should go too far in the direction of superstition; and for his words of warnings of danger he received, as we have seen, the thanks of Pusey. Instead of censuring the *Tracts* which had appeared, he praised them highly; and in order to prevent any misconception as to his meaning, in a footnote to the second edition of his Charge the Bishop wrote :—" As I have been led to suppose that the above passage [cited above] has been misunderstood, I take this opportunity of stating, that it never was my intention therein to pass any *general censure* on the *Tracts for the Times.*" When the Bishop delivered his Charge churchmen everywhere were talking about Froude's *Remains*, its denunciation of the Reformers, and its praise of what ordinary persons called Popery. But on this burning subject the Bishop said nothing. His silence, under such circumstances, was worthy of severe censure.

There was one result of the publication of Froude's *Remains* which its editors never anticipated. It led to the erection of the Martyrs' Memorial at Oxford, in memory of Cranmer, Ridley, and Latimer, who were burnt alive in that city. A prospectus of the proposed Memorial, issued in 1838 by the Heads of Houses in Oxford, stated that it was intended to be " A public testimony of respect for the principles of the Reformation, and veneration for the personal character of the Martyred Bishops." When Pusey first heard of the scheme, he exclaimed that it " is nothing but a cut at us ! "[2] It certainly placed Pusey,

[1] *A Charge delivered to the Clergy of the Diocese of Oxford.* By Richard Bagot, D.D., Bishop of Oxford, 2nd edition, pp. 20, 21. 1838.
[2] *Life of Dr. Pusey*, vol. ii. p. 64.

Newman, and Keble, and their friends in a very awkward and uncomfortable position. They dreaded the public odium which would inevitably fall upon them if they refused altogether to have anything to do with the Memorial; and yet they hated the whole scheme with all their hearts. Pusey informed Keble that he "had spoken strongly lately against the Memorial, as *perhaps* falling within the scope of onr Lord's words against 'building the sepulchres of those whom their fathers had slain,' and AS UNKIND TO THE CHURCH OF ROME, in throwing a hindrance to her reforming herself and healing the schism."[1] It makes one justly indignant to see tender consideration thus shown towards the criminal, and none at all for her innocent victims. If Rome had ever repented of her crimes in burning the Marian Martyrs, it might have been "unkind" to remind her of her former misdeeds; but she never has repented, or ever expressed a single word of regret for burning alive in Mary's reign, five Bishops, twenty-one divines, eight gentlemen, eighty-four artificers, one hundred husbandmen, twenty-six wives, twenty widows, nine virgins, two boys, and two infants. The fact is that the Tractarians had no real respect for the Reformers, and some of them doubted whether they were Martyrs at all. "I cannot," said Keble, "understand how poor Cranmer could be reckoned a *bona fide* Martyr according to the rules of the Primitive Church. Was he not an unwilling sufferer? and did he not in the very final paper of his confession profess to hold in all points the doctrine of that *Answer to Gardiner?* And is not that doctrine such as the ancient Church would have called *heretical?*"[2] So Cranmer was nothing better than a *heretic*, in Keble's estimation, and, therefore, not a Martyr at all! One who was at that time a prominent Tractarian (the Rev. Thomas Mozley), subsequently wrote:—"I have to own that, in spite of the telling illustrations of Mrs. Trimmer's *History of England*, I have never yet succeeded in getting up an atom of affection or respect for the three gentlemen canonised in the 'Martyrs' Memorial' at Oxford. As

---

[1] *Life of Dr. Pusey*, vol. ii. p. 69.
[2] *Ibid.* p. 71.

Lord Blachford once observed to me, 'Cranmer burnt well,' and that is all the good I know about him."[1] What Froude thought about the Reformers I have already cited. And Keble declared:—"Anything which separates the present Church from the Reformers I should hail as a great good."[2] And even Dean Church, when, in later years, he wrote his book on *The Oxford Movement*, went so far as to declare:—"It is safe to say that the Divines of the Reformation never can be again, with their confessed Calvinism, with their shifting opinions, their extravagant deference to the foreign oracles of Geneva and Zurich, their subservience to bad men in power, the heroes and saints of Churchmen."[3] It is evident that men who wrote like this, had they lived in the Reformation period, never would have led a movement against Rome leading to secession from her communion.

Newman and his friends soon found that it was impossible to stop the proposed Memorial; and therefore they directed their energies to a vain attempt to spoil it. Pusey was not at all pleased when he heard that Dr. Sewell talked of placing on the Memorial an inscription bearing the expression "Martyrs for the Truth." Mr. Churton proposed that the Memorial should take the form of a new Church; but Pusey on this point said that "it must not be the Martyrs' Church, canonising them."[4] He thought that the proposed new Church "must be called after some one already canonised, not by individuals." We thus see that Pusey had no objection to honouring in this way some one canonised by the Pope, which was an indirect way of acknowledging the Pope's power to canonise. On this point one of the biographers of Keble informs us that that gentleman, in one of his sermons, asserted of English Churchmen that "*we* are free to reverence all Saints of the Roman Communion."[5]

The *Oxford Protestant Magazine* for 1848, in some valu-

---

[1] *Reminiscences of the Oxford Movement*, vol. ii. p. 230.
[2] *Life of Dr. Pusey*, vol. ii. p. 71.
[3] Church's *Oxford Movement*, p. 39, 1st edition.
[4] *Life of Dr. Pusey*, vol. ii. p. 66.
[5] *John Keble*. By Walter Lock, M.A., p. 149.

able "Hints towards a History of Puseyism," thus refers to the hindrances thrown in the way of the suggested Martyrs' Memorial:—

"The originators and promoters of this design met with almost insurmountable obstacles. Their design, and the methods they adopted, were alike carped at. At a public meeting held in full term, in February 1839, not more than two hundred persons were present, and among these were some who, while professing to support the measure, cavilled and censured, and pronounced it a failure. Such was Mr. Greswell, the Oxford Chairman of Mr. Gladstone's Committee at the late election. Mr. Greswell, besides describing the movement as a 'perfect failure,' £2000 only having been promised, also strongly objected to the use of the word 'Protestant' as applied to the Church; 'the word,' he said, 'was not to be found in the Prayer Book.' Cranmer, he thought, ought not to be praised, but recorded as a penitent."[1]

The Bishop of Oxford paid a special visit to Pusey with a view to persuading him and his friends to help on the Memorial, and intimated that the Archbishop of Canterbury felt the same anxiety for their help. Pusey proposed to the Bishop "to change the Memorial from a commemoration of the Reformers into a thanksgiving for the blessings of the Reformation," and he pressed the Bishop to endeavour to get the Archbishop to recommend this alteration. But it was all in vain; Tractarian efforts to spoil the Memorial by depriving it of its leading characteristic were happily defeated. The beautiful monument to Cranmer, Ridley, and Latimer, still to be seen near St. Mary Magdalene Church, Oxford, was unveiled in 1841. "It was," says Mr. G. V. Cox, in his *Recollections of Oxford*, "a noble proof (though a somewhat tardy one), that Oxford still cherished the memory of those great martyrs to the Reformation. The subscription was a large one (£5000), and was raised with wonderful rapidity; out of it, besides the Martyrs' Memorial, was also built an additional aisle on the north side of Magdalen Parish Church, to be called "The Martyrs' Aisle." It had been found impracticable to get a site in Broad Street, the actual scene of the Mar-

[1] *Oxford Protestant Magazine*, vol. for 1848, p. 597.

tyrdom."[1] On the north side of the Memorial is the inscription, which well merits a place in these pages. It is as follows:—

"To the Glory of God, and in grateful commemoration of His servants, Thomas Cranmer, Nicholas Ridley, Hugh Latimer, Prelates of the Church of England, who, near this spot, yielded their bodies to be burned; bearing witness to the sacred truths which they had affirmed and maintained against the errors of the Church of Rome; and rejoicing that to them it was given not only to believe on Christ, but also to suffer for His sake. This Monument was erected by public subscription in the year of our Lord God, 1841."

---

[1] *Recollections of Oxford.* By G. V. Cox, M.A., 2nd edition, p. 305.

CHAPTER V

Newman in 1839—Influenced by an article in the *Dublin Review*—Remarkable acknowledgments—Corporate Reunion with Rome—Preparing the way for Rome—The Pastor of Antwerp—Breakfasts with Newman and his friends—Startling and treasonable advice given him—Pusey writes on *Tendencies to Romanism*—He pleads for peace in the Church—Dr. M'Crie on the cry for peace—Prayers for the Dead—Breeks *v.* Woolfrey—West *v.* Shuttleworth—Egerton *v.* All of Rode—Moresby Faculty Case—Dr. Pusey begins to hear Confessions in 1838—In 1846 he goes to Confession for the first time—His Protestant notes in the Works of Tertullian—Wiseman hopes the Tractarians will "succeed in their work"—He realises the Roman tendency of their teaching—Extracts from the *Tracts for the Times*—Margaret Chapel as a centre of Tractarianism—Mr. Serjeant Bellasis—Oakeley claims the right to "hold all Roman doctrine"—He is prosecuted by the Bishop of London—His licence revoked—Pusey defends Oakeley—Says the judgment against him has no moral force—Pusey says he believes in Purgatory and Invocation of Saints—Thinks England and Rome "not irreconcilably at variance"—Oakeley secedes to Rome.

THE year 1839 was a memorable one in the life of Newman. It was during the summer of that year that (as he informed the Rev. J. B. Mozley four years later): "It came strongly upon me, from first reading the Monophysite controversy, and then turning to the Donatist, that we were external to the Catholic Church. I have never got over this."[1] Writing to Pusey, on August 28, 1844, he declared:—"I am one who, even five years ago [*i.e.* 1839], had a strong conviction, from reading the history of the early ages, that we are not part of the Church."[2] Writing again to Pusey, on March 14, 1845, Newman tells him:—"My doubts [of the Catholicity of the Church of England] were occasioned by studying the Monophysite controversy—which, when mastered, threw light upon all those which preceded it, not the least on the Arian. I

---

[1] Newman's *Letters*, vol. ii. p. 430. [2] *Life of Pusey*, vol. ii. p. 406.

saw as clear as day (though I was well aware clear impressions need not at once be truths) that our Church was in the *position* towards Rome of the heretical and schismatical bodies towards the Primitive Church. This was in the early summer of 1839; in the autumn, Dr. Wiseman's article on the Donatists completed my unsettlement. Since that time I have tried, first by one means, then by another, to overcome my own convictions."[1] Newman's first impressions on reading Wiseman's article (which appeared in the *Dublin Review*, August 1839) were conveyed by him to his friend, Mr. F. Rogers, afterwards Lord Blachford:—"Since I wrote to you," he tells him, "I have had the first real hit from Romanism which has happened to me. R. W., who has been passing through, directed my attention to Dr. Wiseman's article in the new *Dublin*. I must confess it has given me a stomach-ache."[2]

Now, to any ordinary mind it must seem strange that Newman, who confesses that he felt "strongly," in 1839, that the Church of England was "*external* to the Catholic Church," and who, at that time, had "*clear* impressions" that the position of the Church of England towards the Catholic Church was identical with that of the ancient "heretical and schismatical bodies," could possibly, with a comfortable conscience, remain "external to the Catholic Church" for another six years! But Newman's mind being of a naturally Jesuitical kind, he seems to have set himself right *with himself*, by the following ingenious illustration (written within a fortnight from the time that he got the "stomach-ache") to his friend Mr. F. Rogers, and evidently intended to elicit his opinion of it:—

"Well, then," wrote Newman, "once more; as those who sin after Baptism cannot at once return to their full privileges, yet are not without hope, so a Church which has broken away from the centre of unity is not at liberty at once to return, yet is not nothing. May she not put herself into a state of penance? Are not her children best fulfilling their duty to her—*not by leaving her, but by*

---

[1] *Life of Pusey*, vol. ii. p. 450.   [2] Newman's *Letters*, vol. ii. p. 286.

promoting her return, and not thinking that they have a *right* to rush into such *higher state* as communion with the centre of unity might give them. If the Church Catholic, indeed, has actually commanded their return to her at once, that is another matter; but this she cannot have done without pronouncing their present Church good for nothing, which I do not suppose Rome has done of us. In all this, which I did not mean to have inflicted on you, I assume, on the one hand, that Rome is right; on the other, that we are not bound by uncatholic subscriptions."[1]

There is all the wisdom of the serpent in this scheme, though none of the innocence of the dove; and after reading Newman's statements in subsequent years, I have no doubt that it served to quieten, if not altogether to silence, his own conscience for the next six years. The scheme was a subtle one, known in later years by the designation, "*Corporate* Reunion with Rome," as distinct from individual secession. Members of the Church of England were to "fulfil their duty to her, not by leaving her, but by promoting her return" to "the centre of unity"—the Church of Rome. From this year the idea of Corporate Reunion with Rome seems to have been ever present to Newman, until he seceded to her in 1845. Of the year 1840 he writes:—" I wished for union between the Anglican Church and Rome, if, and when it was possible; and I did what I could to gain weekly prayers for that object."[2] In October of this year he frankly admitted to a friend:—" I fear I must allow that, whether I will or no, I am disposing them [those he influenced by his teaching] towards Rome. First, because Rome is the only representative of the Primitive Church besides ourselves; in proportion then as they are loosened from the one, they will go to the other. Next, because *many doctrines which I have held have far greater, or their only scope, in the Roman system.*"[3] And, therefore, he began to think of giving up St. Mary's Vicarage, Oxford, which he then held, and migrating to the Vicarage of Littlemore, where he might continue to teach, by pen and mouth, those

---

[1] Newman's *Letters*, vol. ii. p. 288.
[2] Newman's *Apologia Pro Vita Sua*, p. 222. [3] *Ibid.* p. 236.

doctrines which, even at that time, he believed had "a far greater, or their only scope, in the Roman system." Was this honest? After making such an important discovery, ought he not at once to have given up all Ministerial duty in the Church of England, and seceded to a Church where his peculiar doctrines have their only honest "scope"? But, if he had at that time done this, what would have become of his schemes for Corporate Reunion with Rome? To a Roman Catholic layman Newman wrote, on September 12, 1841:—"We are keeping people from you [Church of Rome], by supplying their wants in our own Church. We *are* keeping persons from you: do you wish us to keep them from you for a time or for ever? It rests with you to determine. I do not fear that you will succeed among us; you will not supplant our Church in the affections of the English nation; ONLY THROUGH THE ENGLISH CHURCH CAN YOU ACT UPON THE ENGLISH NATION. I wish, of course, our Church should be consolidated, with and through *and in your communion*, for its sake, and your sake, and for the sake of unity."[1]

Only six days before Newman wrote the letter from which my last extract is given, Baron Bunsen described to a friend an incident in which Newman had recently taken part, and in which the Romish sympathies of Newman and his friends came out in a somewhat startling manner:—

"The other day," wrote Baron Bunsen, on Sept. 6, 1841, "Spörlein, the good Pastor of Antwerp, my fellow-traveller, arrived on his pilgrimage to seek comfort in the Church and faith of this country. At Oxford he went to Newman, who invited him to breakfast for a conference on religious opinions. Spörlein[2] stated his difficulties, as resulting from the consistorial government being in the hands of unbelievers, which in the Evangelical Society which he had been tempted to join, the leading members protested against every idea of Church membership. The breakfast party consisted of fifteen young men, whom Newman invited to an expression of opinion and advice; and the award (*uncontradicted*) was that 'Pastor

---

[1] Newman's *Apologia Pro Vita Sua*, pp. 312, 313.
[2] Spörlein had come over to England with a view to joining the Ministry of the Church of England.

Spörlein, as a Continental Christian, was subject to the authority of the Bishop of Antwerp.[1] He objected that by that Bishop he would be excommunicated as a heretic. 'Of course; *but you will conform to his decision?*' 'How can I do that,' exclaimed Spörlein, 'without abjuring my faith?' '*But your faith is heresy.*' 'How? *Do you mean that I am to embrace the errors of Rome*, and abjure the faith of the Gospel?' 'There is no faith but that of the Church.' 'But my faith is in Christ crucified.' 'You are mistaken; you are not saved by Christ, but in the Church.'

"Spörlein was thunderstruck. He looked around, asked again, obtained but the same reply, whereupon he burst out again with the declaration that 'he believed in Christ crucified, by whose merits alone he could be saved, and that *he would not join the Church of Rome*, abhorring her for intruding into the place of Christ.' One after the other dropped away, and Newman, remaining with him alone, attempted an explanation which, however, did not alter the case. I repeated this lamentable story as Spörlein had told it to Hare and myself, and Pusey said it was like telling a man complaining of toothache that the infallible remedy would be cutting off his head."[2]

No wonder that Baron Bunsen exclaimed, after writing the above pitiful story, "Oh, this is heartrending!" It was so indeed. Here was a Protestant Pastor, anxious to join the Ministry of the Church of England, introduced to a party of sixteen members of that Church (probably all clergymen), including Newman, and they, instead of smoothing his path, unanimously tell him to go off to the Church of Rome at once, and submit to the Popish Bishop of Antwerp! Such advice was simply disgraceful to those who gave it. It was the advice of disloyal traitors within the camp. No wonder, too, that Spörlein "was thunderstruck." The high personal character of Baron Bunsen, and his intellectual powers, prevent us supposing for one moment that he was mistaken. I am glad, for Pusey's sake, that he did not see the wisdom of the advice of these thirteen treacherous Tractarians.

We now return to Dr. Pusey, who had greatly

---

[1] Of course, the Roman Catholic Bishop of Antwerp.
[2] *Memoir of Baron Bunsen*, vol. i. pp. 613, 614, 1st edition.

troubled the Bishop of Oxford, by finally refusing to have anything to do with the proposed Martyrs' Memorial. His lordship evidently saw the harm that would be done to the cause of the Tractarians through their conduct in holding aloof, and that its tendency would be to confirm the public in their belief that the whole party hated both the Reformers and the Reformation with all their hearts. So he wrote, on January 19, 1839, an earnest appeal on the subject :—

"Let me then," wrote Dr. Bagot, "entreat you, then, by the love which (in spite of the assertions of your opposers in these days of misrepresentation) I am convinced you feel for our Reformed Church, if you cannot approve the Memorial, to make some declaration at a fit time, and in what you may deem the fittest mode—by letter or by publication of some sort—such as shall stop the accusations of your being in any degree hostile to the Reformation, enable your friends to defend you from such charges, and put to silence the Romanists who wrongly but boldly claim you as countenancing them." [1]

This request led Pusey to write, shortly afterwards, his *Letter to the Bishop of Oxford on the Tendencies to Romanism Imputed to Doctrines Held of Old, as Now, in the English Church.* Within a few months it ran into its fourth edition, to which a special preface on "The Doctrine of Justification" was attached, thus making in all no less than 322 pages, including twenty pages of extracts from the *Tracts for the Times*, the *Lyra Apostolica*, and other publications of the Tractarians, and all with a view to "showing that to oppose Ultra-Protestantism is not to favour Popery." Here I may remark that what the Tractarians, and their successors the Ritualists generally, mean by "Ultra-Protestantism" is Protestantism of the type manifested by such men as Cranmer, Ridley, Latimer, and Jewel ; that is, Protestantism without compromise ; but with abundance of courage to attack unscriptural doctrines. It must be here admitted that *in theory* Dr. Pusey always put himself forward as a friend of the Reformation, though

[1] *Life of Pusey*, vol. ii. p. 72.

he refused to be called a disciple of those Reformers who, under God, were the means of bringing about the Reformation. And he certainly was, down to the day of his death, the warmest friend of Corporate Reunion with Rome to be found in the Church of England. Throughout his *Letter* there appears that mourning over our unhappy divisions, and that cry for peace in the Church, which comes with such a bad grace from the men who, alone, are responsible for the existence of our divisions, and are the real cause of banishing peace from the Church. There is nothing the Ritualists more desire than to be left alone in peace to do their work, and for this purpose they are ever pleading for a liberal and tolerant spirit in their opponents. What Dr. M'Crie says of the enemies of the Church of Scotland at the commencement of the seventeenth century, may be applied to these modern disturbers of the peace of the Church of England. "We can conceive nothing," he writes, "more impertinent and disgusting than the cant of liberality, when assumed by men who, in the act of robbing the Church of her dearest privileges, affect to mourn over the contentions which are the fruits of their own selfish policy." [1]

In his *Letter to the Bishop of Oxford* Pusey states that:— "The charges against us are heavy; disaffection to our own Church, unfaithfulness to her teaching, a desire to bring in new doctrines, and to conform our Church more to the Church of Rome, to bring back either entire or 'modified Popery.'" [2] He expresses the regret of himself and his friends that the Church of England had not "retained more of what was ancient in the Breviary and the Missal, without approximating in any way to the corruptions of *modern* Rome."; [3] and he expresses the opinion that "the revisers of our Liturgy did unadvisedly in yielding some more explicit statements of doctrine to the suggestions of foreign Reformers, whose tone of mind was different from that of our Church." [4] Incidentally he

[1] *Sketches of Scottish Church History.* By the Rev. Thomas M'Crie, p. 156, edition 1841.
[2] Pusey's *Letter to the Bishop of Oxford*, 4th edition, p. 10. 1840.
[3] *Ibid.* p. 15. [4] *Ibid.* p. 20.

mentions that:—"We feel no desire for the meeting of Convocation; we are not even earnest in behalf of a repeal of the Statute of Præmunire, though it would certainly be becoming and just."[1] He claims that the position of the Tractarians is that of the "*via media,*" "in contrast with Romanism on the one hand, and Ultra-Protestantism on the other";[2] and then he proceeds to state what he and his friends did hold. His first point is sufficiently startling to a Protestant Churchman. After stating that as to "the first five Articles" of the Church of England "the Church of Rome is allowed to have transmitted faithfully the doctrine of the Primitive Church," Pusey proceeds:—"Would, my Lord, that there were no signs of unsoundness on any other side! But whereas a traditionary faith would be safe with regard to these essential Articles, in that it would depart neither to the right nor to the left from that which the Universal Church had attested to be the Apostolic and Scriptural Creed, the greater, because unsuspected, danger will beset those who profess to draw their faith, unaided, from Holy Scripture."[3] This, of course, was equivalent to saying that those Protestants who draw their faith direct from the Scriptures are in "greater" danger than those who, like the Tractarians, draw it through the muddy channels of the Church's traditions. We must ever claim our right to draw our faith direct from the fountain head, the Written Word of God; but it is not true to assume that any Protestant does so "unaided." There is the aid of the Holy Spirit of God Himself, given in answer to prayer, and also the important aid obtained by comparing Scripture with Scripture. Pusey warns his readers against "the danger of an over anxiety to recede from Rome,"[4] an offence of which, it must be admitted, neither Dr. Pusey nor his followers have ever been guilty. He declares that "it is *probable* that our Church means that things may be *required* to be believed (provided it be not upon peril of salvation) which are not proved by Holy Scripture; but *certain* that,

---

[1] Pusey's *Letter to the Bishop of Oxford*, p. 21.
[2] *Ibid.* p. 22.   [3] *Ibid.* pp. 22, 23.   [4] *Ibid.* p. 25.

according to her, things not in Holy Scripture may be subjects of belief"[1]—thus opening a door which may lead the unwary to a belief in many of the worst errors of Popery, and all this in a subtle and Jesuitical explanation of Article VI. Pusey was terribly afraid of Private Judgment, and therefore he cautions his readers on this point by assuring them that the "children" of the Church "are not the arbiters, whether she pronounce rightly or no"[2] in expounding Holy Scripture. Apparently they are expected to shut their eyes and open their mouths and take without enquiry what "the Church"—which, to the individual, *practically* means his own clergyman—may choose to give him. "Prove all things" seems to be no part of the Puseyite creed in the Scriptural sense. Apparently they would have been horrified at the conduct of the Bereans of old who, in the exercise of their private judgment, would not believe even what St. Paul taught, until they proved his doctrine to be true out of the Old Testament Scriptures: "These were more noble than those in Thessalonica, in that they received the Word with all readiness of mind, and searched the Scriptures daily, whether those things were so" (Acts xvii. 11). At page 44 Pusey boldly declares that "no real Œcumenical Council ever did" err, and that notwithstanding the clear statement of Article XXI. to the contrary, wherein we read that "General Councils . . . may err, and sometimes have erred, even in things pertaining unto God." He further quotes, with approval, a sermon of Newman in favour of the doctrine of the Infallibility of the whole Catholic Church. "Both we and Romanists," said Newman, "hold that the Church Catholic *is unerring* in its declarations of faith for saving doctrine; but we differ from each other as to what is the faith, and what is the Church Catholic"[3]; and:—"We are at peace with Rome as regards the essentials of faith."[4] Pusey slanders decided Protestants when he most untruly declares that

---

[1] Pusey's *Letter to the Bishop of Oxford*, p. 28. [2] *Ibid.* p. 30.
[3] *Ibid.* p. 50. [4] *Ibid.* p. 51.

"Ultra-Protestants" "prefer what is modern to what is ancient," and "disparage Christian antiquity"[1]; since, as is well known, instead of disparaging it, they are always appealing to *Apostolic* antiquity, as recorded in the Bible, and, as has been well said, "prefer the Grandfathers [the Apostles] to the Fathers." Pusey then makes an attack on the Protestant doctrine of Justification by Faith only, assuring his readers that Lutherans, Wesleyans, "and a section of our own Church"—by which he meant Evangelical Churchmen—"have been taught that Justification is not the gift of God *through His Sacraments*, but the result of a certain frame of mind, of a going forth of themselves, *and resting themselves upon their Saviour;* this is the act whereby *they think themselves* to have been justified."[2] This doctrine Pusey hated with all his heart, and thought it a greater evil than the Roman Catholic system of Justification. That system, he affirmed, had its "corruptions"; but "it bore witness to the holiness of God."[3] The Evangelical system, however, is, he affirms, "altogether a spurious system, misapplying the promises of the Gospel, usurping the privileges of Baptism, which it has not to bestow."[4]

In this *Letter* Pusey professes his faith in the doctrine of the Real Presence, while repudiating the doctrine of Transubstantiation. He says that he believes in "the spiritual unseen Presence of that Blessed Body and Blood, *conveyed to us through the unchanged though consecrated elements*, unchanged in material substance, changed in their use, their efficacy, their dignity, mystically and spiritually. We see not why we need avoid language used by the Fathers . . . that 'the bread and wine is made the Body and Blood of Christ.'"[5] But on this subject, evil as Pusey thinks the doctrine of Rome, he considers the doctrine of Calvin and Zwingle a greater evil:—"For," he says, "deeply as Rome has erred, and much error as she has thereby given occasion to in others, we fear that others have *erred still more deeply*. Not Zwingli alone, but Calvin,

---

[1] Pusey's *Letter to the Bishop of Oxford*, p. 58. [2] *Ibid.* p. 72.
[3] *Ibid.* p. 87. [4] *Ibid.* p. 88. [5] *Ibid.* p. 131.

have, in their way, so explained the mode of Christ's presence, as virtually to explain it away."[1] He asserts that Rome is "presumptuous" in teaching that "Christ is wholly contained under each species"; and he rejects Rome's doctrine that "in the holy Sacrament of the Eucharist, Christ, the Only Begotten Son of God, is to be adored with the outward adoration of Divine worship."[2] As to the Sacrament, as a whole, he writes:—"*Rome, in this respect, has the truth*, though mingled with error, and clouded and injured by it; the Zwingli-Calvinist school *have forfeited it.*"[3] It is evident that much as Dr. Pusey might dislike certain portions of the Roman Catholic religion, he would—even as far back as 1840—greatly prefer being a Romanist to being an "Ultra-Protestant." As to Prayers for the Dead, he considers it "a solemn privilege to the mourner; but not, after that (in consequence of abuses connected with it in the Romish system) it had been *withdrawn from our Church*, to be rashly and indiscriminately revived";[4] and yet although the Church, "for the safety of her children, has relinquished the practice, her doctrine is in accordance with it."[5]

Now it must be said of this *Letter* of Dr. Pusey that it exactly *proves* what it was ostensibly written to *disprove*, viz., that he and his party were labouring to bring back into the Church of England a certain amount of Popery, though not, of course, all of it. Pusey's views, as herein expressed, of private judgment in the interpretation of Scripture, of Tradition, of the infallibility of the Church and of General Councils, of Justification by faith only, of Baptismal Regeneration, the Real Presence, and Prayers for the Dead, were, and are, in the estimation of ninety-nine out of every hundred Protestant Churchmen, distinctly Romish, and tend to Romanism by creating a thirst for that sacerdotal form of religion which the Church of Rome alone can fully satisfy. The set of quotations from Tractarian writings, published at the end of Pusey's pamph-

---

[1] Pusey's *Letter to the Bishop of Oxford*, p. 132. [2] *Ibid.* p. 134.
[3] *Ibid.* p. 144.   [4] *Ibid.* p. 187.   [5] *Ibid.* p. 189.

et, only proved—what at that time nobody denied—that there were certain portions of the Roman system which they rejected. Protestant Churchmen could not see that Tractarians were justified in introducing many Roman Catholic doctrines, merely on the ground that they protested against other Roman doctrines.

In this *Letter* Pusey referred to a judgment of Sir Herbert Jenner Fust, in the case of *Breeks* v. *Woolfrey*, delivered in 1839, in the Court of Arches. The question before the Court was not whether Prayers for the Dead could be lawfully and publicly used in a parish church, but whether it were lawful to inscribe on a tombstone in a parish churchyard the following words:—"Pray for the soul of J. Woolfrey;" and "It is a holy and wholesome thought to pray for the dead.—2 Mac. xii. 46." The tombstone containing these words had actually been set up in Carisbrooke Churchyard, Isle of Wight, by a Roman Catholic lady, Mrs. Woolfrey, widow of the person there buried. The Rev. J. Breeks, vicar of Carisbrooke, entered an action against Mrs. Woolfrey, praying the Court of Arches to compel her to remove the stone. The judge held that if "prayers for the dead necessarily constitute a part of the doctrine of Purgatory, as held by the Romish Church," then "the Court would be bound to monish the party to remove the stone, and to punish her with ecclesiastical censure and with costs." He said that the authorities cited in the case "seem to go no further than this— to show that *the Church discouraged prayers for the dead*, but did not prohibit them; and that the Twenty-second Article is not violated by the use of such prayers." Here I may remark that it seems incredible that the Church should "discourage" such prayers if she thought them good and holy. The learned judge quoted the *Homilies* of the Church of England on prayers for the dead, and said that they "contained the same disapproval of the practice, but no positive prohibition of it." The question may here be asked, how can that Church be supposed to tolerate a practice of which she has expressed her "disapproval"? The passages in the *Homilies* to which the judge referred are found in the *Homily Concerning Prayer*, Part III. :—

"Now," says the *Homily*, "to entreat of that question, whether we ought to pray for them that are departed out of this world, or no. Wherein, if we cleave only unto the Word of God, then must we needs grant, that *we have no commandment so to do*. For the Scripture doth acknowledge but two places after this life; the one proper to the elect and blessed of God, the other to the reprobate and damned souls; as may be well gathered by the parable of Lazarus and the rich man. . . . These words, as *they confound the opinion of helping the dead by prayer*, so do they clean confute and take away the vain error of Purgatory."

"Let these and such other places be sufficient to take away the gross error of Purgatory out of our heads; *neither let us dream any more, that the souls of the dead are anything at all holpen by our prayers;* but, as the Scripture teacheth us, let us think that the soul of man, passing out of the body, goeth straightways either to heaven, or else to hell, whereof *the one needeth no prayer*, the other is without redemption."

No one can read this *Homily* without perceiving that the Church of England is most anxious that her children should *not* pray for the dead. The judge could not quote even one statement of the Church positively in favour of such prayers, and yet he concluded his judgment in these words :—

"I am, then, of opinion, on the whole of the case, that the offence imputed by the articles has not been sustained; that no authority or canon has been pointed out by which the practice of praying for the dead has been expressly prohibited; and I am accordingly of opinion, that, if the articles were proved, the facts would not subject the party to ecclesiastical censure, as far as regards the illegality of the inscription on the tombstone."[1]

In connection with this tombstone case it is well to remember that the judgment was that of an inferior court, and that it has never been appealed against. Had there then been an appeal to the Judicial Committee of the Privy

[1] *Judgments of the Judicial Committee of the Privy Council in Ecclesiastical Cases.* Edited by the Hon. George C. Brodrick, and the Rev. William H. Freemantle, pp. 354-360. London : 1865.

Council, I have no doubt that the judgment of Sir Herbert Jenner Fust would have been reversed. As it is, however, it must be accepted as an exposition of the law until it has been reversed by the Highest Court of Appeal. But let it not be forgotten that it sanctions *only* a request for prayer for the dead when inscribed *on a tombstone*, in a churchyard, and not on a tombstone set up within a parish church. It does not sanction *public* prayers for the dead in a parish church: these are manifestly illegal, since there are no such prayers provided in the Book of Common Prayer, and the clergy are pledged to use only in public prayer and administration of the Sacraments, "the form in the said Book prescribed, and none other, except so far as shall be ordered by lawful authority."[1] I regret the judgment, but it is well to point out that its powers for evil are not so great as is generally supposed.

On this subject there is this further fact, which is worthy of consideration. It has been decided that prayers for the dead are, according to the law of England, superstitious in their character, and that it is unlawful to leave money by will to priests, for the purpose of obtaining their prayers for the dead. In 1835, Sir Charles Pepys gave judgment in the case of *West* v. *Shuttleworth*. In this case the will of a lady was considered, by which she left £10 each to several Roman Catholic priests, for the benefit of their prayers for the repose of her soul, and that of her deceased husband. The judge said:—

"Taking the first gift to priests and chapels in connection with the letter, there can be no doubt that the sums given to the priests and chapels were not intended for the benefit of the priests personally, or for the support of the chapels for general purposes, but that they were given, as expressed in the letter, *for the benefit of their prayers for the repose of the testatrix's soul* and that of her deceased husband; and the question is, whether such legacies can be supported. It is truly observed by Sir William Grant, in *Cary* v. *Abbot* (7 Ves. 490) that there was no statute, making superstitious uses void generally, and that the statute of Edward VI. related only to

---

[1] *The Ecclesiastical Law of the Church of England.* By Sir Robert Phillimore, p. 470, edition 1873.

superstitious uses of a particular description then existing; and it is to be observed, that that statute does not declare such gifts to be unlawful, but avoids certain superstitious gifts previously created. The legacies in question, therefore, are not within the terms of the statute of Edward VI., but *that statute has been considered as establishing the illegality of certain gifts, and amongst others the giving legacies to priests to pray for the soul of the donor* has, in many cases collected in Duke (p. 466) been decided to be within *the superstitious uses* intended to be suppressed by that statute. *I am, therefore, of opinion that these legacies to priests and chapels are void.*"[1]

The question of the lawfulness of Prayers for the Dead, as affected by the case of *Breeks* v. *Woolfrey*, was discussed by the *Solicitors' Journal* of January 16, 1875. Its opinion is worth citing here. It said:—

"Canon Liddon stated last week, in a letter to the *Times*, that prayers for the dead have been expressly declared legal in the Church of England. We presume that this assertion is founded upon Sir H. Jenner Fust's decision in *Breeks* v. *Woolfrey*; but that case certainly does not settle the law upon the question. It was there held that an inscription on a tombstone in Carisbrooke churchyard begging for prayers for the soul of the deceased was lawful; but, as Dr. Liddon would find if the experiment were tried, it is one thing to allow such an inscription to be placed on a monument in a churchyard, and quite another to allow prayers for the dead to be used during the services of the Church. To the latter case the now firmly-established and well-known principle that no omission from or addition to the prescribed form can be permitted is applicable (see *Westerton* v. *Liddell*, 'Moore's Report'). Moreover, prayers for the dead were, it must be remembered, included in the First Prayer Book of Edward VI., and are excluded from the present book, and would, therefore, now be illegal upon the principle on which the mixed chalice, which was ordered by the former Prayer Book, and not ordered in the latter, has already been pronounced illegal. The mistake into which Dr. Liddon has fallen is a very natural one for a writer unacquainted with the legal effect of the more recent decisions in our Ecclesiastical Courts. But any advocate who should attempt to justify prayers for the dead in the Church service on the authority of *Breeks* v. *Woolfrey* would find he had undertaken a hopeless task."

---

[1] *The Statutes Relating to Ecclesiastical Institutions.* By Archibald John Stephens, vol. ii. p. 1508, 2nd edition.

The case of *Egerton* v. *All of Rode* has an important bearing on the question of Prayers for the Dead. In the Consistory Court of Chester, October 26, 1893, before Chancellor Espin, a faculty was applied for by the Rev. John M. Egerton, Rector of Old Rode, to erect in the Parish Church a stained glass window, with the following inscription on a brass plate beneath it :—" De caritate tua ora pro anima Henriettæ Franciscæ viduæ Georgii Hamerton Crump de Chorlton Hall in hoc comitatu mortua die XXIII. Augusti A.D. MDCCCXCII. ætatis suæ LXXV. Et pro anima Johannis Hamerton Crump supradictorum filii majoris mortui die II. Martii A.D. MDCCCLXXXVII. ætatis suæ XXXIII." In giving judgment the Chancellor said :—

"When the proposed inscription was brought before the Court on September 28 last, I referred to the well-known case of *The Office of the Judge Promoted by Breeks* v. *Woolfrey*, and did so on the spur of the moment, not having seen the proposed inscription until just before the Court opened. But on consideration it may be doubted whether that case and the judgment in it would have warranted the Court in sanctioning the proposed inscription being placed in the Church of All Saints at Old Rode. The case of *Breeks* v. *Woolfrey* is a leading case, and the judgment in it is a considered judgment delivered by Sir Herbert Jenner Fust. *But then he did not directly sanction the inscription before him, he only refused to order the tombstone which bore it to be removed. It does not appear that he would himself have authorised the inscription if he had been asked to do so.*

"Then again it might be argued that the proposed Latin inscription in this case, the translation of the portion of which material to the present question is as follows :—' Of your charity pray for the soul of H—— F——, widow of George Hamerton Crump, of Chorlton Hall, in this county, deceased . . . and for the soul of John Hamerton Crump, . . . son of the above, deceased . . .' goes somewhat beyond the inscription placed on the tomb of Mr. Woolfrey in the Churchyard of Carisbrooke. So far as material the latter ran thus :—' Spes mea Christus. Pray for the soul of J. Woolfrey. It is a holy and wholesome thought to pray for the dead.—2 Macabees, xii. 46.'

"It might reasonably be said perhaps that in principle the proposed inscription in this case does not differ from the inscription in

Breeks v. *Woolfrey*. Still the one submitted to this Court does seem to go beyond the one which in *Breeks* v. *Woolfrey* the Dean of Arches refused to displace, and this Court ought in my opinion to govern itself in such a matter somewhat strictly by the decisions and precedents furnished by the Court of Arches. . . .

"Prayers for the Dead are unquestionably associated in the popular mind with the later exaggerations referred to in that [22nd] Article, and it may be added that a bequest made for such prayers being offered up would be void by the common law of the realm as superstitious. And, therefore, though in private such prayers may be offered, as conformable to the ways of the Primitive Church, certainly from the second century and downwards; and however deeply we may sympathise with sentiments of affectionate respect in the bereaved, fired as they often are by strong realising of the Communion of Saints, it does not seem to belong to a Court of first instance to do what the formularies of the Church have abstained from doing; it is not for me here to authorise directly the setting up in a place of public worship of an inscription demanding the prayers of the worshippers for the souls of certain persons who have departed this life.

"In the result I must decline to sanction the inscription brought in on September 28 last, being placed in the Church, and accordingly so much of the application before me as prays that a faculty might be granted for placing such inscription beneath the proposed window must be rejected."[1]

Another faculty case, in which the question of Prayers for the Dead was involved, was decided just as I was about to finish the writing of this book. At a sitting of the Consistory Court of the Diocese of Carlisle, on August 29, 1900, before Chancellor Prescott, D.D., the Vicar and Churchwardens of Moresby applied for leave to affix on the north wall of the said church an ancient memorial brass taken from the north wall of the chancel of the old church, where it had been placed by Thomas Fletcher in memory of his father, Sir William Fletcher, who died in 1703. The brass tablet was said to have been lost in 1840, but was recovered by the late Mr. W. Fletcher from Distington Museum. It bears the following inscription: "Depositum hic jacet in spe futuræ resurrectionis corpus Gulielmi Fletcher ar: Nuper Dom. hujus mannerii qui

---

[1] *The Law Reports*. Probate Division, 1894, pp. 16, 17, 22.

obiit 2do die Martii, Anno Domini, 1703, ætatis suæ 58. Cujus animæ propitietur Deus. Requiem æternam dona ei Domine et lux perpetua luceat ei. Requiescat in pace. Amen. Thomas Fletcher, ar. filius ejus hoc fieri fecit." The Chancellor, in delivering judgment, said:—

"There could be no possible objection to a faculty issuing as desired, all the regulations having been observed, and it being the wish of the parishioners that it should be done. The memorial tablet which it was proposed to put up raised a very important question. When he came to look at it he found that this tablet was on what was called the old church, and had been apparently lost and then found in a museum, and it was now proposed to put it into the new church, it being a memorial tablet to one of the Fletcher family. The inscription on the tablet was in Latin, and there were two expressions in it which called for some remark. One of them was 'Requiem æternam dona ei Domine et lux perpetua luceat,' and the other was 'Requiescat in pace. Amen.' Some persons would call these expressions prayers for the dead; other persons might call them simply the expressions of a pious wish on the part of the friends of the deceased. In any case, these two expressions occurred in the old service-books of the Church of England, the old Sarum books, in the obsequies for the dead. There the first of the expressions was the verse or refrain which occurred over and over again, and the other expression was the final words of the Service for the Burial of the Dead. If this were an application for a faculty for a new memorial tablet, or new monument to be put up in this church, there might be circumstances which would lead the Court to pause a good deal before granting the faculty. . . . If there was anything in this inscription contrary to the doctrine or the laws of the Church, this Court would be bound not to grant the faculty; but he did not think there was anything here contrary to the doctrine or the laws of the Church of England. Whether in later days people were more afraid of superstition with regard to these prayers for the dead than they were about that period at the end of the seventeenth century he was not prepared to say, but, at all events, this proposition was simply to take a memorial tablet which had been in a sacred place, and to place it, not in a secular place like a museum, but in a sacred position in the church. He understood that it was the wish of the family of Fletcher, as well as the expressed wish of the parishioners in Vestry, that this tablet should be placed in the new church. He saw no objection to it, and though it was undoubtedly an important question, and, as he had said, one which if it came before the Court in a different form and under different circumstances might call for a different decision, he had no hesitation in decreeing that the faculty shall issue for the memorial tablet to be placed in the position as requested in the petition."[1]

In his *Letter to the Bishop of Oxford*, first issued in 1839, Dr. Pusey dealt with the subject of sins committed after Baptism, but never recommended Auricular Confession as a remedy. This silence, no doubt, was in accordance with the Tractarian doctrine of "Reserve in Communicating Religious Knowledge."[2] At that early period it would never have done to have recommended Auricular Confession *publicly*, above all in a pamphlet written to refute the charge of Romanising tendencies. Yet, from statements subsequently made by Pusey himself, we learn that he commenced the practice of hearing Confessions in 1838.[3] From that date down to the time of his death he was one of the most active of his party in labours as a Father Confessor. Yet, strange as it may seem to many, although one of the foremost in urging others to practise Auricular Confession, he never went to Confession himself until about eight years after he commenced to practise as a Father Confessor. In 1844 he wrote to Keble:—"I am so shocked at myself, that I dare not lay my wounds bare to any one; since I have seen the benefit of Confession to others, I have looked round whether I could unburthen myself to any one, but there is a reason against every one. I dare not so shock people; and so I go on, having no such comfort as in good Bp. Andrewes' words, to confess myself 'an unclean worm, a dead dog, a putrid corpse.'"[4] He waited for more than two years after writing this

---

[1] *Record*, September 7, 1900, p. 856.

[2] The Rev. John Thomas, writing to the future Lord Selborne, in 1843, after mentioning that he had met the Rev. Frederick Faber at Rome, proceeds:— "This reminds me of the Tract theology. I think you draw too much distinction between the views of the outposts of that school and those of its leaders. I apprehend the only difference to be, that the leaders have the prudence to defer the downright avowal of extreme opinions until things are better prepared for their reception. I never read a writing of Newman in the *Tracts*, in which he did not appear to me to insinuate, 'I could carry the principle much further, but you cannot bear it now.'"—*Memorials, Family and Personal*, 1766–1865, vol. i. p. 387.

[3] *Life of Dr. Pusey*, vol. iii. pp. 269, 335. *Times*, November 29, 1866.

[4] *Ibid.* p. 96.

before he could muster up courage to go to Confession; at last, on December 1, 1846, he made his first Confession to Keble at Hursley.[1]

And here comes in a strange fact. Four years after Pusey had commenced to hear Confessions, he wrote a learned treatise, in the form of a lengthy note to the works of Tertullian, in the *Library of the Fathers*, to prove that in the early history of the Christian Church there is not to be found the slightest trace of private Confession to priests, and that "if a Church have laid it aside, there is no ground for misgiving, as though it had parted with anything essential to the benefits of absolution."[2] But he adds that "it does not follow that because *it was not practised in the early Church*, it may not be a salutary check in the degraded state in which the Church now is"; thus giving to Auricular Confession a purely ecclesiastical and human origin and not any divine authority. It was of man, not of God. From what Pusey has to say about the early Church and Confession of sin to God only, I take the following extracts which, though lengthy, are well worthy of careful study, as proving conclusively that the Primitive Church was thoroughly Protestant on this great and most important subject:—

"*S. Chrysostome* also in the passages cited [by Romanists] to prove private Confession, *shews that the sins of the people were unknown to the priests*. But besides these, there is other distinct evidence that Confession was not regarded as essential to remission. This is chiefly furnished by S. Chrysostome, who yet, as alleged by Bellarmine, recommends public penitence, and himself enforced it; still he most distinctly alleges that Confession to God suffices for forgiveness, and this so repeatedly, and so strongly, as to leave no question as to his meaning. Certainly no words could be used, which should exclude any other meaning, if his do not. Thus he says:— . . . 'Confess to *God alone* thy sins; "against Thee only have I sinned, and done evil before Thee," and thy sin is forgiven.' . . . This language he uses in other places as even with reference to grievous sins, fornication or adultery, 'if he [the sinner] will converse *alone with Him, no one knowing*, and will utter everything accurately, he shall

---

[1] *Life of Dr. Pusey*, vol. iii. p. 103.
[2] *Library of the Fathers: Tertullian*, p. 407. Oxford: 1842.

soon repair his offences'; and putting the words in the very mouth of God, 'I compel thee not, He saith, to come into the midst of a theatre, surrounded by many witnesses. *Tell Me alone thy sin apart*, that I may heal the sore, and free from the pain.' Again, in a passage remarkable for acknowledging what Romanists seem to forget, that there is shame in confessing sin at all, even though man be not by, if any but realise what his defilements are, and how holy God is: ' But thou art ashamed and blushest to utter thy sins, nay, but even were it necessary to utter these things before men and display them, not even thus shouldst thou be ashamed (for sin, not to confess sin, is shame), but now it is not even necessary to confess before witnesses. Be the examination of transgressions in the thoughts of conscience. Be the judgment seat unwitnessed. *Let God alone see thee confessing*' . . . Again, in the same contrast with 'a theatre' and 'witnesses,' he says: 'Within, in the conscience, *none being present except the All-seeing God*, enter into judgment and examination of sins' . . . 'For why art thou ashamed and blushest to tell thy sins? Tellest thou them to man, that he may reproach thee? Confessest thou to thy fellow-servant, that he may make a show of thee? *Thou showest the wound to the Lord*, who careth for thee, The Friend, The Physician' . . . 'I do not bring thee into any theatre of thy fellow-servants, nor compel thee to reveal thy sins to men; *unfold thy conscience to God*, and of Him ask the remedies. . . .'

"There could," continues Dr. Pusey, "if Romanists would fairly consider this, be no way in which *Confession to God alone, exclusive of man*, could be expressed, if not here. S. Chrysostome says, 'to God alone,' 'apart in private,' 'to Him who knoweth beforehand,' 'no one knowing,' 'no one present save Him who knoweth,' 'God alone seeing,' 'unwitnessed,' 'not to man,' 'not to a fellow-servant,' 'within,' 'in the conscience,' 'in the memory,' 'judging thyself' (in lieu of the priest being the judge)."[1]

"The instances, then, being in each case very numerous, *the absence of any mention of Confession in the early Church* under the following circumstances does, when contrasted with the uniform mention of it in the later, *put beyond question that at the earlier period it was not the received practice*. The evidence is given at great length by Daillé. (1) 'Secret confession has, among the modern Latins, a chief place in the religious acts of all the faithful; clergy, monks, lay; princes, private persons; nobles, people; men and women; *but nowhere in the Ancient Church*' (D. iv. 3); 'especially at the close of life, as a bounden duty, it is universal among the moderns,

---

[1] *Library of the Fathers: Tertullian*, pp. 398–401.

unknown among the ancients' (*ibid.* c. 5) ... and certainly the details are given so fully, that it is inconceivable that the practice of Confession should have been so uniformly mentioned with praise in the later, *and* WHOLLY OMITTED *in the earlier Church*, had the practice of the earlier been the same as that of the later."[1]

Now, I may well ask here, could any one who first read this splendid defence of the Protestant position with reference to Auricular Confession, have imagined that its author was at the very period when he wrote hearing Confessions himself? Pusey's treatise, no doubt, tended to blind the eyes of Protestant Churchmen as to what was going on, and to put them off their guard. Who could then have thought it possible that, within a very few years after writing this, Pusey would himself have adopted the full Roman Catholic theory and practice of the Sacrament of Penance? In later life, Pusey never attempted, so far as I am aware, to refute the splendid Protestant arguments against Auricular Confession which he brought forward in his notes to the works of Tertullian.

The Tractarian Movement continued to make rapid progress, greater indeed than its founders had ever anticipated. Young clergymen, filled with High Church ideas, went down from Oxford to their various curacies throughout the length and breadth of the land, and helped to propagate Tractarian views by preaching and private conversation, and especially by assisting in the circulation of each new number of the *Tracts for the Times* as it came out. These were read, not only in Rectories and Vicarages, but also in the Halls of county noblemen and squires. There was a delightful novelty about this new system of religion which pleased and attracted the young, and needless to add, it was very dear to the hearts of the priesthood. It was found peculiarly suited to the spiritual tastes of those who wished to have a high opinion of human merit in the sight of God; and it was soon found, by experience, that it was not inconsistent with a considerable amount of worldliness. Before long the newspapers began to discuss the work going on in Oxford, and

[1] *Library of the Fathers: Tertullian*, pp. 405, 406.

it was even mentioned in Parliament. Publicity is everything for a new cause, and this the Tractarians soon got in abundance. It was not long before they became famous in the United States, and in several of our Colonies. I believe that this success was mainly due to the *Tracts for the Times*, though I do not by any means undervalue the effect of the personal influence of the leaders at Oxford. As years passed on these *Tracts* became more and more Romish in their character, and filled the hearts of the rulers of the Church of Rome with joy and hope. Wiseman was by no means slow to realise that, to a considerable extent, the Tractarians were doing his work, and doing it better than he could ever hope to do it. In the *Dublin Review* for April 1838, he reviewed the first three volumes of the *Tracts for the Times*, of whose authors he asked, "Will they succeed in their work?" To which his answer was: "We firmly believe they will; nay, strange to say, *we hope so.*"[1] "The spiritual and devotional character of the Catholic worship and religion is," wrote Wiseman,[2] "openly avowed" in the *Tracts for the Times;* and in proof of this he cites the following statement to be found at page 4 of *Tract LXXI.*, written by Newman, and published January 1, 1836.

"The same feelings which carry men now to Dissent will carry them to Romanism—novelty being an essential stimulant of popular devotion; and the Roman system, to say nothing of the intrinsic majesty and truth which remain in it amid its corruptions, abounding in this and other stimulants of a most potent and effective character. And further, there will ever be a number of refined and affectionate minds, who, disappointed in finding full matter for their devotional feelings in the English system, as at present conducted, betake themselves, through human frailty, to Rome."

On this statement of Newman's, Wiseman's comment was logical and just. "We have here," he said (including in his remarks the other *Tracts for the Times*), "a clear confession that, upon a dozen points, affecting nothing

---

[1] Wiseman's *Essays on Various Subjects*, vol. ii. p. 29.
[2] *Ibid.* p. 56.

less than the constitution of the Church, and the authority of its hierarchy, the grounds upon which the most solemn dogmas rest, the public offices of the Church, the frequent use of the Eucharistic sacrament, the performance of daily service, the observance of fasting, and other great moral precepts, the Anglican Church, under the mask of a Reformation, *contrived to place things in a worse state than they were before, and than they now exist in the Catholic Church.*"[1] And here it may be useful to give some other quotations from the *Tracts for the Times* which manifest their Romeward tendencies, omitting for the present any reference to *Tract XC.* to be dealt with later on:—

"With these [Foreign Reformers] and the like men Cranmer was surrounded, and paid much deference to them, as a man of no decision is wont to do to those who are bent upon carrying a point. It was probably a fruit of this influence, that there came out from the Council in 1550 *an ill-omened letter*, signed by seven laymen, but by one Bishop only (Ely) besides the Archbishop, *commanding the altars to be taken down*, and tables to be placed in their room."[2]

"Again, from the Prayer 'for the Church militant' we have excluded the more solemn commendation to God, *and Prayer for the Dead;* this is a moving thought, for may we not venture to consider it in this light, that we are by this exclusion, as it were, in some degree disunited from the purer communion of those departed Saints who are now with Christ, as if scarce worthy to profess ourselves one with them.'"[3]

"In speaking of the Rubric, the substitution of the term '*Table*,' '*Holy Table*,' and in the Scotch of '*God's Board*,' for that of '*Altar*,' which is in Edward's First Book (as well as '*God's Board*'), is *a strong instance of this our judicial humiliation.*"[4]

"There is another circumstance now to be observed, of more importance than any which have been hitherto considered, *the entire omission of the use of oil at Baptism and Confirmation.* . . . When we consider these things, surely no one can say [*sic. ? deny*] the greatness of the gifts which are here withdrawn; how much we have thereby fallen from the high appellations of 'a royal priesthood,

---

[1] Wiseman's *Essays on Various Subjects*, vol. ii. pp. 56, 57.
[2] *Tract LXXXI.* p. 16. By Dr. Pusey.
[3] *Tract LXXXVI.* p. 21. By the Rev. Isaac Williams. [4] *Ibid.* p. 26.

a holy nation, a peculiar people': and we have together with it lost the white robe of Baptism."[1]

"In all these things,[2] we have no reason surely to complain of the judicial withholding of privileges, but to lament our unfitness to receive them; the fact is our 'iniquities have separated between us and our God.' 'Our sins have withholden *good things* from us.' The essentials of a Church we have by many merciful interpositions still preserved to us; they are only matters denoting *the highest privileges, royal gifts, that are withdrawn.*"[3]

No one who reads these last quotations can fail to see how dissatisfied the early Tractarians were with the Prayer Book as it is, and how heartily they would have welcomed Prayer Book Revision, provided it were on Tractarian lines. The only Revision to which the Ritualists now object is one on *Protestant* lines.

In the year 1839 an attempt was commenced to influence the wealthy residents of the West End of London in favour of Tractarianism. The Rev. Frederick Oakeley, one of the most zealous and extreme of his party, was in that year appointed to the charge of Margaret Chapel, near Cavendish Square, in which, as he subsequently said, he sought "an opportunity of trying the effect of Tractarian principles upon a practical scale." In a lecture delivered in London in 1855, when he had become a Roman Catholic priest, Mr. Oakeley told his hearers how he began his work in Margaret Chapel:—

"Pulpit and reading desk," he said, "were moved from their former position; and the poor clerk reluctantly took his place in the body of the chapel, although he never succeeded to the last in bringing his 'Amen' into proper tone of subordination. The communion table, now dignified with the name of an altar, exhibited its crimson frontal, its cross, and its candlesticks, whose unlighted candles were standing memorials of Episcopal inflexibility, and emblems of patient hope. Not indeed that they were *always* unlighted; for there came periodically the succession of night to day,

---

[1] *Tract LXXXVI.* pp. 27, 29.
[2] That is, in the removal from the Prayer Book of Prayers for the Dead, and the word "altar"; in the omission from it also of the anointing in Baptism and Confirmation, and the removal of the "anointing of the sick."
[3] *Tract LXXXVI.* pp. 30, 31.

and at times the elements favoured us with a propitious fog. All this, my friends, must sound to you as something inexpressibly absurd. Well, I cannot justify the unlighted candles, and still less, the inordinate attachment to fogs. But, with the exception of a few such trifling extravagances, the whole thing, I assure you, had an earnestness and reality about it; as has been proved, I think you will admit, by its (then most unthought of) results. Margaret Chapel has yielded some scores of converts to the Catholic Church, including four of its successive Ministers; and this, although it never aimed at anything but to promote the cause of the Church of England. It continued to do its work long after I quitted it, and has now merged into one of the most magnificent Churches in England,[1] which I have no doubt will do its work also."[2]

From the biography of Mr. Serjeant Bellasis, who was from the first one of Mr. Oakeley's warmest supporters at Margaret Chapel (and who subsequently seceded to Rome) we learn that "the altar was raised" by the new Incumbent, who at once "commenced intoning parts of the service more after Cathedral fashion."[3] All through Oakeley's troubles while at Margaret Chapel, Serjeant Bellasis was his warmest friend and disciple. How far the Serjeant had gone towards Popery, even seven years before he actually joined the Church of Rome, may be seen in the following extract from a letter he wrote to a friend on March 31, 1843:—"You know my opinion about the Pope. I think he is the Head of the Christian Church, and that Henry VIII. committed a great sin in throwing off the Pope's authority and assuming it himself, and I wish that authority were restored."[4] Six months later Bellasis visited Oxford, and there, amongst the Tractarians (as he wrote from there on September 25, 1843):—"I find *a universal acquiescence in the Council of Trent*, as being the only basis upon which an ultimate reunion will be effected, *and a universal admission that the notion of independent national Churches is absurd*, and that the authority of a Supreme Patriarch is far, very far prefer-

---

[1] All Saints, Margaret Street, W.
[2] *Personal Reminiscences of the Oxford Movement.* A Lecture by Frederick Oakeley, M.A., p. 11. London: 1855.
[3] *Memorials of Mr. Serjeant Bellasis*, p. 35.
[4] *Ibid.* p. 39.

able, to the slavery of the Church to an almost heathen state." [1]

Mr. Oakeley's labours at the Margaret Chapel were soon rewarded with a considerable measure of success. He gathered round him an influential congregation, including many members of the aristocracy, and not a few of those who held high official positions, amongst the latter being Mr. Gladstone, the future Prime Minister,[2] who remained an intimate friend of Mr. Oakeley's until his death. Of Margaret Chapel Mr. Gladstone once said:—"The whole place was so filled by the reverence of Oakeley's ministrations and manner, that its bareness and poverty passed unnoticed. His sermons were always most admirable; they never exceeded twenty minutes."[3] The result was the accession to the ranks of the Tractarians of many perverts of considerable influence in the upper ranks of society. The affairs of the Chapel, under Oakeley's ministrations, appear to have gone on prosperously for several years. Complaints from Protestant Churchmen were heard from time to time, but nothing in the nature of really serious opposition was met with until early in the year 1845. On February 14th of that year the Rev. W. G. Ward was deprived of his degrees by the Convocation of the University of Oxford for having, amongst other offences, affirmed in his book, *The Ideal of a Christian Church*, that, in subscribing the Thirty-Nine Articles, he "renounced no one Roman doctrine." On the very day that Ward was thus degraded, Oakeley wrote a letter to the Vice-Chancellor calling his attention to the fact that, six weeks previously, he had sent to him a copy of a pamphlet which he (Oakeley) had written, and in which occurred the following passage:—"I claim the right, which has been already asserted in another quarter, of holding (as distinct from teaching) all Roman doctrine, and that notwithstanding my subscription to the Thirty-Nine Articles."[4]

[1] *Memorials of Mr. Serjeant Bellasis*, p. 66, *note*.
[2] Purcell's *Life of Cardinal Manning*, vol. i. p. 314.   [3] *Ibid.* p. 314.
[4] *The Subject of Tract XC. Historically Examined.* By Frederick Oakeley, Fellow of Balliol College, Oxford, 2nd edition, p. xiii. Oakeley's pamphlet was

Mr. Oakeley proceeded to state to the Vice-Chancellor:—"If I am allowed, after this plain and public declaration of my sentiments, to retain my place in the University, I shall regard such acquiescence as equivalent to an admission, on the part of the Academical authorities, that my own subscription to the Thirty-Nine Articles is not at variance with good faith.'"[1] The fact that Oakeley had written this letter came to the knowledge of the Bishop of London (Dr. Blomfield), who was so much put out about it that he immediately requested Oakeley to resign his Incumbency of Margaret Chapel. Oakeley's friends wrote to the Bishop in his favour, amongst them being Mr. Gladstone and Mr. Justice Coleridge.[2] While the decision was pending Oakeley wrote and published a letter to the Bishop of London, in the form of a pamphlet,[3] which led his lordship to the decision to prosecute the offender in the Court of Arches. It was open to the Bishop to have withdrawn Oakeley's licence at once, but he thought it would seem fairer to proceed against him by a prosecution. This was the first prosecution brought against a member of the party to which Oakeley belonged, and it is not a little interesting to note that it was initiated by a Bishop, his secretary, Mr. Christopher Hodgson, being the nominal prosecutor. The case came on for hearing in the Arches Court, on June 9, 1845, before Sir Herbert Jenner Fust.[4] The portions of Oakeley's *Letter to the Bishop of London* objected against in the articles included the following passages:—

"I do not deny that it may naturally strike your lordship, as a gratuitous and disturbing movement. Nor, again, could I be sur-

---

ably answered by the Rev. William Goode (afterwards Dean of Ripon) under the title of *Tract XC. Historically Refuted*, 2nd edition, pp. 191. London: Hatchard. 1866.

[1] Mr. Oakeley's letter to the Vice-Chancellor appears in full in the *English Churchman*, February 20, 1845, p. 121.

[2] *Memorials of Mr. Serjeant Bellasis*, p. 41.

[3] *A Letter to the Bishop of London on a Subject Connected with the Recent Proceedings at Oxford*. By the Rev. Frederick Oakeley, pp. 39. London: Toovey.

[4] A *verbatim* copy of the articles brought against the defendant, together with a report of the trial, appears in the *English Churchman*, June 12, 1845, pp. 374-376.

prised to hear that your lordship had been seriously startled by my further declaration of an opinion, that the Articles are *subscribable* in what may be called an ultra-Catholic sense, so as to involve no necessary renunciation on the subscriber's part, of any formal decision of the Western Church, and that I myself, actually so subscribed them."[1]

"And now I wish to draw your lordship's attention to the following point. The distinction in question is, as I contend, wholly irrelevant to my question with the University, for, in the University, it is not the practice of *teaching* certain doctrines which is even apparently impugned, but the claim *to hold them*. Mr. Ward himself never claimed to *teach* Roman doctrine; on the contrary, he urges over and over again that such a procedure would be highly wrong under our circumstances. What he maintains, and what the vote of Thursday seems to deny, is the *honesty* of subscribing the Articles in a certain sense. The University, then, cannot pretend to let me off on the ground of the above distinction; for with respect to it I differ in no way from Mr. Ward, whom it has, by hypothesis, condemned. *Mr. Ward* does not claim to *teach*. *I* claim *to hold*.

"But, *with your lordship*, I contend this distinction ought to, and will, receive consideration. Were I to be found *teaching* Roman doctrine in my public ministrations in your lordship's diocese, I should, as I feel, most deservedly expose myself to your lordship's censure. It is plain that your lordship, as a Bishop of our Church, could not, and would not, suffer it."[2]

At the hearing of the case in the Court of Arches Mr. Oakeley was undefended, but that, of course, was his own fault, since he does not seem to have pleaded any conscientious objections to recognising the Court of Arches. Sir Herbert Jenner Fust delivered his judgment in the case, on June 30, 1845:—

"The learned judge had no doubt that the promoters of the office had sufficiently proved the articles, and that Mr. Oakeley had advisedly maintained and affirmed doctrines directly contrary and repugnant to those of the Church of England, so as to render himself liable to ecclesiastical censure. If the proceeding had been under the statute of Elizabeth, he must, in the first instance, have been called upon to retract his error, and if he refused, be deprived of his preferment; but, as the proceeding was under the general

---

[1] Oakeley's *Letter to the Bishop of London*, p. 11.
[2] *Ibid.* pp. 12, 13.

law, the punishment was left to the discretion of the Court, according to the exigency of the offence.

"What the amount of that punishment should be he had now to consider, and in that consideration he must bear in mind the necessity of inflicting such a punishment as would prevent others from falling into those errors of which Mr. Oakeley was guilty. He believed that the Court would not go beyond the justice of the case if it revoked the licence of Mr. Oakeley to officiate in Margaret Chapel, or elsewhere in the Diocese of London, and if it prohibited him from performing any ministerial offices within the Province of Canterbury until he retracted his errors. He should also condemn Mr. Oakeley in the cost of these proceedings.[1]

The Church of England is much indebted to Bishop Blomfield for the courageous and faithful attitude he assumed towards Mr. Oakeley. The Bishop was not an Evangelical, but rather an old-fashioned High Churchman, yet he could not fail to see a grave danger to the Church in allowing a man like Oakeley to flaunt his defiant Popery in the face of her rulers. The punishment inflicted upon the Minister of Margaret Chapel was severe, but it was thoroughly deserved, and it was effectual in preventing a repetition of the offence. Why is it, we may well ask, that the Bishops of the present generation have not the courage to imitate Bishop Blomfield's example? What an unhappy exhibition of unfaithfulness on their part is revealed in the Archbishop of York's Advent Pastoral, issued in 1899. "It has been widely stated," said the Archbishop, "in various quarters, that the Bishops have determined to prosecute the nonconforming clergy. Such rumours are circulated, from whatever motive, without the slightest authority. *I do not believe that there is a single Bishop who would think of taking such a step*, although, unquestionably, this lies within our power."

Dr. Pusey was made very angry by Sir Herbert Jenner Fust's judgment. He wrote two long letters to the *English Churchman* finding fault with it, and urging that, because Mr. Oakeley was undefended, the judgment "has morally no force upon the conscience, as legally, none as a prece-

---

[1] *English Churchman*, July 3, 1845, p. 422.

dent in law."[1] But here it may be asked what ecclesiastical judgment delivered since 1845 has been considered by Pusey's followers to have any moral "force upon the conscience," when it conflicted with their teaching and conduct? In the very first case of a prosecution against a member of their party, this plea was set up, and against a Spiritual Court too; and it has been set up in every other case tried since then. The plea set up by Dr. Pusey that a judgment has "morally no force upon the conscience," when the prosecuted one wilfully and inexcusably chooses not to defend himself, is simply absurd. If this plea were permitted in criminal courts every prisoner at the bar would escape punishment. And in this Margaret Chapel case Pusey set another bad example to his followers which they were not slow to imitate. He imputed bad motives to the prosecution. He wrote:—"When he (Oakeley) thought it right to give up his cause, he knew that he must be condemned; and whether without any alleged grounds, simply by default, or in other courts, or upon wrong grounds, or on the real grounds, mattered not to him personally. *In any case, he must be crushed*, and then it matters not much to a person, why."[2] In defending Oakeley, Pusey was at the same time defending others who held the same ground. He was anxious to keep men holding this disloyal position within the English Church, and prevent them going over to Rome, their natural home. A few months later, Pusey wrote to Dr. Wilberforce, then Bishop-Elect of Oxford:—

"I did not mean to state anything definitely as to myself, but only *to maintain*, in the abstract, *the tenability of a certain position, in which* VERY MANY *are*, of not holding themselves obliged to renounce any doctrine, *formally* decreed by the Roman Church. And this I knew would satisfy many minds, who do not wish to form any definite opinion on those doctrines, yet still wish not to be obliged to commit themselves against them. But in this I was not speaking of what is commonly meant by 'Popery,' which is a large practical system, going beyond their formularies, varying, perhaps, indefinitely

---

[1] *English Churchman*, October 2, 1845, p. 627.
[2] *Ibid.* p. 627.

in different minds. I mean simply 'the *letter* of what has been decreed by the Roman Church'; and this I have, *for years*, hoped might ultimately become the basis of union between us."[1]

In this same letter Pusey showed to Wilberforce what some of these Romish doctrines were which English Churchmen might lawfully hold, and at the same time he revealed most clearly his intense longing for Corporate Reunion with Rome. "Practically," he wrote, "when people come to me for guidance, I endeavour to withhold them from what lies beyond our Church, although, if asked on the other side, I could not deny that such and such things seem to me admissible. If I may explain my meaning, the remarkable Acts of S. Perpetua and Felicitas, which was beyond question genuine, contain a very solemn vision, which involves the doctrine of a process of purification after death by suffering, to shorten which prayer was available . . . solemn as it was, I could not, taking all together, refuse my belief to an intermediate state of cleansing, in some cases through pain. . . . The effect has been that *I have since been wholly silent about Purgatory* (before I used to speak against it). I have not said as much as this except to two or three friends. Some of my nearest friends do not know of it."[2] Here was undoubtedly a case in which Pusey acted on the doctrine of "Reserve in Communicating Religious Knowledge." And what are we to think of the tactics revealed in the following paragraph of the same letter? "Practically then," said Pusey, "I *dissuade or forbid* (when I have authority) Invocation of Saints; abstractedly, I see no reason why our Church might not eventually allow it, in the sense of asking for their prayers." To "dissuade or forbid" people practising that which he thought might be helpful, if introduced into the English Church, was not a consistent attitude for any Christian minister to assume. It was very much like double-faced conduct. And all this belief in Popery was to be tolerated in the English Church with a view to assisting its Reunion with Rome. "I cannot but think,"

[1] *Life of Bishop Wilberforce*, vol. i. p. 303.
[2] *Ibid.* pp. 304, 305.

wrote Pusey, in the same letter to Wilberforce, "that Rome and we are not irreconcilably at variance, but that, in the impending contest with unbelief, we shall be on the same side, and in God's time, and in His way, one."

A few months after the judgment of Sir Herbert Jenner Fust, Mr. Oakeley seceded to the Church of Rome. Shortly before that event he wrote from Littlemore, on October 23rd, a letter for publication—just a fortnight after Newman had announced his own secession in the same village—in which he stated that he was about to join the Church of Rome, and in which he revealed the object he had in view while labouring as a clergyman in the Church of England:— "*To bring my own Church*," he wrote, "*into the utmost possible sympathy and harmony with the Roman*, while at the same time scrupulously observant of her own express directions, and of the injunctions of authority (as far as I could collect them), this, as you well know, *was my idea of the truest loyalty towards the Church of England.*" [1]

[1] *A Letter On Submitting to the Catholic Church.* By Frederick Oakeley, M.A., 2nd edition, p. 34. London: James Toovey. 1845.

CHAPTER VI

Tract XC.—List of pamphlets on *Tract XC.*—Newman's object in writing the *Tract*—Extracts from it—Rejoicings at Oscott—The letter of the Four Tutors—Dr. Arnold's opinion of the *Tract*—Declaration by the Heads of Houses—Interesting letter from one of the Four Tutors—Newman's *Letter to Dr. Jelf*—Wiseman's attitude towards the advanced Tractarians—Ward's traitorous letter to the *Univers*—An English Catholic's letter to Newman—Wiseman's reply to Newman—Mr. Ambrose Lisle Phillipps' letter—The Bishop of Oxford's difficulties—His correspondence with Pusey and Newman—The *Tracts for the Times* discontinued—Newman's *Letter to the Bishop of Oxford*—Newman withdraws his "dirty words" against Rome—His reasons for doing so—The Rev. William George Ward—Thinks the Reformers guilty of rebellion and perjury—Mr. Percival's defence of the *Tracts for the Times*—Keble's defence of *Tract XC.*—His opinion on Canonical Obedience to the Bishops—Pusey's defence of *Tract XC.*—Manning's dislike for *Tract XC.*—Bricknell's *Judgment of the Bishops upon Tractarian Theology*—What the Bishops said against *Tract XC.*

PROBABLY Newman never created a greater sensation in his life—his secession to Rome excepted—than when he wrote *Tract XC.* The number of pamphlets written on this one *Tract* alone, by friend and foe, was very large. I have not seen them all, but for the purpose of reference my readers may find useful the subjoined list of those in my possession.[1]

---

[1] 1. *Tract XC.* "Remarks on Certain Passages in the Thirty-Nine Articles," pp. 83. London: Rivington. 1841. Reprinted, "With a Historical Preface by the Rev. E. B. Pusey, D.D." London: Parker. 1865.
2. *A Letter to the Rev. R. W. Jelf, D.D., In Explanation of No. 90.* By the Author, pp. 31. Oxford: Parker. 1841.
3. *A Letter to the Bishop of Oxford On Occasion of Tract XC.* By John Henry Newman, pp. 47. Oxford: Parker. 1841.
4. *The Articles Treated on in Tract XC. Reconsidered and their Interpretation Vindicated.* In a Letter to the Rev. R. W. Jelf, D.D. By the Rev. E. B. Pusey, D.D., pp. 217. Oxford: Parker. 1841.
5. *A Letter to the Rev. E. B. Pusey, D.D., On the Publication of No. 90 of the Tracts for the Times.* By William Sewell, M.A., Professor of Moral Philosophy, pp. 13. Oxford: Parker. 1841.
6. *Some Remarks on A Letter Addressed to the Rev. R. W. Jelf, D.D., in Ex-*

It was no new idea of Newman's to write a book about the Thirty-Nine Articles. He had considered the subject more than two years before the start of the Oxford Movement. "I had," he wrote to the Rev. H. J. Rose, on March 28, 1831, "considered a work on the Articles might be useful on the following plan: First, a defence of Articles; then the history of our own. Then an explanation

planation of No. 90. By Ambrose Lisle Phillipps, Esq., pp. 24. London: Charles Dolman. 1841.

7. *A Letter Respectfully Addressed to the Rev. J. H. Newman Upon Some Passages in his Letter to the Rev. Dr. Jelf.* By N. Wiseman, D.D., Bishop of Melipotamus, pp. 32. London: Charles Dolman. 1841.

8. *A Letter to N. Wiseman, D.D., containing Remarks On his Letter to Mr. Newman.* By the Rev. William Palmer, M.A., Worcester College, Oxford, pp. 49. Oxford: Parker. 1841.

9. *Strictures on No. 90 of the Tracts for the Times.* By a Member of the University of Oxford. Part I. pp. 76. Oxford: J. Vincent.

10. *Strictures on No. 90 of the Tracts for the Times.* By a Member of the University of Oxford. Part II. pp. 95. Oxford: J. Vincent. 1841.

11. *Two Letters Concerning No.* 90 *in the Series called Tracts for the Times.* Printed for Private Distribution Only, pp. 31. Oxford: Printed by W. Baxter. 1841.

12. *The Controversy between Tract XC. and the Oxford Tutors*, pp. 32. London: How & Parsons. 1841.

13. *Brief Remarks upon No.* 90, *Second Edition, and some Subsequent Publications in Defence of it.* By the Rev. C. P. Golightly, M.A., pp. 19. Oxford: William Graham. 1841.

14. *The Case of Catholic Subscription to the Thirty-Nine Articles.* By the Rev. John Keble, M.A., pp. 38. "London: 1841. Not Published." Reprinted by Dr. Pusey, in 1865, with *Tract XC.*

15. *A Vindication of the Principles of the Authors of the Tracts for the Times.* By the Hon. and Rev. A. P. Percival, B.C.L., pp. 33. London: Rivington. 1841.

16. *Certain Documents, &c., &c., Connected with the Tracts for the Times No.* 90, pp. 18. Oxford: Printed by W. Baxter. 1841.

17. *Some Documents, &c., &c., Connected with the Tracts for the Times*, 3rd edition, pp. 15. Oxford: W. Graham. 1841.

18. *Oxford or Rome? A Letter to the Rev. J. H. Newman On No.* 90 *of the Tracts for the Times.* By an English Catholic, pp. 32. London: James Ridgway. 1841.

19. *A Letter to the Rev. T. T. Churton, M.A.* By the Rev. H. B. Wilson, St. John's College, Oxford, 2nd edition, pp. 31. Oxford: W. Graham. 1841.

20. *A Few Words in Support of No.* 90, *partly with Reference to Mr. Wilson's Letter.* By the Rev. William George Ward, M.A., pp. 48. London: Parker. 1841.

21. *A Few More Words in Support of No.* 90. By the Rev. William George Ward, M.A., pp. 91. Oxford: Parker. 1841.

22. *Observations Suggested by a Few More Words in Support of No.* 90. By Robert Lowe, Esq., Magdalen College (afterwards Lord Sherbrooke), pp. 24. Oxford: W. Baxter. 1841.

23. *The Thirty-Nine Articles Considered Chiefly with Reference to the Views of Tract No.* 90. A Lecture by Godfrey Faussett, D.D., Lady Margaret Professor of Divinity, pp. 44. Oxford: Parker. 1841.

24. *The Subject of Tract XC. Examined.* By the Rev. Frederick Oakeley, M.A., pp. 84. London: Rivington. 1841.

of them founded on the historical view."[1] He was evidently acquainted at least with the existence of Santa Clara's book (on whose lines *Tract XC.* was written) as early as 1835.[2] Newman says that one motive which he had in view when writing this *Tract* "was the desire to ascertain the ultimate points of contrariety between the Roman and Anglican Creeds, and *to make them as few as possible.*"[3] And then he had a difficulty:—"I was embarrassed in consequence of *my wish to go as far as was possible* in interpreting the Articles *in the direction of Roman dogma*, without disclosing what I was doing to the parties whose doubts I was meeting."[4] Many of his followers could not see how, with the views they held, they could consistently sign the Articles, and consequently they were tempted, for the sake of being honest and consistent, to go over to Rome. *Tract XC.* was written to keep them in the Church of England, so as to further Newman's great scheme of Corporate Reunion with Rome. The italics in the next quotation are Newman's:—

"It was thrown in our teeth," says Newman, "'How can you manage to sign the Articles? they are directly against Rome.' 'Against Rome?' I made answer; 'what do you mean by "Rome"'? *and then I proceeded to make distinctions*, of which I shall now give an account.

"By 'Roman doctrine' might be meant one of three things: 1, the *Catholic teaching* of the early centuries; or 2, the *formal dogmas of Rome* as contained in the later Councils, especially the Council of Trent, and as condensed in the Creed of Pope Pius IV.; 3, the *actual popular beliefs and usages* sanctioned by Rome in the countries in communion with it, over and above the dogmas; and these I called 'dominant errors.' Now Protestants commonly thought that in all three senses 'Roman doctrine' was condemned in the

---

25. *The Subject of Tract XC. Historically Considered.* By the Rev. Frederick Oakeley, M.A., 2nd edition, revised, pp. xvi. 87. London: James Toovey. 1845.

26. *Tract XC. Historically Refuted.* A Reply to the Rev. F. Oakeley. By William Goode, M.A., Dean of Ripon, 2nd edition, pp. iv. 191. London: Hatchard. 1866.

27. *Oxford: Tract No. 90 and Ward's Ideal of a Christian Church.* By the Rev. W. Simcox Bricknell, M.A., 3rd edition, pp. 69. Oxford: J. Vincent. 1844.

[1] Newman's *Letters*, vol. i. p. 239.
[2] *Ibid.* vol. ii, p. 147.
[3] *Apologia Pro Vita Sua*, p. 160.
[4] *Ibid.* p. 162.

Articles: I thought that the *Catholic teaching* was not condemned; that the *dominant errors* were; and as to the *formal dogmas*, that some were, some were not, and that the line had to be drawn between them. Thus, 1, the use of Prayers for the dead was a Catholic doctrine, not condemned; 2, the prison of Purgatory was a Roman dogma,—which was condemned; but the infallibility of Ecumenical Councils was a Roman dogma—not condemned; and 3, the fire of Purgatory was an authorised and popular error, not a dogma—which was condemned."[1]

This explanation, given by Newman himself twenty-three years after *Tract XC.* was written, may be supplemented by a few extracts from the document itself. In the Introduction the author was not ashamed to speak of the Church of England in terms almost of contempt. "Till," he said, "her members are stirred up to this religious course, let the Church sit still; let her be content to be *in bondage;* let her work *in chains;* let her submit to *her imperfections* as a punishment; let her go on teaching with *the stammering lips of ambiguous formularies* and inconsistent precedents."[2] He boldly maintained that "*the Articles are not written against the Creed of the Roman Church*, but against actual existing errors in it, whether taken into its system or not."[3]

"These extracts show not only what the Anglican doctrine is, but, in particular, that the phrase 'Rule of Faith' is no symbolical expression with us, appropriated to some one sense; certainly not as a definition or attribute of Holy Scripture. And it is important to insist upon this, from the very great misconceptions to which the phrase gives rise. Perhaps its use had better be avoided altogether. In the sense in which it is commonly understood at this day,

---

[1] *Apologia Pro Vita Sua*, p. 159.
[2] *Tract XC.*, 1st edition, p. 4. In the 2nd edition this passage was altered to read as follows:—"Till we are stirred up to this religious course, let the Church, our Mother, sit still; let her children be content to be in bondage; let us work in chains; let us submit to our imperfections as a punishment; let us go on teaching through the meaning of indeterminate statements and inconsistent precedents." The passage was toned down because the author felt he had acted unwisely in going so far; but he expressed no regret for his first version, which, I believe, more accurately expressed his real sentiments all through the controversy which it produced.
[3] *Ibid.* p. 59.

Scripture, it is plain, is not, on Anglican principles, the Rule of Faith."[1]

"Now the first remark that occurs on perusing this Article [XXII.] is that the doctrine objected to is 'the *Romish* doctrine.' For instance, no one would suppose that the *Calvinistic* doctrine, concerning Purgatory, Pardons, and Image Worship, is spoken against. Not every doctrine on these matters is a fond thing, but the *Romish* doctrine. Accordingly the *Primitive* doctrine is not condemned in it, unless, indeed, the Primitive doctrine be the Romish, which must not be supposed."[2]

"And further by 'the Romish doctrine' [Article XXII.] *is not meant the Tridentine doctrine*, because this Article was drawn up before the decree of the Council of Trent.[3] What is opposed is the *received doctrine* of the day, and unhappily of this day too, or the doctrine of the *Roman schools;* a conclusion which is still more clear by considering that there are portions of the Tridentine doctrine on these subjects, which the Article, far from condemning, by anticipation approves."[4]

"The pardons, then, spoken of in the Article [XXII.], are large and reckless indulgences from the penalties of sin obtained on money payments."[5]

"This Article [XXV.] does not deny the five rites in question to be Sacraments, but to be Sacraments in *the sense* in which Baptism and the Lord's Supper are Sacraments."[6]

"Here [Article XXXI.] the Sacrifice of the *Mass* is not spoken

---

[1] *Tract XC.* p. 11.   [2] *Ibid.* p. 23.

[3] This assertion is ably and conclusively refuted by Dean Goode, in his reply to a similar assertion made by the Rev. F. Oakeley. "It is quite true," he writes, "that the session of the Council of Trent, in which its decrees respecting Purgatory, Indulgences, Worship of Relics and Images, and Invocation of Saints were laid down, was posterior to the revision of the Articles; the latter being in January 1562-3, and the former in December 1563. But not only was there sufficient evidence what the doctrine of the Church of Rome was upon those subjects from other sources, but in fact as to Purgatory (Sess. vi. can. 30; Sess. xxii. c. 2.), Indulgences (Sess. xxi. c. 9), and Invocation of Saints (Sess. xxii. c. 3), these doctrines had been distinctly recognised in various sessions of the Council that had *preceded* the revision of the Articles. Indeed, out of the twenty-five sessions of the Council, the Decrees of sixteen (including the doctrines of Scripture and Tradition, Original Sin, Justification, and Good Works, the Sacraments, Baptism, the Lord's Supper, &c.) *were well known here before the Articles* were originally drawn up in 1552; and the Decrees of twenty-two must have been well known here before the revision in January 1562-3, the twenty-second session having taken place in September 1562, four months previous. And the only matters connected with our present subject discussed in the remaining three sessions were, the Sacraments of Order and Matrimony, and the points above mentioned. So utterly incorrect is the assertion that 'the Decrees of Trent were drawn up after the Articles'" (*Tract XC. Historically Refuted.* By William Goode, Dean of Ripon, 2nd edition, 1866, p. 77).

[4] *Tract XC.* p. 24.   [5] *Ibid.* p. 31.   [6] *Ibid.* p. 43.

of, in which the special question of doctrine would be introduced; but the 'Sacrifice of *Masses.*'"[1]

"Bishop is superior to Bishop only in rank, not in real power; and the Bishop of Rome, the head of the Catholic world, is not the centre of unity, *except as having a primacy of order.*"[2]

When *Tract XC.* reached the Roman Catholic College at Oscott, the Romanists were delighted. The biographer of Cardinal Wiseman tells us:—"Oscott, as might be expected, rejoiced. At last it seemed that the Tractarians 'meant business.'"[3] Newman wrote the *Tract* to keep his followers contented in the Church of England. It had, as we are told by one of them, who subsequently became a Roman priest [the Rev. W. Lockhart] a directly opposite effect. Lockhart says:—"On us young men *Tract XC.* had the effect of strengthening greatly our growing convictions that Rome was right and the Church of England wrong."[4]

Neither Newman himself, nor Keble, to whom he showed the *Tract* before publication, seem to have anticipated that it would cause any special sensation. It was published on Saturday, February 27, 1841, and at once created a public excitement. As early as the 8th of March, four Tutors of Oxford Colleges addressed an important letter on the subject addressed, "To the Editor of the *Tracts for the Times.*" It was as follows:—

"SIR,—Our attention having been called to No. 90 in the series of *Tracts for the Times*, by 'Members of the University of Oxford,' of which you are the editor, the impression produced upon our minds by its contents is of so painful a character, that we feel it our duty to intrude ourselves briefly on your notice. This publication is entitled, 'Remarks on Certain Passages in the Thirty-Nine Articles,' and, as these Articles are appointed by the Statutes of the University to be the text-book for Tutors in their theological teaching, we hope that the situations we hold in our respective Colleges will

---

[1] *Tract XC.* p. 59.   [2] *Ibid.* p. 78.
[3] *Life and Times of Cardinal Wiseman*, vol. i. p. 373.
[4] Article by the Rev. W. Lockhart, on "Cardinal Newman," in the *Paternoster Review*, October 1890, p. 28.

secure us from the charge of presumption in thus coming forward to address you.

"The *Tract* has, in our apprehension, a highly dangerous tendency, from its suggesting that certain very important errors of the Church of Rome are not condemned by the Articles of the Church of England. For instance, that those Articles do not contain any condemnation of the doctrines—

"1. Of Purgatory,
2. Of Pardons,
3. Of the Worshipping and Adoration of Images and Relics,
4. Of the Invocation of Saints,
5. Of the Mass,

"as they are taught authoritatively by the Church of Rome, but only of certain absurd practices and opinions which intelligent Romanists repudiate as much as we do. It is intimated, moreover, that the Declaration prefixed to the Articles, so far as it has any weight at all, sanctions this mode of interpreting them, as it is one which takes them in their 'literal and grammatical sense,' and does not 'affix any new sense' to them. The *Tract* would thus appear to us to have a tendency to mitigate, beyond what charity requires, and to the prejudice of the pure truth of the Gospel, the very serious differences which separate the Church of Rome from our own, and to shake the confidence of the less learned members of the Church of England in the Scriptural character of her formularies and teaching.

"We readily admit the necessity of allowing that liberty in interpreting the formularies of our Church, which has been advocated by many of its most learned Bishops and other eminent divines; but this *Tract* puts forward new and startling views as to the extent to which that liberty may be carried. For if we are right in our apprehension of the author's meaning, we are at a loss to see what security would remain, were his principles generally recognised, that the most plainly erroneous doctrines and practices of the Church of Rome might not be inculcated in the lecture rooms of the University and from the pulpits of our Churches.

"In conclusion, we venture to call your attention to the impropriety of such questions being treated in an anonymous publication, and to express an earnest hope that you may be authorised to make known the writer's name. Considering how very grave and solemn the whole subject is, we cannot help thinking, that both the Church and the University are entitled to ask that some person, besides the printer and publisher of the *Tract*, should acknowledge himself responsible for its contents.—We are, sir, your obedient humble servants,

"T. T. CHURTON, M.A., Vice-Principal and Tutor of Brasenose College.

H. B. WILSON, B.D., Fellow and Senior Tutor of St. John's College.

JOHN GRIFFITHS, M.A., Sub-Warden and Tutor of Wadham College.

A. C. TAIT, M.A., Fellow and Tutor of Balliol College.

"OXFORD, *March* 8, 1841."

The last to sign this important document, the Rev. A. C. Tait, afterwards became Archbishop of Canterbury. He never repented of the part he then took, Broad Churchman though he was. "Were it all to happen again," he said in 1880, "I think I should, in the same position, do exactly as I did then."[1]

Mr. Tait sent a copy of the Address of the four Tutors to Dr. Arnold, Head Master of Rugby, who, in his reply, wrote strongly, yet justly, in the following terms:—

"I am extremely glad that the *Tract* has been so noticed; yet it is to me far more objectionable morally than theologically; and especially the comment on the 21st Article, to which you have not alluded, is of such a character, that if subscription to the 21st Article, justified by such rules of interpretation, may be honestly practised, I do not see why an Unitarian may not subscribe the first Article or the second. The comparative importance of the truths subscribed to does not affect the question; I am merely speaking of the utter perversion of language shown in the *Tract*, according to which a man may subscribe to an article when he holds the very opposite opinions—believing what it denies, and denying what it affirms."[2]

The letter of the four Tutors, which Newman formally acknowledged (but to whom he did not reveal his name), was speedily followed by the action of the Heads of Houses, at, it is said, the instigation of the Rev. C. P. Golightly of Oriel College. Mr. Golightly was one of the earliest subscribers to the *Tracts for the Times*, and for some years he was considered as one of the Tractarian

---

[1] *Life of Archbishop Tait*, vol. i. p. 87, 1st edition. [2] *Ibid.* p. 86.

party, being on terms of intimate friendship with all the leaders. But, like others, when he discovered whither they were moving, he severed his connection with them. From the publication of *Tract XC.* he became one of the most zealous opponents of the Tractarians, and living to old age, in his later years also he took an active part in opposing the Romanising practices carried on in the Diocese of Oxford. We shall hear of him again later on.

The Heads of Houses held several meetings to consider their action. It is stated by Canon Liddon that Newman privately informed them that he was bringing out in pamphlet form a defence, or apology, for *Tract XC.*, and that he asked them to postpone their decision for one day only until they had had an opportunity of reading his defence. They refused to do so. So far as I can judge they seem to have acted very unadvisedly in this. A day's delay would have done them no harm, and it would certainly have prevented the cry of unfairness which was raised against them. Yet, even if they had waited, I do not think that Newman's pamphlet would have altered their opinion of his *Tract*, which opinion was dated March 15th, and issued on the morning of March 16th. The resolution was in the following terms:—

"At a Meeting of the Vice-Chancellor, Heads of Houses, and Proctors, in the Delegates' Room, March 15, 1841:

"Considering that it is enjoined in the Statutes of this University (Tit. iii. Sect. 2, Tit. ix. Sect. 11 § 3, Sect. v. § 3) that every student shall be instructed and examined in the Thirty-Nine Articles, and shall subscribe to them; considering also that a *Tract* has recently appeared, dated from Oxford, and entitled 'Remarks on Certain Passages in the Thirty-Nine Articles,' being No. 90 of the *Tracts for the Times*, a series of anonymous publications purporting to be written by Members of the University, but which are in no way sanctioned by the University itself;

"Resolved, That modes of interpretation such as are suggested in the said *Tract*, evading rather than explaining the sense of the Thirty-Nine Articles, and reconciling subscription to them with the adoption of errors which they were designed to counteract, defeat the object, and are inconsistent with the due observance of the above-mentioned Statutes.

"P. WYNTER, *Vice-Chancellor.*"

Now with regard to the above resolution of the Hebdomadal Board there is an interesting statement by Mr. Griffiths, one of the four Tutors, in a privately printed letter, which has not hitherto been published, and which I may cite here. He writes on April 5, 1841, to a friend:—

"Now the facts are these. On Friday, March 12, the Board resolved that they ought to censure the *Tract* in some public and official way; and this resolution was carried by nineteen against two. The two were ... One of these two said, that there were certain parts of the *Tract* upon which he did not feel competent to pass an opinion, and therefore he voted against the censure. The other said, that probably no person present could feel more strongly than he did the mischievous tendency of this particular *Tract*, but he thought the *Tracts* as a whole had done good, and he judged the censure inexpedient. Every other person who spoke condemned the *Tract* most strongly. No one, however, spoke as if he was moved to condemn it in consequence of our Letter [*i.e.* of the four Tutors].

"But there were only twenty-one persons then present out of the twenty-six. Three were absent from infirmity or illness, and two by accident. Of the three, one is known to have expressed his opinion that the proceedings taken against the *Tract* were inexpedient, but I also know that he has expressed his opinion that the *Tract* itself was likely to be mischievous: the other two would certainly have been in the majority. Of the two who were absent by accident, one afterwards voted against the proceedings of the Board, alleging as his reason, that he should be as much ashamed of formally disavowing his concurrence with the principles of interpretation suggested in the *Tract* as of formally disavowing his disagreement with any person who might chance to deny that two and two make four: the other afterwards took occasion to express his deep sense of the dangerous tendency of the *Tract*, and his regret that from not knowing the course of the business of the Board he had not been present to give his vote on Friday.

"On that Friday a Committee was appointed to shape the censure, and they reported to the Board on Monday the 15th. Several questions then arose upon details, and divisions were had with various majorities. The first was about an adjournment, for Mr. Newman had informed the Provost of Oriel that the author of the *Tract*, still not named, would publish an explanation of it in two or three days. The minority on this consisted of either three or four; but even he who on Friday opposed the measure as inexpedient, maintained that the Board ought to do whatever it did *at once*. On the subsequent questions, which related chiefly or entirely to the wording of their resolution, I believe that both the members, who formed the minority on Friday, declined to vote. No other division touched the main question.

"All this I state confidently on the direct authority of ear witnesses."[1]

On the same day that the resolution of the Heads of Houses was made public, Newman wrote to the Vice-Chancellor, acknowledging himself the author of the censured *Tract*, and stating that he had not given his "name hitherto, under the belief that it was desired that I should not," and that his opinion remained "unchanged of the truth and honesty of the principle maintained in the *Tract*, and of the necessity of putting it forth." On the same evening Newman's promised explanation was published, but without his name. The title-page stated that it was "By the Author" of the *Tract*, and at the end he placed his initials. In this pamphlet Newman declares that he does consider that the Thirty-Nine Articles "contain a condemnation of the *authoritative teaching* of the Church of Rome" on Purgatory, Pardons, Worshipping, and Adoration of Images and Relics, the Invocation of Saints, and the Mass;[2] but he is careful to explain what he means by the expression "authoritative teaching." "I conceive," he writes, "that what 'all the best writers' say is authoritative teaching, and a sufficient object for the censures conveyed in the Articles, though the decrees of Trent, taken by themselves, remain untouched."[3] Even in this explanation, therefore, he admits that he had not anything to say against what had been defined officially by the Church of Rome, but only against what some of her writers had taught. He knew very well that Rome is not bound by what her "best writers" teach, and that she is free to reject their teaching whenever she likes. He admits that any one who believed that the Church of Rome is infallible ought to join her; but he is careful to

---

[1] *Two Letters Concerning No. 90 in the Series called the Tracts for the Times.* Printed, for Private Distribution Only, by W. Baxter, Oxford, 1841, pp. 13-15.
[2] *A Letter to the Rev. R. W. Jelf, D.D., In Explanation of No. 90.* By the Author, 2nd edition, p. 4. [3] *Ibid.* p. 10.

assure his readers: "I am not aware that this doctrine is anywhere embodied in her formal decrees." He has strong things to say against this teaching of the "best divines." "As to the present authoritative teaching of the Church of Rome," he writes, *"to judge by what we see of it in public,* I think it goes very far indeed to substitute another Gospel for the true one. Instead of setting before the soul the Holy Trinity, and Heaven and Hell; it does seem to me, *as a popular system,* to preach the Blessed Virgin and the Saints, and Purgatory. If ever there was *a system* which required reformation, it is that of Rome at this day, or in other words (as I should call it) Romanism or Popery."[1] As to what the Council of Trent teaches concerning the Veneration of Images, he sees nothing to object against; but he declares that it is better than the popular system of Rome in actual operation:—"The Divines at Trent," he writes, "say that 'to images are to be paid due honour and veneration;' and to those who honour the sacred volume, pictures of friends, and the like, as we all do, *I do not see that these very words of themselves can be the subject of objection.* Far otherwise when we see the comment which the Church of Rome has put on them in teaching and practice. I consider its existing creed and popular worship to be as near idolatry as any portion of that Church can be."[2] Bad as all he objects to is, Newman tries to save the character of the Church of Rome at the expense of her children, for as to the practical abuses condemned in *Tract XC.* he points out that Romanists have protested against them as much as he had:—"At the Council of Trent such protests," he writes, "as are quoted in the *Tract,* were entered against so many of the very errors and corruptions which our Articles and Homilies also condemn."[3] He assures Dr. Jelf that this, his explanation, is not to be taken as withdrawing any opinion he had expressed in *Tract XC.* On the contrary, he tells him:—"Nor can I repent of what I have published."[4] "Nor is this *Letter* a retractation."[5]

---

[1] *A Letter to the Rev. R. W. Jelf, D.D., In Explanation of No.* 90, p. 5.
[2] *Ibid.* pp. 6, 7.   [3] *Ibid.* p. 15.   [4] *Ibid.* p. 27.   [5] *Ibid.* p. 29.

WISEMAN'S SYMPATHY WITH THE TRACTARIANS 159

All through this pamphlet it seems to me that Newman is in reality censuring the Romanists for not being as good as their Church, while he holds that Church responsible for their misconduct. He threatens that if he and his friends are not allowed to have their own way, there will be a "risk of a schism";[1] and he holds up the Church of Rome to the admiration of English Churchmen as having many spiritual blessings of which, in the Church of England, they were deprived.

"The age," he writes, "is moving towards something, and most unhappily the one religious communion among us which has of late years been practically in possession of this something, is the Church of Rome. *She alone*, amid all the errors and evils of her *practical system*, has given free scope to the feelings of awe, mystery, tenderness, reverence, devotedness, and other feelings which may specially be called Catholic. The question then is, whether we shall give them up to the Roman Church or claim them for ourselves. . . . But if we do give them up, then we must give up the men who cherish them. We must consent either to give up the men, or to admit their principles."[2]

In this way Newman glorified the Church of Rome, and tried to frighten the Church of England into admitting the principles of the Tractarians, under the threat that if they were not tolerated the men who held them would go to Rome. Not that Rome was, just at that time, over anxious to hurry them over the border. It suited her schemes that they should for a time remain in the Church of England. Cardinal Wiseman's biographer very frankly admits that:—
"Wiseman's attitude, however, as a whole, was deeply sympathetic towards the spirit and intentions of the Tractarians. . . . He acquiesced in the view that while Newman was satisfied with remaining in the English Church in the hope of ultimately bringing many to unity, *he might do so without being urged to cut short his time of waiting.*"[3] This policy had been adopted before *Tract XC.* was published. Of the previous year Mr. Wilfred Ward writes:—"Corporate Reunion with Rome was more and more explicitly spoken

---

[1] *A Letter to the Rev. R. W. Jelf, D.D., In Explanation of No. 90*, p. 27.
[2] *Ibid.* pp. 25, 26.   [3] *Life and Times of Cardinal Wiseman*, vol. i. p. 381.

of by them [advanced Tractarians] as a practicable prospect, though its nature and extent were somewhat undefined. *The pressing of individual conversions was deprecated, even by the most advanced of the party, as likely to prevent the realisation of any such hope.* The Corporate Movement contemplated soon became limited, however, to a large accession of Tractarians to Rome. The events of 1841 negatived the idea of any action on the part of the National Church; and Newman, Ward, and Oakeley very soon came to see that what was spoken of as 'Reunion' must amount to nothing less than submission to Rome."[1]

To the Roman Catholics on the Continent these subtle plans of the Tractarians were made known by a letter, written soon after the publication of *Tract XC.*, to the Editor of the Paris *Univers*, in which it appeared on April 13th. The letter was written by the Rev. W. G. Ward, and was translated into French by Mr J. D. Dalgairns, of Exeter College, Oxford. Mr. Ward wrote:—

"The charity which you have always shown towards the Anglican Church makes me think you will not refuse to find room in your Catholic journal for the letter of one of the children of *that afflicted Church* which has drunk to the dregs the bitter cup which is now the lot of all the Churches of Christ. The eyes of all Christendom are at this moment turned to England, so long separated from the rest of Catholic Europe; everywhere a presentiment has gone forth that the hour of her reunion is at hand, and that this island, of old so fruitful in saints, is once more about to put forth new fruits worthy of the martyrs who have watered it with their blood. And, truly, this presentiment is not ungrounded, as I shall prove to you by a detail of what is now passing in the University of Oxford. This detail is the more important, inasmuch as the University is indeed the heart of the Anglican Church, the beatings of which make the remotest members of this great body quiver. The only end I propose to myself is to give you a just idea of the present position of the Anglican Church, so that the French Catholics may share the emotions of our souls. And I do not believe that it is possible to give you an idea of them otherwise than by an exposition of a small treatise which has lately appeared. I do not flatter myself that you will approve of all the opinions which I am about to mention. I do not defend them. I am their historian—not their author.

---

[1] *Life and Times of Cardinal Wiseman*, vol. i. pp. 371, 372.

"Mr. Newman, one of our theologians, published, a few days since, the ninetieth number of the *Tracts for the Times*, in which he designs to demonstrate that the Church of Rome has fallen into no formal error in the Council of Trent, that the Invocations of the Saints (the *Ora pro nobis*, for example), Purgatory, and the Supremacy of the Holy See of Rome, are in no way contrary to the Catholic traditions, or even to our authorised formularies; in fine, that the dogma of Transubstantiation should be no obstacle to the union of the Churches, as in this article there is only a verbal difference between them. At the same time he is but little satisfied with our Thirty-Nine Articles, although he maintains throughout that the providence of God hindered the Reformers from openly inserting in them the Protestant dogmas to which they were but too much attached. You will perceive, sir, all the importance of those opinions, and the more so as they are not the opinions of an isolated theologian. I can assure you, that at the same time that an opposition was raised by the elder members of the University (as might be expected, seeing that they lived under the system of the eighteenth century), that very opposition gave me an opportunity of observing that even the most moderate of the Catholic party at Oxford were ready to sustain the author of the *Tract*.

"You see then, sir, that humility, the first condition of every sound reform, is not wanting in us. *We are little satisfied with our position.* We groan at the sins committed by our ancestors in separating from the Catholic world. We experience a burning desire to be reunited to our brethren. *We love with an unfeigned affection the Apostolic See, which we acknowledge to be the head of Christendom,* and the more because the Church of Rome is our mother, which sent from her bosom the blessed St. Augustine to bring us her immovable faith. We admit also that it is not our formularies, nor even the Council of Trent, which prevent our union. After all these concessions, you may ask me, *Why, then, do you not rejoin us? What is it that prevents you?* Is it your formularies? But, according to yourself, you do not look upon them with a very favourable eye. Is it ours?—But, in your opinion, they do not contain any error. My reply to this question will develop to you still more clearly our present position. In the first place, while Mr. Newman expresses himself thus clearly on the purity of the formularies authorised by the Church of Rome, he always makes a distinction between the system of the Council of Trent and another system which exists in that Church. While he returns thanks to God for having preserved that Council from all formal error in matters of faith, he, at the same time, maintains that in practice there are corruptions in the Church against which the Council itself raises its voice, but which nevertheless still exist, and call loudly for reform. Thus he says that 'notwithstanding the errors in practical system, there is no Church but that of Rome which has given a free course to the emotions of adoration, of mystery, of tenderness, of reverence, devotion, and to the other sentiments of that kind, which may so entirely be called Catholic.' He maintains that the theory of the Church is pure; but that, according to certain books of piety which are too widely spread, according to the statements of enlightened travellers, free from all the prejudices of vulgar Protestantism, he fears that there is a system authorised which, practically, 'instead of presenting to the soul of the sinner the Holy Trinity, Heaven, and Hell, substitutes for that the Holy Virgin, the Saints, and Purgatory.' It is true that all that does not form an essential part of the faith of the Church, but he avows that the system loudly calls for reform, and that it would be impossible for the Anglican Church *yet* to cast itself into the arms of that of Rome.

"In the second place, we have a sacred duty to discharge towards the members of our Church. We cannot yet bring ourselves to believe that our dear England is in the same position as *the heretics who boast in the names of Luther and Calvin.* Of a truth, sir, is not the Episcopal order still worth something? A sacrilegious king may indeed have stolen from the altars of Canterbury the sacred bones of St. Thomas, but, think you he had the power to drive away the great soul who, from his throne in the skies, ever watches over the See which he has illustrated by his life, and consecrated by his blood? God forbid that the august line of Lanfranc and of Anselm should ever cease. If we have not preserved it, it is no more; for, of a truth, you will not say that its succession has been kept up by you. There is no Archbishop *in partibus* of Canterbury or York, as there is of Cambysopolis or of Siga. But perhaps you may say that the moment an Archbishop ceases to be in communion with Rome, he also ceases to exist. But permit me here to become a little scholastic, and to borrow the terms with which the schools supply me, in order to give precision to my ideas.

"The Papacy, according to us, is rather the accidental than the essential form of the Church. It resembles rather the vital heat than the life of the Church. The absence of heat is a mark of sickness. Without it the limbs, powerless, are dragged sorrowfully about, and the functions of life languish; but life may still be there. *Thus, union with the Pope is a necessary result of the perfect health of the Church.* The retrenching of this union is a proof that all does not go well. It is a symptom of the presence of a malady which gnaws the entrails of the Church. Her priesthood is, perhaps, deprived of some of its functions, or, as, alas! is too certainly the case with us, the episcopacy is subject to the powers of this world. But life—that is to say, the essence—of the Church is not yet extinct. We have, then, still a duty to perform towards our brethren.

"There are at this moment in the Anglican Church a crowd of persons who balance between Protestantism and Catholicism, and who, nevertheless, would reject with horror the idea of a union with Rome. The Protestant prejudices, which for three hundred years have infected our Church, are unhappily too deeply rooted there to be extirpated *without a great deal of address.* We must then offer in sacrifice to God this ardent desire which devours us of seeing once more the perfect unity of the Church of Christ. We must still bear the terrible void which the isolation of our Church creates in our hearts, and remain still till it pleases God to convert the hearts of our Anglican *confrères*, especially of our holy fathers the Bishops. We are destined, I am persuaded, to bring back many wandering sheep to the knowledge of the truth. In fact, the progress of Catholic opinions in England for the last seven years is so inconceivable, that no hope should appear extravagant. *Let us, then, remain quiet for some years, till, by God's blessing, the ears of Englishmen are accustomed to hear the name of Rome pronounced with reverence.* At the end of this term you will soon see the fruits of our patience.

"But, moreover, I venture to say, that we have besides a sacred duty to fulfil towards Rome. Far from us be that vulgar Protestantism which dares to open its profane mouth, and utter its calumnies against the See of St. Peter. Yes, if I could once be convinced that the Spirit of God had quitted the Church of Rome, I should think at the same time that Christianity was about to be extinguished all over the world. . . .

"And this great heart [of England] once so Catholic, this poor heart, so long torn by the vigour of its own life, exhausted in vain efforts to fill up the frightful void which reigns there, does it not merit some sacrifices on your part, that it may find consolation and healing? Oh, how sweet it was to hear that our Catholic brethren prayed for us. The triumphant army in heaven prays also for us. It has prayed, I am sure, from the beginning of *these three centuries of schism and heresy.* Why have not the prayers of St. Gregory, St. Augustine, and St. Thomas been heard? Because of our sins; the sins not only of England, but of Rome. Let us go and do penance together and we *shall* be heard. During this holy time, in which the Church retires to the depths of the solitude of her soul, following the bleeding feet of her Divine Master, driven *by the Spirit into the desert*, know that many of us stretch out our hands day and night before the Lord, and beg of Him, with sighs and groans, to reunite them to our Catholic brethren. Frenchmen! fail not to aid us in this holy exercise; and I am persuaded that many Lents will not have passed before we shall chaunt together our Paschal hymns, in those sublime accents which have been used by the Divine Spouse of Christ for so many ages."[1]

Roman Catholics as well as Protestants and Tractarians entered zealously into the controversy started by *Tract XC.* Of course it gave them intense joy to witness Newman's gradual advance Romeward, while they held in contempt the logic by which he maintained his position in the Church of England. One who signed himself "An English Catholic" wrote to Newman a stinging letter, in which he said:—"That you should deem it consistent with your station in the Church of England to sanction by your writings a belief in some of the most unpopular doctrines of the Catholic Church is, no doubt, a subject of some surprise to the members of our [Roman Catholic] communion. But however we might wonder, *we*, at least, should have no right to reproach you; nor could your equivocal position afford *us* any ground of complaint, had the question rested here. But, sir, we *have* a right to complain, and we *do* complain, that in order to screen yourself in the adoption of *our* tenets from the obloquy and ruin that your profession of them, *as ours*, would undoubtedly entail upon you, you deliberately distort and misrepresent our faith and practice—that in order to avert the impending storm of Protestant ire from your own devoted head, you erect a counterfeit image of 'Romanism' to serve as an ecclesiastical lightning conductor."[2] As to Newman's attempt, in *Tract XC.*, to reconcile the Council of Trent with the Thirty-Nine Articles, this Roman Catholic writer forcibly remarks:—"If you can only establish the fact that the acceptance of the Decrees of Trent is consistent with a belief in the Thirty-Nine Articles, there is not a Roman

[1] *Catholic Magazine*, vol. for 1841, pp. 310-313.
[2] *Oxford or Rome?* A Letter to the Rev. J. H. Newman on No. 90. By An English Catholic, p. 3.

Catholic in England, Ireland, or Scotland, from his Grace of Norfolk down to your humble correspondent, who may not subscribe these Articles with a safe and easy conscience!"[1]

Dr. Wiseman could not remain an idle spectator of the controversy in which he took the deepest interest. Directly after Newman had published his *Letter to Dr. Jelf*, Wiseman wrote to him about it, and published his letter as a pamphlet. He distinctly repudiated the theory Newman had put forth. "The existence," wrote Wiseman, "of any such *authoritative teaching* at variance with the doctrines of the Tridentine Synod is, to me, a novel idea; and I think it will prove so to all Catholics."[2] But though he criticised, Wiseman had a great deal more to be thankful for than to find fault with, and therefore, at the end of his letter, he expresses his gratitude to Newman in the warmest terms. "In conclusion," he wrote, "I thank you, Rev. Sir, from my heart, for the welcome information which your letter contains, that men, whom you so highly value, should be opening their eyes to the beauties and perfections of our Church, and require such efforts, as your interpretation of the Articles, to keep them from 'straggling in the direction of Rome.'"[3]

Yet one more Roman Catholic pamphlet on *Tract XC*. I must quote before I pass on. It was written by a gentleman who, as we shall see more fully presently, gave the chief energies of his life, from 1841 until his death, to help on the Oxford Movement, because he saw clearly that the fruits of that Movement would be reaped by the Church of Rome. I refer to Mr. Ambrose Lisle Phillipps, who afterwards adopted the name of Ambrose Phillipps de Lisle. *Tract XC.* filled his heart with joy and gladness:—

"It is impossible," he wrote, "to do sufficient justice to the firmness and courage which Mr. Newman has evinced in acknow-

---

[1] *Oxford or Rome?* p. 5.
[2] *A Letter to the Rev. J. H. Newman On Some Passages in his Letter to the Rev. Dr. Jelf.* By N. Wiseman, p. 5.
[3] *Ibid.* p. 31.

ledging the authorship of *Tract No. 90*. I rejoice also to see that, in his subsequent *Letter to Dr. Jelf*, he persists in his noble declaration in favour of so many Catholic truths, no less than in his generous attempt to soften down the differences between the Church of England and the Catholic Church, which to me at least appears a most important step towards the reunion and the peace of distracted Christendom. Above all I hail, with inexpressible joy, and the deepest gratitude towards Him who holds in His hands the hearts of men, and who for the love of mankind turns every event to the good of His Church, the glorious admissions which, both in the *Tract* and the *Letter*, are so fearlessly proclaimed in behalf of that holy Council of Trent, against which for three centuries such absurd and irrational prejudices had taken root in the minds of our separated brethren."[1]

But while Newman and his friends were, on the whole, pleased with *Tract XC.*, the Bishop of Oxford was placed by it in a very uncomfortable position. With the general principles of the *Tracts for the Times* he agreed, but this latest of the series seemed to him to go too far for him to follow. His first step seems to have been that of opening a private correspondence with Pusey, Newman, and the Archbishop of Canterbury on the subject. To Pusey, on March 17th, the Bishop wrote:—" I feel safe in declaring to you more fully the fears which I entertain as to the possible consequences of the recent publication; and you will understand me when I say that I look with anxiety to its effects, not only within the limits of my diocese, but throughout the Church of which I am a Bishop, and in the purity and tranquillity of which I am deeply interested. . . . If he [Newman] could also adopt respectful language (and the more cordial the better) in speaking of the formularies of the Church, he would do much to relieve the minds of many (myself among others) who, with a sincere reverence and desire for Catholic truth, have an unfeigned attachment to the principles of the Church of England."[2] To Newman himself the Bishop wrote on the same day:—" I do feel it my duty

[1] *Some Remarks on a Letter to Dr. Jelf.* By Ambrose Lisle Phillipps, Esq., p. 4.
[2] *Life of Dr. Pusey*, vol. ii. p. 184.

to express my regret at its publication, and to state to you plainly, though generally, my honest conviction of its containing much which I am sure is directly the reverse of what the writer would wish or expect from it, but what would, in my opinion, tend both to disunite and endanger the Church."[1] The Archbishop of Canterbury expressed the opinion that there were passages in *Tract XC.* which were "very objectionable," and that it seemed to him "most desirable that the publication of the *Tracts* should be discontinued for ever."[2] The Bishop of Oxford agreed with the desire of the Archbishop for the suppression of the *Tracts*, and suggested that Newman should write and publish a letter of explanation to his Diocesan. Newman consented to both requests. The result of the discontinuance of the *Tracts* was, in the opinion of Canon Liddon, not altogether satisfactory to High Churchmen. "Looked at from a distance," he remarks, "and taken together, the censure of the Heads of Houses and the discontinuance of the *Tracts* at the request of the Bishop, produced a widespread feeling of discouragement among High Churchmen."[3] Newman's *Letter* to the Bishop is dated March 29th, and filled a pamphlet of forty-seven pages. It could not be termed satisfactory to Protestant Churchmen, and was in no way calculated to remove their reasonable objections. He expressed a sense of "the inestimable privileges" of being a member of that Church over which his lordship presided; that that Church "was a Divinely ordained channel of supernatural grace to the souls of her members"; and that it was "the Catholic Church in this country."[4] But on the other hand, while he had some things to censure in the Church of Rome, he had words of praise for her, and expressed a desire for reunion with that communion. Both criticisms and praise are found in one paragraph.

"They find," he explained, "in what I have written, no abuse, at least I trust not, of the individual Roman Catholic, nor of the

---

[1] *Life of Dr. Pusey*, vol. ii. p. 185. [2] *Ibid.* p. 190. [3] *Ibid.* p. 204.
[4] *A Letter to the Bishop of Oxford On Occasion of No. 90.* By J. H. Newman, B.D., pp. 33, 34.

Church of Rome, viewed abstractedly as a Church. *I cannot speak against the Church of Rome*, viewed in her formal character, as a true Church, since she is 'built upon the foundation of the Apostles and Prophets, Jesus Christ Himself being the Chief Corner Stone.' Nor can I speak against her private members, numbers of whom, I trust, are God's people, in the way to Heaven, and one with us in heart, though not in profession. But what I have spoken, and do strongly speak against, is that energetic system and engrossing influence in the Church *by which* it acts towards us, and meets our eyes, like a cloud filling it, to the eclipse of all that is holy, whether in its ordinances or its members. This system I have called, in what I have written, Romanism or Popery; and by Romanists and Papists, I mean all its members, as far as they are under the power of these principles; and while, and *so far as this system exists*, and it does exist now as fully as heretofore, *I say that we can have no peace with that Church*, however we may secretly love its particular members. I cannot speak against its private members; I should be doing violence to every feeling of my nature if I did, and your lordship would not require it of me. *I wish from my heart we and they were one;* but we cannot, without a sin, sacrifice truth to peace; and, in the words of Archbishop Laud, 'till Rome be other than it is,' we must be estranged from her."[1]

Newman herein affirmed that there could be "no peace" with the Church of Rome, not because of any of her actual doctrines, but because of "this system" within her; but as to the Church of Rome herself, apart from "this system," he declared:—"I wish from my heart we and they were one." In proof of his dislike of "this system," Newman quoted several utterances of his which he had made from time to time, more especially in the *Tracts for the Times*, and his *Lectures on Romanism and Popular Protestantism*. The value of these utterances against the practical evils of Rome and her system may be judged by the reasons he gave, less than two years later, for making them, at the time he withdrew them as "dirty words of mine."[2] "If," wrote Newman to the *Oxford Conservative Journal*, "you ask me how an individual could venture not simply to hold, but to publish such views of a

---

[1] *A Letter to the Bishop of Oxford On Occasion of No.* 90, pp. 20, 21.
[2] *Memoirs of James Hope-Scott*, vol. ii. p. 19.

communion [Church of Rome] so ancient, so wide-spreading, so fruitful of saints, I answer that I said to myself, '*I am not speaking my own words*,[1] I am but following almost a *consensus* of the divines of my Church. They have ever used the strongest language against Rome, even the most able and learned of them. I wish to throw myself into their system. While I say what they say, I am safe. *Such views, too, are necessary to our position.*' Yet I have reason to fear still that such language is to be ascribed, in no small measure, to an impetuous temper, a hope of approving myself to persons I respect, *and a wish to repel the charge of Romanism.*"[2] A week or two later Newman explained more fully to his friend, Mr. J. R. Hope-Scott, his reasons for withdrawing all that he had said against the Church of Rome. Due allowance must be made for any advance of Newman in a Romeward direction between the date when he wrote his published *Letter to the Bishop of Oxford* on March 29, 1841, and February 3, 1843, when he wrote to Mr. Hope-Scott as follows:—

"My reason for the *thing* [that is, for withdrawing his words against Rome] was my *long-continued* feeling of the great inconsistency I was in of letting things stand in print against me which I did not hold, and which I could not but be contradicting by my acting every day of my life. And more especially (*i.e.* it came home to me most vividly in that particular way) I felt that I was *taking people in*; that they thought me what I was not, and were trusting me when they should not, and this has been at times a very painful feeling indeed. I don't want to be trusted (perhaps you may think my fear, even before this affair, somewhat amusing), but so it was and is; people *won't* believe I go as far as I do—they will cling to their hopes. And then, again, *intimate friends have almost reproached me with 'paltering with them in a double sense*, keeping the word of promise to their ear, to break it to their hope.' They have said that my words against Rome often, when narrowly examined, were only what *I* meant, but that the effect of them was what *others* meant."[3]

Though foes many attacked *Tract XC.*, it must not be supposed that Newman was without friends to defend it

---

[1] Yet he published them *as his own words!*
[2] Newman's *Via Media*, vol. ii. pp. 432, 433, edition 1891.
[3] *Memoirs of James Hope-Scott*, vol. ii. pp. 20, 21.

and him. One of the earliest of these to enter the field was the Rev. William George Ward, who himself was, three years later, the object of a successful attack from the Protestant side. I should imagine that Ward's pamphlet, *A Few Words in Support of No. 90*, must have done Newman more harm than good, for it set before the public his real views in altogether too clear a light, Newman's object being to cover his real meaning as far as possible by subtle arguments. The Protestant opposition to *Tract XC.* was certainly not lessened by Ward's explanations, especially as given in his second pamphlet, *A Few More Words in Support of No. 90*. This latter pamphlet dealt at some length with the arguments put forth in an anonymous pamphlet, entitled, *The Articles Construed by Themselves*, the authorship of which is now attributed by his biographer to Mr. Robert Lowe, of Magdalen College, Oxford, since widely known as Lord Sherbrooke.[1] In his *Few More Words* Mr. Ward admitted that it was "a most bitter thought, that the principal advocates of what we are well convinced is God's holy truth, should be really imagined by serious men to advocate a Jesuitical (in the popular sense of that word) and disingenuous principle, by which any thing may mean any thing, and forms may be subscribed at the most solemn period of our life, only to be dishonestly explained away."[2] While criticising an article which had appeared in the *Edinburgh Review*, Ward remarked:—

"2. If we suppose the English Reformation to have severed us from the ancient body of the English Church, we shall be bound in consistency to leave our own communion and join the Church of Rome. The latter of these alternatives the *Reviewer* urges that we are thus bound to adopt: on our principles, he says, 'the Church of England is the offspring of an unjustifiable schism and revolution.' Alter the wording of this a little, and Mr. Newman, at least, would appear not unwilling to admit it. *He intimates, not very obscurely* (*Tract*, p. 79), *that in releasing her from the Roman Supremacy, her then governors were guilty of rebellion;* and considering that they had also sworn obedience to the Pope, for my own part I see not

---

[1] *Life and Letters of Viscount Sherbrooke.* By A. P. Martin, vol. i. p. 123.
[2] *A Few More Words.* By the Rev. W. G. Ward, p. 5. Oxford: Parker. 1841.

how we can avoid adding, of perjury. The point on which Mr. Newman would take his stand is this; that, estimating the sin at the highest, it was not 'that special sin which cuts off from the fountains of grace, and is called schism.' ... Let him *prove* to us that the Church of England *is* a Protestant community; that it was founded on the denial of Catholic doctrines; that it *seceded* from the Ancient English Church which witnessed these doctrines; let him *prove* this; and, though the Articles were as obviously on our side as he considers them overwhelmingly against us, our consciences could not allow us to remain one moment in a communion which had thus forfeited the gifts of grace."[1]

Ward referred to "those whom *we* revere as eminent Saints, the Popes and others of the Middle Ages";[2] but clearly as he showed in this pamphlet his own Romish sympathies, and the contemptible position he considered the English Church to be in, as compared with the Roman Church, he did not in it tell the public *all* that he thought on the subject he was discussing. His full views were revealed to the Paris Roman Catholic *Univers,* at about the same time, as quoted above at pp. 160–164. But in his letter to that paper he was careful not to reveal his name. It was not known that he was the writer of that traitorous letter until after his death, when the fact was revealed in his biography.[3] Mr. Robert Lowe replied to Ward's *Few More Words* by a pamphlet of twenty-four pages, in which he exposed the Jesuitry of what he termed a "dark and thorny labyrinth."

The Rev. and Hon. A. P. Percival, one of the founders of the Tractarian Movement, also came to the aid of Newman, in a pamphlet of thirty-three pages, bearing the title of *A Vindication of the Principles of the Authors of " The Tracts for the Times."* It was dated March 28th. He commenced by giving a wholly inadequate description of the principles held by the writers of the *Tracts* (of whom he was one), and then asked, "Are these principles, or are they not, contrary to the principles of the Reformers, or in any respect forbidden by the Church of England?"[4]

[1] Ward's *Few More Words,* pp. 17, 19.   [2] *Ibid.* p. 33.
[3] *William George Ward and the Oxford Movement,* p. 187.
[4] *A Vindication,* p. 8.

As explained economically by Mr. Percival, I have no doubt there were at the time many loyal Churchmen who would have answered they were not contrary to either the one or the other; but who would at the same time have indignantly repudiated many of the doctrines taught in the *Tracts for the Times,* and especially in *Tract XC.* " With respect to the *Tract XC.,*" said Mr. Percival, " I must confess that I do not see how any member of the Church of England can be blamed for doing what Mr. Newman has there attempted to do, namely, to give to the Articles of the Church of England that interpretation which shall render them most in accordance with that principle of *deference to the Primitive Church of the first seven centuries."*[1] In this, Percival gave an inadequate and misleading representation of Newman's action. What Newman wished was, not so much to prove that the Articles were not in opposition to *"the first seven centuries,"* as that they were not opposed to the official teaching *of the Church of Rome in the nineteenth century.* Yet Percival was constrained to admit of *Tract XC.,* that "There are many things in it which I do not understand, some which I disapprove, perhaps from not understanding them: some statements advanced which I think cannot be maintained: some conclusions drawn, which seem unwarranted by the premises."[2] But "as to the main object aimed at by the *Tract,*" he thought it deserved " the commendation of every member of the Church of England." Yet he cannot conclude without expressing, in a postscript, against protesting the language of Newman (in his *Letter to Dr. Jelf*) in praise of the Church of Rome.

Only five days after Mr. Percival's pamphlet was issued, another champion of Newman's appeared in the field, whose aid he valued more than that of all who had gone before him. This was the Rev. John Keble, who Newman always considered as the real founder of the Oxford Movement. In a privately printed *Letter to Mr. Justice Coleridge,* Keble discussed several important cases of conscience relating to subscription to the Thirty-Nine Articles, which are of as

---

[1] *A Vindication,* p. 16. [2] *Ibid.* p. 18.

great an interest to us in the present day as when they were first written, whatever view we may take of Keble's opinions on the subject. I must say that, in this *Letter*, Keble, on the whole, advocated a course in relation to University and Episcopal authority the honesty of which might well be imitated by the Ritualists of the present day. If Keble's advice were adopted it would lead, in Dioceses under Protestant Bishops, to a wholesale resignation of livings by the Romanising clergy. At the same time there was in Keble's letter a defence of *Tract XC.* open to very grave objection. He frankly admitted, at the outset, that he was "himself responsible, as far as any one besides the actual writer can be, for the *Tract* on which so severe a condemnation has lately been pronounced by the Heads of Houses at Oxford; having seen it in proof, and strongly recommended its publication."[1] He even goes so far as to defend that part of *Tract XC.* which was generally considered one of its most offensive portions, and which the author withdrew in the second edition. He thought it quite right to speak of the Church of England as being "in bondage," working "in chains," and "teaching with the stammering lips of ambiguous formularies"; and he actually affirmed that "until English Churchmen generally sympathise" with Newman in such language, "I see no chance of our Church assuming her true position in Christendom, or of the mitigation of our present 'unhappy divisions.'"[2] "There appears," said Keble, "to be some chance of an authoritative prohibition of the view [of interpreting the Articles], which not this *Tract* only, but a whole army of writers, new and old, recommend: and it becomes a serious question, what ought to be the line of conduct adopted in such case by persons holding that view, and concerned in any way with subscription to the Articles."[3] This important question Keble discusses at considerable length.

"Suppose, *i.e.*," he asks, "that not the Heads of Houses, but the

---

[1] *The Case of Catholic Subscription to the Thirty-Nine Articles Considered.* By the Rev. John Keble. "London: 1841. Not Published," p. 6.
[2] *Ibid.* p. 10.   [3] *Ibid.* p. 12.

Academical Body in Convocation assembled, had determined that interpretations such as have been now (not for the first time), suggested, evade rather than explain the Articles, and are inconsistent with the duty of receiving and teaching them in good faith, to which the University, by express statute, binds her Tutors and other members; how would a College Tutor (to take the simplest case first) have to act under such circumstances, supposing him convinced that the condemned view is the right one? Would it not be a plain breach of a human trust, if he used the authority committed to him for the purpose of teaching that view? and of a still higher trust, if, in compliance with the academical law, he forbore to inculcate it?"[1]

To this question Keble's very proper answer was:—"Such persons would have been met at every turn by the recorded sentence of the University against them: in them it would have been no contumacy, but plain conscientiousness, to withdraw from an engagement which they could not religiously fulfil."[2] Passing from the Tutors to ordinary members of the University, Keble affirmed that "it would be matter of grave inquiry, whether any person, adhering to the Articles in the sense pointed out by the *Tract*, could with an unblemished conscience become a member of the University, or even, without dispensation, continue such. This doubt arises from the acknowledged rule of the best casuists, that all oaths and covenants imposed by a superior, and especially subscriptions required to Articles of religion, *are to be interpreted by the mind and purpose of the parties imposing, and in the sense which they intended.*"[3] According to this important principle, issued with the sanction of the leader of the Oxford Movement, no candidate for Ordination could sign the Thirty-Nine Articles, when imposed by the Bishop about to ordain him, except in the sense held by that Bishop. If this rule were adopted by modern Ritualists, many Romanising wolves would be kept out of the sheepfold of the Church of England.

Keble proceeded to discuss *Clerical* subscription to the Articles. On this he affirms that "The general principles

[1] *The Case of Catholic Subscription to the Thirty-Nine Articles Considered*, p. 13.
[2] *Ibid.* p. 16.
[3] *Ibid.* p. 17.

which regulate Academical subscription must of course be applicable to Clerical subscription likewise; only that all cases of conscience assume a deeper and more awful interest as they come nearer and nearer to the Most Holy Things":[1]—

"If a candidate for Holy Orders, or a clerk nominated to any dignity or cure, were distinctly warned, by the same authority which calls on him to subscribe the Articles, that the Catholic mode of interpreting them would be considered as 'evading their sense,' and 'defeating their object'; the act of signature would evidently amount to a pledge on his part against that mode of interpretation. If, in virtue of a preceding signature, he were already exercising his ministry, his going on, without protest, to do so, after such warning, would virtually come to the same thing: it would be equivalent, as I said before, to a continued signature; unless, indeed, he could obtain from the imposers express or implied dispensation for his own case, which would remove the sin, and, if made public, would remove the scandal also.

"But Clerical Subscription differs from Academical in this important respect: that it is not quite so easy to determine who are the real imposers of it, and what kind of declaration on their part is to be regarded as authoritative. Thus far, however, all Catholics will be agreed: that a Synodical determination of the Bishops of the Church of England, with or without the superadded warrant of the State (on whose prerogative in such cases I would refrain from here expressing any opinion) would be endued with unquestionable authority."[2]

Keble next proceeds to discuss the subject of Canonical Obedience to the Bishops; and here his views, I think, would certainly not, as a whole, be acceptable to his Ritualistic successors of the present day. If Keble could not conscientiously obey his Bishop, he would resign his preferments in the Church, and retire into lay communion, though he would not secede from the Church of England. His words are remarkable, and well worth quoting:—

"Next," he writes, "let it be well weighed how much the Oath of Canonical Obedience imports. No pledge can be more solemn or direct, than that under which we stand bound 'reverently to obey

---

[1] *The Case of Catholic Subscription to the Thirty-Nine Articles Considered*, p. 25.
[2] *Ibid.* pp. 26, 27.

our Ordinary, and other chief Ministers, unto whom is committed the charge and government over us; following with a glad mind and will their godly admonitions, and *submitting ourselves to their godly judgments.*' This latter clause appears to refer, more especially, to doctrinal decisions; and if to any, surely most especially to their explanation of the terms of the engagement, to which they themselves admitted us: as the Church's agents, it is true, and not in any wise by their own independent authority; yet as deliberative, responsible, highly trusted agents, endowed severally with powers of more than human origin, to enforce their 'godly judgments.' So that it would be a very strong step indeed, and one hardly conceivable, but in a case where the very foundation of the faith was unequivocally assailed, for a Catholic priest to go on ministering, when he knew that he was violating the conditions on which his Bishop would allow him to minister. It would be far different from insubordinate conduct here and there, in points of detail: *rather his whole clerical life would be one continued act of disobedience.* Who could endure such a burthen? *What labour could prosper, what blessing be looked for, under it?*"[1]

Keble, of course, was afraid lest the Convocation of the University and the Bishops should censure the line of argument adopted by Newman in *Tract XC.*, and, therefore, in writing his pamphlet he had the possibility of such a censure in view. Unfortunately for the cause of Reformation principles, his fears were groundless. Convocation had before it, on February 13, 1845, a proposition to adopt substantially the vote of censure passed by the Heads of Houses on March 16, 1841. It would, in all probability, have been carried, were it not that the Proctors (of whom the late Dean Church was one), vetoed it. Although most of the Bishops in their charges censured *Tract XC.*, no united declaration against its mischievous principles was issued by the Episcopal Bench. Dr. Pusey issued a bulky pamphlet of 217 pages in defence of *Tract XC.*, in which he strongly advocated the Reunion of Christendom, both East and West. "Who knows," he asked, "but that He who raises us up, may purify Rome too, and St. Peter be the type of the Church of St. Peter, and her Lord yet cast His gracious look

---

[1] *The Case of Catholic Subscription to the Thirty-Nine Articles Considered*, pp. 28, 29.

upon her, and she weep bitterly her fall; and she, being 'converted,' 'strengthen' her 'brethren,' *and deserve to be restored to the pre-eminence*, which, while she deserved, she had."[1] Pusey, in this pamphlet, censured many of the corruptions of Rome, more especially her worship of the Virgin, and the Indulgences granted by the Papal Court. But, as to the *Tract* itself, he declares:—" I have felt no doubt, carefully and conscientiously examining both editions of the *Tract*, that the meaning in which our friend would have them [Thirty-Nine Articles] construed, in conformity and subordination to the teaching of the Catholic Church, is not only *an* admissible, but *the* most legitimate interpretation of them."[2]

Later on in the year, the Rev. C. P. Golightly, of Oriel College, who had been one of the most active workers in getting up the agitation against *Tract XC.*, issued a short pamphlet of nineteen pages on the subject, in which he ably exposed some of Newman's misquotations in the *Tract*, as also the alterations made by him in the second edition. It is remarkable that Manning (afterwards Cardinal), who had become a High Churchman before *Tract XC.* was issued, never approved of its leading principles. Mr. A. W. Hutton, M.A., in his biography of Cardinal Manning, tells us that "Manning never got over the dislike he entertained for *Tract XC.* It always seemed to him of doubtful honesty. When, in the autumn of 1845, after his return from his first visit to Döllinger at Munich, Mr. Gladstone, much perturbed by the grave series of secessions from the Church of England, asked Manning if any one principle could be found that would explain them, the latter said, after reflection:—'Yes; *want of truth.*' At a much later time he said that he thought he must have had in his mind the impression of dishonesty produced by the shifty arguments of the last *Tract*."[3]

In 1845, the Rev. W. Simcox Bricknell, M.A., Incum-

---

[1] *The Articles Treated on in Tract XC. Reconsidered, and their Interpretation Vindicated.* By the Rev. E. B. Pusey, D.D., p. 183.
[2] *Ibid.* p. 148.
[3] *Cardinal Manning.* By Arthur W. Hutton, M.A., p. 252. London: 1894.

bent of Grove, published a thick volume of 753 pages, with the title of *The Judgment of the Bishops upon Tractarian Theology*. It consisted mainly of lengthy extracts from the Charges of the Bishops from 1837 to 1842 inclusive, and was enriched by many useful notes from the pen of Mr. Bricknell himself. From this volume I give the following expressions of Episcopal opinion on *Tract XC.* :—

BISHOP OF HEREFORD (Dr. Musgrave):—" Nothing better, in fact, as all such persons must well know, than sophistry and evasion, could be brought in support of such a thesis. And certainly both are employed in the *Tract*, in as ample measure as any one could be disposed to anticipate." [1]

"In fact, throughout the whole *Tract*, but more especially upon this point [the 'attempt to distinguish between the Romish doctrine, as established by the Decrees of the Council of Trent, and "the authoritative teaching" of the Church of Rome at the time'], the dishonest casuistry to which the Jesuits have given a name, is employed upon a scale to which it would be hard to find a parallel, except in the more notorious of their own writings." [2]

BISHOP OF GLOUCESTER AND BRISTOL (Dr. Monk) :—" The perusal of the *Remarks upon the Thirty-Nine Articles* has filled me with astonishment and concern. The ostensible object of this *Tract* is to show that a person adopting the doctrines of the Council of Trent, with the single exception of the Pope's Supremacy, might sincerely and conscientiously sign the Articles of the Church of England. But the real object at which the writer seems to be labouring, is to prove that the differences in doctrine which separate the Churches of England and Rome will, upon examination, vanish. Upon this point much ingenuity, and, I am forced to add, much sophistry is exerted, and I think exerted in vain." [3]

BISHOP OF EXETER (Dr. Phillpotts) :—" The tone of the *Tract*, as it respects our own Church, is offensive and indecent; as it regards the Reformation and our Reformers, absurd, as well as incongruous and unjust. Its principles of interpreting our Articles I cannot but deem most unsound; the reasoning with which it supports its principles, sophistical; the averments on which it founds its reasoning, at variance with recorded facts." [4]

---

[1] Bricknell's *Judgment of the Bishops*, p. 81.
[2] *Ibid.* p. 85.
[3] *Ibid.* p. 537.
[4] *Ibid.* p. 547.

"This is by far the most daring attempt ever yet made by a Minister of the Church of England to neutralise the distinctive doctrines of our Church, and to make us symbolise with Rome."[1]

BISHOP OF LLANDAFF (Dr. Copleston):—"To speak of the language of the Articles as being capable of two or more senses, and to teach that the subscriber may therefore take them in his own sense, knowing at the same time that the authority which requires his assent understands them in another, is surely a dishonest course, tending to corrupt the conscience, and to destroy all confidence between man and man."[2]

BISHOP OF LONDON (Dr. Blomfield):—"The endeavour to give a Tridentine colouring to the Articles of Religion agreed upon by the Council of London in 1562, and to extenuate the essential differences between the two Churches, is a ground of no unreasonable alarm to those whose bounden duty it is to 'banish and drive away all erroneous and strange doctrines,' and therefore to guard against the insinuation into our Church of any one of those false opinions which she has once solemnly repudiated. It is one of the methods by which the Court of Rome has before sought to beguile the people of this country of their common sense. Bishop Stillingfleet quotes a letter of advice given to a Romish agent, as to the best way of managing the Papal interest in England upon the King's restoration: the third head of which is:—

"'To make it appear, underhand, how near the doctrine, worship, and discipline of the Church of England comes to us (of Rome); at how little distance her Common Prayer is from our Mass; and that the wisest and ablest men of that way (the Anglican) are so moderate, that they would willingly come over to us, or at least meet us half way. Hereby the more staid men will become more odious, and others will run out of all religion for fear of Popery.'"[3]

---

[1] Bricknell's *Judgment of the Bishops*, p. 550.
[2] *Ibid.* p. 559.
[3] *Ibid.* pp. 563, 564.

CHAPTER VII

> Mr. Golightly's letters to the *Standard*—His serious charges against Ward and Bloxam—Palmer of Magdalen anathematises Protestantism—Startling revelations—Mr. Ambrose Phillipps de Lisle—A secret Papal emissary to the Oxford Romanisers—De Lisle intimate with and trusted by the Oxford leaders—Newman's Correspondence with De Lisle—De Lisle hopes to introduce some foreign Theologians to his Oxford friends—He promises to be "prudent and reserved"—Bloxam's fear of publicity—De Lisle's extraordinary letter to his wife—The Oxford men wish "to come to an understanding with the Pope at once"—Their proposals to be sent to the Pope—The Fathers of Charity—A startling suggestion—Cordial meetings at Oxford between the Tractarians and Romanists—Negotiations with Wiseman and Rome—Wiseman visits Oxford—Has an interview with Newman—Wiseman writes to Rome for secret instruction and guidance—He desires to become "the organ of intercourse" between Rome and Oxford—A secret conspiracy—De Lisle's letter to Lord Shrewsbury—It is necessary "to blind" the Low Church party—"Throwing dust in the eyes of Low Churchmen"—"Unpleasant disclosures" in the papers—"A holy reserve"—Ward's double dealing—Remains in the Church of England "to bring many towards Rome"—The ultimate aim "submission to Rome."

EVENTS of great interest were taking place while the controversy as to *Tract XC.* was at its height, of which the English public knew at the time but little or nothing. It is true the veil was partly lifted by the Rev. C. P. Golightly, in the columns of the *Standard*, but his revelations were laughed to scorn by his opponents, as utterly unworthy of credit. Time, however, has served to prove that Mr. Golightly was a truthful witness, for the accuracy of his exposure of Tractarian tactics and underground proceedings, has been amply proved by the biographies of Cardinal Wiseman, Mr. Ambrose Phillipps de Lisle, the Rev. W. G. Ward, and others. In a letter to the *Standard*, dated November 12, 1841, over the signature of "A Master of Arts," Mr. Golightly brought charges of Romanising against certain members of the University, whose names he did not give; thereupon he was challenged by a "D.D. of the University of Oxford," and by the Rev. George Stanley Faber, Master of Sherburn Hospital, and himself a decided Protestant, to give his own name to the public, and also the names of those against whom he had brought such serious charges. In reply to these challenges, Mr. Golightly, over his own proper signature, wrote another letter to the *Standard*, dated November 26th, in which, after thanking those who had challenged him for doing so, he continued:—

"My statement, in allusion to a paragraph which had appeared in the *Morning Post*, was as follows:—

"'I do not insinuate, but I assert, that there is good reason for supposing that there are about ten Members of this University, who, instead of fighting "under their proper banner," have hoisted the flag of Anglicanism, and, under those false colours, are taking advantage of their respective positions, as Fellows of Colleges and Clergymen of the Established Church, to propagate "Romanism," and *oppose* "primitive views."'

"I likewise made a statement respecting the conduct of a Fellow of Balliol, and a Fellow of Magdalen, which I shall repeat in the course of my letter....

"The first witness that I shall cite is the Rev. W. Ward, Fellow of Balliol College, and an intimate friend of Mr. Newman's, who, in the course of the present month, told a friend of mine, opposed to him in opinions, and not in confidential conversation, that a certain party in this place [Oxford University] might now be considered to be divided into disciples of Mr. Newman and disciples of Dr. Pusey —the latter opposed, the former no longer opposed to Rome....

"I now repeat the assertion in my former letter, that the Rev. W. Ward, Fellow of Balliol, was a visitor of Dr. Wiseman's, at Oscott, during the last long vacation (I do not determine the length of his visit), and that the Rev. J. Bloxam, Fellow of Magdalen, was the individual who introduced Mr. Sibthorp to Dr. Wiseman. Previously to his visit to Oscott, Mr. Ward had expressed opinions which induced the Master of Balliol to deprive him of his Mathematical Lectureship, and the Bishop of London to forbid his officiating in his diocese.

"I have also to inform the public, that a Roman Catholic Bishop has been staying at the Mitre Inn, at Oxford, and receiving visits from several Members of the University. Upon communicating this fact to an individual in authority, I found that he had already learned, from other sources of information, that one certainly, perhaps two Romish Bishops had been returning the visits of their friend or friends. . . .

"After what I have written, your readers will not be surprised at the following sayings and doings of some of the more extravagant of the party. A Fellow of Exeter has expressed his belief, that seven years hence the Churches of England and Rome will be reunited; some cross themselves in public worship, others make genuflections, others openly praise the Jesuits, talk of *Saint* Ignatius Loyola, have plans for taming refractory Bishops, and talk over what they shall do, in their day of triumph, with the clergy who reject their views."[1]

The only members of the Romanising party who replied to Mr. Golightly's charges were Ward himself, one of the accused parties, and the Rev. William Palmer of Magdalen College, who must not be confounded with the Rev. William Palmer of Worcester College. Ward frankly admitted that he had paid a visit to Oscott, but he did not add that it was his second visit[2]—Golightly apparently did not know that there had been a previous visit. Ward challenged the accuracy of two or three of Golightly's statements, yet substantially he admitted that they were correct. In acknowledging that he had paid a visit to the Roman Catholic College at Oscott, he explained that he "carefully abstained from taking part in any of their services";[3] yet at the same time he admitted "the very favourable impression produced on my mind by all that I saw there."[4]

Mr. Palmer, who, after several years spent in vain efforts to promote Reunion with the Eastern Churches, afterwards became a Roman Catholic, replied to Mr. Golightly in a published *Letter*, which contained some statements which created quite a sensation:—"I trust," said Mr. Palmer, "others have still stronger grounds for

---

[1] *Correspondence Illustrative of the Actual State of Oxford with Reference to Tractarianism*, pp. 8-13. Oxford: 1842.
[2] *William George Ward and the Oxford Movement*, p. 191.
[3] *Correspondence Illustrative of the Actual State of Oxford*, p. 20.
[4] *Ibid.* p. 19.

viewing and representing it [the Church of England] as a branch of the One Catholic and Apostolic Church, essentially opposed to the principle of general Protestantism, and essentially one with all other Churches of kindred origin, both Greek and Latin."[1]

"Certainly I am for no middle ways," continued Mr. Palmer, "as you will understand when I tell you plainly, that for myself, I utterly reject and anathematise the principle of Protestantism as a heresy, with all its forms, sects, or denominations. And if the Church of England should ever unhappily profess herself to be a form of Protestantism (which may God of His infinite mercy forbid!) then I would reject and anathematise the Church of England, and would separate myself from her immediately as from a human sect, without giving Protestants any unnecessary trouble to procure my expulsion."[2]

"If to desire the restoration of unity with those Churches, and above all with the Church of Rome itself, be Popery, then I for one am a Papist from the very bottom of my soul; but I beg you to take notice at the same time that my Popery is of a kind which takes in not only the Churches now in actual communion with Rome, but also the Eastern Catholic Churches, and the British, if their Protestant members will allow me still to call them Catholic. In conclusion, I once more publicly profess myself a Catholic and a member of the Catholic Church, *and say anathema to the principles of Protestantism* (which I regard as identical with the principle of Dissent), and to all its forms, sects, and denominations, especially to those of the Lutherans and Calvinists, and British and American Dissenters. Likewise to all persons, who *knowingly and willingly, and understanding what they do*, shall assert either for themselves or for the Church of England the principle of Protestantism, or maintain the Church of England to have one and the same common religion with any or all of the various forms and sects of Protestantism, or shall communicate themselves in the temples of the Protestant sects, or give the communion to their members, or go about to establish any intercommunion between our Church and them, otherwise than by bringing them, in the first instance, to renounce their errors and promise a true obedience for the future to the entire faith and discipline of the Catholic and Apostolical Episcopate—to all such I say, *Anathema!*"[3]

---

[1] *A Letter to the Rev. C. P. Golightly.* By William Palmer, M.A., Fellow and Tutor of Magdalen College, p. 7. Oxford: Parker. 1842.
[2] *Ibid.* pp. 9, 10.
[3] *Ibid.* pp. 12, 13.

I may here be permitted to point out that the argument against the Protestantism of the Church of England, based on the omission of the *word* "Protestant" from her formularies, is valueless to the Ritualists. The word on which *they* pride themselves is "Catholic," which of course is also claimed by all true Protestants. Yet this much-prized word "Catholic" *is never found in the New Testament.* Would the Ritualists, I may ask, think me justified in asserting that the "Catholic" religion is not to be found in the New Testament, because the *word* "Catholic" is not found there? I am sure they would never allow that my argument was valid. They would reply that, if the *word* "Catholic" was not there, the *thing* itself was there from beginning to end, and that therefore the New Testament teaches the Catholic religion. But, surely, the argument which the Ritualist would think good for himself, is equally valid for the Protestant Churchman? We argue that if the *word* "Protestant" is not to be found in the Book of Common Prayer, the *thing* itself is there in abundance from cover to cover. In their assertions of Protestant doctrines, and in their protests against Rome and Romanism, the Book of Common Prayer and the Thirty-Nine Articles are amongst the most strongly Protestant documents in the whole world. The historical argument in favour of the Protestantism of the Church of England is ably brought out in a valuable pamphlet by the late Dr. Fleming, entitled *The Church of England is Protestant.*[1]

We must go back to the month of March 1841 for the origin of the Romanising work in part only revealed by Mr. Golightly. Some startling revelations of what then took place have recently been published in the *Life and Letters of Ambrose Phillipps de Lisle*, who in later life changed his name. In 1841 he was known as Mr. Ambrose Lisle Phillipps. He was, as already stated, a county squire residing at Grace Dieu Manor, Leicestershire, of considerable wealth, who in his boyhood had seceded to the Church of Rome,

---

[1] *The Church of England is Protestant:* Historical Testimony to Her Protestantism. By J. P. Fleming, D.C.L., pp. 26. London: Church Association Office.

in 1825, when he was only sixteen years of age. From the birth of the Oxford Movement young Mr. Phillipps took the deepest interest in its proceedings, expecting great things for the Church of Rome from its operations. To help on the Oxford Movement became the great object of his life. Early in 1841 he became, in reality, though not in name, Bishop Wiseman's secret emissary to the leaders of the Movement residing in the University of Oxford; and the medium of communicating their wishes and hopes, through Wiseman, to the Pope himself. His biography, written by Mr. E. S. Purcell, author of the *Life of Cardinal Manning*, is very open indeed in its surprising revelations. Mr. Purcell tells us that :—

"The personal influence of so zealous a Catholic as De Lisle, his sympathy with the Movement and reverence for its leaders, was recognised and felt at Oxford. He was on intimate terms with many of them, with whom he corresponded fully and freely; *he was trusted by their illustrious Leader*, who in many letters of the highest interest discussed the points at issue between the Anglican Church and the Church of Rome. With no other Catholic was Newman *on terms of such intimacy; to no one else did he open his heart so fully* or explain so candidly the motives which guided his conduct or line of action as Leader of the Movement. To no one did he disclose more unreservedly perhaps than to De Lisle the difficulties which stood in the way of reunion, or of the restoration of unity of faith. *For Newman it was easier perhaps to explain to a Catholic than to his immediate disciples the necessity of restraint or of caution* imposed upon him by external circumstances: by fear, on the one hand, of exciting in the University Protestant suspicions; of arousing the ire of the Bishops; or, on the other, of giving scandal to the more timid among his own disciples *by too open an avowal of Catholic principles.*"[1]

This statement shows the importance to be attached to De Lisle's work at Oxford. Newman trusted him more, and more fully opened up to him his secret plans, than to either Pusey or Keble, or any other of his friends in the Church of England. And it is evident to any one reading De Lisle's biography that he was trusted and consulted by most of the other more prominent members

[1] *Life and Letters of Ambrose Phillipps de Lisle*, vol. i. p. 198.

of Newman's followers. One of the chief agents in preparing the way for De Lisle's early visits to Oxford was the Rev. J. R. Bloxam, then Newman's Curate, who was most anxious to promote the Reunion of England and Rome, but who remained within the Church of England until his death nearly fifty years later.

De Lisle was first brought into intimate relations with the leaders of the Oxford Movement early in 1841. On the first Sunday in Lent of that year he sent word to Bloxam that he hoped to visit Oxford in Easter week:—

"I hope," he told Bloxam, "*to be the means of introducing to Oxford some foreign Theologians* who, I assure you, thoroughly appreciate the Catholic Movement there, who admire your admirable treatises, who fully understand the difficulty of your position, who see that humanly speaking the great result to which we look must be distant, the fruit of much labour, much patience, much tribulation, but who feel that God holds in his hands the hearts of men, and that to humble, earnest, believing prayer he will refuse nothing. *In working out our grand object you will find me*, and those whom I hope in a *second* visit to present to the acquaintance both of yourself and your friends, *prudent and reserved;* in fact we shall put ourselves unreservedly in your hands—our only object is to serve you for the love of Jesus Christ, and *for the love of our Catholic Mother*."[1]

Newman at this time entered into confidential correspondence with De Lisle, and also with the Rev. Dr. Russell, of Maynooth College. The latter correspondence was first published in the *Irish Monthly* for September 1892. Of Dr. Russell, Newman says, "He had, perhaps, more to do with my conversion than any one else."[2] Newman saw great difficulties in the way of Reunion. The lack of personal holiness in the Roman Church was one difficulty; the existence of Protestantism in the Anglican Church was another. "This I feel," he wrote on February 25, 1841, "most strongly and cannot conceal it, viz., that while Rome is what she is union is impossible. That we too must change I cannot deny."[3] Mr. Bloxam

---

[1] *Life and Letters of Ambrose Phillipps de Lisle*, vol. i. pp. 203, 204.
[2] Newman's *Apologia*, p. 317.
[3] *Life and Letters of Ambrose Phillipps de Lisle*, vol. i. p. 205.

was fearful lest the public should learn what was going on, and therefore he wrote to De Lisle, shortly before the latter gentleman's visit to Oxford:—" Let me beg of you to consider as most confidential and private whatever may have passed between us. Much mischief has been done by the mention of names."[1] Mr. Purcell says that "Bloxam was the most cautious and timid of men, unwilling to commit himself, a living and moving secret."[2]

At length De Lisle paid his long expected visit to Oxford, and was received with open arms by the Romanisers. To his wife, on May 5th, he related with great joy what up to that date he had seen and heard:—

"You can have no idea," wrote De Lisle, "to what an extent the Catholic Movement in this University has gone; it is impossible to judge of it by printed publications. One thing astonished and delighted me. They have lately printed (*but not published*) a beautiful translation of the Roman Breviary in English, with everything precisely as it is in the Latin. The *Hail Mary* full length, the *Confiteor*, the *Salve Regina, Sancta Maria succurre miseris*, &c., with not an expression changed!!! Is not this wonderful? Nothing can be more determined than they are to reunite their Church to the Catholic; but they will not hear of individuals joining us from *them, though they wish us to convert as many Dissenters as possible;* and they are very glad to hear of Dr. Gentili's doings in that way—even I think they do not object to our converting such of the Church of England as do not hold Catholic views, but they deprecate any noise about it, and above all they deprecate anything like warfare against the Church of England herself. . . . MANY HERE WOULD LIKE TO COME TO AN UNDERSTANDING WITH THE POPE AT ONCE, THAT SO THEY MIGHT BE IN ACTIVE COMMUNION WITH HIM, AND YET REMAIN IN THE CHURCH OF ENGLAND TO LABOUR FOR THE RECONCILIATION OF THEIR WHOLE CHURCH. This is to be taken into solemn consideration; I proposed to them last night that Father Rosmini should come to England and visit Oxford with me *with a view to conveying their sentiments to the Pope himself.* The proposition was well received; but nothing is settled, nor will be yet."[3]

---

[1] *Life and Letters of Ambrose Phillipps de Lisle*, vol. i. p. 216.
[2] *Ibid.* p. 244.
[3] *Ibid.* pp. 248, 249.

The startling expression of opinion, which I have here printed in capitals, seems almost incredible. "It is difficult to conceive," says Mr. Purcell, in commenting on it, "that any of his [De Lisle's] friends at Oxford of sober judgment could have seriously discussed such a plan as that of being in active communion with the Pope, and at the same time remaining in the Church of England."[1] But he does not *deny* that it was seriously discussed; on the contrary, he evidently thinks such a discussion really did take place, for he continues thus: "But we must remember that the Queen herself is always a member of the Scotch Kirk when over the Border, and this without scandal or question of propriety.[2] From the standpoint of the Roman theologian this would, of course, be absolutely unwarrantable, but from the English standpoint of habitual compromise in matters of religion *it is not after all so very startling*, once granted the High Church preamble that the Established Church is essentially Catholic and only accidentally Protestant. And De Lisle's whole plan of action was to foster and encourage every Catholic tendency and move amongst Anglicans, leaving it to the grace of God to correct and harmonise inconsistencies and shortcomings."

In accordance with the principle here laid down by his biographer, De Lisle did "foster and encourage" the traitorous wishes of these Tractarians. Very naturally Mr. Purcell tries to whitewash his own communion, by declaring that "from the standpoint of the Roman theologian this would, of course, be absolutely unwarrantable"; yet, for all this whitewashing, the startling fact remains that the proposal was made, first of all, not by the Tractarians, but by *a Roman Catholic layman*, even De Lisle himself; and it looks very much as though the Jesuitical proposal he made was fostered and actively assisted by no less a "Roman theologian" than Bishop Wiseman!

In proof of this I call attention to the following facts. Mr. Wilfrid Ward, the Roman Catholic biographer of his

---

[1] *Life and Letters of Ambrose Phillipps de Lisle*, vol. i. p. 249.
[2] But she is not *secretly* a member of the Scotch Kirk.

father, the Rev. W. G. Ward, after relating how Mr. Bloxam and De Lisle (or Phillipps) first met by accident, tells us that thereupon—

"A friendship was struck up, and Mr. Bloxam invited him [Phillipps] to Oxford. Here he met Mr. Ward. Zeal for the Reunion of Churches was on both sides a bond of sympathy, and the two men sat up half the night on their first introduction discussing the prospects of Christendom. Mr. Ward was invited to meet a party of Catholics at Grace Dieu, to visit Oscott, and to see the Cistercian Monastery of Mount St. Bernard's. *Informal communications were also opened with Bishop Wiseman.* The conditions of reunion were discussed. *The schemes proposed were Utopian*, and many who were eager for them have in the event remained staunch Anglicans. But they were a witness to the irritation caused by the action of the Heads and Bishops, and to its tendency to drive men towards Rome. Mr. Ward himself, while deeply interested in the subject, was persistent in his opposition to any sudden step, and for a time at least urged that members of both Churches should confine their energies to the reform of the abuses which disfigured each. . . . *Mr. Phillipps had* URGED *that the Fathers of Charity, the Order of the great Italian Reformer Antonio Rosmini*, then represented in England by the excellent and pious Father Gentili, SHOULD OPEN THEIR ORDER AT ONCE TO THE OXFORD SCHOOL, *and adapt its rules to their position and antecedents.*"[1]

Now this was, no doubt, a very daring proposal of De Lisle's. It was nothing less than that the Tractarians should at once become Roman Catholics, and thus, according to his scheme (to quote again his letter to his wife on May 5th), they would "come to an understanding with the Pope at once, that so they might be in active communion with him, *and yet remain in the Church of England* to labour for the reconciliation of their whole Church." Mr. Edwin De Lisle, himself a Roman Catholic, who edited Purcell's *Life* of his father, says:—"From the high Continuity point of view, however, there does not appear to be any valid reason why clergymen upon becoming reconciled to the Holy See should *resign* their livings. They would only be reverting to the position of such admired Church-

---

[1] *William George Ward and the Oxford Movement*, pp. 190, 191.

men as Archbishop Theodore, Stephen Langton, Grosteste, Alfred the Great, or Edward the Confessor. It would *probably* be the duty of their Bishops to *deprive* them."[1] Mr. Wilfrid Ward says that the scheme "resulted only in opportunities for cordial meetings between the Oxonians and the friends of Mr. Phillipps and Father Gentili. The idea itself met with no encouragement from Newman or from the responsible leaders of the party."[2] It is evident to any one who reads De Lisle's *Life* that *he*, at any rate, was under the impression that his scheme was approved by some of the responsible leaders, though not the most prominent of them. It will be remembered that, on the first Sunday of Lent in this year, De Lisle promised Bloxam: "I hope myself to be the means of introducing to Oxford some foreign Theologians." This Father Gentili was one of them. Again, on May 3rd, during his interview with these Oxford conspirators, De Lisle proposed to them "that Father Rosmini should come to England and visit Oxford with me, with a view to conveying their sentiments to the Pope." Rosmini, it seems, did not go to Oxford at that time, but the representative of the Order of which he was head (the Institute of Charity), did go to Oxford, and Mr. Wilfrid Ward shows him to us as present at "cordial meetings" between the Tractarian conspirators and De Lisle. No doubt they discussed together De Lisle's proposal that this Roman Catholic Order of Monks should "open their Order *at once* to the Oxford School." Ward seems to have been in no hurry to adopt the scheme, though he certainly did not object to it, for later on in the year he wrote to De Lisle, on October 28th:—"All this being so, *your* kind communication about the Order of Charity is of less certain and *immediate* importance than it otherwise might be; *though, of course, it might become of the most pressing interest* any single day."[3]

But, as we have seen, the Oxford Tractarians and Father Gentili were not the only persons consulted. "Informal

---

[1] *Life and Letters of Ambrose Phillipps de Lisle*, vol. i. p. 284, *note*.
[2] *William George Ward and the Oxford Movement*, p. 191.
[3] *Ibid.* p. 195.

communications were opened with Bishop Wiseman." These were no ordinary schemes that were proposed to him, but were of a most extraordinary kind. "The schemes proposed," says Mr. W. Ward, "*were Utopian.*" How did Wiseman treat these "Utopian" schemes? Did he reject them as monstrous and impossible, as embodying proposals the Church of Rome could never assent to? There is nothing to show that he acted in this way. On the contrary, all the evidence tends to prove that he became a party to the conspiracy, and gave it his active assistance. Mr. Purcell states that:—

"In these discussions at Oxford *Bishop Wiseman took a lively interest.* But since his conversations with the Oxford men were of a confidential character, De Lisle took care in his communications with Bishop Wiseman not to divulge the more intimate facts or names which had been given to him, *but gave a general purport or outline of his interviews.* Mr. Bloxam was especially careful *to warn De Lisle against letting the fact be known that they were holding direct communications with Catholics.* Bishop Wiseman was fully alive to the value of personal influence, from De Lisle's signal success with the Oxford Divines, *and gladly accepted his offer of a personal introduction to some of the Oxford Leaders.* Bishop Wiseman had already expressed his anxious desire to be in communication with some of the Oxford Divines, but as he wrote to De Lisle he feared embarrassing them by any intercourse, as, should it be known, it would be immediately thrown in their faces." [1]

De Lisle sent word to Bloxam that Wiseman desired to visit Oxford, but Bloxam was timid about it. He said that to himself the visit of "so learned and celebrated a theologian" would be "personally delightful"; [2] but he thought, apparently, that it would scarcely be discreet. Failing to gain Bloxam's consent to the proposed visit, De Lisle informed Newman of Wiseman's desire to visit Oxford and to meet him there. But Newman's subtle mind led him to suggest a way out of the difficulty, which is thus described by Mr. Purcell:—" Newman having a grave objection to receiving Catholics *in the University*, especially a Catholic of such eminence as Bishop Wise-

[1] *Life and Letters of Ambrose Phillipps de Lisle*, vol. i. p. 260.
[2] *Ibid.* p. 261.

man, proposed meeting *in the city of Oxford.*"[1] Accordingly it was arranged that Wiseman should visit Oxford, and there meet Newman; not, however, in the *University*, but in the *city!* "The meeting of two such men," continues Mr. Purcell, "as the leader of the Oxford Movement and the representative champion of the Catholic cause, was an event which appealed to the hearts of both men. Each was frank, candid, and outspoken. Without, however, entering into confidential relations, Wiseman left a favourable impression on Newman's mind."[2] It seems that during this visit Wiseman had an interview with Dr. Pusey. Writing to Lord Shrewsbury, on May 6th, De Lisle remarks:—"I hope Bishop Wiseman was not rude in his manner towards Dr. Pusey the other day, —if he was, he will have done more to keep hundreds of Anglicans (I speak advisedly) back than all my courtesy and charity towards them has done."[3]

But before his visit to Oxford Wiseman had sent to Rome full particulars of what was going on. Referring to the end of April 1841, his biographer says that:— "Wiseman's sanguine temperament was now fired with hopes which those who knew Newman well would not have encouraged. His next plan was to communicate further with the Holy See through his old friend Cardinal Mai, and obtain instructions with a view to *a possibly immediate reconciliation* of Newman and his friends *to Rome.*"[4] Earlier in the month of April, on Good Friday (the 9th), Wiseman had announced his intention of writing to Rome on this subject. There was no need to write to Rome for "instructions for *a possibly immediate* reconciliation" of the Tractarians, if that reconciliation were to be of the ordinary kind. Wiseman knew very well how to receive perverts from the Church of England into the Church of Rome, and required no "instructions" on such a very simple matter. But we can understand that he would very much need "instructions" how to act for "an immediate reconcilia-

---

[1] *Life and Letters of Ambrose Phillipps de Lisle*, vol. i. p. 262.
[2] *Ibid.* p. 262. [3] *Ibid.* p. 280.
[4] *Life and Times of Cardinal Wiseman*, vol. i. p. 391.

tion" with Rome on the lines laid down by De Lisle in his letter to his wife. Only the Pope could grant the Tractarians permission to be "in active communion with him, and yet remain in the Church of England to labour for the reconciliation of their whole Church"; only the Pope could facilitate De Lisle's proposal that the "Fathers of Charity" should "open their Order *at once* to the Oxford School, and adapt its rules to their position and antecedents." What else could Wiseman have had in view than some such secret scheme as this, when he wrote as follows to De Lisle, on Good Friday:—

"I feel that the state of things in England ought to be made known to the Holy Father. On these grounds I have thought of writing a full account of all that is going forward, to one of the discreetest members of the S. College, Card. Mai, *with a request that he will show what I write to none but the Pope*. I would not mention names beyond those publicly known, as Newman's, but would even suppress his name, when referring to what he has privately written. But I will not send off anything till I hear from you, and have your permission *thus secretly* to apply what I know from you for the public good in this way. Let me know that the Vicegerent of Christ approves of my course and understands my motives, and I shall not care for all the world, nor allow differences of opinion to check my exertions"[1]

On May 7th, only two days after De Lisle's startling letter to his wife, already quoted, Wiseman wrote again to him on the same subject, and headed his letter, "Most Confidential":—

"Your last letter has indeed filled me with consolation, and sincere joy. I shall not fail in a second letter to communicate its contents to the Holy Father through Cardinal Mai. But I foresee that it will be almost necessary for me during the vacation to run to Rome. Indeed, I think it probable I shall be desired to do so—AS ANY COMMUNICATION ON THE SUBJECT IN QUESTION IS TOO DELICATE TO BE MADE OTHERWISE THAN ORALLY. Moreover, there are too many other matters on which it would be advisable to have a more intimate communication with *the Holy See*, and as for myself I feel the serious

---

[1] *Life and Times of Cardinal Wiseman*, vol. i. p. 387.

responsibility of becoming (as I at the same time earnestly desire to become) *the organ of intercourse between it and our Oxford friends*, without clear and DISTINCT INSTRUCTIONS, such as I feel cannot be satisfactorily given except on full explanations, and BY WORD OF MOUTH. Again I should like something to emanate from the Pope towards encouraging our views—recommending mildness, prayer, calling on the Bishops for Reforms, &c., and particularly checking all alliance with Dissenters. All this I could probably get done by going on the spot, but not otherwise. I have entered on this matter to ask you what you think of such a plan—*no one, of course, must know of it*. I would go to Paris, and so on to Rome—the Bishop only knowing my plan. He is now in London, so that if you can come over I could see you alone. I must mention that, though I have not said anything to him about your last letter, I have found it necessary to consult *one* most prudent person *under Confessional secrecy*, because I find some advice necessary for my own guidance."[1]

Again, we may well ask *what* could that subject be (if not secret reception into the Church of Rome) any communication as to which to Rome was "too delicate to be made otherwise than orally"; and on which "distinct instructions" could only be given satisfactorily by the "Holy See," and "by word of mouth"? It seems beyond doubt, too, that Wiseman saw nothing morally wrong in such an act of deception, for he actively helped the scheme on which De Lisle had at heart, and even thought it possible that the Pope would grant the permission so earnestly desired. Who, I may well ask, can reasonably blame Protestants, now that so much has been revealed by the Romanists themselves, for taking this view of this secret Conspiracy to bring back England to Rome by unworthy and Jesuitical methods? Of course Wiseman would have preferred that these Tractarian Divines should *publicly* join the Church of Rome there and then; but if they would not come over in that open way, then some other course must be adopted. But whether De Lisle's plans were actually sanctioned at Rome is more than we can definitely say. If they were adopted, however, we may be quite sure that not the slightest trace of it would be permitted to find

[1] *Life and Letters of Ambrose de Lisle*, vol. i. p. 255. *Life and Times of Cardinal Wiseman*, vol. i. pp. 391, 392.

its way into any Roman Catholic biography of the present time. The marvel is that so much has been allowed to come out into the light of day; but I have very little doubt that the authorities of the Papacy in England are far from pleased at the revelations made public in the *Life and Letters of Ambrose Phillipps de Lisle*. What has appeared should certainly open the eyes of Englishmen, and make them anxious to know what is going on underneath the surface at the present time. Negotiations with Rome have been going on, at intervals, ever since 1841, and for all we know we may, at the present moment, be sleeping on the brink of a volcano, which may burst forth at any time, casting spiritual desolation and death around.

There were two other prominent Roman Catholics to whom the secret proceedings going on at Oxford were partly revealed by De Lisle, viz., Lord Shrewsbury and Cardinal Acton. To the former he wrote on May 30, 1841, clearly revealing the Jesuitical cunning of his Tractarian friends:—

"I have been," wrote De Lisle, "for some time now engaged in close correspondence with some of the leaders of the Catholic party at Oxford, to which I can only allude in general terms, as it is strictly confidential; it has, however, been communicated by me to our dear friend *Bishop Wiseman* (*who perfectly concurs with me in everything*) for the purpose of being *in the strictest secrecy* forwarded to Cardinal Mai, *to be by his Eminence communicated to the Holy Father, and to no one else upon any account whatever*. As I said, I cannot at present enter into particulars, but of this you may rest assured, that the reunion of the Churches is certain. Mr. Newman has lately received the adhesion of several hundreds of the Clergy: this is publicly known, and therefore I may state it. Meanwhile the Dissenting party is on the alert, and though they are by no means aware of the extent to which things have gone, they are apprehensive of something: and as they are joined, politically at least, by the Low Church Party, WE FIND IT NECESSARY TO BLIND THEM, the more so as we are not ready to act yet, and probably shall not be for the next three years at earliest. This will account for the great stress still laid by the Oxford men on *practical abuses* supposed to exist in the communion of the Catholic Church: not that I mean to say they do not feel what they state in reference to these (for I know that even they are moved by old prejudices), but feeling as they do, they put it forward more prominently perhaps than they otherwise would do, FOR THE PURPOSE OF THROWING DUST IN THE EYES OF THE DISSENTERS AND THE LOW CHURCH MEN.

"I am very glad you are coming back to England next year. I assure you, if things go on as I expect, you will be wanted then. Meanwhile I beseech you to give us all the assistance you can. *Urge at Rome the necessity* of immense prudence and forbearance, to do everything to encourage, not to damp; *not to call upon these men to quit their own communion to join ours;* but to proceed on courageously with *their holy and glorious intention of reconciling their Church to ours;* remembering that this involves the reconciliation of the Kingdom, of the Aristocracy with all its wealth and power, of the Nation. *A false step* would spoil all, would *produce a Protestant reaction*, and would defeat the hopes of the Holy See for another century. Any use you like to make of this letter, you are perfectly welcome to make: I have said nothing that can commit any *individual;* and yet I have said what would have weight in preparing men's minds. *If you like to read it to the Father General of the Jesuits, you can.*"[1]

In a very long letter to Cardinal Acton, dated "Feast of the Conversion, 1842," De Lisle explained all that had gone on in Oxford down to that time, then over a year after the appearance of *Tract XC*. He informs the Cardinal that "until quite within the last three weeks, owing to the conversions of Mr. Sibthorp and others, the individuals I allude to [the 'Leaders' of the Oxford Movement] felt it both prudent and right to suspend intercourse for a while with either myself or any other Catholics, *the more so as many unpleasant disclosures had been made in newspapers.*[2] . . . Now, however, as that intercourse has been renewed within the last few days, I may have it in my power to give your Eminence some intelligence of a consoling nature."[3] De Lisle proceeds to relate the steps the Tractarians had already taken that "so by God's holy grace, she [Church of England] might regain her ancient Catholic character," and adds :—" In order to bring this

[1] *Life and Letters of Ambrose de Lisle*, vol. i. pp. 217, 218.
[2] No doubt De Lisle here refers to the "disclosures" made by Mr. Golightly in the *Standard* and otherwise.
[3] *Life and Letters of Ambrose de Lisle*, vol. i. p. 231.

about they saw that, as an immense amount of anti-Catholic prejudice still existed in the minds of the generality of Englishmen, it was necessary to bring them on *by degrees, to communicate religious knowledge to them with a holy reserve;* hence they judged that the first step was to prove that the English Church (however committed to Protestant heresy in many respects) was not so Protestant as the popular notion of her implied."[1] Of some of the Tractarians, De Lisle said that :—" Many again liked Catholic ideas, but could not bring themselves to believe that *Rome alone* had any true claim to that glorious title, or that their own Church could only regain the title by reunion with that Church, which, as the Creed of Pius IV. declares, is the Mother and *Mistress* of all other Churches. Those even who saw this great truth the most clearly, saw also *the danger of proclaiming it too openly as yet,* lest the public mind should recoil and an anti-Catholic reaction take place. Hence, even some of the most advanced (as one of them said to me in a letter) thought it right to say all they *honestly* could against Rome, IN ORDER TO BLIND THE EYES OF THOSE WHOM THEY SAW ADVANCING, but yet in a very weak state ; meaning too, when they spoke against Rome, not the *Church* of Rome, not the Council of Trent, but *certain popular notions or opinions* existing within the Church, and dwelt upon more or less even by her Divines, but yet not vouched for by the Church as such ; your Eminence may guess what kind of notions the individuals I allude to implied. Nor indeed did they even mean to reprobate these *popular notions,* except in a *certain sense* which might be objectionable. At all events, I know several individuals, who *by this gradual process* of the Oxford Divines have been brought to the very threshold of truth, and have even crossed her borders."[2] In conclusion, De Lisle asserted that :—
"The devotion of the glorious Mother of God is rapidly increasing, great numbers of the Anglicans now keep her blessed picture with extreme reverence, putting flowers before it, especially on her principal feasts, many

---

[1] *Life and Letters of Ambrose de Lisle,* vol. i. p. 232.   [2] *Ibid.* p. 233.

recite her *Little Office;* a Fellow of Exeter College at Oxford burst into tears when speaking of this Dear Mother of our Saviour. I am confident that next to Jesus they love her above all things. Then they fast most wonderfully, like the Fathers of the Desert; *they take the Discipline;* lie upon hard boards at night; rise at midnight to recite Matins and Lauds; spend whole hours in mental prayer; shed floods of tears over their poor fallen Mother, the Church of England, earnestly imploring of our Lord to restore her, and so their country, to Catholic Unity."[1]

There can be no doubt that the news conveyed to Rome by Wiseman and De Lisle filled the Vatican with joy, and taxed the resources of the Jesuits to the uttermost. It is true that De Lisle was unreasonably hopeful; like most enthusiasts he expected great things, and expected them almost at once. Probably he felt disappointed at first; yet when, in his old age, he looked at the state of the Church of England and the progress in it of Roman ritual and Roman doctrine, he must have felt that he had not laboured in vain. The wonder is that one who, in ordinary private life, would scorn to act otherwise than as a honourable English gentleman, could, when he had to deal with religion, become a party to such unworthy and crooked conduct as that exposed in his own biography. And what must we think of the cause which needed such assistance? De Lisle did not act alone. It was his boast, as we have seen, that "Bishop Wiseman perfectly concurs with me in everything;" and there is no evidence to show that the Pope ever censured either the one or the other for their double dealing; and yet the Pope was made fully acquainted with what they were doing. Later on, when Newman was a Roman priest, he saw clearly the advantage to be gained by Rome through the adoption of one portion of De Lisle's policy, when, on July 1, 1857, he wrote to De Lisle: "I perfectly agree with you in thinking that the Movement of 1833 is not over in the country, whatever be the state of Oxford itself; also, I think it is for the *interest* of Catholicism that in-

[1] *Life and Letters of Ambrose de Lisle,* vol. i. p. 237.

dividuals should not join us, *but should remain to leaven the mass*—I mean that *they will do more for us by remaining where they are than by coming over.*"[1] At the same time Newman felt that there was danger to the individual who adopted such a policy, although the Roman Church would be a gainer by it; for he added: "But then, they have individual souls, and with what heart can I do anything to induce them to preach to others, if they themselves thereby become castaways?"

The Rev. W. G. Ward certainly acted for a time on this policy of aiding the Roman Church by staying within the Church of England, with a view to bringing her back to unity with Rome. His son says of him that, while he was a clergyman of the Church of England:

"He had long held that the Roman Church was the one true Church. He had gradually come to believe that the English Church was not strictly a part of the Church at all. *He had felt bound to retain his external communion with her members, because he believed that he was bringing many of them towards Rome;* and to unite himself to the Church which he loved and trusted, to enjoy the blessings of external communion for himself, if by so doing he thwarted this larger and fuller victory of truth, had seemed a course both indefensible and selfish.

"Still, he had long looked on his present position as only a time of waiting, as a season of Purgatory, as the painful and laborious seed-sowing, endured patiently because of the harvest to come. It was years since he had written that restoration of communion with the one Catholic Church and the See of Peter was 'the most enchanting earthly prospect on which his imagination could dwell.' He had become accustomed to a position similar to that of the missionary, who foregoes the happiness of living among his brethren in the faith, often of approaching the Sacraments, of the sustaining and health-giving presence of Church Liturgy and ordinances, in order that he may lead strangers to see the truth, and to enjoy eventually in his company those helps and blessings which he foregoes for the moment for their sakes."[2]

Is it unreasonable to fear that at the present hour there may be a very large number of Ritualistic clergy in the Church of England acting on the very same principle

---

[1] *Life and Letters of Ambrose de Lisle*, vol. i. p. 368.
[2] *William George Ward and the Oxford Movement*, pp. 356, 357.

which kept Ward for some years within the Church of England? He was for a time the leader of the more advanced Romanisers, and their conduct, it seems, was quite as bad as his. Of these men Mr. Wilfrid Ward writes:—

"Roman doctrine was more and more fully accepted, until in Mr. Ward's work, *The Ideal of a Christian Church*, Rome was practically acknowledged as the Divinely appointed guardian and teacher of religious truth. Finally, the old idea of working towards the Reunion of Churches, and calling for concessions on both sides with a view to this object, disappeared. The Pope was maintained to be normally Primate of Christendom, AND THE ULTIMATE AIM PROPOSED FOR THE ENGLISH CHURCH WAS NOT REUNION WITH BUT SUBMISSION TO ROME.

"On what ground then did the men who held this theory justify their remaining in the Church of England? On the ground (1) that Providence had placed them in it; (2) that its formularies were so loose as to allow the holding of all Roman doctrine within its pale; (3) that the sudden adoption of doctrines new to the moral nature was difficult and undesirable, and that the English Church afforded a good position for gradually drawing nearer to Rome, until some considerable portion of Churchmen should have so far imbibed the spirit of Roman Catholicism, as to feel conscientiously impelled to outward conformity to its communion. For an individual to move prematurely might destroy this prospect; *and, therefore, he was to be, for the present, content with uniting himself in spirit to the Roman Church, without formally joining her.* So long as conscience did not clearly call upon him to take the further step, so long might he hope that he was not cut off from grace by remaining where Providence had placed him."[1]

Of course, this advanced section of Romanisers went beyond Pusey and Keble in a Romeward direction, and therefore I do not accuse them of complicity with their work, though I may mention that of Keble it is recorded by one of his biographers that, on May 14, 1843, he wrote to Newman:—"Certainly there is a great yearning even after Rome in many parts of the Church, which seems to be accompanied by so much good that one hopes if it be right it will be allowed to gain strength."[2]

[1] *William George Ward and the Oxford Movement*, p. 212.
[2] *John Keble*. By Walter Lock, M.A., p. 120.

CHAPTER VIII

The Jerusalem Bishopric—Chevalier Bunsen's mission to England—Puseyite opposition—Hope-Scott's objections—Dr. Hook supports the Bishopric—His description of the Romanisers—Pusey's *Letter to the Archbishop of Canterbury*—Lord Ashley's letter to Pusey—Mr. Gladstone supports the Bishopric—Newman and the Jerusalem Bishopric—He thinks it "atrocious" and "hideous"—His Protest—Contest for Professorship of Poetry—Isaac Williams and *Reserve in Communicating Religious Knowledge*—Extracts from his writings—Mr. Garbett, the Protestant candidate—Samuel Wilberforce on the contest—He denounces the Romanisers—Success of the Protestant candidate—Secessions to Rome—The Rev. F. W. Faber—His visit to the Continent—His *Sights and Thoughts in Foreign Churches*—How he deceived the public—The Rev. William Goode—His Protestant works—His *Case as It Is*—His *Divine Rule of Faith and Practice*—Bishop Bagot's Visitation Charge—Mr. Goode answers it—The Parker Society.

ANOTHER heated controversy arose in 1841 in connection with the establishment of the Jerusalem Bishopric. The first step towards the formation of this Bishopric was taken by the King of Prussia, who was sincerely and earnestly anxious to secure for Protestants of all denominations, residing in Palestine, that protection in the exercise of their religious duties which at that time was greatly needed. Besides this his Majesty was most desirous of promoting the unity of true Protestants of all Evangelical denominations, a unity which he felt would be greatly promoted by the foundation of an Anglican Bishopric in Jerusalem. Having carefully considered the question the King decided on sending Chevalier Bunsen to London, for the purpose of negotiating with the British Government, the Archbishop of Canterbury, and the Bishop of London, with a view to the carrying out of his beneficent plans. Bunsen was instructed by his Royal Master to ascertain :—" How far the Church of England, which is already possessed of a Minister's residence on Mount Zion, and has begun to build a Church on the spot, would be inclined to grant the Evangelical National Church of Prussia rank, as a sister-Church, in the Holy Land?"[1] If the request of the King were granted, he would do all in his power to assist the Bishopric. "Nor will his Majesty," he said in his "Instructions" to Chevalier Bunsen, "impelled by a feeling of Apostolical Catholicity, and expectant of a reciprocal feeling on the part of the Church of England, refrain from expressing his readiness to allow all the clergy and missionaries of his native Church, in every land of Missions where the Church of England has an Episcopate, to unite with it; even to the seeking, if needful, of that Episcopal ordination, which the Church of England requires for admission to the priestly office. And his Majesty will provide that such ordination be duly recognised and respected in his own dominions."[2]

On arriving in England, Bunsen found the authorities in Church and State generally favourable to the King's proposals, which were heartily approved by the Archbishop of Canterbury (Dr. Howley), and the Bishop of London (Dr. Blomfield). The scheme was taken up very warmly by Evangelical Churchmen, Lord Ashley (afterwards Earl of Shaftesbury) taking the lead in removing all difficulties in the way, and furthering the scheme to the utmost. Within five days of his arrival in London Bunsen called on Lord Ashley, who thus recorded his visit in his diary:—"June 24th. My friend Bunsen has just called, and has brought me a most honourable and gratifying message from the King of Prussia. May the blessing of God's saints of old, of David, and of Hezekiah, be on him and his for ever! But all things are now wonderful. The mission of Bunsen is a wonder."[3] Lord Ashley arranged a meeting between Bunsen and Peel. From Lord Palmerston Bunsen received every encourage-

---

[1] *The Jerusalem Bishopric Documents.* By the Rev. Professor W. H. Hechler. London: 1883. Part II. p. 2.
[2] *Ibid.* p. 12.
[3] *Life of Lord Shaftesbury*, popular edition, p. 199.

ment. "Palmerston," wrote Lord Ashley, "went forward with the zeal of an Apostle, did in three weeks what at another time, or, as it seems, under any influence but mine, he would not have listened to in twelve months, fanned the weak embers of willing but timid spirit in the Bishops, and made that to be necessary and irrevocable which his successors would have thought the attribute of a maniac, even in imagination."[1] Before, however, the Jerusalem Bishopric could be founded, it was necessary to pass a special Act of Parliament to legalise it. Special facilities were offered for this purpose, with the result that the Bill speedily passed through both Houses of Parliament, received the Royal assent early in October, and is now known as the Jerusalem Bishopric Act (5 Victoria, chap. vi.), though the word Jerusalem is not once mentioned in it. One half of the money necessary for endowing the Bishopric was supplied by the King of Prussia; the other half was subscribed in England, the London Society for Promoting Christianity amongst the Jews giving £3000. From a *Statement of Proceedings* issued at the end of 1841, and "Published by Authority," we learn that the Archbishop "first consulted the Bishops" about the scheme for a Bishopric. "Its ultimate results cannot be with certainty predicted; but we may reasonably hope that, under the Divine blessing, it may lead the way to an essential unity of discipline, as well as of doctrine, between our own Church and the less perfectly constituted of the Protestant Churches of Europe, and that, too, not by the way of Rome; while it may be the means of establishing relations of unity between the United Church of England and Ireland and the ancient Churches of the East, strengthening them against the encroachments of the See of Rome, and preparing the way for their purification, in some cases from serious errors."[2] The Bishop of Jerusalem, continued the *Statement*, "is specially charged not to entrench upon the spiritual rights

---

[1] *Life of Lord Shaftesbury*, p. 200.
[2] *Statement of Proceedings Relating to the Establishment of a Bishopric in Jerusalem.* Published by Authority, p. 5. London: Rivingtons. 1841.

and liberties of those Churches [of the East]; but to confine himself to the care of those over whom *they* cannot rightly claim any jurisdiction. . . . The Bishop of the United Church of England and Ireland at Jerusalem is to be nominated alternately by the Crowns of England and Prussia, the Archbishop having the absolute right of veto, with respect to those nominated by the Prussian Crown."[1] The *Statement* continues:—

"Congregations, consisting of Protestants of the German tongue, residing within the limits of the Bishop's jurisdiction, and willing to submit to it, will be under the care of German clergymen ordained by him for that purpose; who will officiate in the German language, according to the forms of their National Liturgy, compiled from the Ancient Liturgies, agreeing in all points of doctrine with the Liturgy of the English Church, and sanctioned by the Bishop with consent of the Metropolitan, for the special use of those congregations; such Liturgy to be used in the German language only. Germans, intended for the charge of such congregations, are to be ordained according to the Ritual of the English Church, and to sign the Articles of that Church; and, in order that they may not be disqualified by the laws of Germany from officiating to German congregations, they are, before ordination, to exhibit to the Bishop a certificate of their having subscribed, before some competent authority, the Confession of Augsburg."[2]

The clergyman selected to be the first Protestant Bishop of Jerusalem was the Rev. M. S. Alexander, D.D. The Queen's mandate for his consecration was dated November 6, 1841, and he was consecrated on November 7th by the Archbishop of Canterbury, assisted by the Bishops of London, Rochester, and New Zealand.

The Jerusalem Bishopric was thus founded, with the approbation of the overwhelming majority of English Churchmen. But some there were who murmured.

"But oh!" wrote Lord Ashley, in his diary for October 12th, "the monstrosities of Puseyism! The Bishop of London is beset, and half brow-beaten, by the clamorous and uncatholic race. He showed Bunsen to-day a letter from Dr. Pusey beginning:—'It is

---

[1] *Statement of Proceedings Relating to the Establishment of a Bishopric in Jerusalem*, p. 6.
[2] *Ibid.* p. 8.

now for the first time that the Church of England holds communication with those who are *without the Church!*' This is the holy, Christian, Catholic way in which he speaks of all the congregations of Protestant Germany. Towards the end he adds:—' The Church of England will thus be the protectress of all Protestant communions.' What can be so dreadful? The Puseyite object is this, 'to effect reconciliation with Rome'; ours, with Protestantism; they wish to exalt Apostolical Succession so high as to make it paramount to all moral purity, and all doctrinal truth; we, to respect it so as to shift it from Abiathar to Zadok."[1]

The Jerusalem Bishopric controversy naturally produced a pamphlet war. Mr. James R. Hope (afterwards known as Hope-Scott), Chancellor of the Diocese of Salisbury, a prominent Tractarian, and an intimate friend of Newman and Mr. Gladstone, was greatly disturbed by what had taken place. It shook his faith in the Church of England, and prepared the way for his secession to Rome a few years later. He relieved his feelings by private correspondence with both Newman and Gladstone, and at last, at the close of the year, published a pamphlet on the subject in the form of a *Letter to a Friend*. In this document Mr. Hope candidly indicated his chief objection to the Bishopric. "Above all," he said, "we are bound not to insult those Bishops [in Jerusalem] through whose sufferance our Church there is to exist, by pretending to recognise and participate in their Catholicity, and at the same time by professing religious identity with Calvinism or Lutheranism, both of which they have by name (Synod of Jerusalem in 1675), condemned and rejected."[2] His dislike of the Bishopric was still more clearly revealed in the following passage:—

"And if, on the other hand, it should be determined in law that Bishop Alexander is not subject to the English Metropolitan, or governed in his Diocese by the constitution of the English Church; or if, before a legal decision can be obtained, it should be publicly proclaimed from authority in this country that such is the basis of the new Bishopric, then it will be at once evident that, whatever

---

[1] *Life of Lord Shaftesbury*, p. 201.
[2] *The Bishopric of the United Church of England and Ireland at Jerusalem.* By James R. Hope, B.C.L., 1st edition, p. 45.

title may have been given to Bishop Alexander, he can in no real sense be a Bishop of our Church, nor can his acts in any way implicate us, or affect our credit in the face of Christendom. He must then be held to be an independent Bishop, not in connection with any Catholic body—a fragment struck off from the Rock of the Church. Into the communion of such a Bishop no orthodox Churchman abroad will enter, no orthodox clergyman will submit to his jurisdiction; his orders will not be received in England; the marriages and other rites solemnised by his clergy will be open to serious doubts in our Ecclesiastical Courts; and that these things may not be hid from the world, it will (as I conceive) be the wisdom, if not the duty, of the sister Churches in England, Ireland, Scotland, the Colonies, and America, to proclaim at once and aloud their repudiation of a Prelate, who will have professed openly his design to reject the order of the Church which gave him mission, and whose title and privileges he assumes." [1]

No doubt this is exactly what Mr. Hope and his friends would have liked to have happened. Yet they dared not attempt to bring about such a repudiation of Bishop Alexander by an action in the Courts such as was hinted at in Mr. Hope's pamphlet. This document was answered by the well-known Broad Churchman, the Rev. F. D. Maurice, who declared that:—"It would have been a sin in the Bishops of our Church to let these canonical obligations hinder them from embracing an opportunity, not sought for by them, but offering itself to them unexpectedly, of promoting Catholic unity, and advancing Catholic principles. And that it will be a sin in us, if we allow these canonical objections, supposing no higher and stronger reasons can be produced, to hinder us from giving God thanks for what has been done, and from labouring, so far as in us lies, that it may not have been done in vain." [2]

Several very decided High Churchmen gave their help to the Jerusalem Bishopric. Dr. Hook, Vicar of Leeds, actually subscribed to the Bishopric Fund. No modern Ritualist can point the finger of scorn at Hook, and call him an ultra-Protestant. It was he who, as far back as

[1] Hope's *The Bishopric of the United Church of England and Ireland at Jerusalem*, pp. 55, 56.
[2] *Three Letters to the Rev. W. Palmer.* By F. D. Maurice, A.M., Professor of English Literature at King's College, London, p. 89. London: 1842.

1835, declared that, in his opinion, "the danger now is, not from Popery, but from that snare of Satan, ultra-Protestantism";[1] and who, in 1840, writing to a friend, declared:—"I for one think that a Romanist is far less in error than Owen and Baxter."[2] Yet even Dr. Hook wrote a pamphlet defending the Jerusalem Bishopric against the narrow-minded and bigoted views of his more advanced friends. In the commencement of this pamphlet Dr. Hook sorrowfully acknowledged that:—

"There are, *certainly, many such persons* among our younger brethren at the present time, who are inclined to look upon our Church in the following light:—they regard the Church of England as a Branch of the Catholic Church from which, without peril to their souls, they may not secede; but *they look upon it as injured rather than improved by the Reformation;* they think that if some abuses were corrected, serious errors were introduced; *they agree with the Romanists in maintaining that the Reformation was unnecessary*, at all events, to the extent to which it was carried; and that it was conducted in a manner not to be defended upon Catholic principles. The conclusion which must inevitably be deduced from these premises is this, that the Church of England, as at present constituted, is not the model according to which other Churches are to be reformed; and that we have as much to learn from Rome as Rome has to learn from us. I believe that in this statement I have clearly asserted an opinion *very extensively held* upon this subject. From this opinion I do entirely dissent."[3]

No wonder that those, who so "very extensively held" these unworthy views of the English Church, were bitterly opposed to any approach on her part towards union with non-Episcopal Protestant Churches on the Continent. As to the Jerusalem Bishopric Hook said:—

"The fact of our placing a Bishop of our own Church in Jerusalem, not as an usurper of another Bishop's jurisdiction, but as a representative of the English Church, in a land where such conduct is tolerated with respect to other branches of the Catholic Church, to discharge the ministerial office for those who cannot be received into communion with the Oriental Church, and to watch over the intrigues of the Church of Rome, which certainly can have

---

[1] *Life of Dean Hook*, vol. i. p. 274.
[2] *Ibid.* vol. ii. p. 59.
[3] *Reasons for Contributing Towards the Support of an English Bishop at Jerusalem.* By Walter F. Hook, D.D., p. 3. London: 1842.

no more right to have a representative at Jerusalem than we have; all this cannot have a tendency, as you seem to think, to continue the division which unhappily exists in the Catholic Church." [1]

Dr. Pusey was at first, through conversations with Bunsen, favourable to the proposed Bishopric at Jerusalem. But later on, mainly through the influence of Newman, he altered his mind, and became an opponent. At this period he was very much troubled by the controversy which had arisen in connection with *Tract XC.*, the Episcopal charges against it, and the accusations of a tendency to Romanism which had been brought against the Tractarians. He determined, therefore, to publish a kind of apology for his friends, in which he tried to minimise to the utmost the censures of the Bishops, and at the same time he availed himself of the opportunity to deal with the Jerusalem Bishopric question. He did this in the form of *A Letter to the Archbishop of Canterbury*, which filled a pamphlet of 171 pages. With the earlier portion of this document I have here no special concern, except to call attention to the following remarkable statement, which deserves to be more widely known than it is at the present day:—

"Two schemes of doctrines," wrote Dr. Pusey, "the Genevan and the Catholic, are, probably for the last time, struggling within our Church; the contest, which has been carried on ever since the Reformation, between the Church and those who parted from her, has now been permitted to be transferred to the Church herself; on the issue hangs the destiny of our Church; if human frailty or impatience precipitates not that issue, all will be well, and it will have a peaceful close; *yet a decisive issue it must have;* the one must in time absorb the other; or, to speak more plainly, the Catholic, as the full truth of God, must, *unless it be violently cast out*, in time leaven and absorb into itself whatever is partial and defective; as it has already very extensively." [2]

Translated into plainer language, "Genevan" meant, in Pusey's mind, decided Protestantism; while "Catholic"

---

[1] Hook's *Reasons for Contributing Towards the Support of an English Bishop at Jerusalem*, p. 11.

[2] *A Letter to the Archbishop of Canterbury on Some Circumstances Connected with the Present Crisis in the English Church.* By the Rev. E. B. Pusey, D.D., pp. 84, 85. Oxford: 1842.

meant that imitation of a great deal of Popery with which his name is associated. It is evident from the above quotation that he foresaw that "a decisive issue" between Protestantism and sham Popery must eventually come; but he dreaded lest by "human frailty or impatience" it should come too soon, for then his party might expect to "be violently cast out." But one thing he felt was certain—and in this I agree with him—sooner or later one or other of the two systems of religion, the Protestant or the Sacerdotal, must cease to exist in the Church of England. That is really the issue before the country in the present Ritual Crisis. Unless the Romanising lion be "cast out," it will "absorb" the Evangelical lamb, and that means death to the lamb. We are engaged in a struggle of life or death. The issue will be, either that the Protestant Reformation shall be utterly undone, and the Church go back to her condition in the Dark Ages; or we must go forward in Gospel and Protestant light, until "light shall conquer darkness," and England's Church shall once more be the greatest bulwark against Popery to be found in the world. We are looking forward to times of war, not of peace. We need brave men now, men who will love the glorious Gospel brought back again to life at the Reformation, more than ease, or friends, or life.

As to the Jerusalem Bishopric Pusey threatened the Archbishop in these words:—" But any step which has a tendency to bring her [the Church of England] into relations with foreign un-Catholic bodies, will be unsettling. Any advance to Protestantism will produce a counter-movement towards Romanism."[1] He expressed a fear lest attempts should be made to convert people from the Eastern Church. To act in this way he actually declared would be "encouraging sin,"[2] though he must have known that that Church was steeped in doctrinal corruption and superstition. He had no objection to the

---

[1] Pusey's *Letter to the Archbishop of Canterbury on Some Circumstances Connected with the Present Crisis in the English Church*, p. 112.
[2] *Ibid.* p. 117.

Lutherans being "absorbed into our Church," and he had at first looked forward to such an absorption with hope; but as to this Jerusalem Bishopric:—"Think," he wrote, "only of its effect on the Orthodox Greek communion (apart from the graver and deeper question of the responsibility we should ourselves incur), what suspicion must needs be cast upon us, that we thus, in their very presence, sanction bodies whom they have anathematised, not incorporating them into ourselves nor infusing into them our principles, but joined in an outward alliance with them."[1] And all this dread of alliance with Lutherans was almost solely caused by the fact that they were not Episcopalians. One cannot wonder at the language which Pusey's cousin, Lord Ashley, used when he wrote to him, on January 18, 1842, with reference to the Jerusalem Bishopric:—

"You talk," wrote Lord Ashley, "in allusion to the Bishopric, of 'the grave injury of countenancing heresy'; this is the necessary language, the inevitable issue of your principles; thus you class with the Gnostics, Cerinthians, &c., of old, with the Munster Anabaptists and Socinians of modern days, the whole mass of the Protestant Churches of Europe, except England and Sweden. Every one, however deep his piety, however holy his belief, however prostrate his heart in faith and fear before God and his Saviour, however simple and perfect his reliance on the merits of his Redeemer, is consigned by you, if he be not Episcopally ruled, to the outward darkness of the children of the Devil; while in the same breath you designate the Church of Rome as the sweet Spouse of Christ, and hide all her abominable idolatries under the mantle of her Bishops. This is, to my mind, absolutely dreadful; and I say of your friends, as old Jacob said of Simeon and Levi, 'Oh, my soul, come not thou into their secret.'"[2]

Mr. Gladstone was invited to become one of the Trustees of the Jerusalem Bishopric, and he accepted the post, but subsequently withdrew from it. He was, however, present at a dinner which Bunsen gave on October 15, 1841, at the Star and Garter, Richmond, and at which the new Bishop of Jerusalem and many other friends

---

[1] Pusey's *Letter to the Archbishop of Canterbury on Some Circumstances Connected with the Present Crisis in the English Church*, p. 115.
[2] *Life of Lord Shaftesbury*, pp. 211, 212.

were present. Writing to his wife afterwards Bunsen said:—"Then I arose, and proposed 'The Church of England, and the venerable Prelates at her Head'; and spoke as I felt. M'Caul returned thanks, speaking of Jerusalem, which led to Gladstone's toast, 'Prosperity to the Church of St. James at Jerusalem, and to her first Bishop.' Never was heard a more exquisite speech—it flowed like a gentle and translucent stream."[1]

As to Newman, he took the matter so seriously to heart that, as he tells us in his *Apologia*:—"This was the third blow, which finally shattered my faith in the Anglican Church. That Church was not only forbidding any sympathy or concurrence with the Church of Rome, but it actually was courting an intercommunion with Protestant Prussia and the heresy of the Orientals."[2] To his friends Newman spoke of the Jerusalem Bishopric in such terms as these:—"This *atrocious* Jerusalem Bishop affair";[3] "This *fearful* business of the Bishop of Jerusalem";[4] "It is *hideous*."[5] So he got up a "Protest" of his own against the Bishopric, of which Pusey expressed his approval,[6] and sent it to the Archbishop of Canterbury and the Bishop of Oxford, commencing thus:—

"Whereas the Church of England has a claim on the allegiance of Catholic believers only on the ground of her own claim to be considered a branch of the Catholic Church:

"And whereas the recognition of heresy, indirect as well as direct, goes far to destroy such claim in the case of any religious body advancing it:

"And whereas to admit maintainers of heresy to communion, without formal renunciation of their errors, goes far towards recognising the same:

"*And whereas Lutheranism and Calvinism are heresies*, repugnant to Scripture, springing up three centuries since, and anathematised by East as well as West:

"And whereas it is reported that the Most Reverend Primate and other Right Reverend Rulers of our Church have consecrated a

---

[1] *Memoirs of Baron Bunsen*, vol. i. p. 625.
[2] *Apologia Pro Vita Sua*, p. 248.
[3] Newman's *Letters*, vol. ii. p. 352. [4] *Ibid.* p. 352. [5] *Ibid.* p. 353.
[6] *Memoirs of James Hope-Scott*, vol. i. p. 317.

Bishop with a view to exercising spiritual jurisdiction over Protestant, that is, Lutheran and Calvinist, congregations in the East . . .

"On these grounds, I in my place, being a priest of the English Church and Vicar of St. Mary the Virgin's, Oxford, by way of relieving my conscience, do hereby solemnly protest against the measure aforesaid, and disown it, as removing our Church from her present ground, and tending to her disorganisation."[1]

Opposition of this violent kind raised the indignation of many High Churchmen, including some who approved of the earlier of the *Tracts for the Times*, and made Archdeacon Samuel Wilberforce declare: "I confess I feel furious at the craving of men for union with idolatrous, material, sensual, domineering Rome, and their squeamish anathematising hatred of Protestant Reformed men."[2]

Another event occurred towards the close of 1841, which requires notice in these pages, viz., the contest for the Professorship of Poetry in Oxford University. Two candidates applied for the vacant Professorship, the Rev. Isaac Williams; and the Rev. James Garbett, late Fellow of Brasenose College and Bampton Lecturer-Elect for 1842. The excitement which centred round the election was intense. It became a great party contest, in which the question before the electors was only nominally, which of the two candidates is the best poet? The real question for their decision was, which is the best Churchman? Mr. Williams was the candidate put forward by the Tractarians; Mr. Garbett was the Protestant candidate. The great objection to Mr. Williams was caused by his being the author of two of the *Tracts for the Times* which had raised a storm of indignation throughout the country. Each of these *Tracts* bore the same title, "On Reserve in Communicating Religious Knowledge," the first being No. 80 of the *Tracts for the Times*, and the second No. 87 of the series. The following extracts from these documents contain the passages

---

[1] Newman's *Letters*, vol. ii. pp. 362, 363. Newman's *Apologia*, pp. 251, 252.
[2] *Life of Bishop Wilberforce*, vol. i. p. 213.

THE TRACT ON "RESERVE" 213

which were most objected against by Churchmen. The italics are mine:—

"The object of the present inquiry is to ascertain, whether there is not in God's dealings with mankind, a very remarkable *holding back* of sacred and important truths, as if the knowledge of them were injurious to persons unworthy of them."[1]

"Not only is the exclusive and naked exposure of so very sacred a truth [as the 'Doctrine of the Atonement'] unscriptural and dangerous, but, as Bishop Wilson says, the comforts of Religion ought to be applied with great caution. And moreover to require, as is sometimes done, from both grown persons and children, an explicit declaration of a belief in the Atonement, and the full assurance of its power, appears equally untenable."[2]

"These riches [that is, certain 'sacred truths'] are all *secret*, given to certain dispositions—not cast loosely on the world. . . . The great doctrines which of late years have divided Christians, are again of this ['secret'] kind very peculiarly, *such as the subjects of Faith and Works*, of the *free Grace of God*, and obedience on the part of man. . . . They appear to be *great secrets*, notwithstanding whatever may be said of them, *only revealed to the faithful.*"[3]

"With respect to the *Holy Sacraments*, it is in these, and by these *chiefly*, that the Church of all ages *has held the Doctrine of the Atonement after a certain manner of reserve.* . . . Now here it is very evident at once that the great difference between the two systems [*i.e.* what Williams terms the true Catholic, and the modern Protestant system] consists in this, that the one holds the doctrine *secretly* as it were; and the other in a *public* and popular manner."[4]

"The same may be shown with respect to *the powers of Priestly Absolution*, and the gifts conferred thereby. It is not required for our purpose to show the reality of that power, and the magnitude of those gifts which are thus dispensed. But a little consideration will show, that if the Church of all ages is right in exercising these privileges, *the subject is one entirely of this reserved and mystical character.* Its blessings are received in secret, according to faith: they are such as the world cannot behold, and cannot receive. The subject is one so profound and mysterious, that it hardly admits of being put forward in a popular way, and doubtless more injury than benefit would be done to religion by doing so inconsiderately."[5]

---

[1] *Tract LXXX.* p. 3.   [2] *Ibid.* p. 78.   [3] *Ibid.* pp. 48, 49.
[4] *Tract LXXXVII.* pp. 88, 89.   [5] *Ibid.* p. 90.

We cannot be surprised to learn that the Evangelical and Protestant Churchmen of the day were alarmed at such teaching as this. They, at any rate, would not be a party to the teaching that the doctrines of the Atonement, Faith and Works, the Free Grace of God, and the Sacraments were to be treated as secrets to be imparted only to those who could be trusted. And they had a just reason to dread that this doctrine of Reserve would be used—as it actually was—by the Tractarians to hide their real objects from cautious Protestants. They acted crookedly, as Mr. De Lisle tells us very truly, "for the purpose of throwing dust in the eyes of the Dissenters and the Low Churchmen."[1] Mr. Williams himself, in his *Autobiography*, tells us, when describing the Poetry Professorship contest:—" That the Low Church party as a body should oppose me, as Wadham College did, was all right and natural—my *Tract No.* 80 was against them —*they rightly understood it, there was no mistake.*"[2] And again, Mr. Williams writes:—" With regard to the great obloquy it [*Tract No.* 80] occasioned from the Low Church Party, this was to be expected—it was against their hollow mode of proceeding; *it was understood as it was meant*, and of this I do not complain."[3]

I cannot therefore think that it was any great cause for surprise that, as soon as Mr. Isaac Williams' name was known as a candidate for the vacant post of Professor of Poetry, the Evangelical Party made an effort to oppose it. On November 16, 1841, a circular letter was issued in Mr. Garbett's favour, in which, after calling attention to the fact that Mr. Williams was a writer in the *Tracts for the Times*, and author of the Tract *On Reserve in Communicating Religious Knowledge*, it continued:—" The election of Mr. Williams in Mr. Keble's room would undoubtedly be represented as a decision of Convocation in favour of his party; and the resident members of our College are unanimous in thinking that this would be a serious evil, as well as highly discreditable to the University."[4] The

---

[1] *Life of Ambrose Phillipps de Lisle*, vol. i. p. 217.
[2] *Autobiography of Isaac Williams*, p. 139.   [3] *Ibid.* p. 91.
[4] *Life of Dr. Pusey*, vol. ii. p. 262.

very next day after this letter was written, Dr. Pusey sent out a letter on the same subject to the members of Convocation, with whom rested the election, in which he advocated strongly the candidature of Mr. Williams, and urged them to vote for him. This letter seems to have displeased Williams, because it brought out the controversial question too prominently. "At first," he said, "things went on silently and quietly, without any overt act that stamped it as a religious or party movement. But this comparative quietude was very soon broken up by Pusey, unwittingly, and as it was thought most unwisely, for what he did immediately gave our adversaries all that they desired. This was the printed circular which he issued in my praise and in my favour, complaining of my being bitterly opposed merely and avowedly for my Church principles. Upon this, the opposite party had promises pouring in on all sides, and many, who had been with us, held aloof, and some withdrew their promises. . . . The commotion filled the papers and all parts of the land."[1] Of Pusey's circular, Dean Church writes:—"In an unlucky moment for Mr. Williams, Dr. Pusey, not without the knowledge, but without the assenting judgment of Mr. Newman, thought it well to send forth a circular, in Christ Church first, but soon with wider publicity, asking support for Mr. Williams as a person whose known religious views would ensure his making his office minister to religious truth. Nothing could be more innocently meant. It was the highest purpose to which that office could be devoted. But the mistake was seen on all sides as soon as made. The Principal of Mr. Garbett's College, Dr. Gilbert, like a general jumping on his antagonist whom he had caught in the act of a false move, put forth a dignified counter-appeal, alleging that he had not raised this issue, but adding that as it had been raised and avowed on the other side, he was quite willing that it should be taken into account, and the dangers duly considered of that teaching with which Dr. Pusey's letter had identified Mr. Williams.

[1] *Autobiography of Isaac Williams*, pp. 138, 139.

No one from that moment could prevent the contest from becoming almost entirely a theological one, which was to try the strength of the party of the movement."[1]

The friends of Mr. Williams quite expected that Archdeacon Samuel Wilberforce would vote for him, and the Rev. Sir G. Prevost wrote to him for his support. The Archdeacon's reply is interesting and important, as showing that he had decided to part company with the Tractarians, whose Romeward tendencies began to alarm him.

"I *had* hoped," wrote Wilberforce, "to vote *for* Isaac Williams; and felt sure that I need under no circumstances vote against him; for no mere interest of Poetry, even if a fitter man appeared, could compel me to vote against old friendship. But Pusey's unhappy letter about it has quite altered the circumstances of the case. He has made it a distinct question of peculiar tenets, and thus falls in remarkably with the last *British Critic*. I cannot hide from myself that now it *must* be, whatever one means, simply expressing publicly, aye or no, one's approbation of, or dissent from, the most *peculiar* features of the teaching of the *Tract* writers. With them, as you well know, I have never agreed. Their views on many points (specially the *Tract on Reserve*) have appeared to me so dangerous, that, at all costs, I felt I must bear my feeble testimony against them in my Oxford sermons, &c., &c. Of late, also, they have seemed to me to advance at immense speed. Newman's view of Justification, the language of *Tract XC.*, the *British Critic*, &c., as to Rome; the craving after unity through *some* visible centre; the saying that old Rome was that centre (whereas I believe that to be the central point of the old Papal lie, the seed of everything, the truly putting the Church *for* Christ, instead of showing it as full of Christ, the root of their *opus operatum* in Baptism, Transubstantiation, Tradition, &c., &c.); the fearful doctrine of sin after Baptism, the whole tone about the Reformers, &c., &c., all this has pained and grieved me so entirely, that I have felt daily obliged more and more, from the love of the truth as I saw it, from love to our Church, *whose principles and very life I believe this teaching threatens*, with formality and Romanism on the one hand, and a cold formality and Dissent (by its revulsion) on the other, to take on all occasions a position of more direct opposition to the School than I had of old thought necessary; being content before to feel that, whilst I honoured their zeal, and was abashed by their holiness, and joined heartily in much Church

---

[1] Church's *Oxford Movement*, p. 274.

truth they had brought forward, I myself was of another School of opinion and feeling; but now, feeling that one must contend against what was spreading so widely, and shedding the seeds of Romanism ... How can I, at such a moment, vote for Isaac, with the truth before me that *all* his voters will be men who wish to bear their testimony to their persuasion of the truth of these principles, with which Dr. Pusey's letter has identified him in this contest? Can I escape, at every sacrifice, voting against him?"[1]

It was soon evident that what Mr. F. Rogers (afterwards Lord Blachford, and a warm friend of the Tractarians), termed the "most outrageously injudicious letter"[2] of Pusey had destroyed any chance of the success of Williams' candidature. But the contest was carried on until early in January 1842, when Mr. Gladstone got up a memorial to the rival committees of Garbett and Williams, signed by 253 non-resident members of Convocation, and by the Bishops of Oxford, Exeter, Salisbury, Ripon, and Sodor and Man, requesting the withdrawal of both candidates. Mr. Garbett's committee declined to entertain the proposal, while Williams' committee suggested a comparison of promises made to both candidates. This latter proposal was accepted by Mr. Garbett's committee, and with the result that it was found that 921 members of Convocation had promised to vote for Garbett, while only 623 had promised to vote for Williams. The result was that Mr. Williams withdrew from the contest, and Mr. Garbett was elected as Professor of Poetry in the room of Mr. Keble.

With the year 1842 the tide of secessions to Rome from the ranks of the Tractarians began to flow rapidly. In that year several prominent members of the party seceded. Many of the Tractarians commenced passing their holidays in visiting Continental churches and holding conferences with the Roman prelates and priests they met there. These visits greatly tended to move the more advanced men towards Rome. One of these travellers, who subsequently published a volume describing his travels, was the well-known Rev. Frederick William Faber, afterwards known as Father Faber, of the Brompton Oratory.

[1] *Life of Bishop Wilberforce*, vol. i. pp. 205, 206.
[2] *Letters of Lord Blachford*, p. 106.

I have elsewhere[1] given ample proof of Mr. Faber's outrageously Romanising conduct at this period, and therefore I need not repeat it here; but I may be permitted to mention a startling fact concerning his visit to the Continent in 1841, with which I have only recently become acquainted. Faber published, early in 1842, an account of this visit to the Continent, under the title of *Sights and Thoughts in Foreign Churches*, filling no less than 645 octavo pages. In this book, Faber mentions again and again certain interviews with an imaginary representative of the Dark Ages whom he met during his travels, and whom he terms the "Stranger." He reports the many assertions and arguments which this "Stranger" put forth as a Roman Catholic, in favour of the Church of Rome in the Dark Ages; while, at the same time, he also reports in full the arguments which he (Mr. Faber) brought forward in favour of the Church of England against the Papal claims of the "Stranger." It now appears, on the authority of Faber's biographer, Father J. E. Bowden, of the Brompton Oratory, that in this matter Faber deliberately and intentionally deceived the public. The Popish views which he represented as those expressed by the Romish "Stranger" were in reality those held at the time *by Faber himself*, and many of the views expressed in the book as his own were those to which he was, in reality, strongly opposed. "The 'Stranger,'" writes Father Bowden, "as he is usually called, personates, *in fact*, Mr. Faber's own Catholic feelings and tendencies, against which he appears to contend."[2] And here we may profitably inquire, what were "Mr. Faber's own Catholic feelings and tendencies" thus deceitfully put by him into the mouth of the "Stranger" but which were held by him [Faber], as a clergyman of the Church of England, *four years before he seceded to Rome?* The "Stranger" is represented as saying:—

"To such of you Englishmen as feel the want of it, does not celibacy afford to a priest one of the underhand (by which, not

---

[1] *Secret History of the Oxford Movement*, chapter i.
[2] *Life and Letters of Frederick William Faber, D.D.* By John Edward Bowden, 2nd edition, p. 75.

to be misunderstood, is meant unoffending inwardly realised) ways in which meek hearts may attain to a stronger feeling of communion with the rest of Western Christendom?"[1]

"There has seldom been a family on a throne with so few respectable qualities as the English Tudors. The bitter and narrow-minded *Mary deserves the most esteem; for she*, through principles in which she had faith, *gave up to the Pope* what was nearest and dearest to a Tudor's heart, *unshared supremacy*."[2]

"What! does not the majesty of Rome, that awful Church, so overawe your spirit as to prevent your talking with such curious ingenuity of Rome's penitence?"[3]

"Yet believe me, Rome will be permitted to lie grievously on those who will not reverence her. She is marked, not by her own hand, for reverence."[4]

"Oh, Rome! the city of my times, the place of our glad and lowly pilgrimages, how changed thou art in many things, but still thou art Rome, and hast Rome's prerogative—a tremendous power to ban or bless!"[5]

"The usual Protestant objections to the legends and miracles of the Middle Ages peril authority of the Holy Scripture itself."[6]

"And as to the modification of the Monastic principle embodied in the Order of the Jesuits, you have only to look on the consistent encroachment which Rome has made upon the strongholds of Protestantism ever since, in order to understand and estimate the extent of service performed by that Order for the Holy See. I cannot, therefore, agree with you, that Religious Orders have been failures. On the contrary, a revival of the Monastic spirit seems to be one feature in every crisis of the Church, and to bear fruit abundantly."[7]

"You put forward the highest possible claims for your Church [of England], often in a tone of pharisaical self-conceit, as though the usages and beliefs of the greater part of Christendom were of no account whatever in your eyes; you repeatedly indulge in a very offensive sort of commiseration of Rome, forgetting, on the one hand, that you are very young, and, on the other, that Rome's communion is much more extensive than your own, and comprehends wisdom and holiness which must demand the respect of every thoughtful and modest man."[8]

---

[1] *Sights and Thoughts in Foreign Churches.* By Frederick William Faber, p. 130.
[2] *Ibid.* p. 167.
[3] *Ibid.* p. 170.
[4] *Ibid.* p. 171.
[5] *Ibid.* p. 172.
[6] *Ibid.* p. 276.
[7] *Ibid.* p. 356.
[8] *Ibid.* p. 362.

"But the temper, which would be called the temper of persecution, might be kindled among you [that is, in the Church of England] by Monasteries, *and would be not the least important* BLESSING *which would spring from them.*"[1]

"True, they [Monasteries] have ['ever been nurseries of intolerance and persecution']; and can any virtue be higher than an intolerance of evil, and a hunting it from the earth? Why be frightened at words? Persecution belongs not, strictly speaking, to the Church. Her weapon, and a most dire one, is excommunication, whereby she cuts off the offender from the fountains of life in this world, and makes him over from her own judgment to that of Heaven in the world to come. *But surely it is the duty of Christian States to deprive such an excommunicate person of every social right and privilege;* to lay on him such pains and penalties as may seem good to the wisdom of the law; *or even, if they so judge, to sweep him from the earth. The least which can be done is to make a civil death to follow an ecclesiastical death;* and *this must be done* where the Church and State stand in right positions to each other."[2]

If conduct like this of Faber's, in passing off as the opinions of a Romanist what were really his own opinions; and representing himself as opposed to most of them, can be justified, it will follow that we can never know what an author's opinions really are. To my mind Faber was guilty of shameful and inexcusable deception, which reminds me very forcibly of what another Tractarian clergyman of the period, the Rev. W. G. Ward, used to say to his disciples:—"Make yourselves clear that you are justified in deception, and then lie like a trooper!"[3]

It was in the year 1842 that the Rev. William Goode (afterwards Dean of Ripon) came publicly forward as a learned and able champion of Reformation principles against the Tractarians. Evangelical Churchmen owe a lasting debt of gratitude to Mr. Goode for the many pamphlets and books he wrote against the Romeward Movement. They are of permanent value, and as much needed at the

---

[1] *Sights and Thoughts in Foreign Churches.* By Frederick William Faber, p. 420.
[2] *Ibid.* p. 419.
[3] *William George Ward and the Oxford Movement.* By Wilfrid Ward, p. 31.

present time as when they were first issued. It is a pity that they are not more widely known, for the arguments they contain are as much needed now as when they were first published. Mr. Goode's pamphlet, *The Case as It Is*, issued in 1842, was an able reply to Dr. Pusey's *Letter to the Archbishop of Canterbury*, which I have already noticed. In this pamphlet Mr. Goode clearly proved that he, at least, was alive to the serious nature of the issues which were at stake. His opening sentence shows it. "That the very existence of the English Church," he wrote, "as restored by our Reformers, depends upon the issue of the controversy raised within her by the authors of the *Tracts for the Times*, and their adherents, can hardly be now considered a doubtful matter."[1] Mr. Goode exposes the Romanising character of the doctrines of the Tractarians (whom he terms "Tractators") by copious quotations from their writings; and at the same time gives a startling exhibition of the methods of quotation which they adopted, when citing in their favour the chief writers of the Reformed Church, whose real principles, as he clearly proves, were strongly opposed to those held by the Tractarians. "Isolated sentences from our great divines," wrote Mr. Goode, "have been paraded before the public eye, as evidence of their approval of sentiments which their works, as a whole, show that they abhorred."[2]

Mr. Goode's great work was *The Divine Rule of Faith and Practice*, published this year in two large volumes, of which a second and enlarged edition was published, in three volumes, in 1853.[3] The author showed an extensive and intimate acquaintance, not only with the writings of our great Anglican Divines, but also with those of the Fathers of the Christian Church. His subject was one of the highest importance, and he dealt with it in a masterly manner. It is a pity that the work has never

---

[1] *The Case as It Is; or, a Reply to the Letter of Dr. Pusey*, 2nd edition, p. 5, London: 1842.
[2] *Ibid.* p. 50.
[3] *The Divine Rule of Faith and Practice;* or, "A Defence of the Catholic Doctrine that Holy Scripture has been, since the Times of the Apostles, the sole Divine Rule of Faith and Practice to the Church," 2nd edition. Three vols. London: 1853.

been issued in an abridged form. The late Lord Chancellor Selborne says, in a passage already cited, that "When William Goode, afterwards Dean of Ripon, in his *Divine Rule of Faith and Practice*, called the Fathers themselves as witnesses in favour of the direct use of Scripture for the decision of controversies, some of those who placed confidence in the Oxford Divines, but were themselves ignorant of the Fathers, waited anxiously for answers which never came."[1]

In May 1842, Dr. Bagot, Bishop of Oxford, delivered his fourth Visitation Charge to his clergy, in which at some length he directed attention to the Tractarian Movement. He stated that he saw no reason to alter his sentiments, as to the *Tracts for the Times*, which he had expressed in his third Visitation Charge, in 1838, in which he had called attention to what he conceived to have been good in those *Tracts*, and to "the tendencies in them which" he "considered dangerous"; and in which he had stated that his "fears arose, for the most part, rather from the disciples than the teachers."[2] He again praised the Tract writers for their personal character and conduct, though as to *Tract XC.* he declared:—"I cannot reconcile myself to a system of interpretation, which is so subtle, that by it the Articles may be made to mean anything or nothing."[3] Nevertheless, he asserted of the Tracts as a whole, that they "have, from their commencement, exerted a beneficial influence amongst us in many respects."[4] As to the disciples of the Tract writers, for them he had words of severe censure. "They are," he said, "doing no good service to the Church of England, by their recent publications of manuals of private devotion, extracted from the Breviary and similar sources—by inserting therein no small portion of highly objectionable matter, and tacitly, if not openly, encouraging young persons to be dissatisfied with what God has given them."[5] He thought there was

[1] *Memorials Family and Personal*, 1766–1865. By the Earl of Selborne, vol. i. p. 210.
[2] *A Charge Delivered by Richard Bagot, D.D., Bishop of Oxford*, p. 16. Oxford: 1842.
[3] *Ibid.* p. 17.   [4] *Ibid.* p. 19.   [5] *Ibid.* p. 23.

a very real danger of secessions to Rome, not, however, from amongst the clergy, but from the young and rising generation; and he urged the clergy to do all in their power to prevent such secessions.

It was by no means a satisfactory Charge on the whole, and it seems to have given more pleasure than annoyance to the leaders of the Tractarian party. Newman wrote to Keble about it, on May 24, 1842:—"You will be glad to hear that the Bishop's Charge delivered yesterday was very favourable to us, or rather to our cause, for some of us suffered."[1] The Evangelical Mr. Goode was, however, by no means pleased with the Charge, and, therefore, at once subjected it to a public criticism, in the form of a Letter to the Bishop, who is reminded by Mr. Goode that the Romanists had termed him, as the author of such a Charge, "the apologist of the Tractarians."[2] "Tractarianism," Mr. Goode said to the Bishop, "has been nursed under your eye. It has professed a readiness to act according to your bidding. You have suffered it to spread its principles in all directions throughout the Church. You have permitted it to proceed in its career unchecked."[3] He pointed out the inconsistencies of the Charge. "One part of the Charge seems to be answered by another."[4] It is sometimes supposed that the Tractarians preached the pure Gospel. Mr. Goode did not think so. "My Lord," he wrote to Dr. Bagot, "if the Tractarians are preaching the Gospel of Christ in any degree of purity, their opponents are not so preaching it; and if their opponents are so preaching it, they are not. This they have themselves admitted, nay urged upon us."[5] In conclusion he said:—"The reflection forces itself upon the most unthinking, How different would have been the state of things, if four years ago the admonitions of the Bishop of Oxford had been distinct and decisive! God grant that another four years may

---

[1] Newman's *Letters*, vol. ii. p. 396.
[2] *Some Difficulties in the late Charge of the Bishop of Oxford.* By William Goode, M.A., p. 3. London: 1842.
[3] *Ibid.* p. 5.   [4] *Ibid.* p. 14.   [5] *Ibid.* p. 29.

not force upon your lordship and the Church reflections still more painful."[1]

In this same year the Rev. George Stanley Faber published his most useful *Provincial Letters from the County-Palatine of Durham*, directed against the Tractarians. Mr. Faber was a learned and prolific writer, and his works on the Roman controversy are well worthy of study at the present time.[2]

It was in the year 1842 that the first annual meeting of the Parker Society was held. The Society was formed in 1840, and completed its work in 1855. It was founded for the purpose of "reprinting, without abridgment, alteration, or omission, the best Works of the Fathers and early Writers of the Reformed English Church, published in the period between the accession of King Edward VI. and the death of Queen Elizabeth; secondly, the printing of such remains of other Writers of the Sixteenth Century as may appear desirable (including, under both classes, some of the early English Translations of the Foreign Reformers); and thirdly, the printing of some manuscripts of the same authors, hitherto unpublished."[3] There can be no doubt that the object of the promoters of the Parker Society was to counteract, as far as possible, the influence of certain portions of the *Library of Anglo-Catholic Theology*, issued by the Tractarians, and including the works of several Laudian Divines of the seventeenth century, and the Nonjurors. Lord Ashley became the first President of the Parker Society, and from the commencement of its operations it was most successful. Its first annual report stated that no fewer than upwards of 6000 annual subscriptions of one guinea each had been received. Amongst the subscribers were the Dowager Queen Adelaide, Prince Albert, the King of Prussia, the Dukes of Kent, Sussex, Devonshire, and Sutherland, and the Bishops of London,

[1] *Some Difficulties in the late Charge of the Bishop of Oxford.* By William Goode, M.A., p. 30. London: 1842.
[2] *Provincial Letters from the County-Palatine of Durham*, exhibiting the Nature and Tendency of the Principles put forth by the Writers of the *Tracts for the Times*, and their various Allies and Associates. By the Rev. G. Stanley Faber. Two vols. 1842.
[3] *First Annual Report of the Parker Society*, 1842, p. 10.

Durham, Winchester, Lincoln, Rochester, Llandaff, Chester, Worcester, Ripon, Peterborough, Lichfield, Chichester, Worcester, and Sodor and Man. The second annual report announced that for 1843 7500 subscriptions had come in. In 1849 it was reported that the Duchess of Kent and the Archbishops of Canterbury and York had become subscribers. In issuing the thirteenth and final report the Committee of the Parker Society state that they had published in all fifty-five volumes of the writings of the Protestant Reformers, including an Index Volume to the whole of their publications. These volumes contain the writings of Cranmer, Ridley, Latimer, Jewel, Hooper, Bradford, Nowell, Whitaker, and other prominent men of the sixteenth century. Those who wish to find strong arguments against Ritualistic doctrines, drawn from the Bible and the writings of the Fathers, cannot do better than consult the publications of the Parker Society.

CHAPTER IX

Dr. Pusey's sermon on *The Holy Eucharist*—Denounced to the Vice-Chancellor—The Six Doctors—Their opinion of the sermon—Private negotiations with Pusey—Pusey suspended for two years—His protest—Dr. Hawkins' explanatory letter—Proposed friendly prosecution—Lord Camoys on Pusey's sermon—Curious Clerical Libel Case—An extraordinary Clerical Brawling Case—Protests against Puseyism—The *English Churchman* started by the Puseyites—Newman's progress Romeward—He resigns St. Mary's and retires to Littlemore—Archdeacon Wilberforce on "the insane love for Rome"—Palmer's *Narrative of Events*—Pusey issues "adapted" Roman Catholic books of devotion—Newman tells him they will "promote the cause of the Church of Rome"—Hook thinks "they will make men Infidels"—Extracts from these books—What Pius IX. said about Dr. Pusey—Bishop Blomfield on the effect of adapted Roman books—Puseyites advocate Ecclesiastical Prosecutions of Protestant clergy—The Bishop of Exeter and the Surplice in the Pulpit—Legality of the Black Gown in the Pulpit—Ward's *Ideal of a Christian Church*—Puseyite attack on Dr. Symons—Defeated—Attempt to prosecute the Rev. James Garbett—Failure—Stone Altars and Credence Tables—*Faulkener* v. *Litchfield*—Judgment of the Court of Arches—The Cambridge Camden Society—Denounced by the Rev. F. Close.

THE most important ecclesiastical event in the year 1843 was the sermon on *The Holy Eucharist a Comfort to the Penitent*, preached by Dr. Pusey before the University on the fourth Sunday after Easter, which led to his being suspended from preaching in the University pulpit for two years. In this sermon he taught, in unmistakable terms, the doctrine of the Real Presence in the consecrated elements, and what is termed the Eucharistic Sacrifice. The following extracts from the sermon show what his teaching was on this subject:—

"And we, if we are wise, shall never ask how they can be elements of this world and yet His very Body and Blood."[1]

---
[1] *The Holy Eucharist a Comfort to the Penitent*, p. 7. Oxford: 1843.

"The same reality of the Divine Gift makes It Angels' food to the Saint, the ransom to the sinner. And both because It is the Body and Blood of Christ. Were it *only* a thankful commemoration of His redeeming love, or *only* a showing forth of His death, or a strengthening *only* and refreshing of the soul, it were indeed a reasonable service, but it would have no direct healing for the sinner. To him its special joy is that it is his Redeemer's very Broken Body, It is His Blood, which was shed for the remission of his sins. In the words of the Ancient Church, he 'drinks his ransom,' he eateth that, 'the very Body and Blood of the Lord, the only Sacrifice for sin,' God 'poureth out' for him yet 'the most precious Blood of His Only Begotten.'"[1]

"And this may have been another truth, which our Lord intended to convey to us, when He pronounced the words as the form which consecrates the sacramental elements into His Body and Blood, that that Precious Blood is still, in continuance and application of His One Oblation once made upon the Cross, poured out for us now, conveying to our souls, as being His Blood, with the other benefits of His Passion, the remission of our sins also. . . . 'That which is in the Cup,' S. Chrysostome paraphrases, 'is that which flowed from His side, and of that do we partake.' How should we approach His Sacred Side, and remain leprous still? Touching with our very lips that cleansing Blood, how may we not, with the Ancient Church, confess, 'Lo, this hath touched my lips, and shall take away mine iniquities and cleanse my sins?'"[2]

The Lady Margaret Professor of Divinity, Dr. Faussett, denounced the sermon at once to the Vice-Chancellor (Dr. Wynter), and requested him to apply to Pusey for a copy of his sermon, in order that the soundness of its doctrine might be tested. In sending this request on to Pusey the Vice-Chancellor wrote :—"I do not know that at this period of time it is necessary that I should express my own opinion upon it [Pusey's sermon, which he had heard preached]. But in candour and fairness I think it right to confess that its general scope and certain particular passages have awakened in my mind painful doubts with regard to its strict conformity to the doctrines of the Reformed Church of England."[3] After a delay of a few

---

[1] *The Holy Eucharist a Comfort to the Penitent*, p. 18.
[2] *Ibid.* pp. 22, 23.
[3] *Life of Dr. Pusey*, vol. ii. p. 311.

days, and the insertion by him into the manuscript of certain references to the writings of the Fathers, Pusey sent his sermon as requested, together with a letter, in which he said:—"I felt so entirely sure that I heartily concur with the doctrine of the Church of England, I have so often and decidedly expressed my rejection of the doctrine of Transubstantiation, and the Canons of the Council of Trent upon it, that, neither before nor after preaching my sermon, had I the slightest thought that any could arraign it as contrary to the doctrines of our Church"; and, he added:—"I believe that after Consecration the Holy Elements are in their natural substances bread and wine, and yet are *also* the Body and Blood of Christ. This I believe is a mystery."[1] He concluded with a request that the Vice-Chancellor would "choose that course allowed by the Statute which permits the accused to answer for himself." The Vice-Chancellor thereupon appointed six Doctors as judges to try the case, of whom he was himself one. They met for the first time on May 24th, when the sermon was read to them and discussed. They met again on May 27th, when the greater number of them brought with them separate written opinions on the sermon. One of the number, Dr. Jelf, a personal friend of Pusey's, who had consented to be one of his judges "with the hope of benefiting" him,[2] said that he did not think the sermon contrary to the teaching of the Church of England; but even he had to acknowledge that there was in it "much that is objectionable in tone, and language, and tendency."[3] Having heard the opinion of the Court, the Vice-Chancellor declared that he "considered Dr. Pusey guilty of the charge made against him—namely, that he had preached certain things which were either dissonant from or contrary to the doctrine of the Church of England."[4]

Dr. Pusey's request to be heard personally at the trial was not acceded to. The biographer of Bishop Samuel Wilberforce says that, "The Statute under which the Board

[1] *Life of Dr. Pusey*, vol. ii. p. 313. [2] *Ibid.* p. 315.
[3] *Ibid.* p. 317. [4] *Ibid.* p. 317.

was appointed gave the accused the right to claim a hearing in his own defence"; [1] but this was not the case. One of the three eminent Counsel, later on employed (by Pusey) to give a legal opinion on the case (the Solicitor-General), gave it as his opinion that the Statute "did not necessarily require a hearing." [2] Canon Liddon says expressly that:—" It was true that the Statute did not provide in express terms that the author of a delated sermon should be heard in explanation or defence of his language." [3] Nevertheless it seems that it was open to the Vice-Chancellor to have granted Pusey's request, and I think it is much to be regretted that he did not do so. I do not, however, suppose that if Pusey had thus personally appeared before his judges that it would have altered their decision; and I believe that their judgment when given was a just one. Many a just judgment has been given even after a faulty trial. Yet, strictly speaking, Pusey's friends of the present day are not accurate in saying that he had no "hearing" before judgment was published against him; nor is it correct to state that his judges did not mention to him particular passages of his sermon which they considered unsound. It is true they did not hear his actual *voice;* but they had before them, and seriously considered, a lengthy statement in self-defence and explanation from his *pen;* and in this sense of the word he was *not* condemned unheard. And that written statement of his was based upon particular extracts from his sermons to which his attention had been called privately by the Vice-Chancellor, who requested a retractation of some of the specified statements of Pusey. The two documents forwarded to Pusey from the Vice-Chancellor, containing these extracts, are published in full in the *Life of Dr. Pusey*, pages 323, 324; and his reply, defending and explaining his position, fill four closely printed pages of that *Life*, from page 364 to 368. "On the afternoon of Thursday, June 1," says Canon Liddon, "the Vice-Chancellor and the Six Doctors met for a third time, and in order to consider Pusey's reply. That it did not

---

[1] *Life of Bishop Wilberforce*, vol. i. p. 228.
[2] *Life of Dr. Pusey*, vol. ii. p. 354.   [3] *Ibid.* p. 317.

satisfy them goes without saying."¹ On the following day the Vice-Chancellor published the sentence of suspension of Dr. Pusey from preaching in the University pulpit. On the same day Pusey published and circulated a protest against the sentence, in which occurs the following startling statement:—" I have ground to think that, as *no propositions out of my sermon have been exhibited to me as at variance with the doctrine of our Church*, so neither can they."² The negotiations which had taken place between the Vice-Chancellor and Pusey were, by the former's request, treated as secret and confidential. Were it not for this, I do not think Pusey could ever have dared to make the untrue statement contained in the extract from his protest just given. That Pusey himself thought he had had some opportunity of defending himself is clear from the private letter he sent to the Vice-Chancellor on the day of the sentence and protest:—" It does seem to me," he wrote, " to be so utterly contrary to all principles of justice and equity (not to speak of charity) to afford me *no further opportunity of vindication*, that I can only say I pray that my judges may not, in the Great Day, receive the measure which they have dealt to me."³ He had, therefore, on his own showing, "some opportunity of vindication" of his position, as the words "no *further* opportunity" implies; but he thought the opportunity was not sufficient; and in this, to a certain extent, I am disposed to agree with him. But nothing I have been able to discover justifies him in asserting that no propositions from his sermon had been exhibited to him. Rumours soon got abroad challenging the veracity of Pusey. They troubled him exceedingly, and no wonder. So he thought he would draw a red herring across the trail of his opponents, by shifting the controversy, from the truthfulness of his protest and his own reputation, to the merits of the sermon itself, and this by publishing the much criticised discourse. So, on June 11th, he wrote to Newman:—" Ward told me yesterday evening some statements in the *Morning Chronicle* about my Protest being 'Jesuitical,' 'every one here being dis-

---

¹ *Life of Dr. Pusey*, vol. ii. p. 325.
² *Ibid.* p. 329.   ³ *Ibid.* p. 330.

gusted at it,' &c., which makes it necessary to determine how to act. One line to which I have been inclining this morning, is to let these things die a natural death, commit my own reputation to God, stop privately the Protest in London, *and bring out my sermon, which will at once shift the battle from these grounds to the theological questions.* . . . I feared, as soon as I knew it, that they would make out a plausible case of inaccuracy against me; people will believe just as they wish, and the whole controversy will be about my veracity, which will indispose people to the truths of the sermon when it appears."[1] Tactics such as these were worthy of one who had already obtained a character for Jesuitical conduct. An explanation published by Dr. Hawkins, one of the Six Doctors, on December 31, 1844, in the form of a letter to the Bishop of Exeter, may here be quoted :—

"I will give," wrote Dr. Hawkins, "some account of the proceedings—such as, I hope, may show that, if they were in any way technically informal, they were substantially correct and just.

"It was, of course, our duty to act under the Statute; we had no power to amend it, and having ascertained the sense of the Statute as correctly as we could, with the aid of those recorded precedents to which we had access, we were satisfied that our business in the first instance was exclusively with *the written sermon*. If, indeed, the preacher could produce no copy of his discourse, the Statute expressly provided that he should be called upon to answer personally concerning the matters of which he was suspected or accused; but if (as in this instance) he delivered an authentic copy of the sermon, *there was no room for evidence or cross-examination*, and we had only to consider the sermon itself, not discussing with the writer the doctrines which it contained, but comparing them with the formularies of the Church. This painful duty, accordingly, we endeavoured to discharge as carefully as we could.

" *Yet, in point of fact, we had also before us, at that time, some explanation and defence of the sermon from the author.* For Dr. Pusey sent a letter *with the sermon*, explaining his sentiments at greater length with reference to the passage which was the most likely to be misconstrued; and he both prefaced his copy of the sermon and accompanied it throughout with parallel passages from older Divines

---

[1] *Life of Dr. Pusey*, vol. ii. p. 336.

and from the Fathers, intended to justify the expressions which he had used.

"But the judgment upon the sermon was only the first stage of the proceedings. The Vice-Chancellor, having now to consider the question as it respected *the writer*, could not forget that a writer's meaning might be misapprehended, or his expressions admit of qualification or correction, and even if in themselves censurable, might be no proof that the author entertained 'unsound opinions.' For the purpose of preventing such misapprehensions, therefore, he entered into communication with Dr. Pusey in the interval between the delivery of the judgment upon the sermon (May 27) and the sentence issuing against the preacher (June 2).

"It is true, the Vice-Chancellor, who is as kind as he is upright, did not desire the writer to wait upon him, nor did he call upon the writer, nor did he consider it his duty to enter into controversy with the preacher concerning points of doctrine, and did not *in this sense hear* him; *but he sent to Dr. Pusey*, by his most intimate friend, *written papers, stating the specific objections taken to his discourse*, and giving him opportunity to disclaim any meaning improperly attached to his expressions, and to declare his adherence to those parts of our Articles and formularies with which, under such imputed meanings, his expressions had appeared to be at variance. *Dr. Pusey replied to these communications at some length*, but the papers not having proved satisfactory to him, and his answers having failed to satisfy the Vice-Chancellor, the result was made known to the assessors, and the sentence issued."[1]

In reply to this letter, Dr. Pusey wrote:—"It is my duty to state explicitly that the communications made to me, after my sermon had been condemned, were expressly declared by the Vice-Chancellor to have been made *with a view to recantation, not to explanation.*"[2]

Of course the suspension created a great commotion in the ranks of those who, by this time, had become popularly known as Puseyites; and a great sensation was produced throughout the country. An effort was made to obtain a reversal of the sentence by an appeal to the secular Law Courts; but it fell through. Then a scheme was planned for a friendly lawsuit, in which one of Pusey's friends should be prosecutor and he the defend-

---

[1] *English Churchman*, January 9, 1845, p. 19.
[2] *Ibid.* p. 31.

ant, on a charge of preaching false doctrine in his sermon, contrary to the teaching of the Church of England. Dr. Hook was one of the first to suggest this plan. "I should think," he wrote to Pusey on June 4th, "you ought to demand of the Bishop an investigation under the Church Discipline Act."[1] Consultations with the lawyers took up a considerable time, but at length, on October 12, 1844, seventeen months after the sermon was preached, Pusey wrote to the Bishop of Oxford announcing the proposed friendly prosecution. "A friend of my own (Mr. Woodgate) will apply to your lordship to issue a Commission on my printing a sermon which had been already condemned in the University. Had the sermon been rightly condemned, this would have been a most grave offence, much graver than preaching it originally. I do then most earnestly implore your lordship not to refuse the Commission. I have no anxiety whatever about the issue if you grant it."[2] It is, I may here remark, wonderful to behold the love for ecclesiastical prosecutions early manifested by the Puseyites, when they expected results satisfactory to themselves. The Bishop of Oxford, before giving his decision, sought the advice of the Archbishop of Canterbury. That prelate was strongly against the issue of a Commission. He told the Bishop that the Church Discipline Act gave him the right to veto the proposed prosecution, and he warned him against being a party to "a transaction of rather a dubious character, certainly not straightforward."[3] Acting on this advice, the Bishop wrote to Pusey, on November 5th, declining to grant the Commission asked for :—"I must distinctly state," wrote the Bishop, "that I cannot consent to become a party to what I consider not to be a straightforward proceeding."[4]

It was a great blow to the Puseyite party, but it was nothing more than they deserved. The sermon was distinctly contrary to the teaching of the Church of England, and it could only rejoice the hearts of her avowed enemies. Two years later Newman pointed out that in this sermon, out of 140 texts of the Fathers cited by Pusey, only four

[1] *Life of Dr. Pusey*, vol. ii. p. 349.
[2] *Ibid.* p. 357. [3] *Ibid.* p. 359. [4] *Ibid.* p. 360.

were from the Fathers of the first three centuries.[1] These quotations from the Fathers, together with those from Anglican Divines cited in the appendix to the sermon, were exhaustively dealt with, later on, by the Rev. William Goode, in his work on *The Nature of Christ's Presence in the Eucharist*, published in two volumes in 1856. Of course, Pusey's sermon rejoiced the Romanists. At the annual meeting of the Roman Catholic Institute of Great Britain, held on June 12, 1843, the Chairman, Lord Camoys, said :—

"Look at the controversy now going on in the Established Church, especially at Oxford. (Cheers.) There was one Regius Professor (Dr. Pusey) just condemned and suspended for having advocated the doctrine of the Real Presence in the Eucharist. . . . He had heard at one of the meetings of the Institute a hope expressed that they (the Catholics) might live to see the day when High Mass would be celebrated in Westminster Abbey. (Tremendous cheering.) He knew not how probable such an event might be, but this they knew, that the doctrine of the Mass had been preached in the Cathedral of the University of Oxford—(loud cheering)—and it had been authoritatively declared, that if Dr. Pusey's sermon had not been condemned (as we understood the noble lord), six or seven Colleges of Oxford University were ready to have Mass said directly. (Tremendous cheering and applause.) There was, indeed, a very slender barrier between Puseyism and the Church of Rome." [2]

A curious clerical libel action was heard this year, on March 25th, at Cambridge, before Lord Chief Justice Tindal, in which the Rev. Mr. Belaney sought to recover damages from the Rev. Mr. Totton, Rector of Debden, in consequence of a libellous letter written by the defendant concerning the plaintiff. It appeared that Mr. Belaney had been employed by Mr. Totton as Curate, and that he had altered the services in a High Church direction. This annoyed the Rector very much, and after Mr. Belaney had ceased to be Curate, he wrote the letter complained of, in which he said that : "So long as Mr. Belaney, under the influence of a vile spirit of rancour and revenge, continued to visit the parish, and industriously fomented dis-

---

[1] *Life and Times of Cardinal Wiseman*, vol. i. p. 434.
[2] *Catholic Magazine*, vol. ii. for 1843, pp. 58, 59.

cord, no harmony could exist;" and that "he is, however, what I always thought him, a Papist in disguise." The jury gave a verdict for Mr. Belaney, damages forty shillings.[1]

A singular case of clerical brawling, Langley v. Burder, came before the Judicial Committee of Privy Council this year. The Rev. William Hawkes Langley, Perpetual Curate of Wheatley, Oxon., was, in 1841, prosecuted by the Bishop of Oxford (through his secretary, Mr. Burder), under the Church Discipline Act, for brawling in his own Parish Church during Divine Service! The case was heard in the Court of Arches, before Sir H. Jenner Fust. It was alleged that, on Sunday, May 9, 1841, while conducting Divine Service, and shortly before the conclusion of the Litany, the defendant, "in a chiding, quarrelsome, and brawling manner," addressed the congregation, and said amongst other things:—

"You were, perhaps, surprised at the pause I made at the end of the prayer, but it reminded me of my enemies. I have this morning received a letter from the Archdeacon, offering some clergyman to do duty for me: some one in the congregation has had the audacity to write to the Archdeacon on the subject. Who has had the audacity to do this? Is it a Puseyite, who wants to introduce Popery into the parish? I will, however, take care they never shall, as I will do my duty myself. I have preached the Gospel, and delivered my own soul, whether the people will hear, or whether they will forbear."

Mr. Langley then referred, in indignant terms, to certain charges against his personal character, and denied them emphatically. It was charged against him that "during the delivery of this address, he was in a very excited and impassioned state, and frequently struck the reading desk and the books thereon, in a very violent manner, with his clenched fist, and by such improper and incorrect conduct gave great offence to the congregation then assembled in the church, and reflected scandal and disgrace on his sacred profession." One would have thought that such conduct might easily have been dealt with by the Bishop outside of

---

[1] *English Churchman*, March 30, 1843, p. 199.

Court. The fact that Bishop Bagot's opinions were strongly in favour of the Tractarians, though he did not go with them in every particular, might have induced him to abstain from prosecuting a clergyman for a speech in which he attacked the Puseyites. Of course, it was very indiscreet on Mr. Langley's part to be so impatient. He might have waited until he had got into the pulpit, and then have delivered it in safety from a charge of brawling. Anyhow, the case was heard in the Court of Arches—it was the first case under the new Church Discipline Act—and on June 27, 1842, Sir H. Jenner Fust delivered judgment. The defence had been, he said, that a conspiracy existed against Mr. Langley amongst the parishioners, and that the Bishop was the head of the conspiracy; but he (the Judge) considered the defence an aggravation of the offence, and therefore he sentenced Mr. Langley to be suspended from his living for eight months, and to pay the costs of the case. It was demanded by the plaintiff that Mr. Langley should not be readmitted to his duties until he produced a certificate of good behaviour; but this the Judge very properly refused to grant. Mr. Langley appealed against the judgment to the Judicial Committee of Privy Council, who, on December 4, 1843, delivered judgment, confirming the sentence against him.[1]

I mention this interesting case here, partly to show that the High Church party were the first to put the Church Discipline Act into force, and also because the general question of brawling has of late become very prominent amongst us. I have been unable to find any proof against the personal character of Mr. Langley, though it is evident that charges had been brought against him. I believe that if he had been known to be an immoral man, the Bishop would have gone further, and prosecuted him on that account. I have no doubt that my Ritualistic readers will think me uncharitable, yet I cannot help expressing the opinion that if Mr. Langley had abstained, on that Sunday morning, from attacking the Puseyites, he would have

[1] Brodrick and Freemantle's *Judgments of the Judicial Committee of Privy Council*, pp. 39-43.

escaped with a private Episcopal censure for his conduct. Anyhow, the sentence of suspension for eight months for such an offence was inexcusably severe.

Several public protests against Puseyism were made by Protestant Churchmen during 1843. One of these was from the inhabitants of Blackburn and neighbourhood, and was addressed to the Bishop of Chester (Dr. John Bird). "We feel," they said, "ourselves bound by the ties both of duty and of gratitude to acknowledge our lasting obligations to your lordship for your firm, consistent, and uncompromising resistance to the system of those Tractarian divines, who, true to their self-assumed title of 'Ecclesiastical agitators,' declare their determination 'to intrude upon the peace of the contented, and raise doubts in the minds of the uncomplaining; vex the Church with controversy, alarm serious men, and interrupt the established order of things; set the father against the son, and the mother against the daughter.'" In replying to this address of protest against Puseyism, the Bishop of Chester wrote:—"I rejoice in the proof it affords that the principles established by our Reformers are dear to so many hearts; that so many in whose spiritual welfare I am concerned regard with just horror any departure from the 'truth as it is in Jesus'; whether it be by the way of return to exploded errors, or under the insidious pretence of development of undiscovered mystery."[1] An address from the inhabitants of Bolton was also sent to the Bishop of Chester, protesting against "the evil spirit and false doctrines" of the Puseyites. An address to the Vice-Chancellor and Heads of Houses in Oxford was adopted at a meeting, over which Lord Ashley presided, and was subsequently signed largely, in which "an earnest hope" was expressed "that the authorities of the University will take such steps as are by the constitution of the whole body and of the several Colleges open to them, for protecting the youth committed to their care from the dangerous [anti-Protestant] influence to which we have referred, and for securing to them for the future only such tuition as is in strict accordance with the prin-

[1] *English Churchman*, October 5, 1843, p. 627.

ciples of the Protestant Church and Constitution of these realms."[1]

In this year protests from parishioners against alterations made in the mode of conducting Divine Service by Puseyite clergymen became somewhat numerous. The *English Churchman* newspaper was started by the Puseyites on January 5, 1843, and soon its columns were filled with discussions and comments on such subjects as Altar Coverings, Alternate Chanting, Black Letter Saints, Christian Ceremonial, Copes, Crosses on the Altar, Decoration of Churches, Fast Days, Font Covers, Oblations in the Eucharist, Position of the Celebrant Priest, Reserve, and Stone Altars, thus affording to the public a clear proof of the advance of Puseyism in a Romeward direction. The *English Churchman* still continues to be published, but it no longer advocates the Sacerdotal cause. It has become the most outspoken of all papers against Ritualism.

During 1843 Newman made rapid strides in the direction of Rome. Early in the year he withdrew whatever he had written against the Church of Rome, and expressed his regret for having so written. He told his friend Mr. J. R. Hope-Scott, as we have already seen, with reference to this act, that he had "to eat a few dirty words."[2] On August 30th Newman wrote to a lady:—"We shall not leave the Church as others may. *We have no longings for Rome.*"[3] Only two days later he wrote a letter, marked "Confidential," to the Rev. J. B. Mozley, announcing his forthcoming resignation of the living of St. Mary's, Oxford, and adding:—"The truth then is, I am not a good son enough of the Church of England to feel I can in conscience hold preferment under her. *I love the Church of Rome too well.* Now please *burn this*, there's a good fellow, for you sometimes let letters lie on your mantelpiece."[4] Four weeks later Newman wrote to his sister, on September 29th:—"I do so despair of the Church of England, and am so evidently cast off by her, and, on

---

[1] *English Churchman*, July 27, 1843, p. 467.
[2] *Memoirs of James Hope-Scott*, vol. ii. p. 19.
[3] Newman's *Letters*, vol. ii. p. 421.
[4] *Ibid.* p. 423.

the other hand, *I am so drawn to the Church of Rome*, that I think it *safer*, as a matter of honesty, *not* to keep my living. This is a very different thing from having any *intention* of joining the Church of Rome."[1] With such views most people would have been of the opinion that the only "honest" course would have been to have joined the Church of Rome at once. But he remained in the Church of England for another two years, "loving the Church of Rome" all the time, and with "despair" in his heart concerning the Church of England. Indeed, as early as October 25, 1843, he declared:—"I think the Church of Rome the Catholic Church, and ours not part of the Catholic Church, because not in communion with Rome."[2] In accordance with this inconsistent position he told the Rev. J. B. Mozley, on November 24th :—"I am now publishing sermons, which speak more confidently about our position than I inwardly feel, but I think it right and do not care for seeming inconsistent."[3] Six weeks later Newman wrote to the Rev. T. W. Allies:—"I will say to you, what the occasion makes me say, but which I should not like repeated as from me, that I am not to be trusted. Others say this freely; but I feel it myself too certainly, though it is not well openly to profess it."[4] Newman resigned the living of St. Mary's on September 16th, and removed to Littlemore, the Vicarage of which he retained, however, only for a short time, and then he retired into lay communion. On September 25th he preached at Littlemore the sermon on "The Parting of Friends," which has generally been considered a kind of farewell to the Church of England. The story of the Littlemore Monastery, which at this period was in full operation, I have related elsewhere.[5]

The opinion which Archdeacon Samuel Wilberforce had this year formed of Puseyism and the Romeward Movement, may profitably be quoted here. Writing to his brother Henry, on August 18, 1843, about a Curate, he

---

[1] Newman's *Letters*, vol. ii. p. 425.
[2] Newman's *Apologia*, p. 351.
[3] Newman' *Letters*, vol. ii. p. 430.
[4] *A Life's Decision.* By T. W. Allies, 2nd edition, p. 41. London: 1894.
[5] *Secret History of the Oxford Movement*, chap. i.

said:—"It is so likely that he has been misrepresented, so likely that preaching, it may be injudiciously, against what with him I think *the perils of our Church from the insane love of Rome*, which has possessed many of the followers of the Tract Movement."[1] "For you must," continued the Archdeacon, "remember, dearest H., that your own feelings are here a bad guide. You must remember that men who, like myself, are *not* Low Churchmen, that even we feel in the very centre of our hearts that *the greatest verities of the inner Christian life are absolutely perilled by the Tract system.*"

The Tractarians were made very uncomfortable this year by an exposure of their Romanising work by one who up to that time they had considered as one of their own leaders—the Rev. William Palmer, of Worcester College, Oxford. Mr. Palmer was one of the first to join the Oxford Movement, and therefore the pamphlet he wrote on the subject naturally created a sensation. It was entitled:—*A Narrative of Events Connected with the Publication of "The Tracts for the Times," With Reflections on Existing Tendencies to Romanism.*[2] In issuing this pamphlet, Mr. Palmer withdrew none of the opinions on Church government and doctrine which he had previously held; nor did he in any way censure the *Tracts for the Times;* but he saw clearly that a party had arisen within the Church of England bent on leading her to Rome, and in his pamphlet he proved this by numerous quotations from the writings of the advanced section, more especially from the *British Critic;* and he even went so far as to declare that there were those amongst them who "look on the Papal Supremacy, the Invocation of Saints, &c., as Divinely instituted."[3]

"The *only* difficulty," wrote Mr. Palmer, "with which those who uphold Church principles have had to contend, is the imputation of a tendency to Popery. The continual assertion of our opponents of all kinds has been, that Romanism is the legitimate

---

[1] *Life of Bishop Wilberforce*, vol. i. p. 288.
[2] It was republished by the author in 1883, with a lengthy Introduction and Supplement. London: Rivingtons.
[3] *Narrative of Events Connected with the Tracts for the Times*, 3rd edition p. 64. Oxford: Parker. 1843.

PROGRESS OF THE ROMEWARD MOVEMENT

conclusion of our principles. Romanists, Dissenters, Latitudinarians, and many others have reiterated the assertion, till the world is nearly persuaded of its truth. But what can we say—what defence can be made, when *it is undeniable that Romanism, in its very fullest extent, has advocates amongst ourselves;* that they have influence in the *British Critic;* that they are on terms of intimacy and confidence with leading men; that no public protest is entered against their proceedings by the advocates of Church principles? It is the conviction of the necessity of making some attempt, however feeble, to arrest *an intolerable evil*, which has induced me to publish this narrative of our proceedings."[1]

Yet, after all, though Mr. Palmer could not see it, the Romanising teaching against which he protested, was but the natural development of the sacerdotal teaching of the *Tracts for the Times*. Mr. Palmer's testimony against his former friends is, however, all the stronger, as coming from one who himself was a High Churchman of a decided type. The Oxford Movement made rapid progress towards Rome in 1843.

But still more rapid was the progress in 1844. It was in this year that Dr. Pusey commenced the publication of Roman Catholic books of devotion, "Adapted to the Use of the English Church." He had an idea of translating the Breviary, but only a few small portions were circulated. He asked Newman's advice about it. That astute man at once saw how it would help the Church of Rome. "I am," he wrote to Pusey, "quite of opinion that any Breviary, however corrected, &c., will tend to prepare minds for the Church of Rome. I fully think you will be doing so by your publication . . . I do not think our system will bear it. It is like sewing a new piece of cloth on an old garment. Did I wish to promote the cause of the Church of Rome, I should say, Do what you propose to do."[2] The Rev. W. K. Hamilton (afterwards Bishop of Salisbury), High Churchman though he was, viewed Pusey's adapted books with alarm, and wrote to tell him that they tended to foster an unfilial spirit in members of the Church of England.[3] Archdeacon Samuel Wilberforce disliked them exceedingly.

[1] Palmer's *Narrative of Events Connected with the Tracts for the Times*, pp. 69, 70.
[2] *Life of Dr. Pusey*, vol. ii. p. 390.
[3] *Ibid.* p. 394.

He wrote on April 4, 1844 :—"I opened yesterday Pusey's translation (just out) of Avrillon's mode of keeping Lent, with an introduction by Pusey. I think it fuller of sad and humiliating bits of superstition than anything of his I have yet seen."[1] Dr. Hook was indignant, and declared that one effect of these adapted works would be that they "will make men decided infidels."[2] It may be useful if we here give extracts from some of these adapted Romish books, and from the prefaces Pusey wrote to them, as justifying the dislike to them felt and expressed, not only by Evangelical Churchmen, but by High Churchmen also :—

"For both the large heads, under which these and the like wants would fall—contemplation and self-discipline—*the spiritual writers of Foreign Churches have, as yet, some obvious advantages over our own ;* for the discipline and knowledge of self, through that knowledge of the human heart which results *from habitual confession ;* for contemplation, *in the Monastic Orders*, as joining, in all cases, contemplation and mental prayer with charity and mortification."[3]

"He who hears the word of God without attention, and without respect, is not less guilty than he who by carelessness should allow the Body of Jesus Christ to fall to the ground."[4]

"The most perfect Christians consecrate themselves to God in a Religious State only, that they may be the more separated from the world."[5]

"In vain do we strive to obtain heaven, and *to expiate*, by our repentance, the sins of which we have been guilty, if we are not assisted by Thy grace. We acknowledge our weakness; but we know also that we can do all in Him who strengtheneth us. It is Thou alone who canst give to our labours and our fasts the acceptableness which they need in order *to appease Thy wrath, to efface our sin*, to draw down upon us Thy mercy, *and to obtain eternal life*, which we hope for through the merits of Jesus Christ."[6]

"The rebellion of the body must be mortified by fasts, *Disciplines, Hair Shirts*, vigils, and other similar austerities, as discretion and obedience may teach."[7]

"Never resist the will of thy Superiors, but show them a ready obedience, executing promptly all their commands, and with most

---

[1] *Life of Bishop Wilberforce*, vol. i. p. 236.
[2] *Life of Dr. Pusey*, vol. ii. p. 431.
[3] Avrillon's *Guide to Passing Lent Holily*, Pusey's *Preface*, p. xi.
[4] *Ibid.* p. 270. [5] *Ibid.* p. 282. [6] *Ibid.* p. 278.
[7] Scupoli's *Spiritual Combat*, p. 48.

willingness such as humble thee, and are most opposed to thy natural will and inclination."[1]

"Appearing once *in the form of an infant* to one of His pure and devoted creatures, she asked Him [Jesus] with great simplicity to recite the Angelical Salutation. He readily began: 'Hail Mary, full of grace, the Lord is with Thee, blessed art thou among women,' and then stopped, being unwilling to praise Himself, in the words that follow."[2]

"Before Communion (whatever be our object in receiving It) we must cleanse and purify ourselves, if stained with mortal sin, in the Sacrament of Penance."[3]

"Then as the time of Communion approaches, think What it is thou art about to receive! The Son of God, of Majesty Incomprehensible, before Whom the Heavens and all the powers therein do tremble. The Holy of Holies, the Spotless Mirror, and the Incomprehensible Purity, beside Whom no creature is clean. . . . *Thou art (I say) about to receive God*, in Whose Hand are the life and death of the whole Universe."[4]

"When, thyself, about to communicate, enliven thy faith to see under the accidents of the consecrated elements, the true Lamb of God that taketh away sins."[5]

"*By the law of God we mean* all that is contained in the Decalogue, and all ordinances emanating from a legitimate power, whether written, or authorised and confirmed by custom. We comprehend *also the statutes* and general regulations *made by prelates and ecclesiastical superiors*."[6]

"Happy, at least, is it, if they who think they hold most accurately the corruption of nature, can even understand the language of the self-abhorrence of Saints. Take . . . his who ever prayed that his sins might not bring the vengeance of God on the towns where he preached ['St. Dominic,' Founder of the Inquisition which *slew the Saints of God*]; or of those who wept for their sins, until sight was impaired ['St. Francis of Assisium and St. Ignatius Loyola,' the latter being the founder of the Jesuits]; or his, who, having renounced all the riches and glories of this world, habitually accounted his only fit dwelling to be hell, or being spit upon all night, counted no place fitter than his own face ['St. Francis Borgia,' a Jesuit.]"[7]

"And now, in our entire ignorance of its very nature, the name of '*the Rosary*' or '*Beads*' is associated only with ideas of super-

---

[1] Scupoli's *Spiritual Combat*, p. 47.
[2] *Ibid.* p. 89.
[3] *Ibid.* p. 134.
[4] *Ibid.* p. 141.
[5] *Ibid.* p. 190.
[6] *The Foundations of the Spiritual Life.* By F. Surin, a Jesuit Priest, p. 202.
[7] *Ibid.*, Pusey's *Preface*, pp. xix., xx.

stition, even in minds who, if they knew it, would be shocked at their own thoughts." [1]

"It is almost the inevitable consequence of such compendious or arbitrary selections or substitutions of doctrine, as of 'Justification by Faith,' or even 'The Atonement' for 'Christ Crucified,' that in the end they contract men's faith." [2]

"After the use of the *Exercitia Spiritualia* of St. Ignatius [Loyola] had been introduced into Portugal (among other countries) with a wonderful change of life, it was reported in Coimbra that those who made these holy retreats had strange visions, which led them to extraordinary fervour." [3]

"The *Manuel des Confesseurs*, is a *most valuable* digest of the judgments of some of the most experienced Confessors of the Church, and *of the greatest use*, whether in the receiving of Confessions, or the more ordinary spiritual ministrations." [4]

"CHRIST—That thou mayest be more fully restored to My favour after thus confessing thy unrighteousness to Me, go and show thyself also to the Priest, to whom I have given the power of binding and of loosing. Whoso hideth his wickednesses shall not be put right, but he that confesses and forsakes them shall obtain mercy. My son, be not ashamed to tell the truth for thy soul's sake. There is a shame that bringeth sin, and there is a shame that bringeth glory. Open, then, thy conscience frankly and sincerely to him who is in My Stead, and he shall open Heaven to thee. . . . Master this preposterous shame; humble thyself before My Priest, whom I have appointed in My Place, as My Ambassador, and thy counsellor and physician. Declare thy wickednesses, that thou mayest be justified." [5]

"We pray Thee, also, O Lord, Holy Father, *for the souls of the faithful departed*, especially—that this great Sacrament of Thy Love may be to them salvation, joy, and refreshment." [6]

I have given a great deal of space to these extracts from Dr. Pusey's adapted Roman Catholic works, on the title page of each of which was printed the words:—"Adapted to the Use of the English Church," because he who was responsible for them became, at about this time, and con-

---

[1] *The Foundations of the Spiritual Life*, Pusey's *Preface*, p. xxvi.
[2] *Ibid.* p. xxix. [3] *Ibid.* p. liii. *note*.
[4] *Ibid.* p. lvi. *note*. The book which Pusey thus highly commended, without any qualification, was one of the most filthy of all the filthy Confessional books published in the Roman Church. When Pusey translated it in 1878, he left out the filthy reading as unsuited for English Confessors' circumstances, but he did not condemn the thing itself.
[5] Horst's *Paradise for the Christian Soul*, vol. i. part iii. pp. 15-17. There seems something fearfully wicked in placing such words in the Saviour's mouth, as though Confession to Him were not sufficient. [6] *Ibid.* vol. ii. part v. p. 126.

tinued until his death, the acknowledged leader of what I must term the Romeward Movement in the Church of England. These citations show most clearly how far Pusey had already gone in Popery and superstition, and whither he was leading his deluded disciples. These adapted Popish works had a very large circulation, and undoubtedly did much to lead many to Rome. There was much of truth in what Pope Pius IX. said of Pusey, in an interview with the Rev. A. P. Stanley (the future Dean of Westminster) in 1866. In relating the interview Dean Stanley says:—

"He [the Pope] finally said, 'You know Pusey. When you meet him, give him this message from me—that I compare him to a bell, which always sounds to invite the faithful to Church, and itself always remains outside.'"[1]

The High Church Bishop of London (Dr. Blomfield) in his Charge, delivered in 1846, referred to, amongst others of the same class, these adapted Roman books of Pusey's—though he did not mention Pusey by name. He said:—

"I confess that I cannot understand how any person, professing to be a member of our branch of the Church Catholic, can reconcile it to his conscience to be in any way accessory to proceedings the effect of which, upon the minds of those who are imperfectly instructed, must be to diminish the seeming importance of those fundamental differences which separate the Churches of England and Rome; to make them dissatisfied with the doctrine and discipline of the one, and to habituate them to regard with complacency, and in due time with affection, the worst errors of the other. I can understand this conduct on the part of one of that Society to whom it is permitted to disguise their real sentiments, and to assume any character which best enables them to propagate the errors of Rome; but I cannot comprehend the self-delusion by which any person pursuing this course can persuade himself that he is faithful to his solemn engagements as a clergyman of the English Church. I cannot but regard such a policy as more to be censured and feared than open, honest, undisguised hostility."[2]

During the year 1844 the Puseyites manifested an intense desire to expel some of their opponents from the Church of England by means of ecclesiastical prosecutions.

[1] *Life of Dean Stanley*, vol. ii. p. 358.
[2] *Memoir of Bishop Blomfield*, vol. ii. pp. 75, 76.

Their chief organ, the *English Churchman*, was very energetic in this direction. Some correspondents of that paper started a discussion on this subject early in the year, in consequence of a clerical Declaration in favour of Protestant principles which had just been issued. With reference to this Declaration one of them wrote:—"It is their [the Bishops'] business to punish heresy, it is ours [the laity] to bring it under their notice. Let us, in vindication of our Mother's honour, now act on this principle. If the obnoxious document be really published in any official way, let a fund be immediately raised, and a committee named, for the purpose of proceeding in the Ecclesiastical Courts against the principal signer—say the senior D.D. or the first of that rank on the list—for heresy. I am very ignorant of ecclesiastical law; but of course the first step would be to take counsel's advice as to the proper mode of proceeding."[1] A month later another correspondent wrote:—"I am prepared to raise contributions, from clerical friends and others, with a view to share the expense of bringing to justice, in our Ecclesiastical Courts, those unfaithful Ministers of the Church who have in their late public Declaration proclaimed themselves heretics."[2] The Declaration actually contained not a word of heresy from beginning to end, but a strong affirmation of Protestant doctrines such as any Evangelical clergyman of the present day would gladly sign. But it denied the Puseyite theory of Baptismal Regeneration, Apostolical Succession, and a Sacerdotal Priesthood, and affirmed the doctrine of Justification by Faith only, and that the Bible alone is the sole and only Rule of Faith.[3] It was very largely signed, and if the Puseyites could have had their own way those who signed it would soon have been deprived of their livings and curacies.

Towards the close of September it was publicly announced in Exeter that two Church of England clergymen, the Rev. H. Bulteel, formerly Fellow of Exeter College,

---

[1] *English Churchman*, February 1, 1844, p. 74.
[2] *Ibid.* March 7, 1844, p. 153.
[3] See the document in full in the *English Churchman*, January 25, 1844, pp. 59, 60.

Oxford, and the Rev. J. Shore, M.A., would preach at the opening of the "Episcopal Free Church" in that city. Thereupon the *English Churchman* furiously demanded a prosecution of these clergymen. "The intended schismatical proceedings announced in the following advertisement show the necessity of formally and ecclesiastically *depriving* the rebellious clergy, so that there may no longer be any doubt as to whether they do or do not belong to us. . . . We trust that the Lord Bishop of Exeter will set an example to his brethren, and will proceed canonically against those of his clergy who refuse to conform to the rules of the Church."[1] A month later the *English Churchman* devoted a whole leading article to this subject, and declared:—"To speak plainly, we desire, most earnestly and respectfully, to impress upon their lordships the Bishops, the important fact, that by allowing palpable heresy to be publicly preached and published, without public and personal censure of the offender, they are extensively alienating the confidence and attachment of some most valuable men in the Church. A jealous vigilance to detect the slightest appearance of heresy, and the prompt punishment of heretical teachers, have ever been among the most visible notes of the Catholic Church."[2] Not a word of denunciation was heard, from these Puseyite lovers of prosecution, against the "State Courts," or their interference with the Church, and I am convinced that if they had only consented to interpret the law as the Puseyites desired, their modern successors, the Ritualists, would have been, on the whole, quite content with things as they are. In that case there would not, by this time, have been left a Protestant clergyman in the Church of England. They would have been deprived of their livings long ago as so many heretics.

The High Church Bishop of Exeter was ready enough to put pressure on the Evangelical clergy of his Diocese. On November 19th he issued a Pastoral Letter on "Observance of the Rubric in the Book of Common Prayer," in which he urged a stricter observance of the Rubrics; and ordered all his clergy to wear the surplice in preaching.

[1] *English Churchman*, September 26, 1844, p. 613.
[2] *Ibid.* October 24, 1844, p. 677.

"The law," said the Bishop, "beyond all question which can now arise, requires that the surplice be always used in the sermon, which is part of the Communion Service; and as to all other times, whenever a sermon is part of the ministration of the parochial clergy, there is so little reason for question, that I resolve the doubt by requiring that the surplice be always used."[1]

The opposition to the use of the surplice in the pulpit was, however, too strong for the Bishop, who, within five weeks from issuing it, had to withdraw his order. He had issued an illegal order, founded on a mistaken interpretation of the law. The Black Gown in the pulpit is strictly legal. In the case of *Robinson Wright* v. *Tugwell*, judgment was given in the Court of Appeal on November 28, 1896, by Lord Justice Smith, who said:—

"The 'warrant in law' for the Black Gown is constant use for centuries. Inasmuch as no positive law exists, and no objection against the legality of the Black Gown in the pulpit, which has ranged over three hundred years, can be found, and there is no decision that its use is illegal, I agree with what I understand Mr. Justice North to have held, that its use is not illegal."[2]

The principal ecclesiastical event in 1844 was the publication by the Rev. W. G. Ward of his *Ideal of a Christian Church*, in which he declared that he subscribed the Thirty-Nine Articles "in a non-natural sense," and that in doing so he "renounced no one Roman doctrine." "We find," he exclaimed, "oh most joyful, most wonderful, most unexpected sight! We find the whole cycle of Roman doctrine gradually possessing numbers of English Churchmen." I have given elsewhere[3] a brief history of the controversy which arose out of this publication, and therefore I need say no more about it here, except to give below a list of the leading publications relating to it.[4]

[1] *English Churchman*, December 5, 1844, p. 769.
[2] The Lord Chief Justice of England and Lord Justice Lindley agreed in this judgment, the text of which is printed in the *Church Intelligencer*, January 1897, pp. 5, 6.
[3] *Secret History of the Oxford Movement*, chap. ix.
[4] 1. *The Ideal of a Christian Church.* By the Rev. W. G. Ward, M.A., 2nd edition, pp. xiv., 600. London: James Toovey. 1844.
2. *Selections from a Work entitled "The Ideal of a Christian Church," Illustrative of its Tendency to Promote Dutifulness to the English Church*, pp. 24. London: Toovey. 1844.

PUSEYITE OPPOSITION TO DR. SYMONS

At the beginning of the Michaelmas Term, 1844, Dr. Wynter's term of office as Vice-Chancellor expired. The next in order of succession was Dr. Symons, Warden of Wadham College. Now Dr. Symons was a very decided Protestant, whose opposition to the Oxford Movement was very well known; and besides all this he was one of the Six Doctors who had condemned Dr. Pusey, the previous year, for his sermon on *The Holy Eucharist a Comfort to the Penitent*. This last offence could not possibly be forgiven by Pusey's friends, who determined to show their vindictiveness by opposing the election of Dr. Symons as Vice-Chancellor. Pusey was very zealous in the new campaign against Symons. "I use no concealment now," he wrote to his brother, "if ever I did, that I think Dr. S.[ymons] ought to be opposed as a protest against heresy and heretical decisions. If the University accepted him without a protest, it seemed like making itself a party to it."[1] A prominent member of the Tractarian party wrote to the *English Churchman*, over the signature "N. E. S.":—"It does then seem to me, what I have all along made it, a

---

3. *An Address to Members of Convocation In Protest against the Proposed Statute*. By the Rev. W. G. Ward, M.A., pp. 56. London: Toovey. 1845.

4. *A Letter to the Vice-Chancellor In Connection with the Case of the Rev. W. G. Ward*. By A. C. Tait, D.C.L. (afterwards Archbishop of Canterbury), pp. 22. London: W. Blackwood. 1845.

5. *A Letter to the Bishop of London On a Subject Connected with the Recent Proceedings at Oxford*. By the Rev. Frederick Oakeley, M.A., pp. 39. London: Toovey. 1845.

6. *The New Statute and Mr. Ward*. A Letter by the Rev. Frederick D. Maurice, pp. 31.

7. *Heads of Consideration On the Case of Mr. Ward*. By the Rev. John Keble, M.A., pp. 15. Oxford: Parker. 1845.

8. *The Proposed Degradation and Declaration*. By George Moberley, D.C.L. (afterwards Bishop of Salisbury), pp. 29. Oxford: Parker. 1845.

9. *Suggestions On the New Statute*. By W. Gresley, M.A., Prebendary of Lichfield, pp. 13. London: James Burns. 1845.

10. *A Letter to the Hebdomadal Board On Mr. Ward's Case*. By the Rev. W B. Baxter, 2nd edition, pp. 14. London: James Burns. 1845.

11. *MDCCCXLV. The Month of January*. Oxford. By W. Winstanley Hull, M.A., pp. 18. London: Seeley.

12. *An Earnest Appeal to the Members of the Oxford Convocation*. By Henry Arthur Woodgate, B.D., pp. 9. London: Burns. 1845.

13. *A Defence of Voting against the Propositions to be Submitted to Convocation on February* 13, 1845. By W. F. Donkin, M.A., pp. 7. Oxford: Parker. 1845.

14. *The Claim to "Hold, as Distinct from Teaching," Explained*. By Frederick Oakeley, M.A., pp. 24. London: Toovey. 1845.

15. *Subscription to the Articles*. By George Dudley Ryder, M.A., pp. 42. London: Toovey. 1845.

[1] *Life of Dr. Pusey*, vol. ii. p. 412.

main item in the grounds for opposing Dr. Symons, that he was one of that body who did their best to set the mark of the beast on the Church of England."[1] Dr. Hook, when asked to go to Oxford and vote against the election of Dr. Symons, refused to do so, and gave his reasons in a letter to a friend:—

"Now, after the publication of Mr. Ward's book, which defends Popery on ultra-Protestant principles, and is therefore subversive both of principle and truth; and after various publications which have appeared of late with the evident intention of introducing Mariolatry, in other words idolatry, into our Church, and of defending the very worst abominations of Popery, there are very many persons who, having devoted all the energies of a lifetime to the service of their beloved and holy mother, the Church of England, contending equally against Popery on the one hand, and ultra-Protestantism on the other, would shrink with abhorrence from any appearance of sanctioning these heresies. As we cannot take part against Dr. Symons without seeming to side with the Romanisers, we must stand aloof from the contest."[2]

The efforts of the Puseyites to defeat Dr. Symons were in vain. The election took place on October 8th, when 882 votes were given for Dr. Symons, and only 183 against him. Small as the minority was, it afforded to the public evidence of the growing power of the Puseyites.

In the month of May, the Rev. Charles Marriott, a prominent leader of the Tractarians, wrote to the Vice-Chancellor of Oxford, requiring him to summon a Board of Heresy to examine certain charges which he (Mr. Marriott) had to bring against the Rev. James Garbett, Professor of Poetry, founded on a sermon preached by him before the University. I have not been able to learn what were the portions of Mr. Garbett's sermon against which Mr. Marriott protested as heretical, though I have no doubt it was some Protestant statement. On May 29th the Vice-Chancellor sent the following reply to Mr. Garbett:—

"The Vice-Chancellor begs to acknowledge the receipt of a copy of the sermon which, in consequence of a formal allegation of complaint, he requested Mr. Garbett to deliver to him, under the

---

[1] *English Churchman*, August 29, 1844, p. 549.
[2] *Ibid.* October 10, 1844, p. 641.

provision of the Statute, Tit. xvi. sec. 11. The Vice-Chancellor having had before him, since Friday, the 24th inst., the sermon which has thus been called in question, and having carefully considered what steps it might be his duty to take on the occasion, informs Mr. Garbett, without delay, that in the exercise of the discretion reserved to him by the Statute, he deems it unnecessary to institute any further proceedings."

For the first time in the history of the Romeward Movement, the legality of Stone Altars and Credence Tables was brought before the Ecclesiastical Courts this year. The Cambridge Camden Society had restored the Church of the Holy Sepulchre, Cambridge, commonly known as the Round Church, and towards the end of the year 1843 handed over the Church thus restored to the Incumbent and Churchwardens. On February 14, 1844, the Incumbent, the Rev. R. R. Faulkener, issued a circular in which he asserted that during the restoration the Cambridge Camden Society had introduced into the Church "a Stone Altar, without the knowledge or consent of the Incumbent"; and also a Credence Table. The Churchwardens replied to this circular, taking the side of the Society against the Incumbent. A vestry meeting was next held, at which it was decided to apply to the Ecclesiastical Court for a Faculty confirming the restorations which had been made by the Society. To this Mr. Faulkener replied that he yielded to none of his parishioners in gratitude to the Society for what it had done in restoring his Church, the Stone Altar and Credence Table alone excepted.

"Let these things," said the Incumbent, "be taken away at once. Harmony, peace, love, and goodwill will quickly follow. And why not? What objection can be raised to a plain wooden table, like that which our fathers and we have been so long accustomed to use? Christianity by its very nature requires, and in express words prescribes a Communion Table. And I ask no more. Surely, as Incumbent of the Church, I ought not to have a Stone Altar forced into it against my conscience. God forbid! The Camden Society may offer me one of their Stone Altars, but they shall not, while I have a voice to speak, silence me in protesting loudly against this abomination."[1]

---

[1] *English Churchman*, March 7, 1844, p. 144.

In the Consistory Court of Ely, on July 25, 1844, the Churchwardens applied for a faculty confirming the erection of the Stone Altar and Credence Table. The Court gave judgment in favour of the application. Thereupon there was great rejoicing in the Puseyite camp, whose members knew very well the importance to them of the decision, however much they might, in public, term the dispute an unimportant and trifling one. But their rejoicings were shortlived. The Incumbent gave notice of an appeal to the Court of Arches. This was met by the Puseyites with a howl of indignation and gross personal insult. The organ of the Puseyite party had the indecency to comment on the appeal in the following terms :—

"We might apply to Mr. Faulkener the old alliterative description of a bad wife :—

'Weak and wanton,
Wicked and wilful,
Wrangling and wasteful.'

But then he is wasteful of other people's property; he begs money that he may spend it upon his own fancies and follies, knowing, as he does, that every farthing which he compels his opponents to spend upon him, would, but for him, have been spent to the honour and glory of Almighty God. Thus he robs God as well as man."[1]

But for all this insult, abuse, and bluster, the case came at length into the Court of Arches, and on January 31, 1845, judgment was given by Sir Herbert Jenner Fust, reversing the decision of the Ely Consistorial Court, and declaring Stone Altars and Credence Tables illegal in the Church of England. In delivering judgment he said :—

"I was asked, why should a Stone Font be directed to be used, and a Stone Communion Table be proscribed? To this I answer, the law has sanctioned the one and excluded the other, and for this very obvious reason; to Stone Altars or tables superstitious notions were attached, which did not belong to Stone Fonts."[2]

"After maturely weighing the subject, the conscientious opinion in my mind is, that a structure like the present [*i.e.* the Stone Altar] is not a Communion Table within the meaning of the

---

[1] *English Churchman*, November 28, 1844, p. 758.
[2] Robertson's *Ecclesiastical Reports*, vol. i. p. 255.

STONE ALTARS AND CREDENCE TABLES 253

Rubric; and that the Credence Table, being an adjunct not recognised by our Church, cannot be pronounced for. In coming to this conclusion, I do not go so far as to admonish the Churchwardens to remove them. All I can do is, to refuse to confirm the sentence of the Court below. A question here arises, whether I can so alter the Faculty prayed, as to omit the Stone Altar and Credence Table, and grant it in other respects, confirming all other things not comprised within the former Faculty. I see no objection to that, and such must be the decree of the Court." [1]

Twelve years later the Judicial Committee of Privy Council in the case of *Liddell* v. *Westerton*, on March 21, 1857, confirmed the decision of the Court of Arches in the above case (known as *Faulkener* v. *Litchfield*) as to Stone Altars, declaring them illegal in the Church of England, but reversing the judgment as to Credence Tables. On this latter point the Judicial Committee of Privy Council said:—

"The next question is, as to the Credence Tables. Here the Rubrics of the Prayer Book become important. Their Lordships entirely agree with the opinions expressed by the learned Judges in these cases, and in *Faulkener* v. *Litchfield*, that in the performance of the services, Rites, and Ceremonies ordered by the Prayer Book, the directions contained in it must be strictly observed; that no omission and no addition can be permitted; but they are not prepared to hold that the use of all articles not expressly mentioned in the Rubric, although quite consistent with, and even subsidiary to the service, is forbidden. Organs are not mentioned, yet because they are auxiliary to the singing, they are allowed. Pews, cushions to kneel upon, pulpit cloths, hassocks, seats by the Communion Table, are in constant use, yet they are not mentioned in the Rubric.

"Now what is a Credence Table? It is simply a small side-table, on which the bread and wine are placed before the consecration, having no connection with any superstitious usage of the Church of Rome. Their removal has been ordered on the ground that they are adjuncts to an Altar; their Lordships cannot but think that they are more properly to be regarded as adjuncts to a Communion Table." [2]

The Cambridge Camden Society, which had restored the

[1] Robertson's *Ecclesiastical Reports*, vol. i. pp. 259, 260.
[2] Brodrick and Freemantle's *Judgments of the Judicial Committee of the Privy Council*, p. 153.

Round Church at Cambridge, was founded in 1839, for the purpose of promoting the restoration of Churches on the lines of pre-Reformation times. Perhaps its real object was never more accurately described than by the Rev. Francis Close, Rector of Cheltenham, and afterwards Dean of Carlisle, in a sermon which he preached on November 5, 1844:—

"During the year now drawing to a close," he said, "my attention has been more particularly directed to the same class of [Tractarian] errors and false doctrine promulgated in a still more plausible and attractive form, namely, under the plea of reviving Church Architecture. It will be my object then, on the present occasion, to show that as Romanism is taught *Analytically* at Oxford, it is taught *Artistically* at Cambridge—that it is inculcated theoretically, in Tracts, at one University, and it is *sculptured, painted, and graven* at the other. The Cambridge Camdenians build Churches and furnish symbolic vessels, by which the Oxford Tractarians may carry out their principles."[1]

Dr. Close proved his indictment of the Cambridge Camden Society (which, however, must not be identified with the Camden Society recently united to the Royal Historical Society) by abundant extracts from its publications, showing clearly that the design was to restore Churches so as to make them suited for Popish services and Popish ceremonial. His sermon was subsequently published with the title of *The Restoration of Churches is the Restoration of Popery*. His opponents ridiculed the title, and represented the preacher as opposed to *all* Church Restoration. When reprinting his sermon, in 1863, Dr. Close repudiated such an idea. "No person," he said, "could honestly raise such a charge against him—he will not say who had read the pamphlet—but who had even read the rest of the title-page, which marks as clearly as can be that his assertion was limited to a *special sort* of 'Church Restoration.'"[2] And even in the sermon itself the preacher had explained himself clearly enough. "I affirm," he said, "that I am not opposed to the decoration of Churches, *but to extravagant and gorgeous* decoration; that I am not an enemy to

---

[1] *The Footsteps of Error.* By Francis Close, D.D., Dean of Carlisle, p. 75. London: Hatchard & Co. 1863.
[2] *Ibid.* p. 73.

anything that is beautiful in architecture, while I am, and hope ever to be, *the implacable enemy of all Popish and mediæval restorations.* The best evidence I can allege in support of such assertions are the public buildings in my own [Cheltenham] parish, whose erection I have been permitted either to originate or extensively to promote; they are silent but not inefficacious witnesses that neither with respect to Churches or to Colleges do I desire to see them as 'brick barns.' "[1]

This faithful warning of Dr. Close, in 1844, against the Restoration of Churches on Romish lines, is more needed now than when first uttered, and, perhaps, by no class of men more than by Evangelical Incumbents and Churchwardens. Ritualistic Incumbents know what such Restorations mean, while Protestant Churchmen are, to an alarming extent, blind to the evil. All over the land we find new Churches built, and old ones restored, in a style which can only delight the hearts of the Romanisers, although those Churches are frequently in Evangelical and Protestant hands. Why should Protestant clergymen permit their Churches to be so arranged as to make them ready for a Roman Catholic priest to say Mass in? It would be the wisdom of Protestants never to build a new Church with a Chancel.[2] And what do *they* want with Communion Tables erected on high, like Roman Catholic Altars? And why do they permit Chancel gates and screens to be erected, to separate the supposed Holy of Holies within from where the common laity sit without? Why allow Churches to be so arranged as to convey to the people the idea that the Chancel is holier than any other place? For my part, I believe that there is no portion of a Parish Church which is holier than another part. I am certain that where the poor man kneels, in his humility, at the west end of the Church (if he be a true Christian) is in God's sight quite as holy as where the clergy stand in their glory in the Chancel. We sadly need a wholesale Reform in Church Building and Church Restoration.

[1] Close's *Footsteps of Error*, p. 83.
[2] The majority of Wren's Churches in the City of London were built without chancels.

CHAPTER X

Pusey thinks that God is "drawing" Newman to Rome—Pusey refuses to write against the Church of Rome—Newman secedes to Rome—Father Dominic's narrative of Newman's reception—Pusey on the secession—Newman goes to see the Pope—When and where was Newman ordained a Roman Catholic? Some noteworthy circumstances—St. Saviour's, Leeds—Founded by Dr. Pusey—He insists on an Altar—The distinction between an Altar and a Table—Dr. Hook's anxiety—Dr. Wilberforce appointed Bishop of Oxford—Pusey tries to secure his goodwill for Puseyism—He fails—Pusey's desire for Union with Rome—His subtle tactics with his penitents—Hook believes Pusey is under the influence of the Jesuits—The Exeter Surplice Riots—Debate in the House of Lords—More Puseyite exhortations to prosecute Evangelical clergy—An extraordinary case in Salisbury Diocese—*Extempore* prayers in a Schoolroom "a gross scandal"—The case of the Rev. James Shore—Pusey's Sermon on *The Entire Absolution of the Penitent*—Extracts from the Sermon—Pusey goes to Confession for the first time—The effect of Pusey's Confessional work on his penitents—Testimony of Dean Boyle—Clerical Retreats.

THE year 1845 will ever be memorable in the annals of the Romeward Movement, as the year in which the Rev. J. H. Newman seceded to Rome. The event had long been expected, yet when it came it caused almost as great a sensation as if it had been quite unexpected. In the month of July Pusey seems to have made up his mind that Newman would go over to Rome, but he actually said that he thought that perhaps God was "drawing him" thither! "I have," he wrote to Keble, on July 8th, "looked upon this [expected secession] of dear Newman as a mysterious dispensation, as though (if it be indeed so) *Almighty God was drawing him, as a chosen instrument, for some office in the Roman Church* (although he himself goes, of course, not as a Reformer, but as a simple act of faith), and so I thought that He might be pleased to give him convictions (if it be so) which He does not give to others. At least I have come

THE STORY OF NEWMAN'S RECEPTION

into this way of thinking."[1] In the prospect of Newman's Secession Pusey's friends urged him to take up his pen and write against the Church of Rome; but he refused to do so. "I cannot any more," he said, "take the negative ground against Rome; I can only remain neutral. I have indeed for some time left off alleging grounds against Rome."[2] In the same month of July Pusey wrote to Newman himself with reference to his expected secession: —"I suppose, of course, that, if it is so, *Almighty God is pleased to draw you* for some office which He has for you."[3]

On October 9, 1845, Newman was received into the Church of Rome, in his Littlemore Monastery, by Father Dominic, a Passionist. Three weeks later this gentleman sent to the *Tablet* an account of Newman's reception. He had, he said, previously, on Michaelmas Day, received the Rev. J. D. Dalgairns into the Church of Rome, at Aston Hall:—

"I was," wrote Father Dominic, "on the point of setting out for Belgium, when I received a note from him [Dalgairns], inviting me to pass through Oxford on my way; for, he said, I might perhaps find something to do there. I accordingly set out from here on the 8th of October, and reached Oxford about ten o'clock the evening of the same day. I there found Mr. Dalgairns and Mr. St. John, who had made his profession of Faith at Prior Park on the 2nd of October, awaiting my arrival. They told me that I was to receive Mr. Newman into the Church. This news filled me with joy, and made me soon forget the rain that had been pelting upon me for the last five hours.

"From Oxford we drove in a chaise to Littlemore, where we arrived about eleven o'clock. I immediately sat down near a fire to dry my clothes, when Mr. Newman entered the room, and, throwing himself at my feet, asked my blessing, and begged me to hear his confession, and receive him into the Church. He made his confession that same night, and on the following morning the Reverend Messrs. Bowles and Staunton did the same: in the evening of the same day these three made their profession of Faith in the usual form in their private Oratory, one after another, with such fervour and piety that I was almost out of myself for joy. I afterwards gave them all canonical absolution, and administered to them the Sacra-

---

[1] *Life of Dr. Pusey*, vol. ii. p. 453.
[2] *Ibid.* p. 456.
[3] *Ibid.* p. 458.

ment of Baptism *sub conditione*. On the following morning I said Mass in their Oratory, and gave Communion to Messrs. Newman, St. John, Bowles, Staunton, and Dalgairns."[1]

A correspondent of the *English Churchman* declared, commenting on Newman's secession:—"It has happened that in heart and intention, Mr. Newman, while nominally with us, has during the last four years been a member of the Roman Communion."[2] Pusey wrote a letter, which appeared in the same issue of the *English Churchman*, on Newman's secession, in which he stated that, having heard that the Romanists on the Continent had long been praying to God for Newman's conversion to Rome, he had then begun to fear that "*God will give them* whom they pray for;" and that, as to Newman himself:—"He seems then, to me, not so much gone from us, as transplanted into another part of the Vineyard, where the full energies of his powerful mind can be employed, which here they were not."

Puseyites and Ritualists have never ceased to mourn for the loss of Newman, as though it were some great evil inflicted on the English Church. It was, in reality, nothing of the kind, but a great blessing. A year before it took place, Archdeacon Samuel Wilberforce declared:—"If Newman is to go, the sooner he goes the better, because in going he will lose his power of leading others over with him."[3] The sooner an enemy is removed from the camp, the better it will be for the camp itself, though the enemy personally may be the loser by the change. There are men in the present day who think that if all the Ritualistic clerical rebels against the law of the Church were ejected, the Church of England would suffer loss. Never was there a greater delusion. As well might we argue that a house would become more healthy by retaining in it all who are suffering from fever, and that the epidemic would increase in the house if those who are stricken with it should leave it.

Newman's perversion led to a very large secession to Rome of his followers. He continued to live at Littlemore

[1] *English Churchman*, November 27, 1845, p. 761.
[2] *Ibid.* October 16, 1845, p. 662.
[3] *Life of Bishop Wilberforce*, vol. i. p. 258.

WHEN WAS NEWMAN ORDAINED A PRIEST? 259

for several months after his reception. On November 1st he was confirmed by Bishop Wiseman. On February 23, 1846, he removed to Oscott College. While he was there, Wiseman wrote to Dr. Russell of Maynooth:—"While I am writing this, Mr. Newman is under examination for Minor Orders."[1] The *Univers*, of September 20, 1846, published a letter from Langres, stating that Newman was in that city on his way to Rome. "Mr. Newman," says the writer, "was accompanied by the Rev. Ambrose St. John, who also has been admitted to Minor Orders, and repairs to Rome to receive the priesthood."[2] On October 28th Newman arrived in the City of Rome. The Rome correspondent of the *Daily News*, "Father Prout," in announcing his arrival, added:— "In a few days Mr. Newman, late of Oxford, and his companions, will take possession of chambers in the College of Propaganda, and enter on a preparatory course previous to re-ordination in the Church of Rome."

The question here arises, on *what date*, and *in what building*, was Newman ordained a priest of the Church of Rome? The answer to this question must be—at least until more light is thrown on that mysterious event—*no one knows*, except the authorities of the Church of Rome, *and they have never given the public any information on the subject!* We have seen, on Roman Catholic authority, that he went to Rome expressly for the purpose of being there ordained a priest. There was no necessity for him to go there; he could have been ordained a priest in England by Bishop Wiseman, and have thus saved himself the trouble of the journey. When he died, as Cardinal Newman, in 1890, numerous biographies were published by the Roman Catholic papers, but I have not seen in either of them any information on the point in question. Why this strange and mysterious silence? The event was an important one, such as one would naturally expect to find recorded in any account of Newman's life. But not a line on the subject has, so far as I am aware, been yet written by any Roman Catholic to throw any light on this subject. In 1897, *The*

[1] *Life and Times of Cardinal Wiseman*, vol. i. p. 450.
[2] *Cardinal Newman: A Monograph.* By John Oldcastle, p. 34. London: Burns & Oates.

Life and Times of Cardinal Wiseman was published in two volumes, written by Mr. Wilfrid Ward. The first of these volumes contains several lengthy letters, written from Rome by Newman and his friend Mr. Ambrose St. John, during their residence there (which lasted until towards the end of the year 1847), and addressed to Bishop Wiseman. In these letters they give very full and detailed accounts of their daily life, of their interviews with the Pope and other prominent personages, with ample particulars of all their plans for future work when they returned to England ; *but not one word about an event which would have been the most important in Newman's life—his ordination as a priest in the Church of Rome!* Soon after Newman's death, a brief biography was published by a Roman Catholic, "John Oldcastle," under the title of *Cardinal Newman: A Monograph*. In it we read :—" Newman received Holy Orders at the hands of Cardinal Franzoni, and, in 1847, he announced, in a letter from Rome to Mr. Hope-Scott, the important plans already made."[1] Then follows an extract from the letter alluded to. It was evidently the intention of "John Oldcastle" to convey the impression to his readers that this letter to Mr. Hope-Scott was written *after* Newman's ordination as a priest by Cardinal Franzoni. On turning to the *Memoirs of James Hope-Scott*, where the letter is printed in full, we find that it was dated "Feb. 23, '47 ;"[2] but in the *English Churchman* for *April* 1, 1847, page 234, I find an extract published from the Roman Catholic *Tablet*, of apparently the previous week, and therefore a full month after Newman's letter to Mr. Hope-Scott. And this is what the *Tablet* said :—

"We hear with great pleasure that Mr. Newman is to return to England as a Brother of the Oratory. . . . The story that there has been any difficulty *about Mr. Newman's ordination* is of course a mere fable. *His ordination*, and that of his companions, *may probably be delayed a little* by the noviciate requisite for members of the Oratory, but it will follow, under the direction of the proper authorities, as a matter of course."

It is therefore certain that up to about the middle of

---

[1] *Cardinal Newman: A Monograph.* By John Oldcastle, p. 35.
[2] *Memoirs of James Hope-Scott*, vol. ii. p. 73.

STARTLING ASSERTIONS CONCERNING NEWMAN 261

March 1847—five months after his arrival in Rome—Newman had not, so far as the public were aware, been ordained a priest. In the year 1866 Newman's *Apologia Pro Vita Sua* was replied to by Mr. Charles Hastings Collette, in a volume of 200 pages, entitled *Dr. Newman and His Religious Opinions*. In it the author made some startling statements about Newman's ordination, which, so far as I can ascertain, have never been answered. Certainly they were not replied to by Newman himself, though it would undoubtedly have been worth his while to have done so. It is simply in the hope of forcing, if that be possible, the hands of the Papal authorities into producing the official record of Newman's ordination, together with the date and place where it occurred, that I here reproduce Mr. Collette's statement. Speaking of Newman and Froude's secret interview with Wiseman in Rome, in 1833, to which I have already referred, Mr. Collette writes :—

"Now it is a fact that it was considered at the time, and has been often publicly repeated, that Dr. Newman was at this interview with Dr. Wiseman, in company with Froude, formally ordained a priest of the Roman Church, being then, in fact, a member of that communion. Dr. Newman again visited Rome under the advice of Dr. Wiseman in 1845;[1] after he had *publicly* renounced the communion of the Church of England. He went ostensibly to be inducted into the priesthood, a ceremony that could have been equally well performed in England. It has been confidently asserted that Dr. Newman was not then (1845)[2] ordained a priest of Rome; that his journey was a make-believe. Holy Orders in the Roman Church are accounted a Sacrament, which cannot be repeated without sacrilege. Anglican Orders are void, in the estimation of the Roman Church. If Dr. Newman was secretly ordained in 1833, the ceremony could not be repeated in 1845,[3] and it was publicly alleged at the time that he was not ordained in 1845 [1846], nor ever since. . . . When Dr. Newman publicly declared himself a Romanist, and went to Rome ostensibly for his ordination, a day was proposed for the performance of that ceremony. Great curiosity was excited at the time among the English at Rome, to witness the ceremony. Those who were there at the time well remember the circumstance. But for one reason or another it was deferred, until general interest died away, *and no ordination, so far as the*

---

[1] A misprint for 1846.   [2] 1846.   [3] 1846.

public are aware, took place. One only conclusion was come to; namely, that Dr. Newman had been already ordained a priest of Rome, and was actually a priest while officiating in the Anglican Church. This challenge was, at the time, publicly made, and has never been denied. . . .

"Dr. Newman is now openly an officiating priest in the Roman Church. It was therefore with more than ordinary curiosity that we anxiously awaited the announcement by Dr. Newman, in his biography [the *Apologia Pro Vita Sua*], as to the exact time when, in fact, he had formally taken the vows of the Roman Church as a priest. One would have supposed that the precise date when this important occurrence took place, and the circumstances attending it, and by whom the ceremony was performed, would be duly notified. But we look in vain for this information; all we are told is, that in 1845 he was 'received' into the Church of Rome; and he says 'for a while after my *reception* I proposed to betake myself to some secular calling'; but he nowhere mentions his re-ordination."[1]

Now I know very well that it is quite easy to pooh-pooh Mr. Collette's assertions, and to say that they are not worth a moment's thought. But this is not to answer the question, *When* and *where* was Dr. Newman ordained a priest of the Church of Rome?

The consecration of the new Church of St. Saviour's, Leeds, on October 28, 1845, was an event of more than ordinary interest to the Puseyites. The Church was built for the purpose of carrying the principles of the Oxford Movement into practical operation in a poor parish. Its real founder was Dr. Pusey himself, and up to a certain point he had worked most cordially with Dr. Hook, Vicar of Leeds, in making all necessary arrangements for the new Church. As far back as 1839 Pusey had corresponded with Hook about it, mentioning that a friend (who we now know was Pusey himself) was willing to give £1500 to build at Leeds an "Oratorium," but that he must make it a condition that when erected it should have an inscription with the words: "Ye who enter this holy place, pray for the sinner who built it." The Bishop of Ripon was consulted about the proposed inscription, and he said that on

---

[1] *Dr. Newman and His Religious Opinions.* By Charles Hastings Collette, pp. 47-49. London: J. F. Shaw & Co. 1866.

receiving an assurance that the person referred to was then alive, he would not object to it. Of course, I need hardly point out that as soon as the donor was dead the inscription would then become an invitation to pray for the dead. No doubt this is what Pusey had in his mind when he first proposed its erection. Eventually the foundation-stone was laid on September 14, 1842; but no great publicity was given to the event, through fear of arousing the opposition of the Protestant Churchmen of Leeds. As the building of the Church progressed, it gave rise to a considerable amount of local discussion, so that in November, 1843, Hook told Pusey: "I really dread the consecration."[1] Some members of the Cambridge Camden Society wished that the Ten Commandments, Creed, and Lord's Prayer should not be set up near the Communion Table; but Pusey, to his credit be it said, refused. He thought there was "much good" in having them in such a position. "I cannot but think," he said, "that the Ten Commandments, with their strict warning voice, are far more valuable to us, as attendants on the altar, than images or pictures or tapestry would be;"[2] but he was unwilling, he added, to give up the proposed Altar Cross. As to the material of which the "altar" was to be made, Pusey was very emphatic. He would rather have the consecration of the Church suspended than erect in it a Communion Table. He would have an "altar." "I could not myself," he wrote to a correspondent, "put up what should seem to be a mere table. When truth was not denied, tables were altars, as well as altars holy tables; now they seem to me to involve at least a withdrawal of the truth; and if insisted upon, a denial of it. I dare not myself be any party to putting up a table. I would sooner have the consecration of a Church suspended. I would spare any needless offence; but, if this be one, it seems to me unavoidable. But I hope with a few years it will much diminish, and every altar is a gain."[3] No doubt every "altar" erected in a parish Church is a gain to the Romeward Movement; but at the same time it is a loss to Scriptural truth. The New Testa-

---

[1] *Life of Dr. Pusey*, vol. ii. p. 475.
[2] *Ibid.* p. 477.   [3] *Ibid.* p. 478.

ment knows nothing of an "altar" on which to celebrate the Lord's Supper; and the Church of England orders only a table; but that which she has ordered was not sufficient for Dr. Pusey. On this point the judgment of the Judicial Committee of Privy Council in the case of *Liddell v. Westerton* may be usefully cited. Their lordships said:—

"The distinction between an 'Altar' and a 'Communion Table' is in itself essential and deeply founded in the most important difference in matters of faith between Protestants and Romanists, namely, in the different notions of the nature of the Lord's Supper which prevailed in the Roman Catholic Church at the time of the Reformation, and those which were introduced by the Reformers. By the former it was considered as a Sacrifice of the Body and Blood of the Saviour. The Altar was the place on which the Sacrifice was to be made; the elements were to be consecrated, and, being so consecrated, were treated as the actual Body and Blood of the Victim. The Reformers, on the other hand, considered the Holy Communion not as a Sacrifice, but as a Feast, to be celebrated at the Lord's Table."[1]

Pusey wished the new Church to be known as "Holy Cross Church," but the Bishop of Ripon objected to this, and therefore "St. Saviour's Church" was selected instead. The Bishop refused to consecrate the Church unless a wooden Communion Table were erected, and not either a stone altar or a stone slab resting on a wooden frame. The Rev. Richard Ward was appointed the first Incumbent. He afterwards seceded to Rome. When the selection of special preachers at the Consecration services had to be made, Hook became very anxious. Newman had only just seceded to Rome, and the Vicar of Leeds was naturally fearful lest special preachers should be selected, who might soon after go over to Rome. "If," Hook wrote to Pusey, "any of the preachers fall away into the fearful schism of Rome, against which I am accustomed to preach so very strongly (I am this very day about to denounce the heresy of Rome in praying to Saints), more mischief will be done than I can calculate."[2] At last the consecration took

[1] Brodrick and Freemantle's *Judgments of the Judicial Committee of Privy Council*, p. 144.
[2] *Life of Dr. Pusey*, vol. ii. p. 487.

place, and soon St. Saviour's, Leeds, became notorious throughout the country as a hotbed of Popery, and a nursery of clerical and lay perverts to Rome.

Another event of considerable importance occurred this year, in the appointment of Dean Samuel Wilberforce as Bishop of Oxford, in the room of Dr. Bagot, who had been transferred to Bath and Wells. Churchmen everywhere wondered what would come from such an appointment. Evangelical Churchmen had reason to expect fair play at his hands, though he had refused to be recognised as a member of their party. The Puseyites hoped for the best, yet with fear and trembling. As soon as Dr. Wilberforce's nomination was made public, Dr. Pusey wrote to him, evidently anxious to secure his goodwill for himself and his friends. Wilberforce was elected as Bishop by the Dean and Chapter of Christ Church, on November 15th, and on the same day Pusey opened a correspondence with the Bishop-Elect, in which he explained his own position and work to his future Diocesan. "For myself," Pusey said, "I can too readily think that any apparent connection with myself would rather embarrass you with many; else it would have given me much pleasure if, in the retired way in which I live, my house could be of any service to you at any time that your duties shall call you into Oxford."[1] But Wilberforce was not to be caught in this way. He replied, thanking Pusey for the kind tone of his letter towards himself; but ending with what must have been a bitter pill for Pusey to swallow. "I could not then," wrote Wilberforce, "but say, how very deeply (to go no further back) the letters to which you allude had pained me; and that I cannot feel that the language therein held as to the errors of the Church of Rome is, to my apprehension, to be reconciled with the doctrinal formularies of our own Reformed Church."[2] "It was," says Canon Liddon, "a disagreeable surprise to one in Pusey's anxious position, entertaining, as he had done, such hopeful expectations, to receive thus early a plain intimation that the attitude of his future Bishop was so different from all that he had anticipated, as well as from that of the previous occupant of the

[1] *Life of Bishop Wilberforce*, vol. i. p. 302.   *Ibid.* p. 302.

See."[1] I have already quoted a portion of this correspondence. Pusey's answer to this letter of the Bishop-Elect shows clearly how very far he had gone in helping on the Romeward Movement :—

"I did not," he said, "mean to say anything definitely as to myself, but only to maintain, in the abstract, *the tenability of a certain position, in which very many are, of not holding themselves obliged to renounce any doctrine, formally decreed by the Roman Church.* And this I knew would satisfy many minds, who do not wish to form any definite opinion on those doctrines, yet still wish not to be obliged to commit themselves against them. But in this I was not speaking of what is commonly meant by 'Popery,' which is a large practical system, going beyond their formularies, varying perhaps indefinitely in different minds. I meant simply 'the *letter* of what has been decreed by the Roman Church'; *and this I have, for years, hoped might ultimately become the basis of union between us.*"[2]

Here Pusey's anxious desire for the Union of the Church of England with the corrupt Church of Rome comes out most clearly, as does also his remarkable acknowledgment that he had "for years" previously hoped for such an unholy union. "I cannot but think," he said, in this same letter, "that Rome and we are not irreconcilably at variance, but that, in the great impending contest with unbelief, we shall be on the same side, and in God's time, and in His way, one." I am not exaggerating when I assert that from this period Reunion with Rome became the absorbing passion of Pusey's life. Certainly the "very many," who, in 1845, considered that, although in the Church of England, they were not "obliged to renounce any doctrine *formally* decreed by the Roman Church," would not have felt much pressure on their conscience in accepting Union with Rome on Rome's terms. And even as to Pusey himself there were but few, if any, of the "formal" doctrines of Rome which he would, previous to the Vatican Council, insist on that Church renouncing as a condition of Reunion with the Church of England. He wrote, it is true, strongly against Mariolatry in the Church of Rome, as a part of her "large *practical* system, going beyond their formularies"

---

[1] *Life of Dr. Pusey*, vol. iii. p. 42.
[2] *Life of Bishop Wilberforce*, vol. i. pp. 303, 304.

PUSEY'S DOUBLE DEALING

(and subsequently he wrote against Papal Infallibility); but in this letter of his to Dr. Wilberforce, he showed his faith, even at that early period, in Purgatory and some Invocation of Saints. In what he said on these doctrines his double dealing and Jesuitism are also clearly revealed :—

"Practically," Pusey wrote to Wilberforce, "when people come to me for guidance, *I endeavour to withhold them* from what lies beyond our Church, *although, if asked on the other side, I could not deny that such and such things seem to me admissible.*

"If I may explain my meaning, the remarkable Acts of S. Perpetua and Felicitas, which was beyond question genuine, contain a very solemn vision,[1] which involves *the doctrine of a process of purification after death by suffering*, to shorten which prayer was available. . . . I had interpreted passages (as of S. Basil), as I saw, wrongly, under a bias the other way; solemn as it was, I could not, taking all together, *refuse my belief to an intermediate state of cleansing, in some cases through pain*. . . . The effect has been that *I have since been wholly silent about Purgatory* (before I used to speak against it). I have not said so much as this except to two or three friends. *Some of my nearest friends do not know it.*[2]

"In like manner, I found that some *Invocation of Saints* was much more frequent in the early Church than I had been taught to think, that *it has very high authority*, and is nowhere blamed. This is wholly distinct from the whole system as to S. Mary, as what I said before is from the popular system as to Purgatory. In this way, then, and partly from the internal structure of the Article, I came to think that our Article did not condemn *all* 'doctrine of Purgatory' or 'Invocation of Saints,' but only a certain practical system which the Reformers had before their eyes; *and then I came afterwards to see that the actual Roman formularies did not assert more on these subjects* (as apart from the popular system or 'Popery') *than was in the ancient Church.*

"*Practically, then, I dissuade or forbid* (when I have authority) *Invocation of Saints; abstractedly I see no reason why our Church might not eventually allow it*, in the sense of asking for their prayers."[3]

Double dealing of this kind, on Pusey's part, in relation to St. Saviour's, Leeds, led even that pronounced Tractarian,

---

[1] Fancy a man like Pusey basing his faith in the existence of a Purgatory on "a very solemn *vision!*" There was no basis for it in the Bible.

[2] In this Pusey acted on the doctrine of "*Reserve* in Communicating Religious Knowledge."

[3] *Life of Bishop Wilberforce*, vol. i. pp. 304, 305.

Dr. Hook, to write to him, on December 19, 1846:—"Is this conduct that can be justified by any but a Jesuit? Do not mistake me—I do not think you are a Jesuit; but I believe you to be under the influence of Jesuits. Your own representatives here say as much; they seem to admit that you were only the puppet while others pulled the strings."[1]

Of Pusey's correspondence with Wilberforce Canon Liddon writes:—"Anything more unhappy than such a correspondence as this cannot well be imagined"; and he acknowledges that "there was sufficient in Pusey's letter to excite suspicion in the mind of one who had no closer sympathies with the Tractarian Movement than had Dr. Wilberforce at that moment."[2]

The question of the Surplice or Black Gown in the pulpit came again prominently before the public in 1845. The Bishop of Exeter having withdrawn his order to all his clergy to preach in the surplice only, it was felt by those who used the surplice that this order was not one commanding them to give it up. Amongst those who continued it were the Rev. Francis Courtenay, Vicar of St. Sidwell's, Exeter; and the Rev. Philip Carlyon, Vicar of St. James', in the same city. On January 10th both parishes held a united meeting "to consider the course to be adopted respecting the continued use of the surplice" by the Incumbents of both parishes. Several resolutions were passed (in one of which it was acknowledged that "the use of the surplice in the pulpit was introduced before the present Ministers were appointed") and the Ministers were requested to discontinue the use of the surplice. In reply the Vicar of St. Sidwell's positively refused to grant the request; while the Vicar of St. James' promised to do what the meeting asked for. One result of the refusal by the Vicar of St. Sidwell's was a decision to build a "Free Church" in the district; and the next was that on the following Sunday after his refusal Mr. Courtenay saw, on entering the pulpit in his surplice, two-thirds of the congregation arise and leave the Church in a body. When he left the Church he was hissed and hooted in the streets on his way to his

[1] *Life of Dr. Pusey*, vol. iii. p. 126.
[2] *Ibid.* pp. 48, 49.

residence. The Archbishop of Canterbury tried to allay the public excitement on this and a few other minor matters, which had spread throughout the country, by means of a Pastoral Letter. But inasmuch as his advice was that each side should, for the time being, tolerate the other side, no peaceful results followed from his exhortation. The Vicar of St. Sidwell's, Exeter, continued to preach in the surplice, and this led on several Sundays to riotous proceedings in the Church. The principal inhabitants of the city became alarmed, with the result that a requisition was addressed by the Mayor of Exeter and the Magistrates to the Bishop of Exeter, to use his influence with Mr. Courtenay in the interests of peace. The Bishop thereupon wrote to Mr. Courtenay :—"I advise you to give way, at the request of the civil authorities of Exeter, and not to persist in wearing the surplice in the pulpit, unless conscientiously, and on full inquiry, you have satisfied yourself that your engagements to the Church require you to wear the surplice when you preach."[1] On this Mr. Courtenay very properly gave way, and promised to preach no longer in the surplice. But this concession did not satisfy his parishioners, who, on the day after it was made, held a meeting at which a resolution was unanimously passed, asking Mr. Courtenay to resign the living, and declaring that he "having signified his consent to withdraw the surplice," "any concession *now* is insufficient to restore him to that position which a Pastor should hold among his parishioners." One result of the agitation at Exeter was a petition to the House of Lords from 3200 adult members of the Church of England residing at or near Exeter, complaining of alterations which had been made by the clergy in the mode of conducting the services of the Church, which had "endangered the peace, union, and stability of the Established Church." It was presented by Earl Fortescue, Lord Lieutenant of Devon, on February 23rd, and led to an important debate, in the course of which the Bishop of Exeter defended his conduct as well as he could, and in which the Bishop of Norwich used these words :—

---

[1] *English Churchman*, January 30, 1845, p. 63.

"My Lords, as this question refers to one particular diocese, . . . I forbear from entering into the discussion; but from the general feeling of the country, and particularly from that in my own diocese, I can venture to say that there is a determination to adhere to our Protestant faith, and to resist any innovation, or any approach, in reality or even in imagination, to anything of a Roman Catholic feeling, and I rejoice that these petitions have been forwarded."[1]

All through this year the Puseyites continued to repeat their demand for the prosecution of Protestant clergymen who, in their opinion, had broken the law. I may here remark that there is no reason why Evangelical clergymen should be exempt from prosecution should they break the law of the Church; but at this period it was quite expected that in this way they would be able to suppress those peculiar doctrines of the Evangelicals opposed to the Romeward Movement. In this the Puseyites and their successors, the Ritualists, have been greatly disappointed. A very few of the Evangelical clergy may, here and there, have offended against the law on some minor point of no importance; but these are mere trifles when compared with the serious breaches of the law, in the interests of Sacerdotalism, now constantly perpetrated by the Ritualists, and it is well, in this connection, to remember that Evangelicals should not be held responsible for what Broad Churchmen do. One grave cause of offence to their opponents the Protestant clergy gave at this time, by mixing more freely amongst orthodox Nonconformists, and even giving addresses at public meetings in aid of religious work conducted by Churchmen and Dissenters combined. This exhibition of *Protestant* unity was peculiarly distasteful to men who were sighing for unity with *Rome*. The *English Churchman*, of March 13, 1845, expressed great satisfaction at hearing that the Bishop of London had prevented three London Incumbents from speaking at a meeting of the Welsh Calvinistic Methodist Foreign Missionary Society; and then it continued its comment in the following style:—"So far so

---

[1] *English Churchman*, March 6, 1845, p. 145.

good, as a beginning, and we trust it is only a beginning, on the part of the Lord Bishop of the Diocese. We trust that the meetings of the London City Mission, the Religious Tract Society, and other Dissenting schemes for promoting schism in the Church, will no longer be allowed to boast of the advocacy of the clergy." But there was no praise from the Puseyites for the same Bishop of London (Dr. Blomfield) when, only two years before, he refused to allow a clergyman to officiate in a parish, on the ground that in a sermon he had insisted upon the necessity of Auricular Confession. After quoting passages from the sermon Bishop Blomfield wrote to the preacher:—"I wish to give you an opportunity of retracting or explaining these erroneous positions; but I really do not see how I can safely entrust the care of a large body of poor ignorant people to a teacher who either holds these opinions, or asserts them so broadly and offensively, without a clear understanding of what he says."[1] Would that our Bishops were now as faithful in this gravely important matter as Bishop Blomfield was in 1843. And why should they not be as faithful?

In its issue for September 4, 1845, the *English Churchman* again expressed its delight on hearing that the Bishop of Salisbury had threatened to prosecute two of his Evangelical clergy for what it termed the "gross scandal to the Church" which they had given by actually preaching in an unlicensed building! It seems that during the previous month a Commission appointed by the Bishop of Salisbury, under the Church Discipline Act, met at Upway, for the purpose of making enquiry whether there were *prima facie* grounds for prosecuting the Rev. Samuel Starky, Rector of Charlinch, "in that he has lately, at divers times, committed the canonical offence of preaching *and publicly praying*, in *unconsecrated* places, without the license of the Ordinary thereof;" and for prosecuting the Rev. Octavius Piers, Vicar of Preston, in Dorset, for "having been present at, and aided and abetted the meetings and assemblies lately, and at divers times, held in unconsecrated places *within his*

---

[1] *Memoir of Bishop Blomfield*, vol. ii. p. 84.

said parish of Preston, and at which meetings the Rev. Samuel Starky and other persons had, as alleged, in the presence of the said Octavius Piers, *publicly preached, prayed,* &c."[1] The Commission reported, after hearing evidence, that there was a *prima facie* case for proceeding against the two Evangelical Incumbents.

It makes one justly indignant at the narrow-minded bigotry which would actually prosecute a man, with the hope of his being deprived of his living, or at least suspended for a time, for the sole offence of "publicly preaching and praying" in an unconsecrated building, and that *within his own parish!* And be it noted that, although Mr. Starky preached in Mr. Piers' parish, he did so with the latter gentleman's full knowledge and consent. This is a chapter in the History of the Romeward Movement of which the Ritualists ought to be heartily ashamed, though I sincerely believe that if they had the opportunity they would even now imitate the disgraceful conduct of the Puseyites of 1845. And this is what the Puseyite organ said about the case, when the good news came to its office:—

"The Commission issued by the Lord Bishop of Salisbury, to enquire whether there are grounds for proceeding against Mr. Starky, and the notorious Mr. Octavius Piers, for preaching in unconsecrated places, without the license of the Ordinary. The latter-named clergyman has, for a long time, caused, in various ways, gross scandal to the Church.[2] But the question at issue is of great importance, and an ecclesiastical decision upon it will have a most extensive influence, especially in this diocese, where the practice of extemporary prayer and preaching 'Cottage Lectures' in schoolrooms, hard by the Church, is of common occurrence."[3]

Of course these two excellent Evangelical clergymen had committed no offence against the law whatever. Apparently it was deemed unadvisable to bring the case into Court, for I can find no record of it going any further.

A lawsuit which created a great deal of public interest

---

[1] *English Churchman*, August 28, 1845, p. 544.
[2] I suppose the "gross scandal" was caused by such conduct as preaching and praying in unconsecrated buildings.
[3] *English Churchman*, September 4, 1845, p. 564.

came this year before Sir Herbert Jenner Fust, in the Court of Arches. The real prosecutor was the High Church Bishop of Exeter, who seems to have had a far greater dislike to decidedly Evangelical and Protestant truth, than to any imitations of Popery in his diocese. He prosecuted through his Secretary, Mr. Ralph Barnes. The defendant was the Rev. James Shore, who, until about a year before the commencement of the proceedings, had acted for nearly eleven years as a Minister of Bridgetown Chapel, in the parish of Bury Pomeroy, with the licence of the Bishop who was now his prosecutor. From a correspondence on the case which Mr. Shore published in 1849, while he was in Exeter Gaol through the action of his theological opponents, and from *The Case of Mr. Shore*, written by the Bishop of Exeter, I find that in 1843 the late Incumbent resigned the living, and a Rev. W. B. Cosens was appointed in his room. The Bishop of Exeter sent for Mr. Cosens a few days after his institution, and—to quote the Bishop's own words, given by him on oath at the Exeter Assizes, March 1848—said to him :—" I apprehend you will find a very important part of your parish, or of those souls committed to your charge, to be in such a state that you ought to take especial care whom you appoint as your Assistant Curate at Bridgetown"[1]—of which down to that period Mr. Shore had been for nearly eleven years Curate. Mr. Shore still retained the licence given him by the Bishop when he first entered on the Curacy. There had been a change in the Incumbency meantime, before the arrival of Mr. Cosens, but the licence had not been formally renewed, and *legally* did not require renewal. The Bishop revoked Mr. Shore's licence, and then demanded that he should obtain a new nomination to the Curacy from Mr. Cosens, or cease to officiate in Bridgetown. Of course, after such a hint from his new Diocesan, Mr. Cosens refused to nominate Mr. Shore. The Bishop had for a long time disliked Mr. Shore's decided Protestantism, and was heartily glad to get rid of him. "Doubtless," writes Mr. Shore, "my views of doctrine,

---

[1] *The Case of the Rev. James Shore, M.A.* By Himself. In Reply to the Bishop, p. 16. London : Partridge & Oakey. 1849.

being so opposed to Tractarianism, might have excited a prejudice against me; but there is something further and still deeper. It is evident, from the principal part of the Bishop's pamphlet now before me, that he was very anxious to get the Chapel endowed and consecrated, and thus more certainly under his own control."[1] Had the Bishop succeeded in his ambition, and secured Bridgetown Chapel by having it consecrated—which it had not been—he would very soon have sent Mr. Shore about his business, as a known opponent of the Tractarianism which he (the Bishop) loved so dearly. Mr. Shore tells us, and I see no reason to doubt the statement:—"As showing the Bishop's determination to silence all who oppose the Tractarian Movement, I may here mention that he withdrew his licence from a friend of mine, on account of his having written a note condemning Puseyism. This clergyman waited three years in silence, in the hope of again being able to exercise his ministry in the Establishment, but finding every door shut against him, he built a chapel for himself, in which he is now preaching as a Dissenting Minister."[2] The fact is that the Bishop's nature was tyrannical: he could not endure contradiction or opposition, least of all from the Protestant Churchmen of his diocese.

Mr. Shore, having failed in getting a new nomination from Mr. Cosens, as Curate of Bridgetown Chapel, and having gathered around him a large and deeply attached congregation, had now to face a great difficulty. He was certain that the Bishop would eventually refuse to licence him to any other Curacy in the Diocese of Exeter, and would refuse to sign his testimonials for work in any other diocese, thus shutting him out of any future work in the Church of England, and reducing his victim, together with his wife and family, to a state of abject poverty, if not starvation. What was he to do under such painful circumstances? The Duke of Somerset, who owned Bridgetown Chapel, at this juncture offered him permission to continue the use of the chapel, apart from the jurisdiction of the Church of England, and at the same time secured for him

---

[1] *The Case of the Rev. James Shore, M.A.* By Himself, p. 18.
[2] *Ibid.* p. 18, *note.*

an adequate income as its minister. Mr. Shore decided that he would accept this generous offer, and in order that he might remove, as he thought, every legal difficulty in the way, he had the chapel registered as a Dissenting Chapel, and himself took the necessary oaths declaring himself a Dissenting minister, as required by the Toleration Acts, after which he officiated in Bridgetown Chapel, using the Liturgy of the Church of England. He now thought himself safe from any further interference from the Bishop of Exeter; but in this he was mistaken. The Bishop decided on prosecuting him in the Arches Court, for the offence that he, being still legally a clergyman of the Church of England, had unlawfully officiated in Bridgetown Chapel without the authority, and contrary to the monition of his Diocesan. Of course the Bishop might have left Mr. Shore alone, unmolested by the law, with its pains and penalties. In his pamphlet, Mr. Shore forcibly pointed out that :—"The late Rev. John Hawker, of Plymouth, was not proceeded against by the Bishop. After withdrawing from his lordship's jurisdiction, Mr. Hawker continued, for about fifteen years, to use the services as I use them at Bridgetown—in a chapel, too, which was designed, when erected, for the Establishment; and yet he was left entirely unmolested. I believe, also, that Mr. Hawker did not qualify under the Toleration Act, as I did. Indeed, I have not been able to find one single seceding clergyman who has so qualified except myself; and yet, in every other diocese throughout the land, numbers of seceding clergymen are preaching without let or hindrance, whilst I for doing so am in gaol."[1] It was, therefore, not without reason that Mr. Shore complained of the Bishop's action towards him as "an undue and oppressive exercise of the law."

Greatly to the delight of the Puseyites the action against Mr. Shore was pushed forward, and at length, on June 20, 1846, Sir Herbert Jenner Fust delivered judgment in the Court of Arches. He said :—

"I am of opinion that the proctor for the promoter has proved the articles charging Mr. Shore with having been guilty of publicly

---

[1] *The Case of the Rev. James Shore, M.A.* By Himself, pp. 22, 23.

reading prayers, according to the form prescribed by the Book of Common Prayer, and of preaching in an unconsecrated chapel without a licence; that he has thereby incurred Ecclesiastical censure; and that he must be admonished to refrain from offending in like manner in future. Should he be guilty of a repetition of this offence, it will be not only against his Diocesan, but against the authority of this Court. Though this gentleman is at this moment a minister of the Established Church of this land, from which office he cannot of his own authority relieve himself, still I do not think I am entitled to depose him from the ministry. I content myself by pronouncing that the articles have been sufficiently proved. I admonish Mr. Shore to abstain from offending in like manner in future, in the parish of Bury Pomeroy, and in the Diocese of Exeter, and elsewhere in the Province of Canterbury; and I condemn him in the costs."[1]

Mr. Shore appealed from this sentence to the Judicial Committee of Privy Council. Their lordships gave judgment on February 14, 1848, confirming the sentence of the Court of Arches. Early the next year the Rev. James Shore, still owing to the Bishop of Exeter the sum of £115, 3s. 5d., being a portion of his lordship's costs in prosecuting Mr. Shore, that prelate caused the unhappy defendant to be arrested, on March 31, 1849, and committed to Exeter Gaol, there to remain until he had paid the money. And there he might have remained for all the High Church Bishop cared, were it not that some friends of Mr. Shore subscribed the money needed, and then he was released from prison.

It was not until 1870 that the law was altered under which Mr. Shore suffered. By the Clerical Disabilities Act, 33 and 34 Victoria, c. 91, provision is made by which a clergyman can resign his Orders in the Church of England, free from any penalty. But if he resigns his Orders he can never again, however anxious he may be to do so, officiate in the Church of England.[2]

[1] Robertson's *Ecclesiastical Reports*, vol. i. p. 399.
[2] For further particulars of Mr. Shore's case, see *The Case of the Rev. James Shore, in Reply to the Rev. W. B. Cosens*. By the Rev. James Shore, pp. 25. London: Partridge & Oakey. 1849. *An Appeal to My Fellow-Townsmen on Behalf of the Rev. James Shore*. By Sir Culling E. Eardley, Bart., pp. 24. Torquay: Elliott & Wreyford. 1849.

Dr. Pusey's suspension for two years from preaching in the University pulpit ended in June 1845. Although he did not expect to preach again until the following February, Pusey early began to prepare for it. He sought the advice of friends, some of whom were anxious that he should preach again the sermon for which he had been condemned by the Six Doctors. Pusey's opponents were not idle. On January 5, 1846, the Rev. Charles P. Golightly, of Oriel College, addressed a letter to the Vice-Chancellor, quoting some passages from a letter written by Dr. Pusey, in the previous October, to the *English Churchman*, and demanding that before he preached his forthcoming sermon Pusey should be required to subscribe again to Article XXII. The Vice-Chancellor, however, while disapproving of several of Pusey's statements, did not think there was any necessity to grant that which Mr. Golightly had requested.

The sermon was preached on February 1, 1846, and Pusey took for his subject, *Entire Absolution of the Penitent*. Of course the Cathedral was crowded in every part. "Every inch on the floor of the Church," writes a friendly eye-witness, "was occupied. Dr. Pusey had to move slowly through the dense mass on his way to the corner of the Cathedral where the Vice-Chancellor and Doctors assemble, visible to nobody but those immediately along the line he had to pass; his perfectly pallid, furrowed, mortified face looking almost like jagged marble."[1] He took for his text John xx. 21–23, and in his first sentence referred to the sermon for which he had been suspended: "It will," he said, "be in the memory of some that when, nearly three years past, Almighty God (for 'secret faults' which he knoweth, and from which, I trust, He willed to 'cleanse' me), allowed me to be deprived for a time of this my office among you, I was endeavouring to mitigate the stern doctrine of the heavy character of a Christian's sins." He then proceeded to preach his first sermon advocating Auricular Confession and priestly absolution. He had already taught it in his adapted Roman books: now he preached it from the University pulpit. The time had not

[1] *Life of Dr. Pusey*, vol. iii. p. 59.

yet come for himself to practise what he had so long urged on others. Throughout the sermon it is assumed that Confession to a priest, and priestly absolution, are God's ordinary method of pardoning sin, and cleansing the soul from its stains. It is admitted, in one passage, that those who have perfect contrition, provided they long for absolution, are absolved directly by God without priestly absolution; but this is also the teaching of Rome. All through the discourse Pusey assumes that hardly any such perfectly contrite sinners are to be found on earth. A few extracts from the sermon itself may here serve to give my readers an idea of the thoroughly Popish teaching given in it:—

"And now, brethren, I would proceed to speak of that great authoritative act [of priestly absolution], whereby God in the Church still forgives the sins of the penitent."[1]

"The one object, as I have explained, of this series of sermons, is to minister to one class of souls, those whose consciences being oppressed by the memory of past sin, more or less grievous, long to know how they may be replaced in that condition in which God once placed them; and now, too, my object is, not to speak of discipline in general, or what were best for the Church or for her members generally, but of that mercy which, by the power of the Keys, God pours out upon the penitent. This, then, is probably one ground why so little needed to be said in the New Testament, as to the forgiveness of sins of a Christian very grievously fallen, that our Lord had left a living provision in His Church, whereby [i.e. through Auricular Confession and priestly absolution] all penitents, however fallen, should be restored."[2]

"Those who form to themselves theories of remission of sin distinct from the provision laid up by God in the Church, do 'forsake the Fountain of living waters, and hew them out cisterns, broken cisterns, which hold no water.'"[3]

"Grievous sins after Baptism are remitted by Absolution; and the judgment, if the penitent be sincere, is an earnest of the judgment of Christ, and is confirmed by Him."[4]

"So now, as soon as His Priest has, in His Name, pronounced His forgiveness on earth, the sins of the true penitent are forgiven in Heaven."[5]

---

[1] *Entire Absolution of the Penitent.* By the Rev. E. B. Pusey, D.D., p. 4. Oxford: Parker. 1846.
[2] *Ibid.* pp. 14, 15.   [3] *Ibid.* p. 24.   [4] *Ibid.* p. 26.
[5] *Ibid.* p. 39.

"He hath not left us comfortless, but hath left others with His authority, to convey to sinners in His Name the forgiveness of their sins."[1]

"It may be one of the fruits of the Incarnation, and a part of the dignity thereby conferred upon our nature, that God would rather work His miracles of grace through man, than immediately by Himself."[2]

When the sermon was published, a preface of seventeen pages was printed with it, in which Pusey said that the benefits of Auricular Confession and priestly absolution were not for grievous sinners only; but also "for all who can, through its ministry, approach with lightened, more kindled hearts, to the Holy Communion."[3] He even went so far as to assert that it was open to the Church, even now, to "enforce" private Confession to priests, should she desire to do so. "*It is*," he wrote, "a matter of discipline, *open to the Church, to enforce* public penance, as in the Ancient Church, or *private Confession, as now in the Roman Church;* or to leave the exercise of it to the consciences of individuals."[4] Who, after such a statement as this, can assert that Pusey thought *enforced* Confession wrong *in principle?*

In this sermon Pusey insisted most of all on the benefits of priestly absolution. On the first Sunday in Advent (November 29th) of the same year he preached again before the University, and this time he emphasised, most of all, the supposed advantages of secret Confession to priests. But who, on this occasion, listening to his pressing exhortations to Confession, could ever have dreamed that Pusey—though he had then been hearing Confessions for eight years—had never been to Confession himself? He had urged others to wash and be clean, but he had never washed himself! He was, in this matter, like the Pharisees of old, of whom it is recorded, "they say, and do not." Apparently he lacked the courage which he required of other people. Not the least remarkable portion of Pusey's biography is the story of how he came to go to Confession for the first time, soon

---

[1] Pusey's *Entire Absolution of the Penitent*, p. 39.
[2] *Ibid.* p. 45. [3] *Ibid.* p. viii. [4] *Ibid.* p. xv.

after his second sermon on Confession. On September 26, 1844, Pusey wrote to Keble :—

"I am so shocked at myself that I dare not lay my wounds bare to any one : since I have seen the benefit of Confession to others, I have looked round whether I could unburthen myself to any one, but there is a reason against every one. I dare not so shock people: and so I go on, having no such comfort as in good Bishop Andrewes' words, to confess myself 'an unclean worm, a dead dog, a putrid carcase,' and pray Him to heal my leprosy as He did on earth, and to raise me from the dead : to give me sight, and to forgive me the 10,000 talents; and I must guide myself as best I can, because, as things are, I dare not seek it elsewhere."[1]

This is indeed sad and pitiful language coming from one so intensely in earnest about his own soul's salvation, yet, apparently, thinking that he could not with any certainty obtain the pardon he longed for, *direct* from the Saviour Himself ! He was, truly, a "blind leader of the blind." Later on he wrote a pitiful letter to Keble, which shows how far he had gone wrong, not merely in Popish error, but in Popish *superstition* also. He said that " by God's mercy "—it ought to have been " through my own folly "—he was wearing " *hair cloth* " again, but he would like to wear " some sharper sort " ; and he should " like to be bid to use the Discipline "—a lash of hard knotted cords, with which to whip his bare back ![2] Two days after he preached the University sermon last alluded to, viz., on December 1st, Pusey went down to Hursley and made his *first* Confession to Keble, whom he ever after, until Keble's death, took for his Father Confessor.

The effect of Pusey's Confessional work on his penitents is thus described by Dean Boyle, of Salisbury, who was at Oxford at this time :—" I have, unfortunately, had many friends who submitted themselves to Pusey as a spiritual guide, and fully adopted his theory of Confession and direction, and in nearly every case I have seen traces of enfeebled intellect, and what I must call loss of real moral perception. If the system so zealously advocated by Pusey were ever to

---

[1] *Life of Dr. Pusey*, vol. iii. p. 96. [2] *Ibid.* pp. 100, 101.

be generally adopted, a bad time would come to English homes."[1]

Hundreds of volumes have been written on the subject of Auricular Confession, for and against it. It is manifestly impossible in a work like this to deal adequately with it. Besides, this book is written, primarily, for the use of those whose minds are already made up on this great question on Protestant lines. But I cannot pass away from it without urging my readers to study carefully an invaluable work, reprinted in the *Library of Anglo-Catholic Theology*, and issued under the superintendence of a committee, of which Dr. Pusey himself was a member. It is entitled *The Penitential Discipline of the Primitive Church*. By Nathaniel Marshall, D.D. I know no book which so thoroughly upsets the claims of priestly absolution put forth by Dr. Pusey and the modern Ritualists. There is another work on the subject by an old-fashioned High Churchman, published in 1875, treating the question in a masterly manner, historically and doctrinally, which I cannot too highly commend. It is entitled *An Examination into the Doctrine and Practice of Confession*, and was written by the Rev. William Edward Jelf, B.D. It seems hard to understand how any thoughtful person, with an open mind, can study these two books without rejecting the whole sacerdotal claim of Auricular Confession and Priestly Absolution.

The Bishop of Winchester (Dr. Sumner) had this year to deal with a remarkable application made to him by a clergyman who had seceded to the Church of Rome, but was now anxious to be permitted by his lordship to officiate once more in the Church of England. Since leaving the Church of Rome this clergyman had lived in retirement for three years before making his application. The Bishop replied that he had received his application "with emotions of thankfulness to God," but before granting his request he wished for fuller satisfaction as to the "entire accordance of his present opinions with the doctrines set forth in the Articles and formularies," and "especially in regard to the principal points of difference between our own Church and

---

[1] *Recollections of the Very Rev. G. D. Boyle, Dean of Salisbury*, p. 115. London: 1895.

that of Rome." Before receiving the clergyman's reply a remarkable circumstance was made known to the Bishop, which is thus described by his biographer :—

"Meanwhile, trustworthy information had reached the Bishop that the clergyman in question had been in the habit, within the last few months, of attending a Roman Catholic place of worship. He accordingly wrote to him as follows :—'I think it necessary to acquaint you, that since I last wrote, a statement has been made to me to which I am desirous of calling your attention in the first instance. It is asserted to me, on the authority of a Roman Catholic priest at ——, that so recently as the beginning of the present year, you have attended at the celebration of the Romish service in the chapel of ——. It becomes necessary for me to put to you the explicit question, whether this allegation is true, either in respect of the chapel mentioned, or of any other place of worship of the Romish communion, since the period when you received the Sacrament of the Lord's Supper in —— Church, as a declaration of your desire to return into the communion of the Church of England.'

"In reply, the clergyman, without referring at all to the charge brought against him, begged leave to withdraw his application for permission to minister again in the Church of England."[1]

Conduct like that of this clergyman naturally raises the question, was he simply a Jesuit in disguise?

In this year the Puseyites began to discuss the wisdom of introducing Retreats into the Church of England. Keble wrote on Ash Wednesday about it to the Rev. W. J. Butler, Vicar of Wantage (afterwards Dean of Lincoln):—"Marriott wrote me word that he thought something in the nature of a Retreat might be managed at Leeds, under the clergy of St. Saviour's. But failing that he seemed to say it was not impossible that he might be able to do something towards such a plan, especially if a negotiation succeeded which he was then engaged in with Newman for the loan of the house at Littlemore."[2] Butler hailed the scheme with delight, as a means of propagating the Confessional amongst the clergy. He wrote to Keble, on March 5, 1846 :—

"I was in Oxford for but one day, and that was spent entirely in one place. Indeed, I went there merely to see Dr. Pusey, and to

---

[1] *Life of Bishop Sumner*, pp. 303-305.
[2] *Life and Letters of Dean Butler*, p. 34.

be away from every one; I don't know why I should hesitate to mention it to you; to make a general Confession to him. Of course my thoughts were on this one subject, and though I said something to him some days before in London about the Retreat, yet we did not recur to it. I can only say that I feel more than ever anxious to see something of the kind established. . . . As far as I know, though many are desirous to make a Confession, and to continue it as a habit through life, the thing is all but impossible. Those few who are in the habit of taking general Confessions are fully occupied without the addition of having to act as constant spiritual guides. But men might go to a Retreat periodically, and there receive the advantage of regular Confession, and the continual preparation for it."[1]

---

[1] *Life and Letters of Dean Butler*, p. 35.

CHAPTER XI

Trouble at St. Saviour's, Leeds—Secessions to Rome—Hook's vigorous attack on Pusey—"It is mere Jesuitism"—"A semi-Papal colony"—Hook hopes all the Romanisers will go to Rome—Bishop Phillpotts prosecutes a Puseyite clergyman—The Cross on a Communion Table—The present state of the law on this point—Reducing the distance to Rome—Sackville College, East Grinstead—The Rev. J. M. Neale inhibited—*Freeland* v. *Neale*—The Gorham Case—Judgment of the Court of Arches—Judgment of the Judicial Committee of Privy Council—Puseyite Protest against the Judgment—Dr. Pusey and Keble wish to prosecute Gorham for heresy—Bishop Phillpotts threatens to excommunicate the Archbishop of Canterbury—The Exeter Synod—The case of the Rev. T. W. Allies—His extraordinary and disloyal conduct—His visit to Rome—The Pope tells him that Pusey has "prepared the way for Catholicism"—What Mr. Allies told the Pope—Allies secedes to Rome—Correspondence with Pusey on Auricular Confession—Startling charges against Pusey—"In fear and trembling on their knees before you"—"The rules of the Church of Rome are your rules"—How the Oxford Movement helped Rome—Wilberforce calls Pusey "a decoy bird" for the Papal net—He says that he is "doing the work of a Roman Confessor"—The Papal Aggression—Lord John Russell's Durham Letter—Bishop Blomfield on the Romeward Movement—St. Paul's, Knightsbridge—St. Barnabas, Pimlico—Riots in St. Barnabas' Church—Resignation of the Rev. W. J. E. Bennett—St. Saviour's, Leeds—Traitorous resolutions of twelve clergymen—A Confessional inquiry by the Bishop—The Clergy defend questioning women on the Seventh Commandment.

THE opening of the year 1847 brought with it worry and trouble for Dr. Pusey, and for his friend, Dr. Hook, Vicar of Leeds. On New Year's Day, one of the Curates of St. Saviour's, Leeds, the Rev. R. G. Macmullen, with two laymen from the same parish, seceded to the Church of Rome. It was the same Mr. Macmullen, whose Jesuitical conduct with regard to his Degree at Oxford, has already been described. Pusey had sent him to St. Saviour's, and this was the result. Hook was indignant. He wrote to Pusey two days before the actual reception of Macmullen into the Roman Communion:—"You are aware by this time that Macmullen and his dupes have gone over to the Mother of Abominations, guilty of the deadly sins of heresy and schism. Ward [Vicar of St. Saviour's] and Case remain, I suppose to make more dupes; though strong measures must be taken on my part. I cannot permit a Church and establishment to remain in Leeds for the destruction of souls without seeking to abate the nuisance."[1] Things must have gone very far wrong indeed before such a pronounced High Churchman as Hook could seek to put down as a "nuisance" the first attempt to illustrate Tractarian principles in practice. The Rev. Richard Ward, mentioned by Hook, was the first Vicar of St. Saviour's, and was appointed by Dr. Pusey. He had not been long at Leeds before trouble arose. As late as November 14, 1846, Pusey sent word to Hook:—"I have entire confidence in Ward, as a loyal son of the Church of England;"[2] to which assertion Hook replied most emphatically:—"Ward is *not* loyal to the Church of England. He has himself told me and written to me that to the Church of England he could *not* defer."[3] In this letter Hook complained bitterly of Pusey's conduct:—

"And what do I complain of?" he asks. "I complain of your building a Church and getting a foot in my parish to propagate principles which I detest—having come under the plea of assisting me to propagate the principles I uphold. I complain of your having selected one to oppose me and my principles who approached me as a friend, and who now admits that in so doing he did wrong, and that before he undertook to oppose me by causing a division in Leeds, he ought to have reflected that *he* was not the proper person to be your agent. I have said to him, and he has wept—*Et tu, Brute!* It is really cruel, mere Jesuitism, thus to misrepresent the injured party—the party injured through an excess of charity, as the persecuting party. It is wicked."[4]

Pusey answered by telling Hook:—"You are no more responsible for St. Saviour's than for London"; which was almost equivalent to telling him to mind his own business. But Hook was not the sort of man to be sat upon, or to be

---
[1] *Life of Dr. Pusey*, vol. iii. p. 128.
[2] *Ibid.* p. 119.   [3] *Ibid.* p. 120.   [4] *Ibid.* p. 120.

moved from his purpose by the sickening appeals for peace from the chief cause of the disturbance:—"You tell me," he rejoined, "I have no more to do with St. Saviour's than with London. Be it so. But if my neighbour has a hornet's nest close to my garden gates, and my children are likely to be stung by them, I must ask him to remove the nest, or I send to the constable. And if there be Romanising at St. Saviour's, I shall send to the Right Reverend Constable, come what will."[1] After some further correspondence, in the course of which Hook termed St. Saviour's Church "a semi-Papal colony," whose clergy "proclaim that it is sinful to speak against the Church of Rome"; the Vicar of Leeds again demanded, on December 30, 1846, that Pusey should induce Ward to resign the Vicarage of St. Saviour's:—

"I called upon you most solemnly in the name of the Great God," wrote Hook, "to persuade Ward to resign, and to withdraw your other people. It is now too late to do this entirely, but if you have any sense of honour or of justice, you should withdraw Ward and give the presentation to the Bishop. I must take steps to denounce you and your followers as being in my opinion heretics. I regard you as such from your last letter. If your view of the Eucharist be not that taken by the Church of England, instead of bending your own spirit to the Church, you must, as you say, leave the Church."[2]

The result was that Ward resigned. Pusey asked Archdeacon Manning to suggest a new Incumbent in his room. He does not seem to have nominated anybody, but he expressed in very plain language (on January 23, 1847) to Pusey what was the real tendency of Puseyism. "You know," he said, "how long I have to you openly expressed my conviction that a false position has been taken up in the Church of England. The direct and certain tendency, I believe, of what remains of the original Movement is to the Roman Church. You know the minds of men about us better than I do, and will therefore know both how strong an impression the claims of Rome have made upon them, and how feeble and fragmentary are the reasons on

---

[1] *Life of Dr. Pusey*, vol. iii. p. 122. [2] *Ibid.* p. 128.

which they have made a sudden stand or halt in the line on which they have been, perhaps insensibly, moving for years."[1]

There were those who thought the secession of the Rev. R. G. Macmullen a thing to be deplored by members of the Church of England. Dr. Hook was not one of this class. "To true-hearted members of the Church of England," said Hook, "the departure of Mr. Macmullen and his disciples is a satisfaction and relief; *we may hope that all Romanisers will follow his example.* I have no sympathy with the cant of those who urge us to retain such persons in the Church, by permitting them to revile at will the principles of the English Reformation. I am told that Mr. Macmullen would have laboured in the Church if he had been permitted to act thus. I rejoice to think that he is gone."[2]

Mr. Gladstone urged Pusey, in view of the secessions to Rome from St. Saviour's, Leeds, to set himself right with public opinion by some explicit and public statement against the Church of Rome. But he refused to do so. On February 8, 1847, he wrote to Mr. Gladstone:—"If I did say anything publicly about the Church of Rome, it would be that no good can come of this general declamation against it, without owning what is good and great in it. Many feel this, who love the Church of England deeply."[3] Pusey's kindly feeling towards Roman Catholics was shown the previous year, in the statement he made to his brother on the question of the endowment of Roman Catholicism:—"For myself, I hope that everything done *for* the Roman Catholics will work to good, both in doing away irritation at present, and tending ultimately to bring us together. I do not see anything to object to in giving seats to Irish Roman Catholic Bishops, or endowing Colleges for them, or paying their clergy if they would receive it. I do not see anything amiss, or any principle violated, in doing anything *positively* for the Roman Catholics."[4] In *this* respect Pusey was, beyond doubt, a very true friend to the Church of Rome.

[1] *Life of Dr. Pusey*, vol. iii. p. 135.
[2] *Life and Letters of Dean Hook*, vol. ii. p. 200.
[3] *Life of Dr. Pusey*, vol. iii. p. 146.　　[4] *Ibid.* p. 171.

In the month of May 1847, the Bishop of Exeter prosecuted one of his Puseyite clergy, the Rev. W. G. Parks Smith, Incumbent of St. George's Chapel, Torquay, for a breach of the law in setting on the Communion Table two Vases of Flowers, and a Cross two feet high, wreathed with flowers. The Bishop had for several years attended and taken part in the services in this Chapel, and had again and again entreated, and even enjoined Mr. Smith to abstain from all changes in matters not required by the Rubric or other law of the Church; but Mr. Smith had paid no attention to his Bishop's wishes. The result was that his lordship issued a Commission, under the Church Discipline Act, to inquire into the charges brought against Mr. Smith. The Commission met in the Chapter House of Exeter Cathedral, and after hearing evidence, and counsel for the defence, decided that a *prima facie* case had been made out against the defendant. Thereupon, it was announced, on behalf of Mr. Smith, that to prevent further legal action he would consent that the Bishop should pronounce sentence. This his lordship did, on May 28th. He declared that Mr. Smith had acted contrary to the law of the Church, admonished him not to offend again in like manner, and ordered him to pay the costs of the proceedings. The following brief extracts from the judgment are interesting:—

"If one person may at his pleasure decorate the Lord's Table with a Cross, another may equally claim to set a Crucifix upon it —whilst a third might think it necessary to erect some symbol of Puritan doctrine or feeling—to mark his reprobation of his Romanising neighbour."

"The only direction in the Rubric is, 'that the Table at the Communion time have a fair white linen cloth upon it;' and the 82nd Canon 'appoints, that the Communion Table shall be covered in time of Divine Service, with a carpet of silk, or other decent stuff, and with a fair linen cloth at the time of ministration.' This must be holden virtually to exclude all else, except what is used, or may be used, in the service itself. If any one ventures to go further—to add anything which he may deem an ornament—he does it at his peril."

"Such a thing [as the use of the material Cross on the Lord's

Table] was never heard of, during more than the first three centuries of the Christian era; and Durandas, the authority relied on by the defendant's advocate, for saying, that 'the proper place for the Cross is the Lord's Table,' was a Bishop and Canonist of the thirteenth century; therefore very little entitled to our attention on a question respecting the present law of our Church, even if the reasons stated by him were as solid as they are, in truth, shadowy and contradictory."[1]

The part taken by the Bishop of Exeter in this case shows that, however domineering his nature might be, he was prepared to prosecute those he thought law-breakers, quite apart from their ordinary theological views. The present state of the law as to the use of the Cross on the Communion Table is thus explained by Mr. Whitehead:—"It must not, however, be attached to the Communion Table or placed upon a ledge immediately over the Table, so as to appear to form one structure with it, and it makes no difference whether it is fixed or moveable. It may, however, be placed on the sill of the eastern window, five feet above the Communion Table, or it may surmount a Chancel screen. Of course, in no case may it be an object of superstitious reverence, or carried in processions, or otherwise used ceremonially."[2] The Bishop's judgment as to the use of Vases of Flowers on the Communion Table was overruled in the Court of Arches, by the judgment of Sir Robert Phillimore, in the case of *Elphinstone* v. *Purchas*, delivered on February 3, 1870.[3]

The leading Puseyite newspaper, the *English Churchman*, in a leading article, very clearly revealed the real object of the Puseyite party. It said:—" With those who seek to *reduce the distance which separates us from Rome*, to the narrowest limits which a due regard to Catholic faith and practice will admit of, we readily and heartily avow our sympathy."[4]

---

[1] *English Churchman*, June 3, 1847, where a *verbatim* report of the judgment is printed.
[2] Whitehead's *Church Law*, p. 103, 2nd edition. London: Stevens & Sons. 1899.
[3] Phillimore's *Ecclesiastical Judgments*, pp. 191, 192.
[4] *English Churchman*, October 7, 1847, p. 745.

The Bishop of Chichester (Dr. Gilbert) felt it necessary to take notice of the affairs of Sackville College, East Grinstead, an institution founded early in the seventeenth century as a kind of almshouses, consisting of a Warden, two Assistant Wardens, five brethren, six sisters, and fourteen probationers. In the month of May 1846, the Rev. J. M. Neale, M.A., was appointed Warden, and as such conducted Divine Service, and administered Holy Communion to the inmates in the College Chapel. Early in 1847 a complaint was made to the Bishop of Chichester as to the proceedings in the Chapel, which stated that a Vulgate Bible and a copy of the Roman Breviary were seen there, that there was a "suspicion" that the English Bible in the Chapel was the Douay, and that a large Cross was erected on the Chancel screen. Mr. Neale, in reply, proved that the English Bible was the authorised edition with notes; and asserted that there could be no valid objection to having a Latin Vulgate Bible for his own private use; and that as to the Roman Breviary, he was engaged at the time in Liturgical studies which required the use of the Breviary, and that it had been accidentally left in the Chapel by mistake. On April 12, 1847, the Bishop wrote to Mr. Neale requesting him to have the goodness to communicate with him before he officiated "in any Church or Chapel" in the Diocese. Mr. Neale thereupon informed the Bishop that Sackville College was outside his jurisdiction, and therefore no licence was needed to officiate in it, since he was only doing so as the head of a private family. On May 7th the Bishop had an interview with Mr. Neale in the vestry of East Grinstead Church, of which the latter gentleman subsequently published a report. Mr. Neale informed him that he personally would prefer to have his lordship's licence to officiate, but his wishes had been overruled by the authorities of the College; on which the Bishop remarked :—"I ought to say that I probably might not have been disposed to grant the licence. I could not, if the reports which I have heard of Romanistic proceedings in the College be true." Later on in the day the Bishop went with Mr. Neale and a "Mr. H." —who had first called the Bishop's attention to what was going on—to the College Chapel. What took place therein is thus reported by Mr. Neale:—

"BISHOP—'I am not here with visitatorial authority; if I were, I should sweep away all that'—(pointing to the altar).

"Mr. H.—'Flowers and all, my Lord?'

"I SAID—'The Altar, my Lord?'

"BISHOP—'I know nothing of Altars; the Church of England knows nothing of Altars or sacrifices. I would retain a decent low Table. I would not feed Christ's little ones with the wood of the Cross.'"[1]

On the very next day the Bishop sent Mr. Neale a formal Inhibition "from celebrating Divine Worship, and from the exercise of clerical functions in my Diocese." With the Inhibition he sent the following letter:—"I cannot transmit to you the following Inhibition without adding a fervent prayer that God may be pleased to open your eyes to the dishonour done to Him by supposing that His spiritual service can be promoted by presenting to the eyes and thoughts of worshippers the frippery with which you have transformed the simplicity of the Chapel at Sackville College into an imitation of the degrading superstitions of an erroneous Church."[2]

Mr. Neale simply ignored the Inhibition, and went on conducting the services in the Chapel as though nothing had happened. The Bishop seems to have left him alone for five months, but then, finding him still rebellious, he sent the case on for trial in the Court of Arches. On June 3, 1848, the case—Freeland *v.* Neale—was heard by Sir H. Jenner Fust, who delivered judgment the same day. He said:—

"I should like to have heard some authority for the statement that a number of persons constituting a corporation, as the inhabitants of Sackville College are said to be, is a private family. It is possible that the inmates of the College may be under one continuous roof, that they have one common table, but those circumstances will not render them a private family or household; each member has, I presume, his separate apartments allotted. ... It is impossible then to say that this was an assemblage of a private

---

[1] *A Statement of Proceedings against the Warden of Sackville College*, p. 9. London: Joseph Masters. 1853.
[2] *Ibid.* p. 9.

family. In *Barnes* v. *Shore* I said, what I now repeat, that where two or three are gathered together, who do not strictly form a part of a family, there is a congregation, and the reading to them the service of the Church is a reading *in public*. I am of opinion that Mr. Neale is proved guilty of an ecclesiastical offence."[1]

The Judge thereupon admonished Mr. Neale not to offend any more, and condemned him to pay the costs of the proceedings. It was remarkable that the very law which the Puseyites had put into operation against the Rev. James Shore, should now be used against one of their own party. Both were charged with and condemned for the same offence ; the only difference being that Mr. Shore admitted that he officiated *in public*, which Mr. Neale denied, though his denial had no effect upon his Judge. When the Protestant Mr. Shore was condemned, the Puseyites shouted for joy; but when Mr. Neale was condemned, they howled with indignation.

I respectfully suggest that the case of Mr. Neale has its lesson for our own day and generation. In almost every Diocese private Chapels and Oratories are set up in Convents and Monasteries, where lawless and thoroughly Romanising services are performed. All such services are, as we have seen, illegal without the consent and licence of the Bishop of the Diocese. But what do we find? Instead of Inhibiting the clergy who officiate in these Oratories, the Bishops actually grant them their licences to officiate. It is within their power to put a stop, with a stroke of their pen, to all the Romanising extravagances which take place in these buildings; but they do nothing at all, unless it be to grant the law-breakers their Episcopal permission to officiate. After which they have the daring to go into the House of Lords, and tell the country that the Bishops are doing everything in their power to put down lawlessness!

The commencement of the celebrated Gorham Case dates from the month of August 1847, when the Lord Chancellor Cottenham nominated the Rev. George Cornelius Gorham to the living of Brampford Speke, in the Diocese of Exeter. Mr. Gorham was a scholar of repute,

[1] Robertson's *Ecclesiastical Reports*, vol. i. pp. 650, 651.

having been formerly a Fellow of Queen's College, Cambridge. He had been in Holy Orders thirty-six years at the time of his nomination, had served in six dioceses, and bore an unblemished character and a high reputation. In 1846 he had been presented by Lord Chancellor Lyndhurst to the living of St. Just-in-Penwith, at that time in the Diocese of Exeter, and while there had incurred the wrathful indignation of his Diocesan, Bishop Phillpotts, by advertising for a Curate "free from Tractarian error." When, in the following year, Mr. Gorham was presented to Brampford Speke, his Bishop had neither forgotten nor forgiven his alleged offence; and showed his displeasure by refusing to institute him, until after he had examined him as to his soundness in the faith. The Bishop's doubts centred round one point of doctrine only. He believed that Mr. Gorham held Evangelical views as to Baptismal Regeneration, and he considered that any one holding such views had no right to minister in the Church of England. Hence arose one of the most important theological contests which the Church of England had witnessed since the Protestant Reformation. On its issue depended the question whether Evangelical clergymen should be banished from the Church of England. It could not be disputed that men holding their views as to Baptismal Regeneration had officiated in our Reformed Church since the Reformation, nor that the overwhelming majority of the Reformers held their views. What the Puseyites aimed at was the capture of the Church of England for themselves, and to banish for ever decided Protestantism from its fold. I have no doubt that these results would have followed the victory of their cause in the Gorham Case. But, thank God, they failed, and victory remained on the side of God's truth and Evangelical principles.

Mr. Gorham humbly submitted to the Bishop of Exeter's examination, though he might, considering his learning and past career, have justly objected to being treated as though he were some ignorant young curate just fresh from College. When Mr. Gorham had thus placed himself in the Bishop's hands, he found it no easy task to get out again. The examination was inquisitorial and prolonged. It began on December 17th, and was continued at intervals until the 10th of March, 1848, during which time Mr. Gorham had to write answers to no fewer than 149 questions on the single subject of Baptismal Efficacy! It looked as though the Bishop wanted to worry his victim to the utmost of his power. The day after the examination ended, the Bishop signified his decision to refuse to institute Mr. Gorham to the living of Brampford Speke, on the ground of unsoundness of doctrine, as revealed by him in the examination.

As quickly as possible after the Bishop's refusal to institute, the case was brought into the Court of Arches. The Dean of Arches (Sir H. Jenner Fust) thereupon issued a monition to the Bishop of Exeter to show cause why he should not institute Mr. Gorham within fifteen days—failing which the Dean would himself proceed to institute him. The case did not come before the Court on its merits until February 17, 1849. On August 2, 1849, Sir H. Jenner Fust delivered a lengthy judgment, concluding as follows:—

"Therefore I say, that as the doctrine of the Church of England undoubtedly is, that children baptized are regenerated at Baptism, and are undoubtedly saved if they die without committing actual sin, Mr. Gorham has maintained and does maintain opinions opposed to that Church of which he professes himself a member and Minister. The only remaining question is, has the Bishop shown sufficient cause why he should not institute Mr. Gorham to the Vicarage of Brampford Speke? I am clearly of opinion that the Bishop has, by reason of the premises, shown sufficient cause; that consequently he is entitled to be dismissed, and must be dismissed, according to the usual course, with costs."[1]

Of course Mr. Gorham appealed against this judgment to the Judicial Committee of Privy Council, and it was well for the Evangelical cause that he did so. The case was heard before the Judicial Committee on December 11, 1849. The proceedings lasted four days. The case of the Bishop of Exeter rested on a book which Mr. Gorham had published, containing the replies he had given in the

---

[1] Robertson's *Ecclesiastical Reports*, vol. ii. pp. 103, 104.

MR. GORHAM'S DOCTRINE

Bishop's examination.[1] It is impossible, nor is it necessary, to find room here for the very lengthy passages in this book relied on by the Bishop to prove that Mr. Gorham held unsound doctrine as to Baptismal Regeneration. A summary of Mr. Gorham's views on this important subject was given by the Judicial Committee in their judgment on March 8, 1850, which will serve to supply my readers with an idea of what he held, and for holding which he was acquitted by the Court. I know the Bishop of Exeter subsequently denied its accuracy, but in this I venture to differ from him. Anyhow, it is the teaching which the judgment declared was not contrary to the Church of England:—

"The doctrine held by Mr. Gorham," said the Judicial Committee, "appears to be this—that Baptism is a Sacrament generally necessary to salvation, but that the grace of regeneration does not so necessarily accompany the act of Baptism, that regeneration invariably takes place in Baptism; that the grace may be given before, in, or after Baptism; that Baptism is an effectual sign of grace, by which God works invisibly in us, but only in such as worthily receive it—in them alone it has a wholesome effect; and that, without reference to the qualification of the recipient, it is not in itself an effectual sign of grace. That infants baptized, and dying before actual sin, are certainly saved; but that in no case is regeneration in Baptism unconditional.

"These being," continued their lordships, "as we collect them, the opinions of Mr. Gorham, the question which we have to decide is, not whether they are theologically sound or unsound—not whether upon some of the doctrines comprised in the opinions, other opinions opposite to them may or may not be held with equal or even greater reason by other learned and pious Ministers of the Church; but whether these opinions now under our consideration are contrary or repugnant to the doctrines which the Church of England, by its Articles, Formularies, and Rubrics, requires to be held by its Ministers, so that upon the ground of those opinions the appellant can lawfully be excluded from the benefice to which he has been presented."[2]

The judgment entered at great length into the argu-

[1] *Examination before Admission to a Benefice by the Bishop of Exeter.* By the Clerk Examined, George Cornelius Gorham, B.D., pp. xlvii., 230. London: Hatchard & Son. 1848.
[2] Brodrick and Freemantle's *Judgments of the Judicial Committee of the Privy Council*, p. 89.

ments which had been brought forward in the case both for and against Mr. Gorham. It will be sufficient for my purpose to give from it the following extracts:—

"The Services abound with expressions which must be construed in a charitable and qualified sense, and cannot with any appearance of reason be taken as proofs of doctrine. Our principal attention has been given to the Baptismal Services; and those who are strongly impressed with the earnest prayers which are offered for the Divine blessing, and the grace of God, may not unreasonably suppose that the grace is not necessarily tied to the rite; but that it ought to be earnestly and devoutly prayed for, in order that it may then, or when God pleases, be present to make the rite beneficial." [1]

"This Court, constituted for the purpose of advising her Majesty in matters which come within its competency, has no jurisdiction or authority to settle matters of faith, or to determine what ought in any particular to be the doctrine of the Church of England. Its duty extends only to the consideration of that which is by law established to be the doctrine of the Church of England, upon the true and legal construction of her Articles and Formularies; and we consider that it is not the duty of any Court to be minute and rigid in cases of this sort. We agree with Sir William Scott in the opinion which he expressed in Stone's case, in the Consistory Court of London—'That if any Article is really a subject of dubious interpretation, it would be highly improper that this Court should fix on one meaning, and prosecute all those who hold a contrary opinion regarding its interpretation.'

"In the examination of this case, we have not relied on the doctrinal opinions of any of the eminent writers, by whose piety, learning, and ability the Church of England has been distinguished; but it appears that opinions, which we cannot in any important particular distinguish from those entertained by Mr. Gorham, have been propounded and maintained, without censure or reproach, by many eminent and illustrious prelates and divines who have adorned the Church from the time when the Articles were first established. We do not affirm that the doctrines and opinions of Jewel, Hooker, Usher, Jeremy Taylor, Whitgift, Pearson, Carlton, Prideaux, and many others, can be received as evidence of the doctrine of the Church of England; but their conduct, unblamed and unquestioned as it was, proves, at least, the liberty which has been allowed of maintaining such doctrine." [2]

---

[1] Brodrick and Freemantle's *Judgments of the Judicial Committee of the Privy Council*, p. 101. [2] *Ibid.* pp. 102, 103.

"His Honour the Vice-Chancellor Knight Bruce, dissents from our judgment, but all the other members of the Judicial Committee, who were present at the hearing of the case (those who are now present, and Baron Parke, who is unavoidably absent on circuit), are unanimously agreed in opinion; and the judgment of their lordships is, that the doctrine held by Mr. Gorham is not contrary, or repugnant to the declared doctrine of the Church of England as by law established, and that Mr. Gorham ought not, by reason of the doctrine held by him, to have been refused admission to the Vicarage of Brampford Speke." [1]

Of the three Episcopal Assessors in the case, two agreed with the judgment (the Archbishops of Canterbury and York), and one dissented from it—the Bishop of London. Amongst those who were in Court during the delivery of this important judgment were Baron Bunsen and Cardinal Wiseman. The former sent his son, on the same day, an account of the proceedings, from which I take the following interesting extract:—"I am this moment come from the Privy Council, and have heard the most remarkable judgment pronounced, which since the Reformation and the Civil Wars has ever been given in this country on a great point of faith. . . . I sat on the Privy Council seats, behind the right hand side of the judges, along with Dr. Wiseman! Going out I met W. Goode (the protagonist of the Evangelicals), with whom I shook hands, and who was *blissful;* then my way was stopped in the lobby by two persons—and who were they? Archdeacon Wilberforce and Hope. They drooped their heads, and after some silence, going on and I following them, Archdeacon W. said, 'Well, at least, there is no mistake about it.' In which I heartily concur." [2]

The immediate effect of the judgment on Archdeacon Manning and his friends was related by him many years later, when he was a Roman Cardinal:—

"I remember well," he said, "I was in London when it was given. I went at once to Gladstone, who then lived in Carlton Terrace. He was ill with influenza and in bed; I sat down by his bedside and told him of the judgment. Starting up and

---

[1] Brodrick and Freemantle's *Judgments of the Judicial Committee of the Privy Council*, p. 105. [2] *Memoirs of Baron Bunsen*, vol. ii. pp. 245, 246.

throwing out his arms, he exclaimed :—'The Church of England has gone unless it releases itself by some authoritative act.' We then agreed to draw up a Declaration and get it signed. For this purpose we met in the vestry of St. Paul's, Knightsbridge. There were present Bennett, Hope, Richard Cavendish, Gladstone, and Dr. Mill, I think, and some others. They made me preside. We agreed to a string of propositions, deducing that, by the Gorham judgment, the Church of England had forfeited its authority as a divine teacher. The next time we met, Pusey and Keble, I think, were there. They refused this, and got it changed to 'If the Church of England shall accept this judgment it would forfeit its authority as a divine teacher.' This amendment was accepted because it did not say whether the Church of England had or had not *de facto* accepted the judgment. Hope said :—'I suppose we are all agreed that if the Church of England does not undo this we must join the Church of Rome.' This made an outcry; and I think it was then that Keble said :— 'If the Church of England were to fail, it should be found in my parish.'"[1]

The Declaration to which Cardinal Manning refers was, of course, a strong protest against the judgment. It consisted of nine clauses, of which the fifth, sixth, and seventh were as follows :—

" 5. That, inasmuch as the faith is one, and rests upon one principle of authority, the conscious, deliberate, and wilful abandonment of the essential meaning of an article of the Creed destroys the Divine foundation upon which alone the entire faith is propounded by the Church.

" 6. That any portion of the Church which does so abandon the essential meaning of an article, forfeits, not only the Catholic doctrine in that article, but also the office and authority to witness and teach as a member of the Universal Church.

" 7. That by such conscious, wilful, and deliberate act such portion of the Church becomes formally separated from the Catholic body, and can no longer assure to its members the grace of the Sacraments and the remission of sins."[2]

Those who signed this Declaration had not long to wait before they discovered that the Church of England tacitly accepted a judgment which, according to the Declaration,

---

[1] *Life of Cardinal Manning*, vol. i. p. 528.
[2] *Ibid.* p. 532. *Life of Dr. Pusey*, vol. iii. pp. 240, 241.

"formally separated her from the Catholic body," and made her no longer able "to assure to its members the grace of the Sacraments and the remission of sins." Of course there were protests against the judgment in abundance, but, in her official character, who can doubt that the Church of England has *practically* accepted the Gorham judgment? Has any Bishop since its delivery dared to refuse institution to a clergyman on the ground that he held Mr. Gorham's views as to Baptismal Regeneration? To be consistent, every one of the fourteen gentlemen who signed the Declaration ought, after a reasonable interval, to have seceded to Rome. Six of the number certainly saw the inconsistency of their position, after signing such a document, in remaining in the Church of England for any lengthy period, and therefore they seceded to the Church of Rome. Those who seceded were, Archdeacon Manning, Archdeacon Robert J. Wilberforce, the Rev. W. Dodsworth, the Rev. Henry William Wilberforce, Mr. Edward Badeley, and Mr. James Hope (afterwards Hope-Scott). Those who signed, but remained in the Church of England, were, Archdeacon Thomas Thorp, Dr. Pusey, Dr. Mill, the Rev. John Keble, the Rev. William J. E. Bennett, Mr. John C. Talbot, Mr. Richard Cavendish, and the Rev. (afterwards Archdeacon) George Anthony Denison.

There had been a steady stream of secessions to Rome from the ranks of the Puseyites ever since 1841, but after the delivery of the Gorham judgment the stream became for a time something like a flood. A list of the names of the seceders may be read in Browne's *Annals of the Tractarian Movement*, and in Gorman's *Converts to Rome*.

Of course, before the delivery of the judgment, there had been many anxious discussions amongst the Puseyites as to what they should do when it was delivered. One proposal found great favour, and was warmly welcomed by Pusey and Keble. It was nothing less than to *prosecute* Mr. Gorham for heresy! On February 19, 1850, Keble wrote to Pusey:—"I still find myself driven back to the notion of *prosecuting him* [Gorham] *for heresy*; which, however, I fear is not practical, as you say no more of it, and Coleridge does not answer my questions about it."¹ Canon Liddon tells us that :—"*Pusey acquiesced* in Keble's proposal for a prosecution of Mr. Gorham for heresy, and suggested this course to the Bishop."² On February 23, 1850, Keble again wrote to Pusey on the subject :—"I am ashamed to say nothing has been done yet about the prosecution for heresy. I will try and write to Badeley by next post. I did not know till last night that you consented to that step."³ No member of the Church Association has ever been more anxious to prosecute law-breakers than Pusey and Keble were, at this time, to prosecute the Evangelical Mr. Gorham. But, alas for their hopes! "Mr. Badeley," says Canon Liddon, "thought it impossible at the time to prosecute Mr. Gorham for heresy."⁴ No doubt, if it had been possible, poor Mr. Gorham would have been prosecuted, and the Evangelicals, as a consequence, would have been banished from the Church of England. Had such a result followed such a prosecution, we should never have heard one word from modern Ritualists about the supposed wickedness of ecclesiastical prosecutions.

And what effect had the Gorham judgment on the Bishop of Exeter? The Judicial Committee of Privy Council did not order him to institute Mr. Gorham, or, possibly, he might have been sent to prison for contempt. It remitted the case to the Court of Arches, and the Dean of Arches, acting for the Archbishop of Canterbury, instituted Mr. Gorham to the Rectory of Brampford Speke, notwithstanding the opposition of the Bishop of Exeter. It was a sore point with the Bishop that the Dean should act, in this capacity, as the representative of the Archbishop of Canterbury. So, before the actual institution took place, Dr. Phillpotts wrote, and published as a pamphlet, a not very respectful *Letter to the Archbishop of Canterbury*, concluding with the following strong protest :—

"I have one most painful duty to perform. I have to protest not only against the judgment pronounced in the recent cause, but also against the regular consequences of that judgment. I have to

---

¹ *Life of Dr. Pusey*, vol. iii. p. 223.   ² *Ibid*. p. 223.
³ *Ibid*. p. 226.   ⁴ *Ibid*. p. 227.

protest against your Grace's doing what you will be speedily called to do, either in person, or by some other exercising your authority. I have to protest, and I do hereby solemnly protest, before the Church of England, before the Holy Catholic Church, before Him who is its Divine Head, against your giving mission to exercise cure of souls, within my diocese, to a clergyman who proclaims himself to hold the heresies which Mr. Gorham holds. I protest that any one who gives mission to him till he retract, is a favourer and supporter of these heresies. I protest, in conclusion, that I cannot without sin—and by God's grace I will not—hold communion with him, be he who he may, who shall so abuse the high commission which he bears."[1]

The Rev. William Goode replied to the Bishop of Exeter in a forcible and well-written pamphlet of 107 pages. On the passage from that prelate's letter which I have just cited, Mr. Goode remarked:—

"My Lord, if by these words you mean that you are about to retire to a more suitable communion than the Church of England, be it so. You will not ask us to lament your departure. Nor shall you hear from me words of exultation or insult. Or if you mean that you will withdraw from the Primate the light of your presence, and the blessing of your communion and 'affectionate friendship,' why then, my Lord,—if you have really made up your mind—so it must be. And I will only hope that his Grace may be enabled to bear the deprivation with equanimity.

"But if you mean, what your words appear to mean, that, retaining your position in this Church and country as the Bishop of Exeter, you will set at defiance your Primate and your Sovereign; that you will place yourself in a state of open rebellion against the laws of your country; then, my Lord, I leave you, without fear, to reap the due reward of broken vows and violated oaths; feeling well assured that the majesty of the law will obtain as easy a triumph over Devonshire and Cornish rebels *now*, as it did three centuries ago."[2]

Any one reading the pamphlet of the Bishop of Exeter must admit that he had the courage of his convictions. It was, indeed, a daring thing to do—to practically excom-

---

[1] *A Letter to the Archbishop of Canterbury.* By the Bishop of Exeter, p. 90. London: John Murray. 1850.
[2] *A Letter to the Bishop of Exeter.* By William Goode, M.A., p. 97, 3rd edition. London: Hatchard & Son. 1850.

municate his own Primate. But he went further, and tried to blacken Mr. Gorham's theological character in the eyes of his new parishioners at Brampford Speke, by a published letter to the Churchwardens of that parish. In this document Dr. Phillpotts most unjustly affirmed that "truths on which the whole teaching of the Church rests" "were directly contradicted by your new Vicar in his examination before me, his Bishop."[1] The Churchwardens were assured that:—"You have already too strong reason to apprehend that your new Vicar may endeavour to spread the poison of heresy among his people";[2] and that Mr. Gorham was "one who himself believes not the saving truths which he has undertaken to teach."[3] The Churchwardens were exhorted to act as spies on their Vicar's preaching, and if he taught from the pulpit anything contrary to the Bishop's view of Baptismal Regeneration, they were to make a note of his words, and send them to the Archdeacon, in order that they might be dealt with by the Bishop. In that case the Bishop promised to prosecute Mr. Gorham for heresy.

Now there can be no question that a letter like this was well calculated to stir up the parishioners of Brampford Speke against their new Vicar. It certainly was not a case of trying to pour oil on the troubled waters. And, moreover, it was in defiance of the law. The next step taken by the Bishop was to convoke what he termed a "Synod" of his clergy, mainly to consider this question of Baptismal Regeneration. His lordship, however, did not invite *all* of the clergy to take part in it; had he done so the proceedings would not have passed off as smoothly as he desired. So he invited the clergy of every Rural Deanery to elect two only of their Deanery as their representatives; and to these were added the Dean of Exeter and the Greater Chapter, the Bishop's Chaplains, and the officials of the Archdeacons.[4] The laity were left out altogether. Had *they* been admitted the Bishop knew very well that he would have had a very disagreeable time in the Synod. The Synod met on June

---

[1] *A Letter to the Churchwardens of Brampford Speke.* By the Bishop of Exeter, p. 10, 2nd edition. London: John Murray. 1850.
[2] *Ibid.* p. 14.   [3] *Ibid.* p. 15.
[4] *Acts of the Synod of Exeter*, p. 1. London: John Murray. 1851.

25, 1851, and the proceedings lasted three days; but a portion of the second day only was devoted to the real object for which it was convened. Now there was not a man at that Synod who did not know very well that, were he to get up and speak against the Declaration on Baptism submitted to it, he would be a marked man by the Bishop from that day out. The names of those who were present were not printed in the official report of the proceedings subsequently issued "By Authority," and therefore I cannot tell whether there were any Evangelical clergymen in the Synod. If they were there they ought to have spoken out, and voted against the Declaration, which was so strongly on the side of the Bishop's views as to Baptismal Regeneration that, when it was declared carried unanimously, the Bishop exclaimed:— "Thank God for this: let His Holy Name be praised."[1]

One result of the Gorham Case was the publication of two important books on Baptismal Regeneration. One, published in 1862, was entitled, *A Review of the Baptismal Controversy*, and was written by the Rev. J. B. Mozley, a High Churchman, and subsequently Regius Professor of Divinity in the University of Oxford. The object of this work is thus explained by its learned author in his preface: —"I have, however, in the present treatise, confined myself to two positions: one, that the doctrine of the regeneration of all infants in Baptism is not an article of the faith; the other, that the formularies of our Church do not impose it." The other work, published in 1849, while the Gorham Case was still undecided, was written by the Rev. William Goode, and bore the title of *The Doctrine of the Church of England as to the Effects of Baptism*. I would strongly recommend both of these valuable and important works to the Evangelical clergy and laity, and also to those who wish to know what can be said in support of the Gorham judgment. The Baptismal Regeneration controversy is not studied now as much as in former years, and yet it is needed now more than ever. Its importance for Evangelical Churchmen cannot be over-estimated.

Coming back to the year 1849 we find the Bishop of

---

[1] *Acts of the Synod of Exeter*, p. 57.

Oxford endeavouring to exercise Episcopal discipline over one of his Romanising clergymen—the Rev. T. W. Allies, Rector of Launton, Oxon. This case shows how audacious some of the clergy had already become in their march to Rome. Several years before this, while officiating for the Rev. W. J. Bennett, that gentleman had given Mr. Allies a copy of the Roman Missal, and ever since his Romeward sympathies had developed rapidly. In 1840 Mr. Allies was appointed Chaplain to Dr. Blomfield, Bishop of London, an office which he held until June 1842. Soon after he became Rector of Launton. We learn from Mr. Allies' autobiography that early in 1844 he had come to the conclusion " that post-Baptismal sin required Sacramental Confession and Absolution."[1] He fitted up his Church with open oak pews. It was reopened on September 1, 1844. "*Before* that time," says Mr. Allies, "*all my trust in Anglicanism was gone.*"[2] And yet he remained officiating within the Anglican Church, as one of her clergy, for seven years and a half afterwards! How he could do it with a comfortable conscience is indeed a mystery. On February 12, 1845, he wrote in his diary:—" Since my last birthday one very important change of view has developed itself—a secret and yet undefined dread that we are in a state of schism."[3] He wrote a book in 1846 entitled *The Church of England Cleared from the Charge of Schism*, of which he brought out a second edition in February, 1848; and this is how he describes its publication:—" I had become, both practically and theoretically, more and more *disgusted* with the Anglican Church, more and more struck with what I saw of the action and conduct of the Catholic Church abroad. And so it came to pass, that I was publishing the second edition of a book, written in the utmost good faith, with daily prayers for enlightenment, *in ostensible defence of a communion which I thoroughly hated.*"[4] It must have required an immense quantity of Jesuitical casuistry to have enabled him to continue ministering for two and a half years more

---

[1] *A Life's Decision.* By T. W. Allies, p. 50, 2nd edition. London: Burns and Oates. 1894.
[2] *Ibid.* p. 51.   [3] *Ibid.* p. 53.
[4] *Ibid.* p. 115.

in a communion which he "thoroughly hated." What part had any sense of truth and honour in such conduct? Early in 1849 Mr. Allies published his *Journal in France*.[1] On February 19th he wrote in his diary:—"Received to-day the first copies of my *Journal in France*. I went into the garden and read the whole conclusion. The publishing this book gave me great gratification. It so exactly sets forth my mind; *it pays a debt which I seemed to owe to the Roman Church;*" and again, on the following day, he wrote in the same diary, with reference to this book:—"I seem to have discharged a *sacred* debt to the Roman Church."[2] The Rev. Charles Marriott, writing from Oriel College, on Easter Monday 1849, to thank Allies for a copy of the book, said that, in what he had written about Invocation of Saints, "so far you have exercised a laudable subtlety."[3] There can be no doubt about the "subtlety," but I do not believe that it was "*laudable*." Almost everything in Romanism was held up by Mr. Allies to admiration in this book. The following extracts from it will give some idea of how far its author had gone towards Rome:—

"Most intimately connected with the dogma of the Incarnation, and its symbol, the Real Presence, is that of the Intercession of all Saints, especially of the Blessed Mother of God; nay, this may be said to be the continuation and carrying out of the Real Presence, so that wherever that is truly and heartfully believed, this will be, within due bounds, cherished and practised."[4]

"And may not we ask you, who dwell in sight of the Eternal Throne, but who once, like ourselves, bore the burden and heat of the day in this earthly wilderness, may we not ask you to turn your regards on us, to intercede for us before Him, whose members ye are in glory, and we in trial?"[5]

"Christ is present in His Church, for the Priest in the tribunal of penitence is as God himself."[6]

"Among minor things, which yet we have suffered loss and harm

---

[1] *Journal in France in* 1845 *and* 1848. By Thomas William Allies, M.A., Rector of Launton, pp. xii. 388.
[2] *A Life's Decision*, p. 125.
[3] *Ibid.* p. 148.
[4] Allies' *Journal in France*, p. 334.
[5] *Ibid.* p. 335.
[6] *Ibid.* p. 338.

in giving up, may be reckoned the custom of crossing with Holy Water on entering a Church."¹

"A still more to be regretted omission is that of the Crucifix, which might, with much edification, appear prominently at least in one part of the Church, over the Rood Screen or over the altar."²

"If the Anglo-German race be ever restored to the communion of the Latin Church, as *I fervently pray that mercy may be reserved for them* by God."³

The Bishop of Oxford read the book soon after its publication, and gave his opinion of it in the most emphatic terms on March 8th. "It is," he declared, "the most undisguised, unblushing preference for Rome I almost ever read."⁴ Nine days later he wrote to the author of the book, calling his attention to the variance which existed "between its language and the dogmatic teachings of the Church of England;" and adding that no particular extracts could "*fully* exhibit this contradiction, because the general tone" of the book was "more at variance with the teaching of our Church" than any particular extracts. His language concerning the Mass contradicted the explicit teaching of Article XXVIII. The tone of the book towards the Church of England was "deprecating, and even insulting," while it contained "unbounded eulogies of the Papal system." The Bishop enclosed a set of extracts from the book, and called on Mr. Allies for an explanation or an unqualified retractation.⁵ The author's reply was not considered satisfactory, and therefore the Bishop wrote to him again on March 24th, pointing out that he had not replied to his chief objections against the book:—"The part of my communication," wrote Dr. Wilberforce, "which needed the most direct reply you have left almost untouched, under the allegation that my letter closes with a threat. I think that if you look again at it, you will perceive that it contains nothing but a declaration that if you cannot show that your statements do not contradict the Articles, and will not retract them, I shall appeal to your own conscience as to whether

---
¹ Allies' *Journal in France*, p. 340.   ² *Ibid*. p. 340.
³ *Ibid*. p. 344.
⁴ *Life of Bishop Wilberforce*, vol. ii. p. 17.   ⁵ *Ibid*. pp. 17, 18.

THE CASE OF MR. ALLIES

it is honest to maintain your position as a paid teacher of doctrines you formally deny."[1]

The case of Mr. Allies worried the Bishop not a little. "I have great trouble with Mr. Allies," he wrote to his sister-in-law; "he has given me most evasive answers to the questions I have been obliged to put to him. He wishes to make out that he may hold all Roman doctrine, except the Pope's Supremacy, and remain with us. I am now taking an opinion whether his *words* make his *meaning* plain enough for me to proceed in the Courts against him."[2] The legal opinion referred to in this letter was given to the Bishop a week later by the well-known ecclesiastical lawyer, Dr. Lushington. He said that he was satisfied that "a prosecution would be attended with success." There were evils in such prosecutions, but it would in this case be a greater evil not to prosecute. The Bishop decided to send the case to the Court of Arches, but at the last moment Baron Alderson persuaded him not to do so, on the ground that a lawsuit would tend to a schism in the Church, while the tendencies of the Romanisers would "die out if judiciously left alone"— an opinion which the results have not justified. The Baron's appeal was backed up by a letter from his friend, Mr. Allies, addressed to the Bishop, in which he expressed regret that anything in his book "should appear to my Diocesan to be contrary to the Articles of the Church of England, or calculated to depreciate that Church in comparison with the Church of Rome; and I undertake not to publish a second edition of the work. I declare my adherence to the Articles in their plain, literal, and grammatical sense, and will not preach or teach anything contrary to such Articles in their plain, literal, and grammatical sense."[3] This, be it observed, was not an acknowledgment that he *had* written anything in his book contrary to the Articles, but that he was sorry the Bishop should think so. It was very wrong of Bishop Wilberforce to yield to the advice of Allies' friends in withdrawing the prosecution, and it was not long before

[1] *Life of Bishop Wilberforce*, p. 19.
[2] *Ibid.* p. 20. [3] *Ibid.* p. 26.

he had cause to regret his decision. In his old age, writing as a Roman Catholic, Mr. Allies frankly acknowledges:—"Simply taking the passages in my *Journal* quoted by the Bishop, they certainly appear to me irreconcilable with the letter, and still more with the spirit, of the Anglican Articles;"[1] and, he adds, that he has "no doubt whatever that he [the Bishop] would have got a judgment against me."[2]

On July 26, 1849, Mr. Allies, accompanied by a friend, started on a journey to Rome. Writing as a Roman Catholic he says:—"It was quite necessary for my health and spirits to seek for a time a total change of scene, and I could think of nothing so attractive as a visit to Rome, and especially to the Pope.... I felt that I had not a shred to love in Anglicanism, yet all the while the speculative difficulty on the side of the Roman Supremacy remained."[3] Of course while at Rome he had an interview with Pope Pius IX., who seems to have had a great admiration for Dr. Pusey. His opinion of that divine, as given by Mr. Allies in his report of this interview, is very interesting:—

"Then he asked after Dr. Pusey. '*He has done*,' said the Pope, '*much good;* HE HAS OPENED THE DOOR; he has set before his countrymen the principle of authority, which is the first thing in religion; *he has prepared the way for Catholicism.*'"[4]

So much for Dr. Pusey. And this is what Mr. Allies told the Pope about himself, and some of his Puseyite friends he had left behind in England:—"I consider it a blessing to have the opportunity of expressing personally to your Holiness, that some ecclesiastics at least amongst us— I may say, several—deeply feel *how great a calamity it has been to England, and to the whole British realm, that she has been separated from the Holy See.* They ardently desire her reunion with it." Mr. Allies adds that the Pope "expressed his joy at this. I asked if he would give us his blessing, 'That I will do with all my heart,' he replied, 'and I will pray for you, and for your friends, and for all England.' *He also, at our request, blessed two Crucifixes* which I held

---

[1] *A Life's Decision*, p. 197. [2] *Ibid.* p. 198.
[3] *Ibid.* p. 199. [4] *Ibid.* p. 203.

in my hand, *and also those in Wynne's;* he seemed merely to touch them. We then knelt, and he pronounced the blessing."[1] And all the while this man, thus kneeling before the Pope, humbly seeking his blessing for himself and his crucifixes, was professedly a clergyman of the Church of England, receiving her pay, and bound to her by oaths of allegiance! Truly there are many crooked things in the History of the Romeward Movement! "I then," writes Mr. Allies, "returned by sea to Marseilles, leaving Wynne at Genoa, and on Thursday, September 13th, was again in England, *and carrying about with me the Pope's present as a safeguard against all evil.*"[2] He must, indeed, have fallen deep into the mire of superstition ere he could have believed that the Pope's present would defend him "against all evil!" A year later, on September 8, 1850, Allies announced his resignation of the living of Launton, and the day after he was received into the Church of Rome by Newman.

A few weeks before his secession, Mr. Allies joined two of his friends, the Revs. W. Dodsworth and W. Maskell, in sending to Dr. Pusey a joint letter on the subject of Auricular Confession, which greatly disturbed the latter gentleman:—

"We wish," these gentlemen wrote to Pusey, "to put you a question on a point nearly concerning our own peace of mind, and that of others. It is this—What authority is there for supposing that the acts of a priest are *valid* who hears Confessions, and gives Absolution, in mere virtue of his orders, *without ordinary or delegated jurisdiction from his Bishop?* We believe it to be the undisputed law of the Church that acts flowing from Order, though done wrongly and illicitly, are yet, when done, *valid;* the reason of which is, that the power of Order, being given by consecration and indelible, cannot be taken away: but that acts flowing from Jurisdiction, if done upon those over whom the doer has no Jurisdiction, are absolutely *invalid* and *null.*"[3]

"But what we wish to know is, whether there be any authority for considering *valid* the Absolution of a priest, who has neither

---

[1] *A Life's Decision,* p. 203. [2] *Ibid.* p. 206.
[3] *A Letter to the Rev. Dr. Pusey On His Practice of Receiving Persons in Auricular Confessions.* By William Maskell, M.A., pp. 8, 9. London: William Pickering. 1850.

received such ordinary Jurisdiction in the cure of souls, nor such delegated Jurisdiction, or, again, who, having the cure of souls, absolves not only his own parishioners, but others also, without licence from their own parish priest or Bishop."[1]

"It would certainly follow from all this, as it seems to us, that the authority which for some time past has been exercised by some among us, *and especially by yourself*, not only in our own dioceses, but in other dioceses—often without the knowledge, and probably (were it known) it would be against the consent, of both the parish priest and Bishop—has not been based upon true and sufficient foundation: nay more, has been (however ignorantly) in opposition to Catholic rules from the first ages to the present time. And further—a point to which we allude with reluctance and sorrow—it would follow likewise that the vast majority of those persons, to whom you and others have given Absolution in this manner, are still, so far as the effect of any such Absolutions is concerned, under the chain of their sins, because they have not made Confession to priests who had duly received power to absolve them. Hence, we cannot suppose that you will be surprised that we should earnestly desire from you an elucidation of this matter."[2]

This letter seems to have disturbed Pusey very much. He complained of its tone, and especially of its reference to his own practice—a very delicate point—and he asked the writers to alter, before publication, the wording of their letter. This, however, they declined to do, and pressed for an answer. Of course they had put to him a very difficult and awkward question. He had been wandering about the country—especially in Devonshire—hearing Confessions on the sly, as Mr. Maskell pointed out to him later on. If he could have produced Episcopal leave for hearing these Confessions, and also the leave of the Incumbents of those parishes where he had heard them, he would have had an answer at hand, which must have satisfied Messrs. Maskell, Allies, and Dodsworth, so far, at least, as his own practice was concerned. But as he could not do this, he wrote and published a large volume of 312 pages, the title of which really was his answer to the

[1] Maskell's *Letter to the Rev. Dr. Pusey On His Practice of Receiving Persons in Auricular Confessions*, p. 10.
[2] *Ibid.* pp. 13, 14.

questions put to him: *The Church of England Leaves Her Children Free to Whom to Open Their Griefs.* Ever since then the Ritualistic Father Confessors seem to have acted on the principle laid down by Dr. Pusey in justification of his own practice. The controversy over Jurisdiction has very little, if any, practical interest to Protestant Churchmen, who never need to practise Auricular Confession to human priests, having a much better Confessional to resort to, in which the Great High Priest sits to hear Confessions and give His all-satisfying Absolution; but this correspondence is important to them for this reason. The controversy led to an exposure of Pusey's practice, which was most useful in opening the eyes of Englishmen to the thoroughly Romish character of Auricular Confession, as conducted by the leader of the Puseyites. I quote these exposures with confidence, since Pusey was unable to contradict any one of the charges brought against him, excepting only that which affirmed that he had "enjoined" Confession on his penitents. I should here mention that Messrs. Maskell, Allies, and Dodsworth seceded to Rome soon after their united letter to Pusey. As to Pusey's denial of having "enjoined" Auricular Confession, Mr. Maskell wrote to him:—

"In p. 6 of your letter to Mr. Richards, you blame Mr. Dodsworth for having said in his published letter to you, that you have 'enjoined' Auricular Confession; and you say that you could not *enjoin* Auricular Confession. Suffer me to say, that, in connection with the other words of the same sentence, Mr. Dodsworth's use of the word *enjoin* was just and reasonable. He does not use it simply, and without limitation; he says that you have 'encouraged, if not enjoined,' Auricular Confession: by which it is evident that, in the sense of compulsion, he knew, as well as yourself, you *could not* possibly enjoin Auricular Confession. And he knew also, *as I know*, that to say merely that you have *encouraged* it, would fall as far short of what your actual practice is, as the word *enjoin*, in the sense of *compelling*, would exceed it. He knew that you had done more than *encouraged* Confession in very many cases; that you have warned people of the danger of deferring it, *have insisted on it as the only remedy*, have pointed out the inevitable dangers of the neglect of it, and have promised the highest blessings in the observance, *until you had brought penitents in fear and trembling upon their knees before you.*"¹

"To conclude, in hearing Auricular Confessions, in giving Absolution, and in assuring those who come to you that the grace which they so receive by your ministry is Sacramental, and effective of the removal of the guilt of mortal sin—in thus speaking and thus acting, *you cannot have any other guide, or authority, or teacher, than the* [Roman] *Catholic Church. To her documents, canons, and decisions*, and to the voice of her theologians in their books upon the subject, *you must and do refer.* Whatsoever you hold upon this great Christian Sacrament is derived from that source, *and from that source alone;* and if this be so, as regards your *theory* of Absolution, much more is it as regards your *practice* in hearing Auricular Confessions. I shall not enter into this last point. It would give you as well as myself sorrow to be obliged to do so. All that need be said is that THE RULES OF THE CHURCH OF ROME, AND NO OTHER, ARE YOUR RULES."²

In the following year Mr. Dodsworth published two or three more controversial pamphlets. In one of these he said :—

"I knew, what was also known to hundreds of other persons, that clergymen of the Established Church (I myself was one) were in the habit of doing what is here described; that is, of receiving Confessions, both from men and women, of their whole lives, *in details as minute as any that can possibly be made to a Catholic Priest;* of enjoining penance, and giving Priestly Absolution. Dr. Pusey (I mention it to his honour), was one of the foremost to commend the restoration of this salutary practice, both by precept and example. He was the first Anglican clergyman who spoke to me of its revival in the Established Church, and I know of many persons whom he has led into the practice. With regard to what English Protestants most object to—the minute details of sins in Confession—it is only right to say, so far as I know, that Confession is required to be at least quite as minute, where observed in the Established Church, as it is in the Catholic Church."³

The Revs. W. Maskell, W. Dodsworth, and T. W. Allies had been for years the friends of Dr. Pusey, and were intimately acquainted with the inner working of the Rome-

---

¹ Maskell's *Letter to the Rev. Dr. Pusey On His Practice of Receiving Persons in Auricular Confessions*, pp. 17, 18. ² *Ibid.* p. 50.
³ *A Few Comments on Dr. Pusey's Letter to the Bishop of London.* By William Dodsworth, M.A., pp. 5, 6. London: William Pickering. 1851.

ward Movement in the Church of England. They testified to that which *they knew*, and therefore their testimony—not having been since contradicted on any material point—is of great importance, as proving, beyond the possibility of a doubt, the thoroughly Romish character of the Confessional as worked by Dr. Pusey. It was to them, as it has always been, a great instrument of priestly power; and as we have seen, it "brought penitents in fear and trembling upon their knees" before their spiritual lords and masters. Mr. Dodsworth had been Perpetual Curate of Christ Church, St. Pancras, and soon after his secession to Rome he addressed a published letter to his late congregation, explaining why he had left them. In this document he frankly acknowledged the great assistance the Oxford Movement had already been to the Church of Rome. What would he have said of these services, had he lived to the year 1900? Of "the Oxford Movement of 1833" Mr. Dodsworth said:—

"*I think its tendency towards Rome has been very decisive and very extensive.* Look at the Church of England as it was fifty years ago, or even thirty. At that time it would have been thought Popish to speak of the Real Presence; the doctrine of the Eucharistic Sacrifice was scarcely known in the teaching of the Church. Auricular Confession, counsels of perfection, the Conventual Life, as well as less important matters, such as the use of the Crucifix, &c., were all identified with Popery. But now these doctrines and usages are quite current amongst Anglicans. May we not appeal to the common-sense of men to say whether these things are not *a decisive approximation to Rome?* Nay, more, are not Anglicans indebted to Rome for them? . . . And then, if it be admitted, as it must be, that they enter vitally into the truth of our holy religion, and have a most decisive influence upon religious practice, must it not also be admitted that the revival of these things amongst Anglicans *is so far a witness in favour of Rome?*"[1]

Mr. Dodsworth's exposures of Dr. Pusey's Confessional practices brought the latter gentleman into trouble with his Diocesan. But it was not his work as a Father Confessor only which brought down on Pusey the censures of Bishop Wilberforce. His adapted Roman books, and his teaching concerning the Lord's Supper, seemed to the

[1] *Anglicanism Considered in Its Results.* By William Dodsworth, M.A., pp. 91, 92. London: William Pickering. 1851.

Bishop of Oxford to have a distinct tendency Romeward. There was a lengthy correspondence between the Bishop, Pusey, and Keble on the subject, which may be read in the *Life of Bishop Wilberforce*, and in the *Life of Dr. Pusey*. Wilberforce considered that Pusey was a "decoy bird" who led people into the Papal net, which he had no intention of entering himself. "I do not mean that he intends any such thing; I am quite sure that he does not."[1] Still, however good Pusey's intentions may have been, the result was, in the Bishop's opinion, the same. So at last he had to privately inhibit him from officiating in the Diocese of Oxford, except in the parish of Pusey, for two years. "You seem to me," the Bishop wrote to Pusey, "to be habitually assuming the place and doing the work of a Roman Confessor, and not that of an English clergyman. Now I so firmly believe that of all the curses of Popery this is the crowning curse, that I cannot allow voluntarily within my charge the continuance of any ministry which is infected by it."[2]

The great public excitement connected with the Papal Aggression commenced towards the close of 1850, by the publication of the Papal Bull dividing England into Dioceses to be filled by Bishops of his own choosing. The Protestant opposition to the Pope's action found but little support from the Puseyites: several of them, in fact, actively opposed it. This attitude is partly accounted for by the action of Lord John Russell, the Prime Minister, who, in his famous Durham Letter, attacked, not only the Pope, but also his imitators in the Church of England. His lordship's opinion of the Oxford Movement is thus explained by his biographer, Mr. Spencer Walpole:—"Lord John had always regarded with deep distrust the progress of the great religious Movement which is associated with the names of Cardinal Newman and Mr. Pusey. Its votaries, he thought, were not merely traitors to the Church, but guilty of 'shocking profanation.' They were, consciously or unconsciously, initiating a Movement which was leading to Rome, and they were simultaneously turning a service

---

[1] *Life of Bishop Wilberforce*, vol. ii. p. 86.   [2] *Ibid.* p. 90.

LORD JOHN RUSSELL'S DURHAM LETTER

of remembrance into an offensive spectacle."[1] It is evident from this that Lord John Russell ever looked upon Tractarianism as a Romeward Movement. He feared that "nothing but the erection of a priestly supremacy over the Crown and people would satisfy the party in the Church who now take the lead in agitation."[2] In his letter to the Bishop of Durham his lordship said :—

"There is a danger, however, which alarms me much more than any aggression of a foreign Sovereign. Clergymen of our own Church, who have subscribed the Thirty-Nine Articles and acknowledged in explicit terms the Queen's supremacy, have been most forward in leading their flocks 'step by step to the very verge of the precipice.' The honour paid to Saints, the claim of Infallibility for the Church, the superstitious use of the sign of the Cross, the muttering of the Liturgy so as to disguise the language in which it is written, the recommendation of Auricular Confession, and the administration of penance and absolution—all these things are pointed out by clergymen of the Church of England as worthy of adoption, and are now openly reprehended by the Bishop of London in his Charge to the clergy of his diocese.

"What then is the danger to be apprehended from a foreign prince of no great power, compared to the danger within the gates from the unworthy sons of the Church of England herself?

"I have little hope that the propounders and framers of these innovations will desist from their insidious course. But I rely with confidence on the people of England; and I will not bate a jot of heart or hope, so long as the glorious principles and the immortal Martyrs of the Reformation shall be held in reverence by the great mass of a nation which looks with contempt on the mummeries of superstition, and with scorn at the laborious endeavours which are now making to confine the intellect and enslave the soul."[3]

The words cited in this letter, "step by step to the very verge of the precipice," were a quotation from the Charge of the Bishop of London, delivered on November 2nd. In that Charge Dr. Blomfield, as a High Churchman, expressed his strong disapproval of the Gorham judgment, and advocated the doctrine of Baptismal Regeneration. He then went on to make a strong attack on the Puseyite party, who

---

[1] *Life of Lord John Russell.* By Spencer Walpole, vol. ii. p. 115.
[2] *Ibid.* p. 117. [3] *Ibid.* p. 120.

he held responsible mainly for the many secessions to Rome which had recently taken place:—

"But," said the Bishop, "there is another very important consideration suggested to us by the recent lamentable secessions from our Church. It may well occur to us to enquire how far the way may have been *paved for them*, in some instances at least, by the growth of opinions and practices in our own Reformed Church, at variance, if not with the letter, yet with the spirit, of its teaching and ordinances. I am unwilling to condemn, without reserve, the motives of those among the clergy who have thought themselves at liberty to imitate, as nearly as it is possible to imitate, without a positive infringement of the law, the forms and ceremonies of the Church of Rome. . . . Concessions to error can never really serve the cause of truth. If some few have been thus retained within the pale of our Church, many others have been gradually trained for secession from it. A taste has been excited in them for forms and observances which has stimulated without satisfying their appetite, and they have naturally sought for fuller gratification in the Church of Rome. They have been led, step by step, to the very verge of the precipice, and then, to the surprise and disappointment of their guides, have fallen over. I know that this has happened in some instances. I have no doubt of its having happened in many.

"Then, with respect to doctrine, what can be better calculated to lead the less learned, or the less thoughtful, members of our Protestant Church to look with complacency upon the errors which their Church has renounced, and at length to embrace them, than to have books of devotion put into their hands by their own clergymen, in which all but Divine honour is paid to the Virgin Mary? A propitiatory virtue is attributed to the Eucharist—the mediation of the Saints is spoken of as a probable doctrine—Prayer for the Dead urged as a positive duty—and a superstitious use of the sign of the Cross is recommended as profitable; add to this the secret practice of Auricular Confession, the use of Crucifixes and Rosaries, the administration of what is termed the Sacrament of Penance, and it is manifest that they who are taught to believe that such things are compatible with the principles of the English Church, must also believe it to be separated from that of Rome by a faint and almost imperceptible line, and be prepared to pass that line without much fear of incurring the guilt of schism.

"Then with regard to the mode of celebrating Divine worship, it has been a subject of great uneasiness to me to see the changes which have been introduced by a few of the clergy, at variance, as

I think, with the *spirit* of the Church's directions, and, in some instances, with the *letter*. . . . These innovations have, in some instances, been carried to such a length as to render the Church service almost *histrionic*. I really cannot characterise by a gentler term the continual changes of posture, the frequent genuflexions, the crossings, the peculiarities of dress, and some of the decorations of Churches to which I allude. They are, after all, a poor imitation of the Roman ceremonial, and furnish, I have no doubt, to the observant members of that Church, a subject, on the one hand, of ridicule, as being a faint and meagre copy of their own gaudy ritual; and, on the other hand, of exultation, as preparing those who take delight in them to seek a fuller gratification of their taste in the Roman communion."

In all this the Bishop had only stated the truth. There was nothing of exaggeration in his description of what was taking place. No doubt he had specially in his mind what was going on at the moment in St. Barnabas' Church, Pimlico, under the Rev. W. J. E. Bennett, Vicar of St. Paul's, Knightsbridge, of which St. Barnabas' was then a District Chapel-of-Ease. From a *Farewell Letter to his Parishioners*, issued by Mr. Bennett after his resignation of St. Paul's, I learn that he was appointed to work in the parish in 1840, that he assisted in building the new Church of St. Paul's, Knightsbridge, and that not very long after complaints as to his mode of conducting Divine Service were frequently forwarded to the Bishop of London, and many more were made directly to himself. "On one occasion," said Mr. Bennett, "a person coming from abroad informed me that, for all the world, the Church of St. Paul's was nothing more than he had just seen at Paris and at Rome. To which I replied, How happy it was that members of the Church of England could be in any way like the great bulk of Christendom, for it seemed like the beginning of unity."[1] In the year 1849, during a pestilence in London, Mr. Bennett printed and circulated a Form of Prayer, to be used privately, containing Prayers for the Dead. The Bishop of London wrote to him about it, and strongly objected to such

[1] *A Farewell Letter to his Parishioners.* By the Rev. W. J. E. Bennett, p. 24. London: Cleaver. 1851.

prayers. A lengthy correspondence followed;[1] but Mr. Bennett, notwithstanding his oath of obedience to his Bishop, refused to yield to his clearly expressed wishes. On June 10, 1850, the new Chapel-of-Ease, afterwards known as St. Barnabas' Church, Pimlico, was consecrated by the Bishop of London. It was not long before Ritualistic practices, which were then thought very advanced, were observed in the new Church. One of the Curates, finding things going so far wrong, could endure it no longer, and went to the Bishop of London with a view to his resignation, not to complain of Mr. Bennett, who alone was responsible for what went on at St. Barnabas'. The Bishop, of course, questioned him as to the matters he objected to, and having thus learnt what was going on, he wrote on July 1st to Mr. Bennett, stating that he had been informed upon authority he could not doubt, that in St. Barnabas' Church (1) at Holy Communion he celebrated standing in the centre of the west side of the table, with his back to the congregation; (2) that he did not give the cup into the hands of the communicants, but put it to their lips; (3) that in some instances he had not given the bread into the hands of the communicants, but had put it into their mouths; (4) that he prefaced the sermon with an invocation of the Trinity; (5) that at this invocation before the sermon the clergy rose up and crossed themselves; and (6) that he had administered Extreme Unction to a young lady. To this letter Mr. Bennett replied on July 15th, denying absolutely the last charge, and admitting the truth of all the other charges, except that as to not putting the elements into the hands of the communicants; this was, he explained, true only of six communicants, and that by their special request, but that since receiving his lordship's letter he had spoken to the six, who had agreed to give up the practice complained of. Mr. Bennett, at some length, defended these practices, but did not promise to give up more than the last named, and he said to the Bishop:—"If you think, upon reading what I have said,

---

[1] Bennett's *Farewell Letter to his Parishioners*, pp. 44–61.

that the picture of my mind is not that which could justify my remaining in the cure of souls in your lordship's diocese, I am ready and willing to depart."[1] After writing this letter Mr. Bennett says that three months elapsed before he received any reply, during which "all the practices complained of were continued without variation."[2] On October 18th the Bishop wrote again, expressing himself as not at all satisfied with Mr. Bennett's explanations and defence, and requiring him to give up the practices to which he objected. To this Mr. Bennett replied on October 30th:—"It grieves me to say that, after having conscientiously considered all the bearings of the matter, I find that I am unable to withdraw or alter anything that I have said or done," and he offered to resign his living if the Bishop called on him to do so.[3] Soon after Mr. Bennett presented a young gentleman to the Bishop to be ordained to the Curacy of St. Barnabas', but his lordship refused to ordain him on Mr. Bennett's nomination. The Bishop of London's Charge was delivered, as already stated, on November 2nd, condemning the Puseyites in strong terms. On November 5th, Lord John Russell's letter to the Bishop of Durham, dated November 4th, was published in the daily papers. On Sunday, November 10th, riots broke out in St. Barnabas' Church, which were renewed on the following Sunday—a method of protest with which, I may be permitted to state, I have no sympathy whatever. It has ever been injurious to the Protestant cause, and can only benefit the Romanisers. Here were a number of, I suppose, Protestant people, going to Church to protest against lawlessness by committing acts of violent lawlessness themselves. The principle of taking the law into our own hands, as separate individuals, seems to me to be the root evil of Anarchy.

On December 4th, Mr. Bennett sent in his resignation, by demand of the Bishop, of his living. A few days before this Mr. Bennett published *A First Letter to Lord John Russell*, which is remarkable for its unsparing and just exposure of

---

[1] Bennett's *Farewell Letter to his Parishioners*, p. 84.
[2] *Ibid.* p. 86.   [3] *Ibid.* pp. 91, 92.

the way in which his lordship had been supporting Popery for many years, and for its acknowledgment that Auricular Confession, as practised by the Puseyite clergy, was in itself identical with that of the Church of Rome. On this latter point, Mr. Bennett's words are :—" Sufficient it is to me to call your attention to the fact, that Confession to a priest (commonly called Auricular Confession), is advocated and pronounced useful by the English Church. *The only difference* you will observe between the Church of Rome and ourselves being this, that Rome makes such Confession absolutely necessary for salvation ; the other leaves it as a voluntary act, to be used or not used, according to the spiritual needs of the penitent."[1] A few weeks later Dr. Pusey had the audacity to say that :—" I am not aware that any Divine or Bishop in our Church, since the Reformation, has excepted against anything, except making Confession compulsory."[2] The truth is, that almost all our Divines and Bishops since the Reformation, down to the commencement of the Oxford Movement, were deadly enemies of the Confessional itself, as conducted by Pusey, excepting only the Laudian Divines. A large number of Mr. Bennett's congregation took his part in his controversy with the Bishop, and an effort was made to keep him in the living by an appeal to a Court of law. A legal opinion was taken on this question, but as it was decidedly adverse to any appeal to a Court, the proposed proceedings were necessarily dropped.

Towards the end of 1850, another fierce controversy arose at St. Saviour's, Leeds. The Bishop of Ripon had had painful experience of the evasive and Romanising conduct of the clergy of that church. In June 1850, his lordship informed one of its clergy that " the proceedings of the clergy of St. Saviour's were of such a character as to destroy all my confidence in them ; and that their study seemed to be how far they could evade their Bishop's known wishes, without violating the letter of the law."[3] In the month of

---

[1] *A First Letter to Lord John Russell.* By the Rev. W. J. E. Bennett, p. 43. London : Cleaver. 1850.
[2] *A Letter to the Bishop of London.* By the Rev. E. B. Pusey, D.D., p. 3. Oxford : 1851.
[3] *A Letter to the Parishioners of St. Saviour's, Leeds.* By the Bishop of Ripon, p. 29. London : Rivington. 1851.

October 1850, a meeting of twelve clergymen was held at St. Saviour's, at which the two following resolutions, which clearly show the traitorous spirit of those who passed them, were carried *unanimously* :—

"That the very existence of the English Church involves the principle of her submission, in matters of faith, to the Church Catholic."

"That her national history, previous to the Reformation, indicates that *such submission can only be made through the medium of the Papal See.*" [1]

Of course these were thoroughly dishonest resolutions, which reflected the utmost disgrace on the clergy of the Church of England who passed them, and fully justified the strong remarks of the Bishop of Ripon about the clergy of St. Saviour's, in his letter to the parishioners :—"For my own part," said the Bishop, "I shall refrain from saying more than that their conduct has verified, in a remarkable and very painful manner, the statement which I had made in my Episcopal Charge three months only previous, that 'the nearer persons approach to the Roman system, the more will their powers of judgment be perverted, *their moral sense blunted*, and an obliquity of moral vision superinduced, blinding them more and more to the simplicity of Christian truth, and estranging them more and more from the sincerity of Christian practice." [2]

The Rev. J. H. Pollen, who for a time was one of the Curates of St. Saviour's, frankly admits that this meeting was held, and he says that the clergy present "came to resolutions to the effect that the English Church was subject to the Catholic Church as regards the faith. That *now* was a time when she needed to refer to that tribunal for support and guidance—that the Apostolic See had hitherto been the only access to that voice." [3]

Early in December a majority of the clergy of Leeds requested the Bishop of Ripon to hold a commission for the purpose of investigating certain charges to be brought against the clergy of St. Saviour's. Dr. Hook, Vicar of

---

[1] *A Letter to the Parishioners of St. Saviour's, Leeds.* By the Bishop of Ripon, p. 29. [2] *Ibid.* p. 15.
[3] *Narrative of Five Years at St. Saviour's, Leeds.* By the Rev. J. H. Pollen, p. 166. Oxford: J. Vincent. 1851.

Leeds, shortly before had publicly separated himself from the advanced section of his party. In a preface to two sermons he had preached, the Vicar of Leeds said:—"I take leave to make a wide distinction between a Romaniser and a High Churchman."

"But when," wrote Dr. Hook, "I now find them [the Romanisers] calumniators of the Church of England, and vindicators of the Church of Rome; palliating the vices of the Romish system, and magnifying the deficiencies of the Church of England; sneering at everything Anglican, and admiring everything Romish; students of the Breviary and Missal, disciples of the Schoolmen, converts to mediævalism, insinuating Romish sentiments, circulating and republishing Romish works; introducing Romish practices in their private, and infusing a Romish tone into their public devotions; introducing the Romish Confessional, enjoining Romish penances, adopting Romish prostrations, recommending Romish Litanies; muttering the Romish shibboleth, and rejoicing in the cant of Romish fanaticism, assuming sometimes the garb of the Romish priesthood, and venerating without imitating their celibacy; defending Romish miracles, and receiving as true the lying legends of Rome; almost adoring Romish saints, and complaining that we have had no saints in England since we purified our Church; explaining away the idolatry, and pining for the Mariolatry of the Church of Rome; vituperating the English Reformation, and receiving for truth the false doctrines of the Council of Trent; when I hear them whispering in the ears of credulous ignorance, in high places as well as low, that the two Churches are in principle the same; when they who were once in the pit on the one side of the wall, have now tumbled over on the other side, and have fallen into 'a lower deep still gaping to devour them'; I conceive that I am bound as a High Churchman to remain stationary, and not to follow them in their downfalling. I believe it to be incumbent upon every High Churchman to declare plainly that it is not merely in detail, that it is not merely in the application of our principles themselves, that we differ from the Church of Rome; and that no man can secede to Rome, the system of which is opposed to the truth as it is in Jesus, without placing his soul in peril, and risking his salvation. . . . It is not against *Romanists* but against *Romanisers* that we write; against those who are doing the work of the Church of Rome while eating the bread of the Church of England."[1]

---

[1] *Life of Dean Hook*, vol. ii. pp. 278, 279.

THE LEEDS CONFESSIONAL CASE

The Bishop of Ripon held his inquiry concerning St. Saviour's Church in the vestry of Leeds Parish Church, on December 14 and 15, 1850. Dr. Hook was present, and the inquiry extended itself into all the Romanising practices and doctrines of the accused clergy. But the chief subject considered was a charge against the Rev. H. F. Beckett, one of the Curates, of hearing the confession of a married woman (who appeared as a witness), without the knowledge of her husband, and then asking her shockingly indelicate and indecent questions. Of this witness the Bishop subsequently stated:—" Every attempt was made, but in vain, to invalidate her simple, straightforward testimony; and no imputation was ever cast upon her general integrity."[1] After the inquiry the Bishop wrote to Mr. Beckett:—" It appeared in evidence which you did not contradict, and could not shake by any cross-examination, that Mr. Rooke, who was then a deacon, having required a married woman who was a candidate for confirmation to go for Confession to you as a priest, you received that female to confession under these circumstances, and that you put to her questions which she says made her feel very much ashamed and greatly distressed her, and which were of such an indelicate nature that she would never tell her husband of them."[2] Mr. Beckett replied to the Bishop's letter, but he did not dare to deny the truth of the charges brought against him. He made, however, one remarkable assertion, which husbands whose wives go to Confession would do well to bear in mind. "*No woman,*" he said, "*would, I suppose, ever tell her husband what had passed in her Confession*";[3] and as to asking questions of the penitent, he wrote:—"*The asking of questions* according to the discretion of the Confessor is, your lordship must see, *absolutely necessary* to make Confession of value to those who have recourse to it."[4]

It was thought absolutely necessary by the Bishop of Ripon (afterwards Archbishop of Canterbury) to print some of the indecent questions which this Puseyite priest put to

---

[1] *A Letter to the Parishioners of St. Saviour's, Leeds.* By the Bishop of Ripon, p. 31.
[2] *Ibid.* p. 37.   [3] *Ibid.* p. 38.
[4] *Ibid.* p. 39.

this woman in the Confessional.[1] All that I can say about them here is that if any husband, be he Protestant or Ritualist, knew that his wife was asked those questions in Confession by her Ritualistic Confessor, the next time that Confessor came to that husband's house he would knock him down flat, and afterwards kick him out of the house. I do not say the husband *ought* to act thus: I only affirm that he could not very well help doing so. And I am quite certain that the filthy-tongued Confessor, who asked such obscene questions, would deserve all that he got from an outraged and justly indignant husband. Ordinary men of the world would be ashamed to ask such questions; but these brazen-faced Puseyite priests of St. Saviour's, Leeds, gloried in their shame. They issued a *Statement* of their case, in which they had the audacity to justify Father Confessors in asking penitents, male or female, indecent questions. As this, to my ordinary readers, will seem almost incredible, I give their justification of such dirty conduct in the priests' own words:—

"We now come," said the clergy of St. Saviour's, "to the second charge, relied on by the Bishop, against Mr. Beckett. The same witness states that certain questions which he asked her were very indelicate.

"To those who do not recognise the presence of Almighty God in the ministrations of the Confessional, it may seem that an 'indelicate' question may be a wrong one. But we believe that He who has created physicians for bodily sickness, and by them is pleased to effect many merciful cures, has ordained other physicians in His Church for the relief of men's spiritual disorders; and that there is an analogy between the discretion which we willingly concede to those whom we consult for the health of our bodies, and that which must be exercised by the physicians of the soul. If this be true, a question in itself indelicate ceases to be so when it is known to be important to the safe treatment of the sufferer's case; and woe be to those who countenance the vicious refinement of this generation, and abet the world in its unceasing efforts to place a false delicacy between the soul and its salvation. It would doubtless be indelicate, were it not in the highest degree necessary, to drag sin from its lurking-place, and expose it to the sinner's view;

---

[1] *A Letter to the Parishioners of St. Saviour's, Leeds.* By the Bishop of Ripon, p. 32.

but that there is often a paramount necessity for doing this, will be doubted by none whose earnest thoughts of sin and of repentance, of God's wrath and of acceptance with Him, have not been checked and stunted, chilled or blasted, by the breath of Lutheran heresy and Socinian unbelief. Whether such a necessity existed in the case which has led the Bishop to visit Mr. Beckett with his severest displeasure, is known, and will be known, to none but God and Mr. Beckett himself. He was asked by Mr. Randall, at the 'investigation,' whether he would have put the same questions to his (Mr. Randall's) wife? to which he replied that under the same circumstances he would have put the same questions, not only to Mr. Randall's wife, but even to Mr. Randall himself."[1]

A defence of this kind is simply a slander on an honourable profession. No medical man of honour would ever ask a patient such questions as those put to this woman in the Confessional. And even if, in some points, the analogy were to hold good, yet it would fail in this. The priest in the Confessional is not a physician but a quack, who kills souls, instead of curing them. The whole system of Confession on these indelicate lines is abhorrent to every enlightened Christian. It pollutes both Confessor and penitent.

The result of the Bishop's investigation was that all the clergy of St. Saviour's, with one exception, seceded to the Church of Rome. Out of fifteen clergy who had laboured in that Church since its consecration in 1845, no fewer than nine had now seceded to the Church of Rome. So much for the first attempt to exhibit the Oxford Movement *in operation*.

---

[1] *The Statement of the Clergy of St. Saviour's, Leeds, in Reference to the Recent Proceedings Against Them*, p. 9. Leeds: S. Morrish. 1851.

CHAPTER XII

The Bristol Church Union—Pusey objects to a protest against Rome—Archbishop Tait on the Church Discipline Act—The Judicial Committee of Privy Council—Lay Address to the Queen—Her Majesty's action in response—Lay Address to the Archbishop of Canterbury—The appeal to the Bishops—An Episcopal Manifesto—A Clerical and Lay Declaration in support of the Gorham judgment—The Confessional at Plymouth—Revival and reform of Convocation—Prosecution of Archdeacon Denison—The power and privileges of examining chaplains—The Archbishop's Commission of Inquiry—The Archbishop's judgment at Bath—How the Archdeacon evaded punishment—Pusey hoists the flag of rebellion—The protest against the Bath judgment—The Society of the Holy Cross—The Association for the Promotion of the Unity of Christendom—Startling revelations as to its early history—Secret negotiations with Rome—De Lisle's secret letter to Cardinal Barnabo—The Cardinal's answer—Newman consulted by De Lisle—The conspirators meet in London—Their secret, traitorous, and treacherous message to the Pope—The case of *Westerton* v. *Liddell*—Judgment—A Ritualistic rebel.

A NUMBER of independent "Church Unions," formed by the Tractarians, had been in existence for several years when the Papal Aggression commenced. The first of these, called the Bristol Union, was formed in 1844, to which were subsequently affiliated a number of local Church Unions throughout the country, all having the promotion of High Church principles as their chief object. In addition to these, but working independently on similar lines, were the Metropolitan Church Union, and the London Church Union. One of the chief promoters of the Bristol Church Union was the Rev. William Palmer, whose *Narrative of Events Connected with the Tracts for the Times*, published in 1843, was, as I have already stated, the first effectual exposure of the Romanising party which had appeared up to that date. At the time of the Papal Aggression Mr. Palmer was very much alarmed at the prospect of the extreme division of the Puseyites, under their leader Dr. Pusey, capturing all the

Church Unions throughout the country. He wished these Unions to be regulated by those High Church principles which had ever guided his own conduct. The London Church Union, which was then managed by the extreme section, was anxious to become the centre of the whole of the Church Unions of the country, and thus bring them all under the guidance of men in whom moderate High Churchmen could place no trust. That Mr. Palmer's fears were not without foundation is proved by a letter written to Mr. A. Beresford Hope, M.P., by Dr. Pusey, on October 3, 1850. The Metropolitan Church Union, to which he refers at the commencement of his letter, was not, at that time—so Mr. Palmer states[1]—under Tractarian (though it was under High Church) guidance.

"MY DEAR HOPE,—All hope of reconciliation with the Metropolitan is now plainly at an end. But something must be done to prevent their absorbing the whole Church Movement into their hands, at which they are evidently aiming. Some are ambitious for the Metropolitan; Palmer wishes to get rid of J. K.[eble] and myself; Dr. Biber to put forward himself.

"Might not the London Union unite itself more closely with some of the others? as the Bristol, the South-Eastern, the Yorks, &c. . . .

"One great Union, such as Badeley suggests, which should take in all England, and have leading clergy or laity from every diocese on its Committee (the distrusts would not often be then) would be immense strength.

"The members of this great Union in each diocese might assemble in their diocese, at any time, or regularly as now, and any member in the diocese, who was a member of the Central Committee, might be the chairman.

"This (which B. suggested) would have much greater moral strength than the existing Unions.

"I wish that you would think of this, or some similar plan. I sent you Badeley's opinion, which was sent to J. K.[eble] relatively to the plan we were hoping might be carried out, that all Unions might be fused into one.—God bless you. Yours most faithfully,
"E. B. PUSEY."

"LONDON, *Oct.* 3."

---

[1] *A Statement of Circumstances.* By William Palmer, M.A., p. 21. London: Rivington. 1850.

The idea here suggested by Pusey was eventually carried out several years later by the formation of the English Church Union. Palmer's suspicions were therefore well founded, and so to prevent, if possible, what he considered would be a disaster to the High Church cause, he gave notice that at the forthcoming Annual Meeting of the Bristol Church Union on October 1st, he would propose that a "Statement of Principles" should be adopted by the Union, containing a protest against the Church of Rome and her errors. On hearing of this proposal Pusey was greatly alarmed. A protest against Rome was what he hated with all his heart. He was afraid that his Father Confessor, Keble, would approve of this protest, so he wrote to him:—" If you go along with this plan I shall withdraw my name from the Bristol Union, by a letter to the Chairman, in order not to have any responsibility in the matter."[1] Canon Liddon tells us that:—" Dr. Mill suggested a resolution expressing love and allegiance to the English Church, 'as reformed in the sixteenth century.' Pusey would prefer to omit the allusion to the sixteenth century. It would introduce a large controverted subject, and would repel many minds. Pusey would have as simple a statement as possible; a positive statement of love for the Church of England, *without a negative statement about the Church of Rome.*"[2] Keble at length came over to Pusey's view, and therefore wrote:—" I cannot join in any Anti-Roman Declaration that I have yet seen, not even in my own, now that I find the terms of it are equivocal."[3] At length the day arrived (October 1st), on which the Bristol Church Union held its annual meeting. And what, it may be asked, was this declaration which Pusey and his supporters so dreaded and hated? It was proposed by the Rev. William Palmer, and seconded by the Rev. Prebendary Clarke, and was as follows:—

"STATEMENT OF PRINCIPLES.

" 1. That the English branch of the One Holy Catholic and Apostolic Church, which has reformed herself, taking primitive

---

[1] *Life of Dr. Pusey*, vol. iii. p. 275.
[2] *Ibid.* p. 275.   [3] *Ibid.* p. 280.

Christianity as her model, has a claim upon the undivided and faithful allegiance of the whole English people.

"2. That the Roman Church (including the other Churches in communion with her) having repudiated communion with all the Churches which do not recognise the claims of the Bishop of Rome, and having by formal decrees and other authoritative acts, and in her popular practice, corrupted the primitive faith and worship of the Holy Catholic Church, and persisted in the said claims and corruptions, communion with the Roman Church, on the part of Churches, and therefore of individuals, of the English Communion, cannot, consistently with the laws of Christ, be restored, until the Roman Church shall have relinquished her pretensions; and sufficient provision shall have been made for the maintenance of Christian truth in all its purity and integrity.

"3. That the serious dangers to the faith, arising from the abuse of private judgment, and from a mere negative Protestantism, having of late years been greatly aggravated by the insidious propagation of Rationalistic notions, and by the encroachments of a Latitudinarian State policy, it is the duty of all members of the Church of England to offer to these several abuses, errors, and pernicious principles, the most active and uncompromising opposition."[1]

The wording of the third section of this *Statement* shows that Mr. Palmer was no lover of decided Protestantism; nor can there be a reasonable doubt that if there were nothing more in the Declaration than this section it would have been carried unanimously. But, as we have seen, the Corporate Reunion of the Church of Rome had been the chief object of the leaders of the Oxford Movement from its very birth. How, then, could they agree to a Declaration censuring either that Church, its doctrines, or its practices? And why should they be called upon to demand that Rome should "relinquish her pretensions," or give up any of her doctrines, as a condition of England's union with her? It is true that no reasonably loyal Churchman could consistently object to sign the second clause of the Declaration; but these were not consistent or loyal Churchmen, as their conduct on this occasion amply proved. They were more anxious to shield and protect the Church of Rome from her enemies than to defend the Church of

[1] Palmer's *Statement of Circumstances*, p. 74.

England, and, therefore, Lord Forbes proposed, and Mr. A. Beresford Hope, M.P., seconded, the following amendment, which was carried by a large majority:—

"That whereas the Bristol Union was designed to be a union of all Churchmen desirous of co-operating in the promotion of certain defined objects, it cannot consent to narrow the basis of its constitution by identifying itself with an organisation which is founded upon the acceptance of a Declaration of faith over and above the existing formularies of the English Church, which it desires to make the rule of its proceedings."[1]

Amongst those who spoke in favour of this amendment, in addition to the mover and seconder, were Dr. Pusey and the Rev. J. Keble. Amongst those who spoke in favour of Mr. Palmer's motion was the Rev. G. A. Denison, afterwards so well known as Archdeacon Denison. The objection to signing a Declaration of faith "over and above the existing formularies," came with a bad grace from those very men who signed Declarations of faith soon after "over and above the existing formularies" in defence of Baptismal Regeneration, as against the Gorham judgment. Two days after the Bristol meeting, Dr. Hook replied to an invitation to join the Yorkshire Church Union. He declined to do so.

"I do not," he wrote, "see how members of the Church of England can be called upon to form a Union, except on the principles, and in vindication of the principles, of the English Reformation. Those principles are both Catholic and Protestant—Catholic as opposed to the peculiarities of Rationalism, and Protestant as opposed to the Mediævalism of the Romanist. I do not see how a consistent High Churchman can, after what has transpired, join your Union, unless you state one of your objects to be 'to maintain and propagate the principles of the English Reformation; to uphold Scriptural and primitive truth in opposition to mediæval heresies; and to preserve the middle position of the Church of England in opposition equally to Rationalistic scepticism and Romish superstition.' If this were to be one of the avowed objects of your institution, it would exclude Romanisers as well as all Rationalists."[2]

One result of the Gorham judgment was seen this year in an organised attack on the Judicial Committee of Privy

[1] *English Churchman*, October 3, 1850, p. 675.
[2] *Ibid.* October 10, 1850, p. 685.

THE BISHOPS AND THE CHURCH DISCIPLINE ACT

Council as the final Court of Appeal. It was the desire of the Puseyites that not only should the Church's laws be made by the clergy only, but that they alone should be judges in ecclesiastical causes. Their wish was to bring the Church once more into priestly bondage. It is remarkable that the Act of Parliament which made the Judicial Committee of Privy Council the final Court of Appeal (viz., 3 & 4 Victoria, chap. 86), was passed with the consent of the Bishops. Archbishop Tait, on this subject, wrote, while Bishop of London :—

"It is important to observe that this Act was framed with the concurrence of the Bishops. The Lord Chancellor, in introducing it, expressed a hope that it would reconcile all differences upon the subject. The Archbishop of Canterbury, on the part of the clergy, gave his cordial approbation to the Bill; the Bishop of Exeter, also, entirely and heartily concurred in the measure. There is no record of any debate upon the Bill, beyond a very few suggestions by independent members in either House; and the acquiescence with which it was received on all sides was doubtless owing to the agreement of the Bishops in supporting the measure. It seems clear, therefore, that the rulers of our Church at that time saw no reason to object to the Judicial Committee as a Court of Appeal in matters of ecclesiastical discipline, whether relating to faith or morals. It would be a serious reflection upon the character of men like Archbishop Howley, and Bishop Blomfield, and Bishop Kaye, were it to be supposed that they were ignorant of the nature of a tribunal which they had themselves assisted in founding, or that they were careless of the interests with which they were now, after trial, entrusting it, or that they deliberately sanctioned an institution against which any objection of principle could be raised."[1]

During this year, the Bishop of London introduced a Bill into the House of Lords, which received the assent of the Archbishop of Canterbury, the object of which was to deprive the Judicial Committee of Privy Council of its powers as the final Court of Appeal, and to transfer them to the Upper House of Convocation. Happily it was defeated on its second reading, on June 3, 1850, by 84 to 51, and from that day to this the Judicial Committee remains the final Court of Appeal. It will be a dark day for Protestantism

[1] Brodrick and Freemantle's *Judgments of the Judicial Committee.* Introduction by the Bishop of London, p. lxxi.

should Parliament ever make the Bishops the final Court of Appeal. The opinion of Lord John Russell on this important subject was wise and worthy of remembrance. He wrote to the Bishop of London on February 25, 1850:—"What I think essential to the Queen's Supremacy is that no person should be deprived of his rights unless by due interpretation of law. If the Supreme Court of Appeal in heresy were formed solely of the clergy, their opinions would probably be founded on the prevailing theological opinions of the Judicial Bishops, who might be one day Calvinistic and the next Romish. Especially if three senior Bishops and two Divinity Professors were to form part of the tribunal, we might have superannuated Bishops and University intolerance driving out of the Church its most distinguished ornaments."[1] It was on this same subject of a final Court of Appeal that his lordship wrote the sentence which I have already cited:—"I fear that nothing but the erection of a priestly supremacy over the Crown would ever satisfy the party in the Church who now take the lead in agitation."[2]

The Papal Aggression led to a great increase of Protestant opposition to Puseyism throughout the country. By this time the Puseyite clergy had made considerable progress in the adoption of Ritual which had not been seen in English Churches since the Protestant Reformation. Protests were heard on every hand, and addresses to the Bishops were multiplied. Of these, the most remarkable was the outcome of a great Protestant meeting held in the Freemasons' Hall, on December 6, 1850, over which Lord Ashley presided. An important Lay Address to the Queen on the subject of the Papal Aggression was presented to her Majesty, signed by 63 Peers, 108 Members of Parliament, and 321,240 lay members of the Church of England. In this Address, an earnest protest was made against the Romanising work going on in the Church of England. From it I give the following extracts:—

"But we desire also humbly to represent to your Majesty our conviction, confirmed by the recent testimony of several Bishops of

---

[1] *Life of Lord John Russell*, vol. ii. p. 116.   [2] *Ibid.* p. 117.

our Church, that the Court of Rome would never have attempted such an act of aggression had not encouragements been held out to that encroaching power by many of the clergy of our own Church, who have for several years past shown a desire to assimilate the doctrines and services of the Church of England to those of the Roman Communion. While we would cheerfully contend for the principles of the Reformation against all open enemies, we have to lament that our most dangerous foes are those of our own household; and hence we feel that it is to little purpose to repel the aggressions of the foreigner, unless those principles and practices which have tempted him to such aggressions be publicly and universally repudiated.

"We are conscious that the evils to which we allude are deeply seated, and have been the growth of a series of years, and hence we entertain no expectation that they can be suddenly eradicated. But we humbly entreat your Majesty, in the exercise of your Royal Prerogative, to direct the attention of the Primates and the Bishops of the Church to the necessity of using all fit and proper means to purify it from the infection of false doctrine; and, as respects external and visible observances, in which many novelties have been introduced, to take care that measures may be promptly adopted for the repression of all such practices.

"While we feel deeply conscious that the true and effectual remedy for the dangers which beset our Protestant Church belongs to no human power, but only to the Supreme Head of the Church whose Almighty aid is to be sought by humble, persevering prayer, we are thankful that, by the Constitution and the existing laws, there is vested in your Majesty, as the Earthly Head of our Church, a wholesome power of interposition; which power we entreat your Majesty now to exercise. The records of the reigns of your Majesty's illustrious predecessors, both before and since the glorious Revolution, furnish many examples of the manner in which the mischiefs and abuses which at various times have sprung up in the Church have been dealt with by the exercise of the Royal Authority.

"That it may please your Majesty, on a view of the peculiar perils in which our Protestant Church is now placed, to interpose for its defence, is our humble petition."

A record of some of the instances, referred to in this petition, in which evils in the Church have been dealt with by the exercise of the Royal Prerogative, may be read in Cardwell's *Documentary Annals of the Reformed Church of England*. It gave great pleasure to those who signed this petition to the Queen to find that it had been acted on by her Majesty. By her command a copy was sent to the Archbishop of Canterbury, to be by him communicated to the Archbishop of York and the Bishops, with a request that they would do all in their power to prevent innovations. Sir George Grey's letter, conveying the Royal commands to the Archbishop, is important, not only for what it contains, but as a possible precedent in the not distant future. It was as follows :—

"WHITEHALL, 1st April, 1851.

"MY LORD ARCHBISHOP,—I have received the Queen's commands to transmit to your Grace the accompanying Address, which has been presented to her Majesty, signed by a very large number of lay members of the United Church of England and Ireland, including many Members of both Houses of Parliament.

"Her Majesty places full confidence in your Grace's desire to use such means as are within your power to maintain the purity of the doctrines taught by the clergy of the Established Church, and to discourage and prevent innovations in the mode of conducting the services of the Church not sanctioned by law or general usage, and calculated to create dissatisfaction and alarm among a numerous body of its members.

"I am, therefore, commanded to place this Address in your Grace's hands, and to request that it may be communicated to the Archbishop of York and to the Suffragan Bishops in England and Wales, who, her Majesty does not doubt, will concur with your Grace in the endeavour, by a judicious exercise of their authority and influence, to uphold the purity and simplicity of the Faith and Worship of our Reformed Church, and to reconcile differences among its members injurious to its peace and usefulness.—I have the honour to be, my Lord Archbishop, your Grace's obedient servant, G. GREY.

"HIS GRACE THE ARCHBISHOP OF CANTERBURY."

On March 19, 1851, Lord Ashley presented an address to the Archbishop of Canterbury, signed by 239,860 clerical and lay members of the Church of England, stating that the Papal Aggression had been "invited, encouraged, and facilitated" by the state of things in the English Church produced by Tractarianism, and calling upon the Bishops to give "the desired relief." The Archbishop, in his reply, said:—"It will be vain to deny what our adversaries have themselves avowed, that the aggressive measures on the part of Rome, against which this country is protesting, have been encouraged by symptoms of approach towards Romish doctrines and Romish usages which have appeared of late years within the Church of England. It is also certain that the principles which have been loudly maintained and zealously propagated, under the equivocal title of Church principles, have a tendency to lead those who embrace them to reconciliation with the Church of Rome, as the Church in which those principles are most perfectly carried out and established."[1] In conclusion, his Grace promised, on behalf of the Episcopal Bench, that they would do their duty in preventing practices and innovations in public worship, which had their origin in error and superstition. I have no doubt that his Grace meant all that he said, but, alas! the Protestant petitioners looked to the Bishops in vain for any effectual remedy for the evils of which they complained. And so it has been ever since to the present day. There have been some noble exceptions to the general rule with regard to the attitude of the Bishops in their own dioceses, but taking the Episcopal Bench as a whole they have lamentably failed in their duty. We have had plenty of words, and many promises, but for all this, little or nothing has been done to satisfy the just demands of the loyal and aggrieved laity. What was the immediate result of the Archbishop of Canterbury's promise of Episcopal action in 1851? Scarcely anything but an Episcopal Manifesto, which, however, was not signed by the Bishops of Bath and Wells, Exeter, Manchester, and Hereford. It was about as mild and harmless a document as could well be imagined. It was simply an exhortation to the clergy to make no innovations in Divine Service which should give offence to the congregation, even if legal; and to do nothing contrary to the law of the Church. They did, however, denounce the principle which had been laid down by some of the clergy, that "whatever form or usage existed in the Church before the Reformation may now be

---

[1] *Guardian*, March 22, 1851, p. 212.

freely introduced and observed, unless there can be alleged against it the distinct letter of some formal prohibition." As to this principle their lordships declared that:—"It is manifest that a licence such as is contended for is wholly incompatible with any uniformity of worship whatsoever, and at variance with the universal practice of the Catholic Church, which has never given to the officiating Ministers of separate congregations any such large discretion in the selection of ritual observances."[1] From this document it is evident that the overwhelming majority of the Bishops of that day accepted the principle that "omission is prohibition."

Later on in the year, another Declaration was signed by no fewer than 3262 clergymen, including seven Deans and twelve Archdeacons, in favour of the Royal Supremacy, and expressing approval of the judgment of the Judicial Committee of Privy Council in the Gorham case. It was forwarded to the Archbishops of Canterbury and York. Those who signed it declared that they felt called upon "under present circumstances (whether holding or not the view which called forth the judgment) humbly to state our conviction that it was a wise and just sentence, in accordance with the principles of the Church of England. And we respectfully, but firmly, protest against any attempt, from whatever quarter it may proceed, to bring into contempt a judgment so issued; and to charge with false teaching, and discredit with their flocks, those whose doctrine has been pronounced by that judgment to be 'not contrary or repugnant to the declared doctrine of the Church of England.' And we respectfully, but firmly, protest against any attempt, from whatever quarter it may proceed, to bring into contempt a judgment so issued." Amongst those who signed this very proper declaration, was the Very Rev. A. C. Tait, Dean of Carlisle, and afterwards Archbishop of Canterbury. From the Archbishop of Canterbury a reply to the Declaration was received, expressing "much satisfaction" at receiving it, while from the Archbishop of York a letter was received expressing approval of the Declaration.[2]

[1] *Guardian*, April 2, 1851, p. 251. [2] *Ibid.* January 14, 1852, p 28.

A PLYMOUTH CONFESSIONAL CASE

A great deal of excitement was created in Plymouth during the year 1852, in connection with some Confessional scandals alleged to have taken place at St. Peter's Church in that city. The Bishop of Exeter was asked to hold a judicial inquiry on oath as to the alleged facts, but he declined to do so. In the month of September, however, he held an inquiry into the case at the Royal Hotel, Plymouth, but refused to consider it as judicial, nor would he consent to grant the urgent entreaties of the Protestant accusers of the Vicar of St. Peter's, that the witnesses should be sworn before giving their evidence. The principal charge against the Vicar was that of hearing the Confessions of young girls from the institutions of Miss Sellon's Sisters of Mercy, and then asking them indecent questions. During the inquiry a letter was read from Miss Sellon, the Mother Superior of the Sisterhood, denying that any of the girls under the care of the Sisters were " in anywise compelled or constrained to confess," but admitting that they were allowed to go " of free choice " ; and that " it is *our constant practice* to advise them to see their Minister, either for this purpose [Confession], or for receiving such higher counsel and spiritual aid as it is not ours to give them, for their soul's good."[1] The principal witness examined was a girl whose character, as it appeared at the inquiry, was far from satisfactory, nor would it, I think, have been right to have condemned the Vicar on such evidence, more especially as he appeared personally before the Bishop and in the most solemn manner denied that he had ever even so much as received the girl to Confession at all, much less put disgusting questions to her. There were other cases to be brought against the Vicar, and it was certainly unfortunate, for both parties, that time was not allowed to bring them forward. In the result, the Bishop entirely acquitted the Vicar as to the whole of the charges brought against him, and declared that he was free, not merely from blame, but " even of indiscretion in receiving the Confessions made to him." There was, however, a remarkable letter from the accused Vicar to the Bishop, which was read at the inquiry, which contained a startling statement worthy of notice here

[1] *Guardian*, September 29, 1852, p. 647.

Referring therein to his practice in the Confessional—he in no way denied that he heard Confessions—he declared:— "On the Seventh Commandment I trust I have been most cautious not to suggest evil to the penitent, *but judicious questions.*"[1] This was a frank acknowledgment that, in some cases, he asked questions about the Seventh Commandment—one of the most objectionable features of the Confessional to an enlightened Protestant mind. If a girl has a trouble on this subject it would be far wiser, and more modest, to consult one of her own sex for advice. Later on in the year Dr. Pusey wrote to this same Vicar that:— "It is (as you know), a mere dream, that any father, mother, husband, wife, or child, would be pained by any question we put in Confession, apart from the pain that sins have been committed."[2] In reply to this very bold statement, it may be sufficient to ask any husband or father reading these pages—Would *you* like your wife or daughter questioned in the Confessional as to sins of word, thought, and deed against the Seventh Commandment? You would, in such a case, be something more than "pained"; you would be highly and justly indignant, if a wife or daughter of yours had been thus subjected to the indecent talk of a Father Confessor, who might be far from immaculate. The whole thing is disgusting and intolerable. I should be sorry to accuse Ritualistic Confessors generally of doing this sort of dirty work from evil motives; but it is dirty work none the less, whose natural tendency is to corrupt both priest and penitent. God, the Holy Ghost, in his Word, exhorts us concerning sin against this commandment:—"Let it not be once named among you, as becometh saints"; and I am not aware that any exception is given in favour of a Father Confessor—an official wholly unknown in the New Testament.

A very important event took place on November 12, 1852, when the Convocation of Canterbury met for the despatch of business, for the first time in 135 years. A persistent agitation for freedom to transact business had gone on for several years, and a "Society for the Revival of Convocation" had been formed in the previous year.

[1] *Guardian*, September 29, 1852, p. 647.   [2] *Ibid.* November 24, 1852, p. 788.

The founders of this Society, some time before its formation, endeavoured in vain to secure the adhesion of the National Club to an address to the Queen in favour of the revival of Convocation. This Club, I may here remark, was formed in 1845 for promoting the cause of Protestantism in the Established Church, and is still in existence with a very large number of members. The movement for the Revival of Convocation was mainly conducted by High Churchmen, and was not fully successful until March 20, 1861, when the Convocation of York also met for the transaction of business. And now, after nearly forty years, we are met face to face with an agitation, not for the Revival, but for the Reform of Convocation, and a Bill has been prepared to enable it to reform itself. Unfortunately, there are so many Romanisers in Convocation that Protestant Churchmen cannot safely entrust them with such an important task, nor should any reform be considered satisfactory which does not give to the laity an adequate representation, with a voice on all questions, whether matters of doctrine or discipline. But this is what the extreme Ritualists will never, if they can help it, permit the present Convocations to accept, and to allow the Convocations of Canterbury and York to become a real Parliament of the Church, without granting to the laity even as much power as they already possess in the Established Church of Scotland, would be to place the Church of England under sacerdotal bondage as real as that from which our forefathers escaped at the Protestant Reformation.

During the years 1853 and 1854 not many events of great importance took place in the History of the Romeward Movement, with the exception of the prosecution of Archdeacon Denison for false doctrine, and the first steps in the case of *Westerton* v. *Liddell*. Yet during this period the Ritualists were by no means asleep or idle. They were quietly pushing their way into many a hitherto peaceful parish, causing in numerous instances heartburns, dissension, and frequently energetic opposition. "Altar Lights" were slowly introduced, and the way prepared for the use of the Romish vestments. Occasionally notes of defiance were heard from the Puseyite camp. The Rev. James Skinner, Senior Curate of St. Barnabas', wrote to the *Times* challenging a prosecution. "The worship of St. Barnabas'," he said, "is the worship of the Church of England. We challenge this issue in the Courts of the Church of England, if any such there be. If it is not the worship of the Church of England, the sooner it is put down the better."[1] We do not hear challenges like this in the year 1900. The Ritualists now dread nothing so much as prosecutions. A brother Curate of Mr. Skinner's at St. Barnabas', the well-known Rev. Charles Lowder, when opposition again arose in that parish, in 1854, was of a somewhat militant nature. A placard was being carried one day, about the parish, urging people to "Vote for Westerton," the Protestant Churchwarden, which greatly angered a youthful cousin of Mr. Lowder. "Charles," says his biographer, "bade him not to throw dirt or stones, but gave the boys sixpence to buy rotten eggs. They were not slow in using them, carrying the war into Ebury Street, and the bespattered 'sandwich' complained to his employers, who speedily invoked the aid of the law against the assailants. Charles [Lowder] was interrogated, and took all the blame of inciting the boys to bedaub the inscription. Before the police magistrate he repeated publicly the admission of indiscretion and sorrow for it, which he had already made privately, and the case was dismissed, with more than acquiescence on the part of the prosecution." But the Bishop of London did not let Mr. Lowder off so easily, for he suspended him from his duties as Curate for six weeks, as a punishment for his offence, which he subsequently mitigated at the request of the Vicar, the Hon. and Rev. R. Liddell, who had succeeded to the Rev. W. J. E. Bennett, then Vicar of Frome. The latter gentleman wrote to Mr. Lowder in his trouble:—"I have no doubt I myself have done, or might have done, a similar thing."[2]

In the month of January 1853 a controversy arose between Bishop Spencer (late of Madras), Assistant-Bishop to

[1] *Charles Lowder: A Biography*, 1st edition, p. 49.
[2] *Ibid.* pp. 57-60.

the Bishop of Bath and Wells, and the Rev. G. A. Denison, Archdeacon of Taunton, and Examining Chaplain to the Bishop of Bath and Wells. It arose in this way. A young Deacon, the Rev. William F. Fisher, wrote to Bishop Spencer to inform him that Archdeacon Denison had refused to present him for priest's orders at his lordship's next Ordination, on the ground that he held views as to the Lord's Supper, which, in the Archdeacon's opinion, were erroneous. To this the Bishop replied, giving at some length his own views as to the Real Presence, which were decidedly Protestant, and then he wrote to the Archdeacon on the subject. After reminding him of an interview he had had with him on April 15th, Dr. Spencer proceeded to say that :—" It would be highly dishonest and improper on my part to ordain a candidate holding such an opinion" as that of Archdeacon Denison's. The latter gentleman replied, giving an outline of his doctrine :—

" To you, as a kind friend and a Bishop of the Church, I am ready to state, that I hold the doctrine of the 'Real Presence,' as taught and declared by the Church of England, to be this:—First, *Negatively*.—That there *is not* a corporal presence of the Body and Blood of Christ in the Sacramental Bread and Wine; that the Sacramental Bread and Wine remain still in their very natural substances, and therefore may not be adored.

" Secondly, *Affirmatively*.—That there *is* a Real Presence of the Body and Blood of Christ in the Sacramental Bread and Wine, in a manner which, as Holy Scripture has not explained, the Church has not defined. That the Body and Blood of Christ, being really present in the Sacramental Bread and Wine, are *given* in and by the outward sign to *all*, and are received by all."[1]

Bishop Spencer, of course, was not satisfied with this explanation, which was followed by an intimation from the Archdeacon that if the Bishop attempted to counter-examine any of the candidates at the forthcoming ordination, he should "most positively" decline to have anything to do with the presentation of any of the candidates. The result was that Bishop Spencer resigned his commission as Episcopal Assistant to Bishop Bagot, and soon after Archdeacon Denison resigned the office of Examining Chaplain. When

[1] *A Letter to the Bishop of Bath and Wells.* By Bishop Spencer, pp. 20, 21. London: Rivington. 1853.

writing his autobiography, the Archdeacon declared that the Bishop of Bath and Wells was in error in supposing that he had imposed, "of my own authority," his doctrine of the Real Presence on the candidates for Holy Orders.[1] This was not an absolute, but a qualified denial of the charge. He admits that he *did* impose his doctrine as to Baptismal Regeneration on all the candidates, refusing to pass those who did not accept it. In conduct like this we discover one of the reasons why there are so few Evangelical candidates for the Ministry at the present time. It is no easy matter, in some cases, for an Evangelical of decided views to pass an examination at the hands of men who are advanced Romanisers, as, unfortunately, several Examining Chaplains are.

Soon after these events, Archdeacon Denison preached in Wells Cathedral three sermons on the Real Presence, which led to legal proceedings being taken against him for false doctrine. They were preached respectively on August 7, 1853, November 6, 1853, and May 14, 1854. The prosecutor was the Rev. Joseph Ditcher, Vicar of South Brent, Somerset. These sermons were subsequently published by the Archdeacon. As the Bishop of Bath and Wells was patron of the living of East Brent, of which the Archdeacon was Vicar, it was necessary to apply to the Archbishop of Canterbury to issue a Commission of Inquiry. On November 3, 1854, his Grace served on the defendant a formal notice that the Commission would shortly be appointed, but it did not meet until January 3, 1855, when the proceedings lasted four days. On January 10th, the Commissioners reported that there were *prima facie* grounds for proceeding. In the unanimous opinion of the Commissioners:—
"The proposition of the Venerable the Archdeacon, 'that to all who come to the Lord's Table, to those who eat and drink worthily, and to those who eat and drink unworthily, the Body and Blood of Christ are given, and that by all who come to the Lord's Table, by those who eat and drink worthily, and by those who eat and drink unworthily, the Body and Blood of Christ are received,' is directly contrary or repugnant to the doctrine of the Church of England,

[1] Archdeacon Denison's *Notes of My Life*, p. 230.

and especially to the Articles of Religion, and that the doctrines set forth in the aforesaid sermons, with reference to the Real Presence in the Holy Eucharist, are unsupported by the Articles taken in their literal and grammatical sense, are contrary to the doctrines and teaching of the Church of England, and have a very dangerous tendency."[1] The passage from the Archdeacon's sermon thus selected for condemnation is found in the first of the three sermons objected against.[2]

After the finding of the Commissioners, several legal difficulties arose in the way of proceeding with the case, but eventually these were overcome. The case was argued on its merits at the Guildhall, Bath, on July 22, 1856, and the five following days, before the Archbishop of Canterbury, Dr. Lushington, the Rev. Dr. Heurtley (Margaret Professor of Divinity at Oxford), and the Dean of Wells. After the hearing the Court adjourned, and on August 12th Dr. Lushington delivered an interlocutory judgment condemning the Archdeacon, but allowing him time until October 1st to revoke his errors. As this judgment was subsequently confirmed by the Court, it is important to give here the following extract from it, condemning Archdeacon Denison's doctrine on the Real Presence:—

"Whereas it is laid in the said ninth article filed in this proceeding, that the said Archdeacon, in a sermon preached by him in the Cathedral Church of Wells, on or about Sunday, August 7, 1853, did advisedly maintain and affirm doctrines directly contrary and repugnant to the 25th, 28th, and 29th Articles of Religion, referred to in the statute of 13 Eliz., c. 12, or some or one of them. Among other things, did therein advise, maintain, and affirm, 'That the Body and Blood of Christ, being really present after an immaterial and spiritual manner in the consecrated Bread and Wine, are therein and thereby given to all, and are received by all who come to the Lord's Table';[3] and 'That to all who come to the Lord's Table, to those who eat and drink worthily and to those who eat and drink unworthily, the Body and Blood of Christ are given; and that by all who come to the Lord's Table, by those who eat and

---

[1] *Guardian*, January 17, 1855, p. 57.
[2] *The Real Presence.* A Sermon Preached on August 7, 1853. By George A. Denison, Archdeacon of Taunton, p. 20. London: Masters. 1853.
[3] *Ibid.* p. 18.

drink worthily and by those who eat and drink unworthily, the Body and Blood of Christ are received'—his Grace, with the assistance and unanimous concurrence of his Assessors, has determined that the doctrine in the said passages is directly contrary and repugnant to the 28th and 29th of the said Articles of Religion and the various statutes of Queen Elizabeth, and that the construction put upon the said Articles of Religion by the Venerable the Archdeacon of Taunton, viz., that the Body and Blood of Christ become so joined to and become so present in the Consecrated Elements by the act of consecration, that the unworthy receivers receive in the elements the Body and Blood of Christ, is not the true, nor an admissible construction of the said Articles of Religion; that such doctrines are directly contrary and repugnant to the 28th and 29th Articles, and that the true and legal exposition of the said Articles is, That the Body and Blood of Christ are taken and received by the worthy receivers only, who, in taking and receiving the same by faith, do spiritually eat the Flesh of Christ and drink the Blood of Christ; whilst the wicked and unworthy, by eating the bread and drinking the wine without faith, do not in anywise eat, take, or receive the Body and Blood of Christ, being void of faith, whereby only the Body and Blood of Christ can be taken, eaten, and received. . . .

"Whereas it is pleaded in the said 14th article filed in these proceedings, that divers printed copies of the sermons or discourses, in the 12th article mentioned as written or printed, or caused to be printed, by the said Archdeacon, were, by his order and direction, sold and distributed, in the years 1853 and 1854, within the said diocese of Bath and Wells; and whereas the said sermon or discourse contains the following amongst other passages: 'And to all who come to the Lord's Table, to those who eat and drink worthily, and to those who eat and drink unworthily, the Body and Blood of Christ are given; and that by all who come to the Lord's Table, by those who eat and drink worthily, and by those who eat and drink unworthily, the Body and Blood of Christ are received'; and 'It is not true that the consecrated bread and wine are changed in their natural substance, for they remain in their very natural substance, and therefore may not be adored. It *is* true that worship is due to the Real, though invisible and supernatural presence of the Body and Blood of Christ in the Eucharist, under the form of Bread and Wine'—his Grace, with the assistance of his Assessors, has determined that the doctrines of the said passages are directly contrary and repugnant to the 28th and 29th of the said Articles of Religion mentioned in the various statutes of Queen Elizabeth."[1]

---

[1] *Guardian*, August 13, 1856, pp. 649, 650.

On October 22, 1856, the Court again met, when the Archdeacon was called upon to retract his errors. He delivered a paper of explanations, which the Court considered a mere reiteration of his offence, after which the Archbishop of Canterbury's judgment was read by the Registrar, confirming and approving the interlocutory judgment of August 12, and concluding as follows :—

"Having maturely deliberated upon the proceedings had therein, and the offence proved, exacting by law deprivation of ecclesiastical promotion, [we] have thought fit to pronounce, and do accordingly pronounce, decree, and declare, that the said Venerable George Anthony Denison, by reason of the premises, ought by law to be deprived of his ecclesiastical promotions, and especially of the said Archdeaconry of Taunton, and of the said Vicarage and Parish Church of East Brent, in the county of Somerset, Diocese of Bath and Wells, and Province of Canterbury, and all profits and benefit of the said Archdeaconry, and of the said Vicarage and Parish Church, and of and from all and singular the fruits, tithes, rents, salaries, and other ecclesiastical dues, rights, and emoluments whatsoever, belonging and appertaining to the said Archdeaconry, and to the said Vicarage and Parish Church; and we do deprive him thereof accordingly by this our definite sentence or final decree, which we read and promulgate by these presents." [1]

The Archdeacon at once gave notice of appeal against this judgment, and bitterly complained afterwards that the Court did not give him credit for his assertion, in his sermons, that he taught that while in Communion the good and wicked eat the same Body and Blood of Christ, the one eats it to his salvation, while the other eats it to his damnation. But surely this statement in no way affected the charge brought against him, which had nothing to do with the results of eating, but with the reality of what is eaten. And so the Archdeacon appealed to the Arches Court, but when the case came before that Court, on April 20, 1857, it was found that it was not an appeal on the merits of the case, but an attempt to evade punishment by raising a side issue. It was pleaded by the Counsel for Archdeacon Denison that all the proceedings in the case were null and void, because more than two years had elapsed

[1] *Guardian*, October 29, 1856, p. 840.

between the commission of the last alleged offence, and the citation to appear before the Archbishop at Bath, contrary to the Act under which the prosecution was undertaken. On April 23, 1857, the Dean of Arches gave judgment in favour of the Archdeacon. Mr. Ditcher, the prosecutor, appealed to the Judicial Committee of Privy Council, which gave its judgment on February 6, 1858, dismissing the appeal, but carefully guarding itself by the statement:—" Of course it is understood that upon the question of heterodoxy, the question whether the respondent [Archdeacon Denison] has at any time uttered heretical doctrine or committed any ecclesiastical offence, their lordships have intimated no opinion."[1]

The Archdeacon was afraid to make an appeal on the merits of the case, and therefore the judgment of the Court at Bath still remains an unrefuted exposition of the law of the Church of England, which has in no way been upset by the Bennett judgment. Indeed, the Archdeacon, in later life, seems to have held the Bennett judgment in as great contempt as the Archbishop's judgment at Bath. "The Judicial Committee of Privy Council," he said, "has done what it could, first in the Gorham case, then in the Bennett case, to ruin the teaching of the Doctrine of the Sacraments."[2] And what, it may be asked, were the Archdeacon's reasons for not appealing, *on the merits of the case*, from the Archbishop's judgment at Bath, depriving him of his living, as a teacher of doctrine condemned by the Church whose bread he ate? He writes:—

"I despised throughout the imputation that I was shielding myself under 'legal objections,' when, if I had been an honest man, I ought to have waived all such things and gone at once to 'the merits.' I despised the imputation as dishonest: I laughed at it as ridiculous. If there had been so much as the shadow of a shade of a decently fair tribunal, rather I should say, if there had been *any* tribunal in England recognised by the constitution in Church and State as competent to pronounce in matter of Doctrine (the same has to be said now [in 1878] in respect of matter of Worship), I might possibly have considered about taking

---

[1] Brodrick and Freemantle's *Judgments of the Privy Council*, p. 175.
[2] Denison's *Notes of My Life*, p. 192.

the case *simpliciter* upon its 'merits.' But fairness and competency were alike lacking."[1]

In other words, Denison would appeal against the Bath judgment on "its merits" when a Court came into existence which would take his side. A very convenient policy for the defendant, no doubt, but one which can only be allowed in a country where law has ceased to exist, and every man is allowed to do that which is right in his own eyes. It is evident from what he said that, if every existing Court of Law in England had given judgment against him, the Archdeacon would have been as much a rebel as he was to the Bath judgment. There was not, it seems, in 1856, in existence a tribunal "competent to pronounce in matter of doctrine;" and, in 1878, when he wrote his *Notes of My Life*, matters were still worse, for then there did not exist a Court competent to pronounce a judgment even "in respect of matter of worship." Of course, all this sort of talk was simply the language of an anarchist, which left every clergyman in the Church free to be a law unto himself. The Ritualists are acting on the lines of Archdeacon Denison at the present moment, and frankly tell us that even the Church of England, as a whole, has no power to forbid certain Romish doctrines and practices which they hold dear, though they are disliked and opposed by the overwhelming majority of loyal Churchmen. We have been reminded again and again of late that the Church of England is not an independent Church, but is subject to the rest of what is somewhat vaguely termed "the Catholic Church." The Archbishop's Court at Bath was a purely spiritual Court; yet it was treated with as much contempt and rebellion as though it were the most Erastian tribunal ever set up by a State anxious to oppress the Church.

No sooner was Archdeacon Denison condemned than a great hue and cry was heard throughout the length and breadth of the land. The Puseyites were furious; but all they could do was to rally round the Archdeacon and practically, though not in so many words, declare: "We are one with you. There shall be not one rebel, but a small

[1] Denison's *Notes of My Life*, p. 242.

army of rebels on your side." Dr. Pusey boldly wrote:—
"The only course open to us is, publicly to apprise those *in authority* over us, that *we cannot obey them in this*, and to go on as before, leaving it to them to interfere with us, or no, as they may think fit."[1] This was done by means of the celebrated Protest against the Bath judgment, signed by Pusey, Keble, Bennett, Carter, Neale, Isaac Williams, and other members of the party. Those who signed this document identified themselves with the views for which Denison had been condemned, and appealed against the Archbishop's judgment, not to any existing Court of Law, which they knew very well would condemn them, but "to a lawful Synod of all the Churches of our communion," which had no existence, and which, as a matter of fact, has had no existence from that day to this. These protesters against Protestantism affirmed their belief that: "The wicked, although they can 'in no wise be partakers of Christ,' nor 'spiritually eat His Flesh and drink His Blood,' yet do in the Sacrament not only take, but eat and drink unworthily to their own condemnation the Body and Blood of Christ, which they do not discern." Surely this is a self-contradictory paragraph? If, as is here clearly asserted, the wicked "eat and drink" the Body and Blood of Christ, surely they must at the same time be "partakers of Christ," whom they are supposed to have eaten with their bodily mouths. The protesters also declared: "We appeal from the said opinion, decision, or sentence of his Grace, in the first instance, to a free and lawful Synod of all the Churches of our communion, when such by God's mercy may be had."[2]

Of course, this Protest against the Bath judgment was equivalent to a challenge to those in authority to prosecute the men who signed it. It is much to be regretted that the challenge was not accepted. I have no doubt whatever that the final decision would have been against the Romanisers, and an effectual blow would thus have been inflicted on the Puseyites, from which they would not have recovered. But our rulers in the Church of England have

[1] *Life of Dr. Pusey*, vol. iii. p. 444.
[2] *Ibid.* pp. 440–442.

never been noted for an excess of courage, and so they let the grand opportunity slip by. Will it ever come again?

The year 1855 witnessed the formation of the first secret Society of the Romanisers. The Society of the Holy Cross was formed on February 28, 1855, and its first secret Synod was held on the 3rd of the following May. From the very first it loved darkness rather than light, dreading nothing so much as publicity. As its Master said, at its Synod, held in May 1876: "The bond of union between the Brethren was to be as strict as possible. None but themselves were to know their names, or of the existence of the Society, except those to whom it might be named to induce them to join: but this only with leave of the Society."[1] For the first eight years of its existence its statutes and rules existed only in manuscript; the authorities were afraid to commit them to print. The names of the Brethren for the first ten years "were only to be found in a written book kept by the Secretary";[2] and when, at last, in 1865, they were printed for the first time, every care was taken to prevent a copy falling into Protestant hands, a precaution which is still adopted, for there is nothing the members more dread than that their names shall be known to the public. The Society of the Holy Cross is very influential, and is more secret, more Romanising, and more dangerous now than ever it has been before. An exposure of its history and work, based on its own secret documents, may be read in the second chapter of my *Secret History of the Oxford Movement*, and therefore I need not say anything more about it here.

Two years later, in 1857, the Association for the Promotion of the Unity of Christendom was formed by members of the Church of England, the Church of Rome, and the Greek Church. Its members are expected to pray that all those three Churches may become united and form one Church again. It would be a bad day for England were such a request granted. Some years after its formation the Pope ordered all the Roman Catholics to leave the Association, though I see from one of its recent reports

[1] S.S.C. Master's Address, May Synod, 1876, p. 2.
[2] *Ibid.* p. 4.

that some Roman Catholics are still members. Since the publication of my *Secret History of the Oxford Movement*, in the tenth chapter of which the Romanising character of this organisation is proved from its own documents, some startling revelations as to its early history have been given to the world in the *Life and Letters of Ambrose Phillipps de Lisle*, who was one of its principal founders. The way had been carefully prepared for the formation of such an Association. In 1857 Ritualism had made considerable progress. A Roman Catholic barrister, writing to the *Union*—a new paper representing the advanced Romanisers—remarked :—"The Oxford Movement is still doing its work, and spreading the true principles of Anglicanism; which, if carried out, are, as all allow, almost identical with those of Catholicism. Go to such churches as St. Barnabas', Pimlico; and St. Mary, Osnaburg Street (both of which I have recently visited to see with my own eyes, and to judge for myself, instead of letting the converts judge for me, as they do for most Catholics) *and tell me in what they differ from our own?*"[1] By this time Roman Catholic Vestments had been restored by a small section of the clergy, and the Mass, though as yet without the *name*, was exalted in certain quarters as highly as in the Church of Rome.

"Our firm conviction," said the *Union*, in a leading article, "is that, until the Sacrifice of the Altar takes its legitimate and appointed place in our Sunday worship, we shall only remain hampered by Puritan traditions, and be hindered in our great work of Catholicising England. If this were done, the charge about 'unlighted Altars and unstoled priests' would fall to the ground. Those who are led to underrate this revival must seek to accomplish it effectually. Everything should give place to this. The Altar should be duly raised and effectively vested and adorned. Cross, lights, flower vases, pictures, book-rest, chalice, and corporal should all be provided. The Sacred Vestments should be used to distinguish the ordinary office from the Tremendous Sacrifice. Then shams and empty ceremonies, 'table prayers,' Ten Commandments, and the 'form and ceremony' of going to the Altar to 'read the Epistle and

---

[1] *Union*, August 14, 1857, p. 102.

Gospel' would cease to be perpetuated. Then would our flocks learn what true worship is."[1]

The anxiety herein manifested to get rid of the Ten Commandments, as a part of the service called "the Sacrifice of the Altar," is very instructive. It shows that the Ritualists are not on terms of good friendship with them. They must feel very uncomfortable when, in church —as I have frequently witnessed—a clergyman reads out the Second Commandment against the use of images in worship, while the ends of his surplice are, perhaps, touching one of the God-condemned articles, let in to the frontal of the Communion Table, while other images are seen scattered throughout the chancel. In these dangerous days we may well be thankful for the law of the Church, which commands the placing of the Ten Commandments in a prominent position in every parish church, from which, alas! many Ritualistic priests remove them, thus showing themselves to be the enemies of God and the Church.

Next to the so-called "Sacrifice of the Altar," the Romanisers threw considerable energy, at this time, into propagating the Confessional. Nothing of a modified character would please them: they must have Auricular Confession as in the Roman Catholic Church, or go without it altogether. In a leading article, the new organ of the advanced section boldly and unblushingly declared :—

"Every one knows that the only difference between Confession in the Roman and English Churches is that, in the former, it is compulsory; and in the latter not so. The mode of making and receiving a Confession is substantially identical; the same questions are asked; the same kind of penances given; the same consolation offered; and it appears to us somewhat dishonest to pretend that it is otherwise."[2]

A month later the *Union* repeated its assertion, which, unfortunately, is as true now as when first uttered, except that the word "Ritualists" should be substituted for "England":—"We continue to maintain that there is

---

[1] *Union*, December 4, 1857, p. 353.
[2] *Ibid.* August 20, 1858, p. 540.

no virtual distinction between the doctrine of Rome and England as regards the Ordinance of Confession."[1]

In this way the Romeward Movement was being actively carried on. The Church of England was being made ready to reunite with Rome, by teaching Roman doctrine and, as far as possible, turning the parish churches into imitations of Roman Catholic places of worship. The work had, as we have seen, been really going on ever since 1833, but now the time had arrived when the conspirators felt themselves powerful enough to band together into a society, having for its real object the submission of the Eastern churches and the Church of England unto the Church of Rome. But before such an organisation could be founded, a great deal of subtlety had to be called into action, and, above all, the Pope and his Propaganda had to be consulted. Of course, all the preliminary work had to be done in the dark, and the utmost possible secrecy was enjoined on all who were called upon to organise the new, daring, and united movement towards Rome. The negotiations with the Propaganda at Rome were undertaken by Mr. Ambrose Phillipps de Lisle, as a devout and humble servant of the Pope. On May 18, 1857, he wrote a long and confidential letter on the subject to Cardinal Barnabo, Prefect of the Propaganda :—

"I write to you," said De Lisle, "most eminent and reverend Cardinal of the Holy Roman Church, concerning a matter of great importance, *but of great secrecy and delicacy*, which I humbly pray your Eminence to lay before our most holy Lord the Pope. I will briefly explain the matter if you will give me your ear.

"There is at this moment a large party in the Established Church of this realm (called the Anglican Church) which have conceived the idea of reuniting their National Church with the holy Mother Catholic, *and also of placing the same under canonical obedience to the authority of the holy Apostolic See*, which for three hundred years heretical malice has so miserably delighted to cast away.

"Persons of great dignity, who are the heads of this party, with whom I am related either by blood or by marriage or by friendship have communicated their idea to me, and their longing, begging me

---

[1] *Union*, September 17, 1858, p. 601.

to open and reveal to your Eminence the matter, in order to its being known to his Holiness the Pope, and if it be lawful *to beg of him in all humility his Apostolic blessing* upon the matter taken up and already begun.

"These persons have designated me, although unworthy, to communicate this business to the Holy See, partly *because they wished to act most secretly* on account of the intimate relations of their Church with the civil power of this realm, and because Her Majesty's Government at this moment is directed by Viscount Palmerston, a man by no means friendly to the Catholic Church and things Catholic; partly because they were unwilling on account of political reasons to divulge the matter to our holy Father the Archbishop Cardinal of Westminster, our Catholic Primate, there being a certain suspicion in existence, not without natural causes, between the National Anglican Church and the local Catholic Church, as your Eminence will easily apprehend.

"This Party, therefore, wish to show your Eminence *their sincere desire to reconcile as soon as possible their own Church with the Holy See.* But so great an undertaking cannot be carried through all at once. The Party which has taken up the matter numbers two thousand priests and ten Bishops, joined together in this idea. ... Now the ten Bishops who favour union are Salisbury, Oxford, Chichester, London, Exeter, in England, all in the Province of Canterbury; the other four are in Scotland, the Bishop of Brechin with three others. To these Bishops are united two thousand priests, amongst whom are some Archdeacons, Deans, and Canons, some Rectors of Collegiate Churches, others parish priests and vicars. To this section of the Anglican clergy belong a very large body of men of the richest and noblest families of the realm, amongst whom are some most illustrious persons very closely bound to myself, who held office under the Crown in 1852, in the Government of the Earl of Derby. They have made it known to me that they wish the business begun to succeed.

"Accordingly, this Party of the Anglican Church humbly desires ecclesiastical reunion of the National Church of the whole British Empire with the holy Catholic Mother, by embracing without any ambiguity all the articles defined in the sacred Council of Trent and the whole Orthodox Faith; also the latest definition of the Immaculate Conception of our Lady, the holy Virgin Mary, Mother of God; and *by submitting their Church to the divine authority of the holy Apostolic See*, with all affection of the heart and most faithful canonical obedience.

"But, as your Eminence will easily understand, this Party in the

National Anglican Church, as yet a minority in the whole kingdom, can for the present do no more than, *with all prudence but zeal, dispose the people* to take up so grand an object in the future . . . *For such an end* they already teach amongst the people the whole of the Catholic doctrine, not less explicitly than we Catholics ourselves are able to do it, and with the greatest reverence. It is indeed wonderful, and for so many centuries quite unhoped for! They teach the Sacrifice of the Mass, the true presence and Transubstantiation, the oblation of the most holy Body and Blood of our Lord for the quick and the dead; the Invocation of the Blessed Virgin and the Saints, the veneration of sacred images; also, *so far as they prudently can*, concerning the Primacy of the holy Apostolic See . . . Whatever may come to pass, they requested me to lay the matter before your Eminence, O most excellent Cardinal, requesting your generous prayers for its success, and also (if it be lawful) *desiring with their whole heart and soul some word of encouragement from our most holy Lord the Supreme Pontiff* that all things may turn out well."[1]

No doubt the writer of this very remarkable letter was an enthusiast in the cause to which he had devoted his life, and somewhat too hopeful as to the immediate future, and I think he was probably misinformed as to the English Bishops being a party to the scheme. Yet I have no doubt that he was perfectly sincere in conveying this information to Cardinal Barnabo, and that he had only too much reason for rejoicing at what was being done in the English Church by the traitors within her camp, whose dearest and disgraceful ambition it was to hand her over, bound hand and foot, to the bondage of her bitterest enemy, the Church of Rome. Mr. De Lisle soon received a favourable reply from Cardinal Barnabo, who wrote to him :—

"MOST HONOURED SIR,—The subject brought to my notice by your letter of the 18th of May last *has given me the deepest consolation*. For nothing could be better, or more in accordance with my prayers as Prefect of this Sacred Congregation, than the accomplishment of the designs which your letter declares to be of not insuperable difficulty.

"And this matter, which I at once commend in my prayers to the Omnipotent God, I shall be most happy to place before our

---

[1] *Life and Letters of Ambrose Phillipps de Lisle*, vol. i. pp. 375-377.

most holy Lord Pius IX. on his return to Rome, so that what is already a subject of hope may soon be brought to a happy issue for the glory of God and the eternal salvation of souls.

"Moreover, I return my thanks over and over again, and I shall pray for all things to turn out favourably according to our wishes.

"Your Lordship's most obliged,

"ALEXANDER, CARD. BARNABO, *Prefect*."[1]

With this encouraging letter in his possession, De Lisle next approached Dr. Newman, and laid the whole plan, in strict secrecy, before him, asking for his opinion and guidance. Newman replied :—"I thank you very much for your most confidential letter, and the very interesting information it contains. . . . I am still somewhat uneasy lest persons who *ought* to be Catholics should allow themselves to *bargain* and *make terms*. Should not they have some presumption from the Holy See—or in some formal way surrender themselves?"[2] There is something mysterious as to what Newman meant when he asked thus, "Should not they have some presumption from the Holy See?" Three days before this he wrote to De Lisle :—"I perfectly agree with you in thinking that the Movement of 1833 is not over in the country, whatever be the state of Oxford itself ; also, *I think it is for the interest of Catholicism that individuals should not join us, but should remain to leaven the mass. I mean that* THEY WILL DO MORE FOR US BY REMAINING WHERE THEY ARE THAN BY COMING OVER, but then they have individual souls, and with what heart can I do anything to induce them to preach to others, if they themselves thereby become castaways?"[3]

Thus encouraged, with the approval of the Cardinal Prefect of the Propaganda and Dr. Newman, the conspirators held a meeting in London on July 4, 1857, at which they passed the following six resolutions (to be sent to the Pope), which were kept as a profound secret from the public for forty-two years, until the publication of De Lisle's biography, at the close of 1899. I can understand

---

[1] *Life and Letters of Ambrose Phillipps de Lisle*, vol. i. p. 378.
[2] *Ibid.* p. 369. [3] *Ibid.* p. 368.

Roman Catholics voting for these resolutions, but how English Church clergymen, with a spark of common honesty, could approve of them is more than I can comprehend:—

"1. To express their gratitude and respect for the person of his Eminence they vote a golden chalice studded with jewels and a paten of beaten Australian gold, to be presented to Cardinal Barnabo as a pledge of the hoped-for Reunion between the English and Roman Churches.

"2. To carry out the wishes expressed in the Cardinal's letter, they determine never to rest until they have done everything possible to reunite the said two Churches, AND RESTORE THE AUTHORITY OF THE HOLY SEE IN ENGLAND.

"3. They express the opinion that after the lapse of some years the plan will become feasible.

"4. They resolve that a treatise, exact, statistical, and historical, dealing with the vexed question of Anglican Orders, shall be drawn up by one of their own body, and *submitted to Pope Pius IX. for his supreme and authoritative judgment.*

"5. They propose to organise a select body of learned preachers to bring forward, and expound and recommend, the godly reunion of all dissident Churches with their holy Catholic Mother Church, in all Churches and Colleges and Cathedrals where the Bishop's licence to do so can be obtained.

"6. They propose to establish *a Society or Association of Prayer to promote this sacred object*, of which the only obligation shall be to recite daily the Lord's Prayer once, and the Liturgical Prayer for Peace and Unity, '*ut ecclesiam secundum Voluntatem Tuam pacificare et coadunare digneris*,' and beg of his Holiness to attach an Indulgence to this prayer, to be extended even to Anglicans not in external communion with the Holy See, should it seem good and be within the limits of the power of the Supreme Pontiff to do so."[1]

It must be admitted by every honest man that these resolutions were a disgrace to every member of the Church of England who agreed to them. The Oxford Movement has no reason to be proud of those of her children who thus acted in a way which puts to shame every idea of honesty and honour. And so "to promote this sacred object," of bringing the English Church to bow the neck once more to Rome, the Association for the

---

[1] *Life and Letters of Ambrose Phillipps de Lisle*, vol. i. pp. 379, 380.

Promotion of the Unity of Christendom was actually founded, at a private meeting held in the parish of St. Clement Danes, Strand, London, on September 8, 1857. Since then it has continued its Romeward progress, and although, as I write, Mr. De Lisle's biography has been before the public for ten months, I have yet to learn that the A.P.U.C. has uttered one word of censure of the document which led to its formation, or denied its authenticity. Scores of churches are placed at its disposal every year for celebrations of Holy Communion on behalf of its objects. It is understood to have over 10,000 clerical and lay members scattered throughout the English Church, but nobody knows who they are, except the officials at its head office in London.

The Hon. and Rev. Robert Liddell, who succeeded Mr. Bennett as Vicar of St. Paul's, Knightsbridge, was quite as far removed from Protestantism as his predecessor. Instead of diminishing he added to the Ritual and ornaments of the Church. Intense dissatisfaction was created in the parish by these changes, and at last the parishioners decided to elect a Protestant Churchwarden to look after their interests. The gentleman they selected was Mr. Westerton, who had all the courage of his convictions, and soon made things very uncomfortable for the Vicar. Early in 1854 Mr. Westerton wrote to the Bishop of London (Dr. Blomfield) requesting him to order the removal of certain ornaments from St. Paul's Church; but this the Bishop declined to do, pleading that he doubted whether he possessed the power to order their removal, except through a decree in the Consistory Court. Some of the ornaments complained of were, he believed, not illegal. At about the same time Mr. Beal, a resident in the district of St. Barnabas, Pimlico (a District Church in the charge of Mr. Liddell), applied to the Consistory Court for a monition to the Chapelwardens to remove certain ornaments from St. Barnabas' Church. Mr. Westerton also applied to the same Court for a monition as to the ornaments in St. Paul's Church. The two cases were argued together in the Consistory Court, and at length judgment was delivered by Dr. Lushington, on December 5, 1855. The following were the subjects with which he had to deal, together with his decisions thereon :—

1. A High Altar of carved wood, raised on platform in St. Paul's Church—*Being of wood, Legal.*
2. A High Altar of stone in St. Barnabas' Church —*Illegal.*
3. A Credence Table—*Legal.*
4. Candlesticks and Candles, used when not needed for light—*Illegal.*
5. Coloured Cloths on Communion Table changed according to the seasons—*Illegal.*
6. Embroidered lace cloths on Communion Table at time of Communion—*Illegal.*
7. Crosses—*Illegal.*

From this judgment Mr. Liddell appealed to the Court of Arches, where, on December 20, 1856, Sir J. Dodson gave judgment confirming in every respect the judgment of the Consistory Court. Under these circumstances what was the Vicar to do? Two purely Spiritual Courts had decided against him. There was only an appeal to the Judicial Committee of Privy Council open to him. But this Court was, in the estimation of the Puseyites, a purely State tribunal whose decisions had no weight in conscience. Yet if Cæsar would only upset the decisions of the Spiritual Courts, then to Cæsar they would go. It was not a consistent position to take up—there is not an atom of legal consistency in the whole Romeward Movement—but it was a convenient one. To appeal to the Judicial Committee on such a subject was to acknowledge its competency and right to decide. So to the Judicial Committee Mr. Liddell went, hoping it would overthrow the Spiritual Courts' authority, when blessings would be upon it; but if it failed in this respect, why, then, the sooner the Judicial Committee was pulled down, and a Court of Appeal more favourable to the Ritualists erected in its place, the better it would be for the law-breaking clergy.

The appeal of Mr. Liddell was heard before the Judicial Committee of Privy Council on February 9, 10, 11, 12, 13, 14, and 16, 1857. Judgment was delivered on the 21st of

March 1857. From it I give the following extracts, dealing with the seven points mentioned above:—

1 and 2. *Tables and Stone Altars.*—"The Rubric of the present Prayer-Book provides only that at the Communion time, the table, having a fair white linen cloth upon it, shall stand in the body of the Church or chancel, where Morning and Evening Prayer are appointed to be said; and the priest is to commence the service standing at the north side of the table. The term 'Altar' is never used to describe it, and there is an express declaration at the close of the service against the doctrine of Transubstantiation, with which the ideas of an Altar and Sacrifice are closely connected. Under these circumstances, the first question is, whether the stone structure at St. Barnabas is a Communion Table within the meaning of the Canons and the Rubric; and their lordships are clearly of opinion that it is not . . . Their lordships, therefore, are satisfied that the decision upon this point [that Communion Tables must be made of wood] in *Faulkener* v. *Litchfield* is well founded, and they must advise her Majesty that the decree as to the removal of the stone structure at St. Barnabas, and the Cross upon it, and the substitution of a Communion Table of wood, ought to be affirmed."

3. *Credence Tables.*—For the text of the judgment on this subject, and a further extract on Altars, see above, chapter ix. p. 253. "As to the Credence Tables, their lordships therefore must advise a reversal of the sentence complained of."

4. *Candlesticks and Candles.*—The Consistory Court declared lights illegal when not needed for light, but did not order the removal of either candlesticks or candles. Their lordships now said:—"The judgment complained of has not ordered the removal of the table [in St. Paul's] or of the candlesticks, but only of the Cross, the Credence Table, and the cloths. There is no appeal against this order as far as it permits the table and candlesticks to remain, and it is therefore not open to their lordships to consider the judgment with reference to the articles not ordered to be removed."

5. *Coloured Cloths on Communion Table.*—"In this case their lordships do not see any sufficient reason for interference, and they must therefore advise the reversal of the sentence as to the cloths used for the covering of the Lord's Table during the time of Divine Service, both with respect to St. Paul's and St. Barnabas."

6. *Embroidered Lace on Communion Table.*—"With respect to the embroidered linen and lace used on the Communion Table at the time of the ministration of the Holy Communion. The Rubric and the Canon prescribe the use of a fair white linen cloth, and both the

learned Judges in the Court below have been of opinion that embroidery and lace are not consistent with the meaning of that expression, having regard to the nature of the table upon which the cloth is to be used. Although their lordships are not disposed in any case, to restrict within narrower limits than the law has imposed, the discretion which, within those limits, is justly allowed to congregations by the rules both of the Ecclesiastical and the Common Law Courts, the directions of the Rubric must be complied with ; and upon the whole their lordships do not dissent from the construction of the Rubric adopted by the present decree upon this point; and they must therefore advise her Majesty to affirm it."

7. *Crosses.*—"Upon the whole, their lordships, after the most anxious consideration, have come to the conclusion that Crosses, as distinguished from Crucifixes, have been in use, as ornaments of churches, from the earliest periods of Christianity; that when used as mere emblems of the Christian faith, and not as objects of superstitious reverence, they may still lawfully be erected as architectural decorations of churches; that the wooden Cross erected on the Chancel screen of St. Barnabas is to be considered as a mere architectural ornament; and that as to this article, they must advise her Majesty to reverse the judgment complained of."

"Next, with respect to the wooden Cross attached to the Communion Table at St. Paul's. Their lordships have already declared their opinion that the Communion Table intended by the Canon was a table in the ordinary sense of the word, flat and movable, capable of being covered with a cloth, at which or around which the communicants might be placed in order to partake of the Lord's Supper, and the question is, whether the existence of a Cross attached to the table is consistent with the spirit or with the letter of those regulations. Their lordships are clearly of opinion that it is not; and they must recommend that upon this point also the decree complained of should be affirmed."[1]

By this appeal to the Judicial Committee of Privy Council, Mr. Liddell gained the following points:—(1) The carved wood table in St. Paul's, (2) the Credence Table, (3) Coloured "Altar" cloths, changeable according to the seasons, (4) the Cross on the Chancel Screen. On the other hand, it was declared by the highest Court of Appeal illegal (1) to erect a Stone Altar, (2) to use Embroidered Lace on the Communion Cloth, and (3) to erect a Cross

[1] *The Judgment of the Judicial Committee in Liddell v. Westerton.* Edited by A. F. Bayford, LL.D., pp. 105-136. London: Butterworths. 1857.

attached to the Communion Table. A fifth point, which was not appealed against, was that it was declared illegal to burn lights when not needed for light. As to how these points are affected by later judgments, it seems that they are all still illegal. The illegality of "Altar Lights" is not affected by the judgment of the Archbishop of Canterbury in the Lincoln Case, since his, as an inferior Court, could not upset the decision of the Judicial Committee in the case of *Martin* v. *Mackonochie* (1868). When the judgment of Archbishop Benson subsequently came before the Judicial Committee, their lordships did not reverse their previous judgment on lights given in 1868, and therefore it still stands as the declared law of the Church.

To his credit be it recorded, Mr. Liddell at once accepted the judgment, and in a letter to his parishioners expressed his opinion that it had "clearly defined some points of ritual which were previously deemed ambiguous, and has established beyond contradiction the Church's Law, to which I, for one, have ever desired to yield loyal and unswerving obedience."[1] Not so, however, with all his brethren. There were rebels in their rank. One of these was the Rev. E. Stuart, Vicar of St. Mary Magdalene, Munster Square, and one of the founders of the English Church Union. To him, on March 5, 1858, the new Bishop of London (Dr. Tait) wrote:—"I have very carefully considered what passed at my interview with you yesterday in London House, and I feel myself obliged to adhere to the opinion I then expressed. I must, therefore, *lay my commands upon you* to discontinue the practice you have introduced without any authority in St. Mary Magdalene, Munster Square, of lighting the candles on the Communion Table in broad daylight, except when they may reasonably be considered necessary or convenient for purpose of light."[2] To this Episcopal command, Mr. Stuart, notwithstanding his oath of obedience to his Bishop, bluntly and rebelliously replied:—"I write to acknowledge the receipt of your letter of the 5th instant, containing a command to

---

[1] *A Letter to the Parishioners of St. Paul's, Knightsbridge.* By the Hon. and Rev. Robert Liddell, pp. 3, 4. London: Hayes. 1858.
[2] *Life of Archbishop Tait*, vol. i. p. 220.

me to discontinue the use of lights at the celebration of the Sacrament. *I must respectfully decline to obey this command*, as I believe that in issuing it you have (unintentionally, of course) transgressed the limits of that authority which the Church of England has committed to her Bishops. I believe that you have done this by forbidding what the law of the Church distinctly authorises."[1] To this Bishop Tait replied :—" I greatly regret that you should think it right to disobey my command on your own private interpretation of what you deem to be the law. Had you read the judgment of the Privy Council in the Knightsbridge Case, and Dr. Lushington's previous judgment on the same, with the care that they deserve, you would, I doubt not, have seen your error as to the point of law."[2] The pity is that the Bishop did not prosecute this rebellious Vicar; but he seems to have dreaded the trouble and worry, and consequently Mr. Stuart was left to do as he liked, practically triumphant over his Bishop. This claim of Mr. Stuart to refuse obedience to a Bishop, if he, in the exercise of his own opinion, thinks he understands the Church's law as to doctrine and ritual better than the Bishop and all the Courts of Law, is still a very common one. Born of conceit, pride, and self-will, it ought not to be allowed. On this subject it may be well to quote here the wise words of Lord Stowell in his judgment on the Stone Case :—

"But that any clergyman should assume the liberty of inculcating his own private opinions, in direct opposition to the doctrines of the Established Church, in a place set apart for its own private worship, is not more contrary to the character of a National Church than to all honest and rational conduct. Nor is this restraint inconsistent with Christian liberty; for to what purpose is it directed, but to ensure, in the Established Church, that uniformity which tends to edification; leaving individuals to go elsewhere according to the private persuasions they may entertain. It is, therefore, a restraint essential to the security of the Church, and it would be a gross contradiction to its fundamental purpose to say, that it is liable to the reproach of persecution, if it does not pay its Ministers for maintaining doctrines contrary to its own."[3]

---

[1] *Life of Archbishop Tait*, vol. i. p. 221.   [2] *Ibid.* p. 222.
[3] *Considerations on the Exercise of Private Judgment*. By James Parker Deane, D.C.L., p. 43. London: Parker. 1845.

CHAPTER XIII

The Convent Case at Lewes—Charges against the Rev. J. M. Neale—Riot at Lewes at the burial of a Sister of Mercy—Bishop of Chichester's letters to Mr. Scobell and the Mother Superior—The Bishop withdraws his patronage from St. Margaret's, East Grinstead—Threatening the Bishop—Mr. Neale's pamphlet—His underhand conduct—Confession on the sly—The Case of the Rev. Alfred Poole—His licence withdrawn—His admissions—Remarkable assertions at a Communicants' Meeting—Mr. Poole appeals to the Archbishop of Canterbury—His Judgment—The Lavington Case—Romanising books—Theological Colleges—Attack upon Cuddesdon College—Mr. Golightly's *Facts and Documents Showing the Alarming State of the Diocese of Oxford*—An exciting controversy.

SOME events of minor importance, but not without interest, have now to be recorded. Considerable excitement was created at Lewes, Sussex, towards the close of the year 1857, in consequence of the publication of a pamphlet by the Rev. John Scobell, Rector of All Saints, Lewes, and Hon. Canon of Chichester, containing serious charges against the Rev. J. M. Neale, Chaplain and Father Confessor of St. Margaret's, East Grinstead, Sisterhood. These charges were first privately made in a letter addressed to Mr. Neale by Mr. Scobell, in February 1857, and were as follows :—

"1. That you have been carrying on by letter, under cover to the Mistress of my Infants' School, a clandestine correspondence with my eldest daughter while in my house.

"2. That you hold clandestine and secret meetings with her, of some hours' duration, in the private apartments of my Infants' Schoolhouse, situate in my parish of All Saints, Lewes.

"3. That you there usurp, dishonourably and unlawfully, the office of parish priest of All Saints, Lewes; wearing a surplice; exercising Liturgical offices; receiving Confession and pronouncing Absolution.

"4. That you assume to yourself, and allow yourself to be viewed by my daughter and parishioner in the character of her spiritual guide and adviser, to my detriment as her natural parent and lawful parish priest; that you receive in that character, at her hands, the letters of me, her father, for your perusal; that you animadvert, and dictate how they shall be replied to—how far complied with—how far resisted.

"5. That you seek to hold and keep up a lasting spiritual influence over my daughter living in my house. That you seek to guide her future course of life. That your advice is to her, that she quit my house, that she persevere in demanding my consent to so doing, and that she join and give herself, and whatever income or property she may have, to an establishment, at or near East Grinstead, or some other similar establishment; and, under your guidance and tutelage, there to resign her will, her person, her services, her property, to your or others' will and pleasure.

"6. That in the prosecution of these designs you have never made one word of communication to me, her natural parent, the guide of her youth, and constituted spiritual pastor; that the whole is clandestinely and surreptitiously carried on and continued now by letter during her absence from home, to the injury of my family peace and to the infringement of my public rights.

"I make these charges distinctly and deliberately, and I ask for your distinct and definite reply."[1]

Mr. Neale formally acknowledged the receipt of Mr. Scobell's letter, stating that he declined replying to his questions, although his silence was not to be taken as an acquiescence in the correctness of his statements, but as taken from motives "of the most friendly character towards" Mr. Scobell.

The facts of the case were not made public until the following December, after the funeral of Mr. Scobell's daughter, who died at St. Margaret's, East Grinstead, from fever, on November 13, 1857, after she had been a Sister there for a few months. Great indignation was felt at Lewes when some of the circumstances became known, immediately after the young lady's death, and with the result that at her funeral, on November 18th—which took place at Lewes—something approaching to a riot took place. At the conclusion of the funeral service, the body having been buried in a vault within the Church, a dis-

---

[1] *The Rev. J. M. Neale and the Institute of St. Margaret's, East Grinstead.* Statement by the Rev. J. Scobell, p. 9. London: Nisbet & Co. 1857.

THE LEWES RIOTS

graceful attack was made upon Mr. Neale and the Sisters of Mercy who accompanied him. Amid cries of "No Popery," Mr. Neale was knocked down, and parts of the dresses of the Sisters were torn off, the whole party from East Grinstead being hustled about by the mob, until rescued by the police. Such conduct on the part of the Protestants was, I believe, wholly without excuse, and was a disgrace to the cause it was ostensibly got up to promote. There was grave cause for public indignation, but not for mob violence on defenceless women.

About three weeks after this riot Mr. Scobell published the pamphlet containing the six charges against Mr. Neale, which I have quoted above. Meanwhile Mr. Scobell had received from the Bishop of Chichester a letter of sympathy, dated November 22nd :—"You may," wrote his lordship, "be well assured of the deep-felt sympathy of every upright candidly religious man. I beg to offer you and your family the sincere expression of mine and Mrs. Gilbert's. I have felt it my duty to write to the Lady Superioress and the Society of St. Margaret's at East Grinstead, the letter, with a copy of which I thus briefly intrude upon your sorrows. He must be heartless who could have permitted himself to add to them as that infatuated man from East Grinstead has done"[1] (that is, Mr. Neale). To the Mother Superior of the Sisterhood the Bishop wrote as follows :—

PALACE, CHICHESTER, *Nov.* 21, 1857.

"MADAM,—Your Society was first formed as an association of ladies, who should engage themselves and train others to minister to the bodily wants of their fellow-Christians, by nursing them in sickness. Such an institution I regarded as praiseworthy and Christian in its object, and I authorised the use of my name in connection with it. It has for some time past submitted itself to the unlimited influence of Mr. Neale, a clergyman, in whose views and practices it is well known I have no confidence. Especially it is well known that I deny that the Church of England sanctions the habitual practice of Confession. She acknowledges it only in rare and exceptional cases, and Mr. Neale is unwarranted in using it in

---

[1] *The Rev. J. M. Neale and the Institute of St. Margaret's, East Grinstead.* Statement by the Rev. J. Scobell, p. 13. *The Lewes Riots.* A Letter to the Bishop of Chichester. By the Rev. J. M. Neale, p. 36, 5th edition. London: Masters. 1857.

the frequent and regular way in which he applies it. Those who admit such application of it to themselves, manifest thereby the inadequacy of their direct faith in Christ's promises. Their resort to this unauthorised remedy, by a righteous retribution, issues in a continuous increase of weakness, and an accumulation of obstructions in the way of the true influences of grace upon their hearts. They trust more and more in man, and are less and less able, without man, to hope in Christ, *i.e.* truly hope in Him. I desire, therefore, that henceforth neither you nor any of your Sisterhood will state that I approve of, or have any connection with, your Institution and Sisterhood of S. Margaret's. I desire that any circulars or printed copies of your rules in which my name is introduced, may be cancelled and not used with my name in future. Whatever expense is brought upon the Institution by the consequent loss of the copies you may have by you, I will fully repay.—I remain, Madam, your faithful Pastor,

(Signed) "A. T. CICESTR.

" MISS GREAME, or the Lady Superioress
of S. Margaret's, East Grinstead."

On Sunday, November 29th, Mr. Scobell preached in All Saints' Church, Lewes, a special sermon on the treatment his deceased daughter had received at the hands of Mr. Neale, in the course of which he announced his intention to publish a narrative of what had taken place. On December 3rd the Mother Superior of St. Margaret's Convent appeared at the door of the Palace of the Bishop of Chichester, and sent in a letter requesting an interview. This document has the appearance of having been written under dread of Mr. Scobell's forthcoming pamphlet. It was, in fact, a threatening letter, evidently written in the hope of frightening the Bishop into using his influence to prevent Mr. Scobell publishing his exposure. "Mr. Neale," wrote the Mother Superior to the Bishop, in the letter which she handed in at the door, "is extremely anxious to spare the feelings of that unhappy parent, and he hoped that after I had seen you, an arrangement would be made by which the public might be disabused of their false impressions *without an exposure in the papers.*"[1] I do not wonder that the Bishop refused to see a lady who brought him such a threatening letter. But he wrote her

[1] *The Lewes Riots.* By the Rev. J. M. Neale, p. 37.

a letter, which has not been published, to which the Mother Superior sent a rude and sneering reply. On December 2nd Mr. Neale himself wrote to the Bishop, expressing a hope that he would not compel him, "in absolute self-defence, to expose Mr. Scobell."[1] But the Bishop would not yield, so in a letter, bearing date December 4, 1857, Mr. Neale published his "exposure" of Mr. Scobell. In this pamphlet Mr. Neale quotes numerous documents, amongst them being one he wrote to Miss Scobell, on January 21, 1855, containing the following statement:—"I should advise you to act thus. To tell your father (perhaps it would be better to write it) that, while you shall always be ready to go to the very furthest length you can in obeying him, there are some points on which you feel that you have a higher duty. That you feel that you need that counsel from a priest, and that Absolution which the Church clearly allows you to have; that you intend, however painful it must be to disobey him, to avail yourself of it."[2] On February 22, 1855, he wrote to her:—"I cannot feel happy about the state in which matters stand as regards your father. It is a sad necessity (if it be a necessity) for me to write, as this letter must be sent, *under cover, to a third person*."[3] Again, on the following November 27th he wrote to her:—"This kind of correspondence ought not to go on, because it is in your power to end it. Only be firm now, only insist on an answer, and one way or the other it will be terminated. *I never direct to you under cover to Miss Parker* without pain." It may have caused him pain, but he continued to do it. The Miss Parker here mentioned was Mr. Scobell's Infant Schoolmistress. These letters, from which I have just quoted (published by Mr. Neale himself), fully prove Mr. Scobell's charge against him of "carrying on, by letter, under cover to the Mistress of my Infants' School, a clandestine correspondence with my daughter while in my house." Mr. Neale did not dare to deny that he had "secret meetings" with Miss Scobell in her father's Infant School House, or that he there, vested in surplice,

---

[1] *The Lewes Riots.* By the Rev. J. M. Neale, p. 39.
[2] *Ibid.* p. 10.   [3] *Ibid.* p. 10.

clandestinely heard her Confessions, and never wrote a word himself to her father about it. Not until two years after her first Confession did Miss Scobell's father know the name of her Father Confessor, and even then not through her action, or that of Mr. Neale, but through a penitent letter from Miss M. B. Parker, the Infant Schoolmistress. She wrote to her Rector on February 10, 1857, to acknowledge her double dealing :—"I have for a long time," she said, "been labouring under the weight of an evil conscience, inasmuch as I promised to be faithful to the trust placed in me by yourself with reference to one of your family. Out of kindness to Miss Scobell, I have been induced to allow her the use of my sitting-room, to meet a person [Mr. Neale] whom I never before saw in my life; and what is more I deceived you in this thing, in that I ought to have told you, but I did not see the harm in it then, but I have since, and do now, to my sorrow."[1] On the receipt of this letter Mr. Scobell at once wrote to Mr. Neale the letter containing the six charges quoted above.

And what, it will be asked, was Mr. Neale's defence; what were the charges which he, in return, had to bring against Mr. Scobell? Briefly, it was that he and the Sisters of Mercy who had enticed Miss Scobell into the Sisterhood, were justified in doing so, because Mr. Scobell had been tyrannical and unkind to his daughter. But on looking through the evidence produced, I find that the supposed tyranny consisted in a firm refusal to give his consent to his daughter going to Confession, or becoming a Sister of Mercy. And why should he be compelled to give his consent, against both his reason and his conscience? He was a decided Protestant, and conscientiously he believed that Auricular Confession and the Conventual life would not be for the spiritual benefit of his child. There was eloquence, faithfulness, and true fatherly affection in his letter to his daughter, on December 8, 1855, giving her his refusal to sanction her conduct in going to Confession to Mr.

[1] *The Rev. J. M. Neale and the Institute of St Margaret's, East Grinstead.* By the Rev. J. Scobell, p. 8.

Neale, of which he had just heard from her, though he did not for long after know the name of her Confessor:—

"It is," he wrote to her, "my duty to tell you this, even if you give me an unwilling ear. You shall not sin in ignorance. But the question to myself is—can I bear it? For almost thirty years, God knows, I have lived for my children—so did their mother. There was nothing we would not have denied ourselves and borne for them. But there are things which man or woman cannot resolve—cannot effect. I do not feel it to be in my power to promise to bear what you now propose to me. For me to live at home without family privacy—to live in fear and subjection to another man—to live in the bondage of distrust—to fear or to think it possible, that my own words, my private thoughts, my most unguarded actions, if they relate to you, are noting down, to be laid at the feet of another man by my kneeling, captive, misdoing daughter! and this, a proposal, not for a week, for a month, but for years, and for life! 'Tis more than I can promise to bear and endure with patience, with contentment, with reconciliation, with fulness of family love. . . . Be wise, my dear Emily, in time. Retrace your steps. You have begun to do so in small things, advance upon greater. . . . I must not write more; my heart yearns to you. Dismiss 'secrets' and secrecy; never did good come of them when interrupting the natural love between father and child, husband and wife. Increase and renew your confidence. Put away jealousy and pride and every insubordinate temper and practice, and seek without pain and without mortification to be loving and amiable, faithful and obedient. Do this; pray for this; obtain this, and all will be well. God will sanctify everything to your use and improvement. Be strong in faith, and you shall subdue these mountains. Be in spiritual bondage to no man. Live in patience and godly resolution, and be willing in your own sphere, and your own proper calling, to take up your cross daily, and follow the Lamb whither He goeth."[1]

Is this, I ask, the letter of a tyrant, a cruel and unfeeling father? Rather is it not full of affection and anxiety for the welfare of a beloved daughter? It is certainly decided. Mr. Scobell was, undoubtedly, a firm man, and it may be that from time to time he manifested the irritability of firm men. He had to deal with a daughter who, being in her early childhood an invalid, had been petted and made

---

[1] *A Reply to the Postscript of the Rev. John M. Neale.* By the Rev. J. Scobell, p. 8. London: Nisbet. 1858.

much of by her affectionate father. When other children came he divided his love with them, with the result that this one became peevish, jealous, and often sulky. Mr. Neale further pleaded, in self-defence, that he had urged Miss Scobell to tell her father that she had been to Confession. Just so. He was quite willing that *she* should bear the brunt of her father's displeasure; but he took good care, so far as he could, to keep himself safe from her father's wrath. There was nothing very courageous in this. On this point, it may be well to cite here the testimony of three trustworthy witnesses. The first is that of Hannah Potter, who made a special declaration on the subject, dated December 11, 1857, in the course of which she said :—

"Miss Scobell first spoke to me of Confession as applying to some third person, and asked my opinion of it. Afterwards she told me it was herself, and said Mr. Neale had come to her, and she had made one Confession to him. She said it was a very hard and long Confession; that he said he must know all or he could advise her in nothing. That she had drawn up a paper from four years old and upwards, and read it, as a Confession, to Mr. Neale. That she had suffered very much in doing this in body and mind, and from the questions arising out of it. Having done this she thought she had done all. But Mr. Neale said, 'No! having done thus much you must go on and continue to confess.' If he would have been satisfied, I gathered from her that she would rather not. She wished to tell her father all this. At first Mr. Neale made no objection to this being told to her father; but then he wrote *and forbade his name being mentioned*, and that was the reason why all Mr. Neale's letters were sent under cover to the Infant Schoolmistress, and not direct to her. Miss Scobell *persevered in wishing and requesting that Mr. Neale's name should be made known to her father*, with all else that had occurred. *Mr. Neale opposed that*, and promised at some future time to give the reason why, and added that *if she did disclose his name contrary to his wishes*, she might confess, but *he would not absolve her*. . . . After this her Confessions went on without informing her father."[1]

It makes one burn with indignation to thus witness this cowardly Father Confessor trying to suppress the honour-

[1] *A Letter to the Rev. John M. Neale.* By the Rev. John Scobell, p. 10. London: Nisbet. 1857.

able desire in this young lady's breast to be open and above-board with her father. He had to resort to threats to accomplish his wishes, threats to withhold his absolution, which she was not strong enough to resist. Why was he ashamed and afraid to be found out? He had no objection to act like a snake in the grass, but he trembled with a cowardly fear at exposure in the light of day. And now we come to the testimony of Miss Parker, the Infant School-mistress, dated December 10, 1857:—

"I distinctly remember Miss Scobell's wish and desire, strongly expressed to me, that both she and I should make known to her father, the Revd. J. Scobell, the fact of Mr. Neale's visits to her in my sitting-room, and of her practice of Confession to him, and of receiving Absolution from him. This was not long after her first Confession to Mr. Neale. She said she would rather do this herself, but if that could not be allowed, she wished I could do it. She said she had made this her desire known to Mr. Neale, and requested his permission to do so, but that *Mr. Neale positively forbade it, and threatened that if she did so, he would not give her Absolution.* She would not therefore tell her father, or allow me to do so; for, she said, Mr. Neale's wish ought to be her and my wish also."[1]

Early in December 1855, Miss Scobell wrote a letter to her father stating that she had been to Confession, but not giving the name of her Confessor. She wrote this letter in the presence of Miss Parker, and when the father's reply came back it was sent on to Mr. Neale to read, who at once, fearing, no doubt, that he would lose his penitent, sent word that he would come over from East Grinstead to Lewes to see Miss Scobell. Miss Parker states that when Miss Scobell heard from her that her Father Confessor was coming to see her—

"She was very sorry, and cried, and said, 'Oh dear, he is coming again! What shall I do! I suppose I must see him.' On Friday the 21st December he did come, sent to say he wished to see her, and they had another *long interview, from two to half-past five p.m.*, at my room. When he went away I went in, and she was weeping and in an exhausted state and hysterical. I was frightened, and cried too. I made her coffee and quieted her. She was not

---

[1] *A Letter to the Rev. John M. Neale.* By the Rev. John Scobell, p. 9.

able to walk home alone, she shook so violently; she could not have got along without my arm. I went back to tea and returned again to the Rectory in the course of the evening, and sat with her two or three hours in her bedroom; she was very weak, and cried again more than once. She said 'she could not have her own way in anything.' She said 'he overpowered her,' and she supposed it was right to give up her own will, for she must do as he bid her; I understood this to mean that else (as before) he would not give her absolution. And thus I understood that the hope of returning to a good understanding with her father was given up by her for lost."[1]

Thus do these Ritualistic Father Confessors come in between daughters and their parents, and disturb the peace of families, acquiring thereby a greater power in the household than is possessed by either father or mother. Who can wonder that when Mr. Scobell came to quote this last declaration of Miss Parker, in his published *Letter to the Rev. John M. Neale,* he should comment on it in the following righteously indignant terms:—" *This* was the oppression that was intolerable—an evil angel had stepped in and the waters were as troubled as before. You [Mr. Neale] were an incubus which no effort or cry of mine could dislodge, and you truly say it was possible I might, as a last remedy, have broken up my establishment, and gone to another land for refuge. I felt a stabbing in the dark! a hidden voice replying—another's eye lurking—another hand guiding—a relentless heart plotting against a child, whom for more than twenty years of her short life [2] I had loved with uninterrupted and fullest affection, returned by her with all the ardour of an enthusiastic temperament. Oh, for the love of God and man desist—rash man, desist—with all who act with you or like you, and never drive another fellow-creature to agony and desperation by your boasted, but empty, evil-working, ungodly 'Confessions.'"[3]

As to the third witness, another daughter of Mr. Scobell, I give her testimony in the words of her father:—" As regards the matter of 'secrecy.' In addition to what has been already said, I give the testimony of a daughter. She has often

---

[1] *A Letter to the Rev. John M. Neale.* By the Rev. John Scobell, p. 17.
[2] Miss Scobell was 27 at her death.
[3] *A Letter to the Rev. John M. Neale.* By the Rev. John Scobell, p. 17.

heard her deceased sister say, that the reason why she so often refused her father the name of her guide, was the unwillingness of that unknown gentleman to have his name mentioned; and that her sister believed the reason to be his dread of the further displeasure of the Bishop."[1]

There was one statement in the fifth section of Mr. Scobell's indictment of Mr. Neale which he was unable to prove. It was contained in these words:—"And give herself and whatever income and property she may have, to an establishment at or near East Grinstead." I happen to know that one of the rules of the Sisterhood at that time was that a Sister was not compelled to give *all* her property to the Sisterhood. Before entering the Convent, Miss Scobell promised three of her relatives that she would not leave, by will, any of her property to the St. Margaret's Sisterhood; it should only have her annual income during her life. But on her deathbed she made a will giving the Sisterhood £400 (the rest she gave to a brother), and making Mr. Neale and the Mother Superior her sole executors, instead of her father. Mr. Neale declared that he in no way interfered in the matter of making the will, and was not present when it was made by a solicitor who was sent for. But the question here arises, how far was she influenced in the Confessional? Some of the Sisters, at least, were certainly expected to mention the disposal of their property, to their Confessors, in the Confessional. Only the year after Miss Scobell died, Mr. Neale himself gave a secret address on the subject to the Sisterhood, which was subsequently printed for their secret use, and of which I possess a copy:—"A Sister coming to us," said Mr. Neale, "and able to pay the dowry of this House, is at perfect liberty to dispose of the rest of her money as she pleases, provided it be not on herself. She may give it to whom she will, without mentioning the subject even in Confession. A Sister coming to us, and not able to pay any, or all, of the dowry of this House, *is then bound to mention in Confession why not, and to tell the Priest how she disposes of her income.*"[2] Here, then, is a case in which the priest uses the Con-

---

[1] *A Reply to the Postscript*, p. 9.
[2] *The Spirit of the Founder*, p. 11.

fessional to interfere with the money and property of the Sister. Can we, for one moment, suppose that this is the only case in which it is used for this purpose? And is there not grave reason to fear that, even outside of Convent walls, the Confessional is used for the same purpose?

I have devoted a considerable amount of space to this case, because I am not without hope that it will serve as a warning to parents, leading them to keep a watchful eye on the proceedings of any Father Confessor who may be seeking to influence their daughters.

The question of Auricular Confession was very much discussed in London and the provinces in 1858, in consequence of the Bishop of London (Dr. Tait) having withdrawn the licence of the Rev. Alfred Poole, Curate of St. Barnabas', Pimlico, under the Hon. and Rev. Robert Liddell, Vicar of St. Paul's, Knightsbridge, the mother parish. The licence was withdrawn on the ground that Mr. Poole had advocated systematic Confession to priests, and had asked females improper questions on the Seventh Commandment. A statement of this case, on behalf of Mr. Poole, was published in 1864,[1] on which I mainly rely for my account of the proceedings and facts.

A formal complaint against Mr. Poole was forwarded to the Bishop of London, on February 26, 1858, by the Hon. Rev. F. Baring, together with the written evidence of three women who had been to Confession to Mr. Poole. The Bishop thereupon sent for the latter gentleman, and read to him the statements of the women. "Mr. Poole," says the document issued in his defence, "denied before the Bishop most solemnly that he ever put to the women, whose statements are above referred to, or to any persons, the objectionable questions contained in them, or any questions of a similar import; and he asserted to the Bishop, that the statements, so far as they express that he did so, were entirely and deliberately false."[2] At this interview the Bishop questioned Mr. Poole upon the general subject of Confession. Later on, Mr. Poole had a

[1] *An Authentic Statement and Report of the Case of the Rev. Alfred Poole*, pp. 140. London: Joseph Masters. 1864.
[2] *Ibid.* p. 4.

second interview with the Bishop, who again questioned him as to his views and practice, taking on this occasion written notes of his replies. The result was that on May 8, 1858, the Bishop wrote to Mr. Poole:—

"While I fully admit that the statements you have made to me, tend to make me look with much suspicion upon the particular evidence laid before me, I regret to say, that quite independently of that evidence, *I am led by your own admissions* to regard the course you are in the habit of pursuing, in reference to Confession, as likely to cause scandal and injury to the Church. I feel especially, that this questioning of females on the subject of the violations of the Seventh Commandment is of a dangerous tendency; and I am convinced, generally, that the sort of systematic admission of your people to Confession and Absolution, *which you have allowed to be* your practice, ought not to take place.

"Under these circumstances, I feel I ought to mark my sense of the impropriety of what *you describe* as your practice, and I shall therefore feel myself bound, though with great pain, to withdraw your licence as Curate of S. Barnabas', and shall send you formal notice accordingly."[1]

To this letter Mr. Poole replied, on May 11th, asking the Bishop to "point out what are the particulars, either as regards my admissions, to which you refer, or anything I have done, on which your lordship's severe animadversion is founded." Two days later the Bishop answered:—"I have already stated that what I object to in the course which *you admitted to me* that you pursue, is, that questioning, especially of females, on the subject of violations of the Seventh Commandment, which seems to me of very dangerous tendency, and a systematic admission of your people to Confession and Absolution, going beyond anything contemplated by the services or teaching of our Church."[2] To this statement Mr. Poole replied:—"The only admission I have made upon this point is, that I asked questions in the particular instance alluded to, *because I was requested by the person to do so*—knowing beforehand that these were the very sins which she came to confess. Am I to understand that your lordship condemns me without previous

[1] *An Authentic Statement and Report of the Case of the Rev. Alfred Poole,* p. 6. [2] *Ibid.* p. 8.

advice or remonstrance given on so difficult a point of discretion, in which I am borne out by the approval of *my Incumbent*, viz.—that of asking any questions on a certain Commandment, when requested to do so by the penitent herself, and when the refusal to do so might hinder the penitent from 'opening her griefs?'"[1] Three days later the Bishop sent Mr. Poole notice that unless he could "show cause to the contrary" either personally at London House, or "in writing," he should at once withdraw his licence. The accused preferred to show cause in writing, and did so in a letter dated May 21st, in which he remarked:—

"The ground upon which your lordship intimates your intention to withdraw my licence is, that 'admitting females to Confession, I address to them questions of a character calculated to bring scandal on the Church.'

"This charge is made in general terms, and I do not know in what way I can meet it, unless it be by a general, but a solemn and entire, denial of its truth. I admit that when persons, male or female, have sought my ministry in Confession, I have put to them such questions as have been suggested by the matters confessed, which have appeared to me necessary, in order to enable me to give the 'counsel and advice' which the case required. But I solemnly assert that I have never put any questions of a nature, or in a manner, or in language 'calculated to bring scandal on the Church,' or otherwise, than was calculated to assist the penitent, and to enable him or her to receive more effectually the consolation or advice which, as the minister of the church, it was my duty to impart."[2]

Mr. Poole concluded by demanding, as of right, "that my accusers may be brought before me, and that I may meet them face to face, and be allowed such assistance as I may require for my defence; and for this purpose I request your lordship to allow me to be furnished with a statement in writing of the particular charges which I may be required to meet." As a matter of fact, Mr. Poole had already, as we have seen, been furnished by the Bishop with a written statement of charges, and as to the other demands the Counsel for the Bishop, when the

[1] *An Authentic Statement and Report of the Case of the Rev. Alfred Poole*, p. 10. [2] *Ibid.* p. 12.

case was being subsequently heard before the Archbishop, said:—"It had been asked, why was not Mr. Poole afforded the opportunity of showing that the statements of the witnesses were untrue, and putting a different complexion on the matter? Now, as there were no persons present but Mr. Poole and the women, Mr. Poole was the only person who could reply to their statements; and the Bishop handed the depositions to Mr. Poole, who made such comments upon them as he thought desirable; and these comments and the admissions made by Mr. Poole himself were, in the opinion of the Bishop, inconsistent with the law and practice of the Church, and quite sufficient to show that Mr. Poole had been guilty of grievous indiscretion in the performance of the duties of his office."[1]

The Bishop, in his letter of May 8th, had practically cast off the evidence of the women witnesses, and had only acted on it so far as it had been confirmed by Mr. Poole himself. As to one of these witnesses, the Bishop's Counsel said:—"With respect to the questions which the woman stated to have been put to her, he did not ask the Court to believe anything further than the admissions of Mr. Poole himself on that subject."[2] And again, the Counsel said:—"His learned friends had stated their inability to discover whether the Bishop had acted upon a belief of the evidence of these women. This seemed rather unfair towards the Bishop, when he stated that he was acting on Mr. Poole's own admissions, and when it was perfectly clear that he was only acting on their evidence so far as it was confirmed by Mr. Poole himself. The Bishop, therefore, was not acting on conflicting, but on concurrent testimony, *and surely Mr. Poole had no right to complain of being judged on statements which he was not prepared to deny.*"[3] From his first interview with Mr. Poole the Bishop had accepted fully his denial that he had ever put to the women the particular questions specified. His lordship could not well have acted otherwise, for the women were persons of notoriously immoral character, whose evidence could not

[1] *An Authentic Statement and Report of the Case of the Rev. Alfred Pool* p. 73.
[2] *Ibid.* p. 75.
[3] *Ibid.* p. 77.

be accepted by itself. And therefore he relied on what the counsel termed "the admissions of Mr. Poole himself." It is important and right to bear in mind that throughout the whole of the proceedings no charge was brought by the Bishop or any one else, against Mr. Poole himself, nor was it suggested in any way that he had acted from evil or prurient motives. On the contrary, writing to the Churchwardens of St. Barnabas' on June 24, 1858, in reply to an address in favour of Mr. Poole, sent by the Communicants, his lordship emphatically said:—"I beg to thank you for the opportunity you have given me of stating that I fully believe him to be a conscientious and upright man."[1]

If I be asked why I devote so much space to this particular case, I reply that I do so because of its importance in the present day, when the Confessional, in its most objectionable form, is far more prevalent than it was in 1858; and the evil complained of—questioning women on the Seventh Commandment—far greater than ever before. In this particular case, when disguise was no longer available, it was thrown off; the fact that women were questioned in this way by Puseyite Confessors was unblushingly avowed, and actually defended by one of Mr. Poole's Counsel, in the Archbishop's Court. A meeting of the Communicants of St. Barnabas' was held on June 29th, at which it was unanimously resolved to send to the Bishop a letter on this case of Mr. Poole, which, amongst others, contained the following statement:—

"It is true also that in your correspondence you specify as objectionable Mr. Poole's questioning of females admitted to Confession; but this also is manifestly only a general charge, and it appears to us that the propriety or impropriety of such a practice must depend on the prior and larger one, of the propriety of Confession altogether. For if the practice of Confession be, as we hold it is, the *Right of the People*, which the clergy *may not* refuse when 'any come to' them for it, *then it cannot be more improper to question them upon the violation of the Seventh than of any of the other Commandments; or, to question females upon it*, if they present themselves for Confession, *than males.*"[2]

---

[1] *An Authentic Statement and Report of the Case of the Rev Alfred Poole,* p. 20. [2] *Ibid.* p. 21.

This is plain speech, at any rate, and I trust that it will not be forgotten. It was the best argument which could be devised in defence of Mr. Poole's conduct; and the only wonder is that the Communicants were not ashamed to make it. Mr. Poole's Vicar, the Hon. and Rev. Robert Liddell, agreed with them on this point. In his published letter to the Bishop of London, he wrote as follows:—

"Your lordship has stated, in your condemnation of Mr. Poole, that you consider the questioning, especially of females, on the subject of violations of the Seventh Commandment, to be of very dangerous tendency. Putting aside, as denied by Mr. Poole, and not yet [August 1858] proven, the particular questions with which he was charged, I most readily admit the difficulty of this part of our duty, the need of much prayer and self-discipline, and the great impropriety, nay, sin, on the part of the Confessor, of asking any questions on this Commandment, *which do not strictly arise out of matters confessed*, or out of the circumstances of the penitent, otherwise known to him; because *his duty is simply to aid the penitent in an unreserved Confession* of past acts of sin, not to suggest fresh evil.

"I hope I may be permitted to consider that this is your lordship's general meaning; for I cannot conceive your lordship to imply that God's ministers are to be more silent upon one part of His holy law than upon another; or that sinners' consciences are to be *least* probed upon that Commandment, which, in spirit and in letter, is, by general admission, most violated."[1]

This, of course, was a defence of asking questions in Confession on the Seventh Commandment, whether of men or women, though with great care on the part of the Confessor. Protestant Churchmen strongly object to any questions whatever being put in Confession on such a subject, to persons of an opposite sex. It is an unmitigated evil, though, as we have seen, defended and glorified in by the Puseyites. Even Mr. Coleridge, in his speech for Mr. Poole before the Archbishop, defended the objectionable practice. He said:—

"If a person wished to confess, the Scriptural course [Where is there 'Scriptural' authority for confessing to priests?] was to place

---

[1] *A Letter to the Bishop of London On Confession and Absolution, with Special Reference to the Case of the Rev. Alfred Poole.* By the Hon. and Rev. Robert Liddell, p. 26. London: J. T. Hayes. 1858.

the precepts of the Decalogue before him, and ask him to examine himself upon those precepts. In that case must the Seventh Commandment be omitted? Where was the authority to be found for such an omission? He admitted the delicacy of the case, and that a prurient person ought to be scouted out of society; but, admitting the *bona-fides* of the person administering the Confession, where was the authority for leaving out one Commandment more than another? If Confession was to be anything more than a mere mockery, *it was impossible to avoid* going into those very questions respecting which the penitent was seeking relief and assistance."[1]

The Bishop formally withdrew Mr. Poole's licence on May 25, 1858, who thereupon appealed to the Archbishop of Canterbury. This was done, says Archbishop Tait's biographer, "with the Bishop's entire approval, and even encouragement."[2] The Archbishop, unfortunately, gave his decision without a formal hearing of Mr. Poole, and confirmed the decision of the Bishop of London on July 9th. On this Mr. Poole applied to the Court of Queen's Bench for a *mandamus* to compel the Archbishop to hear him. In this he was successful, and as a result the case was heard by his Grace on February 18 and 19, 1859, Dr. Lushington, as Dean of Arches, being his Assessor. Counsel were heard on both sides at considerable length, and on March 23, 1859, Dr. Lushington delivered, at Lambeth Palace, his report on the case as Assessor, after which the Archbishop gave his judgment in the following terms :—

"With the able assistance of my learned Assessor, I have given the merits and circumstances of this Appeal my most serious and careful consideration. I am of opinion that the proved and admitted allegations afford in the language of the Statute good and reasonable cause for the revocation of this licence, and that the Lord Bishop of London has exercised a sound discretion in revoking the same.

"And I am further of opinion that the course pursued by the Appellant is not in accordance with the Rubric or doctrine of the Church of England, but most dangerous and likely to produce most serious mischief to the cause of morality and religion."[3]

These two spiritual authorities having dealt with Mr.

[1] *An Authentic Statement*, pp. 69, 70.
[2] *Life of Archbishop Tait*, vol. i. p. 224.
[3] *An Authentic Statement*, p. 95.

THE LAVINGTON CASE

Poole's case, and having decided it against him, the inconsistent Puseyites at once determined to appeal to what they considered a purely State Court, the Judicial Committee of Privy Council, in the hope that it would upset the decision of the Archbishop's Spiritual Court. When the State is willing to put down the Protestant cause, the Ritualists are quite willing to support its decisions, but if it dare to remove one of their pretty ribbons from their backs, the whole party is up in arms directly, protesting with all their power against the State's audacious profanity. The fact is the Ritualists hate and oppose every Court, spiritual or State, and every authority, which dares to contradict and condemn them, no matter how guilty they may be. Mr. Poole appealed to the Judicial Committee, but he did so in vain. After hearing arguments on both sides, their lordships delivered judgment on March 13, 1861, dismissing the appeal, and declaring that, by law, there really was no appeal against the Archbishop's decision, which was final.

At Lavington, Sussex, of which Cardinal Manning was once Rector, and of which parish Bishop Samuel Wilberforce was at the time the Squire and Patron, a controversy broke out as to the alleged Romanising practices of its Rector, the Rev. R. W. Randall. The Rector had as Curate the Rev. E. Randall, who, though bearing the same surname, was in no way related to him. This Curate, though a moderate High Churchman, could not approve of his Rector's advanced teaching. The *National Standard* of August 28, 1858, in calling attention to the controversy which had arisen, said:—" The Rector of Lavington, as we learn, is a clergyman of the most extreme views. During the time that Mr. Edward Randall was his Curate, he was guilty of gross violations of the Rubric, and of sundry most unchurchmanlike irregularities. For instance, it was his habit to cross himself during divine service, to make the sign of the Cross upon the water at Baptism, to mix water with wine at the Eucharist, and to bow to the elements after consecration. . . . On one occasion Mr. E. Randall, while catechising the children at the school, asked them what other name there was for the Lord's Supper? To his astonishment they answered 'The Mass.' Upon his remarking that that was the name the Pope called it by, they informed him that they had been so taught by the Rector. He then asked them how many Sacraments there were? They answered 'Seven,' and enumerated the Romish Sacraments. He called upon the Rector, and informed him of what the children had said, and of the manner in which he had corrected them. The Rector rebuked him, and expressed his determination to go to the school, and unteach the Curate's instruction." Subsequently, the Rev. E. Randall made a statement, asserting the above facts as true, at the office of the Protestant Defence Society, in the presence of five clergymen.[1] A few days after the above-mentioned interview with the Rector, Mr. E. Randall again went into the school, when the schoolmaster put into his hands a paper, in the Rector's handwriting, containing instruction on the Seven Sacraments, which, he said, had been given to him in December 1857 by the Rector, in order that its contents might be taught by him to the school children. This paper was as follows:—

"BAPTISM.—A Sacrament instituted by Christ for the spiritual regeneration of men, which is performed by the washing of water, with the expressed invocation of the Holy Trinity.

"CONFIRMATION.—A Sacrament in which, by the laying on of hands, according to the prescribed form, fresh strength is given to the baptized, that they may believe firmly, and more constantly and bravely contend for the faith.

"EUCHARIST.—A Sacrament of the new law, instituted by our Lord, for the heavenly nourishment of our souls, in which the Body and Blood of Christ are truly and really present under the form of bread and wine.

"PENANCE.—A Sacrament instituted for the forgiveness of sins, after Baptism, by the Absolution of the priest.

"EXTREME UNCTION.—A Sacrament of the new law, consisting of unction with oil and the prayer of the priest, by which salvation of the soul is conferred on a Christian grievously sick, and even health of the body, if that be good for the soul.

"ORDERS.—A Sacrament of the new law, in which spiritual power is given to the ordained.

---

[1] *A Statement Respecting the Romish Doctrines and Practices of the Rev. R. W. Randall.* By An English Churchman, p. 21. London: Hatchard. 1858.

"MATRIMONY.—A Sacrament of the new law, in which a baptized man and woman naturally give themselves each to the other to live together continually.

"SACRAMENTS.—Outward ceremonies instituted to give grace.

"CONFIRMATION.—A Sacrament given by a Bishop to strengthen and confirm our faith."[1]

The Curate sent this paper to the Bishop of Chichester, in the absence from home of his Rector, and was severely censured by his lordship for doing so without first having waited until he could discuss the matter with his Rector on his return home. The Bishop wrote to the Rector on the subject, and in a letter to the Curate (dated February 23, 1858), declared himself satisfied with the Rector's explanation. What that explanation was remained unknown to the public until September 16th, when the Rector wrote to the *Brighton Gazette* of that date:—"The very paper of notes from which you quote [that is, the document quoted above] was intended to be used in the school, not by itself, but together with other more detailed papers, for the purpose of showing what the Church of England believes, and, at the same time, of guarding the children against the Romish errors which she has rejected."[2] The extraordinary document in question was shown to be substantially a translation into English from Den's *Theology* and the *Catechism of the Council of Trent*. The Rector's letter to the *Brighton Gazette* brought a reply in the next issue of the same paper, dated September 18th, from Mr. H. R. Harding, Choirmaster of Lavington Church, in the course of which he said:—

"Alarmed at this state of things I went [on February 3rd] to the Schoolmaster, who produced the paper of which I enclose an exact entire copy [see above]. This paper, bearing plain evidence that it was intended to be taught, by the fact of the five questionable Sacraments being repeated, was in the handwriting of the Rector, and the Schoolmaster assured me it had been given to him *to be taught in the school*. He was very clear, it was the last and only paper he had received from the Rector for many months, and that it was not intended to be modified by any other paper or any other teaching. He also asserted again and again that the words the

---

[1] *A Statement Respecting the Romish Doctrines and Practices of the Rev. R. W. Randall*, pp. 31, 32. [2] *Ibid.* p. 24.

Rector used on giving him the paper were, 'The former papers would be a guide for *me* in teaching the Sacraments, but they are not sufficiently explicit for *you*; this paper is what I want you to teach.' . . . In the evening of that day [February 7th] the Rector came to me, to satisfy my mind about the paper. The Schoolmaster was present. The discussion lasted a long time, *and the paper was fully defended by the Rector*, and certainly he neither brought out that the paper was intended to have been taken with others, nor to illustrate the Church of Rome. At the conclusion of this interview, the Rector said to the Master, 'If your mind is not made up to the paper, I don't wish you to teach it,' and asked for the paper."[1]

To this letter of the Choirmaster, who had resigned his situation in consequence of the Rector's Romanising, the latter gentleman made no reply, and so far as I can ascertain, never publicly denied the truthfulness of the statements it contained. The ex-Choirmaster's letter was followed, a month later, by one written to the *National Standard*, by the Schoolmaster, Mr. William Marigold, enclosing a letter which he had addressed to the Rector, on October 21, 1858, in the course of which he said:—

"Every statement with reference to the teaching which appears in your letter to the *Brighton Gazette* of the 16th September I utterly contradict; and every word of Mr. Harding's letter to the same paper of 23rd September, in reply to yours, I fully confirm and accept as my own.

"You know well that you did give me that paper containing the Seven Sacraments *to teach as it stands*. You know well that you used every means to convince me the paper as it stands is consistent with the Church of England's teaching, and that the Bishop had accepted it as such. You know well that when I spoke to you in consequence of the reports which were in circulation, that you had satisfied the Bishop by telling his lordship you had given the paper merely to show what the Church of Rome teaches, you arose from your seat pale and trembling with emotion, and exclaimed, '*That's a lie.*' . . .

"You will perhaps say I am *prompted* to this course, or that I have some prospect of advantage in it. 'Tis not so. I have no situation in view, nor any place to turn to when I leave you. But I will not be a party to such a system, nor to such conduct."[2]

---

[1] *A Statement Respecting the Romish Doctrines and Practices of the Rev. R. W. Randall*, pp. 28, 29. [2] *Ibid.* p. 34.

The Rector never, so far as I can ascertain, gave any public denial to the statements made by the Schoolmaster, any more than before he had given to those of the Choirmaster, men, both of them, of unblemished reputation, and who were certainly not moved by any feelings of personal ill-will towards the Rector. Nor did the Rev. R. W. Randall deny that his Curate had received the alleged answers from the school children as to the Mass and Seven Sacraments, nor that he had adopted the ritual and ceremonies complained of, though he gave up those portions of his ritual to which the Bishop objected. He had, it is true, two Bishops on his side, viz., those of Oxford and Chichester. Since then the former Rector of Lavington has developed his anti-Protestant views greatly, and has become a Vice-President of the Romanising and rebel English Church Union, and a leading man in the Romanising Confraternity of the Blessed Sacrament, established for the special purpose of bringing back the self-same Sacrifice of the Mass which our Protestant Martyrs died to put down. And he has obtained also great favour and honour at the hands of the State. In 1892 he was made Dean of Chichester, an office which he still holds.

The Bishop of Chichester was requested to issue a Commission, under the Church Discipline Act, with a view to a prosecution of the Rev. R. W. Randall for teaching false doctrine, and for illegal practices; but he declined to do so. Thereupon the Rev. C. P. Golightly applied to the Court of Queen's Bench for a writ of *mandamus* commanding the Bishop of Chichester to issue a Commission under the Act. The case was heard on June 6, 1859, and judgment was delivered on June 15th, refusing to grant the application.

MR. JUSTICE HILL said:—"If it were necessary to give an opinion on the construction of the 3rd Section of the Statute [Church Discipline Act], I should have thought that the writ ought to issue, so that a question of such importance might be decided on the return in such manner that the judgment of this Court might be reviewed by a Court of Error. I am not satisfied that it is a mere matter in the discretion of the Bishop whether he will issue a Commission if a proper complaint be made by a party who is entitled to complain. But it appears to me not necessary to give any opinion on the construction of the Statute. This is an application to the discretion of the Court to issue the prerogative writ of *mandamus*. That the Court has a discretion whether the writ shall be issued or not was distinctly recognised by *Ashurst J.* in *R.* v. *Bishop of Chester* (1 T. R. 403). In the case before the Court the party applying for the writ of *mandamus* is a total stranger to the Diocese of Chichester, and in no way interested in the matter charged against Mr. Randall, more than any other Clerk in Holy Orders in the most remote part of the kingdom. I think it would be productive of the greatest inconvenience and mischief if this Court were to lend its aid to any stranger to compel a Bishop to issue a Commission in any particular case, and that this Court ought not to interfere upon the application of a party who is not shown to be a party aggrieved or to have some connection with the parish or Diocese. On this short ground, therefore, I think the rule should be discharged."

MR. JUSTICE WIGHTMAN said:—"The real question in the case is, whether the Bishop has any discretion in the matter, or whether, under the provisions of the Church Discipline Act, 3 & 4 Victoria, chap. 86, he is absolutely bound, without previous examination or inquiry himself, to issue a Commission of Inquiry as directed by that Statute, if any clergyman of his Diocese is charged with an offence against the laws ecclesiastical. . . . I cannot think that such can have been the intention of the Legislature, but that it was intended, when this new mode of procedure was instituted, to invest the Bishop with a power to cause inquiry to be made in cases where it appeared to them that the interests of the Church and the public required it, and in the belief that such power would be duly and properly exercised whenever a proper case arose; and that it was better for the interest of religion and the public that the Bishop, who is the overseer or superintendent of religious matters in the Church, should be intrusted with a discretion as to the propriety of issuing a Commission of Inquiry in such cases, than that it should be left entirely, as expressed by Sir W. Scott, to the judgment or passions of private persons, who, under the influence of zeal, or prejudice, or fancy, might call peremptorily upon the Bishop, without any real or substantial ground, upon a mere scandal or evil report, to institute proceedings which would cause at once expense, trouble, and vexation, and tend to create disturbance and scandal in the Church. I am, therefore, of opinion that the Bishop might exercise his discretion as to the propriety of issuing a Commission in this case, and that the present rule for a *mandamus* should be discharged."[1]

Mr. Justice Wightman's opinion, that the Church Dis-

[1] *Guardian*, July 6, 1859, p. 583.

cipline Act gave to the Bishop the right to veto proceedings under that Act, was upheld by the House of Lords on March 23, 1880, in the case of *Julius* v. *Bishop of Oxford.* The Episcopal Veto has thus been legally established; but there is at present a widespread and rapidly-growing feeling in the country that the Bishops have greatly and inexcusably misused the Veto, by shamelessly barring the Courts of Justice to those who had a right to enter, and whose case was a strong one. They have used the Episcopal Veto to protect flagrant law-breakers from the just punishment which was their due, and have thus encouraged the very lawlessness which they ought to have been the first to suppress. It is felt that it is no longer safe to entrust them with the power of vetoing ecclesiastical prosecutions. The fact that they are so costly and wearisome is alone sufficient to prevent any man, or any body of men, from taking up the part of prosecutor without a strong *prima facie* case in hand. The Episcopal Veto is at present the shield of lawlessness, and the oppressor of justice. It must be swept away, and the sooner the better.

For many years the Puseyites had been adding to their stock of literature of a Romanising tendency, which had become more Romish as the years went on. Some of the works which they produced were privately printed, and were circulated with great care, lest they should fall into Protestant hands. One of the most remarkable books of this class was printed in 1855, primarily for use in the Scottish Episcopal Church, but also adapted for use in the Church of England. It was written by the Rev. William Wright, LL.D., who died before it was printed, and it bore the title of *Directorium Scoticanum et Anglicanum.* The book simply reproduced the directions of the Church of Rome as to what Vestments Ministers should wear at Holy Communion, and what ornaments of the Church were required; together with the directions of the Papal Church as to rites and ceremonies. The book was, in brief, unblushing Popery. At length, in 1858, the Rev. John Purchas, M.A., published his now well-known *Directorium Anglicanum,* containing all the superstitions and extravagances of the Sacrifice of the Mass, as found in the Roman Church. At about the same time Mr. Purchas printed for private circulation a translation of the Cautels of the Mass from the Sarum Missal,[1] which were so extraordinary that I gave a selection of them in the last chapter of my *Secret History*, as they appeared in the fourth edition of the *Directorium Anglicanum*. These Cautels were secretly circulated for seven years before it was considered safe to give them to the public. They were published for the first time, in the second edition of the *Directorium*, in 1865. This latter book created a great sensation when it first appeared, was sold out within six months, and remained out of print until 1865. The last edition, the fourth, was issued in 1879, edited by the Rev. F. G. Lee, one of the Bishops of the notorious and secret Order of Corporate Reunion. The work has had a very large circulation amongst the clergy, and this fact affords ample evidence of the wide extent to which Roman Catholic ritual has spread amongst the clergy in the pay of the Church of England.

At about this period the subject of Theological Colleges occupied a great deal of public attention. As far back as 1853, Mr. James Bateman, F.R.S., a Staffordshire gentleman, called attention to this important subject at a meeting held at Stoke-on-Trent, to consider the advisability of founding a new Theological College at Lichfield. He proved clearly that Wells Theological College and Chichester Diocesan College were already under Tractarian control, and asserted that there was grave reason to fear that the proposed College at Lichfield would turn out a similar institution, a fear which the subsequent history of that College has more than justified. "This Lichfield scheme," said Mr. Bateman, "is but part of an extensive scheme of Tractarian policy, which contemplates the creation of similar establishments in every Diocese throughout the land, and which—whenever the ecclesiastical *cordon* shall have become complete—would effectually exclude from the walls of our

---

[1] *A Translation of the Cautels of the Sarum Ritual.* By John Purchas, M.A., pp. 14. 4to. Privately printed. 1858.

Church, every Minister holding to the pure principles of the Reformation."[1]

As years went on, the need of Mr. Bateman's warning became more and more apparent. A Theological College had been established at Cuddesdon, near Oxford, which had given cause for anxiety to the decided Protestants of the Diocese. They perhaps suspected more than they could actually prove at that time, but when, in January 1858, the *Quarterly Review* made an attack on Cuddesdon, the Rev. C. P. Golightly took the subject up with all the ardour for which he was famed. He issued a circular letter to the clergy and laity of the Diocese of Oxford, calling attention to the article in the *Quarterly Review*, summarising its allegations against Cuddesdon College, and declaring that the tendency of the teaching given therein was "to sow broadcast the seeds of Romish perversion in the counties of Oxfordshire, Berkshire, and Buckinghamshire."[2] The Bishop of Oxford (Dr. S. Wilberforce), lost not a day in dealing with the charges, which were as follows:—" 1. That the Chapel of the College is 'fitted up with every fantastic decoration to which a party meaning has been assigned.' 2. That the so-called Altar 'affects in every particular the closest approximation to the Romish model.' 3. That the service of the Sacrament of the Lord's Supper is 'conducted with genuflexions, rinsings of cups in the piscina, and other ceremonial acts, foreign to the ritual and usages of the Church of England.' 4. And, lastly, that a service-book is in use in the Chapel 'concocted from the seven Canonical Hours of the Romish Church.'"[3] The Bishop promptly called the atttention of the Principal of the College (the Rev. Alfred Pott), to these accusations, who replied, denying the truth of the charges altogether, and requesting his lordship to appoint a Commission, consisting of the three Archdeacons of the Diocese, "to examine into the truth of Mr. Golightly's allegations, and report officially to you thereon, as the Visitor of the College." To this request the Bishop agreed, and appointed the three Archdeacons accordingly,

---

[1] *The Tractarian Tendency of Diocesan Theological Colleges.* By James Bateman, Esq., M.A., F.R.S., p. 27. London: Seeleys. 1853.
[2] *Guardian*, February 3, 1858, p. 86.
[3] *Ibid.*

forgetting that the Protestant party would have had more confidence in the Commission, if it had been partly composed of men who were not the officials of the Visitor of the College. However, they made their inquiries, and after they had had an interview with Mr. Golightly, they made their report in February. They dealt with the charges in the order in which they were made:—(1., 2.) "We see no reason for imputing a party meaning to any of these decorations—nevertheless we think it right to express our opinion that there is too lavish a display of ornaments, and we consider that excess of decoration in the Chapel of such an institution has a tendency, on the one hand, to strengthen a prejudice which already exists in some minds against Theological Colleges, and, on the other hand, to encourage in the students a disproportionate regard for the mere accessories of public worship, and to invest them with an over-prominent importance'. The 'so-called altar' is a movable table of wood. It has on the side next the east wall a raised shelf, on which stand two candlesticks. The candles in these are never lighted, except when the Chapel is lighted throughout. . . . At the time of the celebration of Holy Communion the table is covered with a fair linen cloth, without lace or other ornament. A cloth with lace was formerly used; but the use has been discontinued in consequence of the recent judgment of the Privy Council. We find that at one period a small metal cross stood on the shelf of the table. It was given; and was placed there by the donor without objection on the part of the heads of the College; but was removed about a year ago by your lordship's directions." 3. The truth of this charge the Commissioners denied altogether, though they admit that "it was at one time the custom to rinse the Sacramental vessels in the piscina of the Chapel;" but that this practice had "for some time been abandoned." 4. As to the Service-Book in use in the Chapel—"We have examined the prayers and hymns, and think them not only unexceptionable, but highly valuable. The book is certainly not 'concocted from the Seven Canonical Hours of the Romish Church,' nor, in our judgment, does it contain or suggest any doctrine at variance with that of the Church of England. It has, however, been cast in a form which *bears an unfortunate resemblance to the Breviary of the Church of Rome;* and we think it would be much improved if the compilers would abandon the title of Antiphon, and the obsolete designation of the Hours."[1]

The Bishop, in sending on his Archdeacons' report to the Principal of Cuddesdon, actually said :—" I am rejoiced to see that it negatives completely every charge brought against you by my gossiping friend, Mr. Golightly;"[2] though how that could be, when it acknowledged the accuracy of several of his facts, it is hard to see. Mr. Golightly had certainly proved to the Archdeacons that there was need for reform. There was more going on in the College than Mr. Golightly was then aware of. The Bishop himself was by no means satisfied with the existing state of things. He wrote to a friend :—" Then there are things in the actual life [in Cuddesdon College] I wish changed. The tendency to crowd the walls with pictures of the *Mater Dolorosa,* &c., their chimney-pieces with Crosses, their studies with Saints, all offend me and all do incalculable injury to the College in the eyes of chance visitors. The habit of some of our men of kneeling in a sort of rapt prayer on the steps of the Communion Table, when they cannot be *alone* there; when visitors are coming in and going out and talking around them: such prayers should be 'in the closet' with the 'door shut'—and setting apart their grave dangers, as I apprehend them to be to the young men, they really force on visitors the feeling of the strict resemblance to what they see in Belgium, &c., and never in Church of England Churches."[3] The Rev. H. P. Liddon, afterwards widely known as Canon Liddon, of St. Paul's Cathedral, was at this time Vice-Principal of Cuddesdon College, and the Bishop was not satisfied with his teaching and influence—in fact, he was anxious to get rid of him on this account. "It was," says the Bishop's biographer, "a far graver and greater question than one of mere forms

---

[1] *Guardian,* March 3, 1858, p. 183.
[2] *Ibid.*
[3] *Life of Bishop Wilberforce,* vol. ii. p. 368.

and ceremonies which lost to Cuddesdon College the services of its able Vice-Principal. The Principal, in one of his letters to the Bishop, says:—'On the Eucharistic question I feel that, although I and Liddon have never had a word like dispute since we have been together, we are mutually conscious of a difference on this point, and so are our men.' The Bishop, in a letter written about this time, says:—'Our (that is, Liddon's and mine), theological standpoint is not identical. On the great doctrine of the Eucharist we should use somewhat different language and our Ritualistic tendencies would be all coloured by this. On Confession, and its expedient limits, we should also, I think, differ. The Principal entirely agreed with me.'"[1]

And so Mr. Liddon was induced to resign—the Principal had already done so—but the Bishop was anxious that the public should not know the real reason. So he wrote to the Rev. W. J. Butler, Vicar of Wantage, and afterwards Dean of Lincoln:—"Now no reason need be given but that after full deliberation the coming of the new Principal necessitated a new Vice-Principal."[2] The biographer of Bishop Wilberforce denies that Golightly's attack was the cause of Liddon's resignation; but a warm friend of the Oxford Movement, in his sketch of Canon Liddon's life, distinctly asserts that "on account of the attacks that were made upon the College, after five years of laborious and loving work, Liddon resigned."[3] Mr. Golightly's attack was, therefore, not without satisfactory results. Another satisfactory result was seen at the annual festival of the College that year. The *Union*, in giving a friendly notice of the proceedings, remarked that, "evidently in consequence of Mr. Golightly's attack," several changes were made—"A Cross and flowers on the altar, banners, a second celebration, Gregorian music, and a procession up the village have been given up."[4] This organ of the advanced section of the Romanisers was

[1] *Life of Bishop Wilberforce*, vol. ii. p. 366.
[2] *Ibid.* p. 371.
[3] *Five Great Oxford Leaders*. By the Rev. A. B. Donaldson, p. 237. London: Rivingtons. 1900.
[4] *Union*, June 5, 1858, p. 362.

furious at Bishop Wilberforce and the Principal for yielding to the Protestant demands, and charged them with trimming and compromising.

The Oxford Protestant Crusade against Tractarianism was renewed in January 1859, but this time it was directed not specially against Cuddesdon College, but against the Ritualistic Movement throughout the Diocese of Oxford, and included a severe attack on the administration of the Bishop of Oxford himself. The attack was again led by the Rev. C. P. Golightly, in an anonymous pamphlet (the authorship of which was at once widely known), entitled, *Facts and Documeuts Shewing the Alarming State of the Diocese of Oxford*. The author termed himself "neither a High Churchman nor a Low Churchman," but "simply a Protestant, and a true son of the Church of England." He quoted largely from the *Directorium Anglicanum*, because its author, Mr. Purchas, acknowledged his obligations for assistance in compiling that Romanising work to the Rev. T. Chamberlain, Vicar of St. Thomas', Oxford; to the Rev. F. G. Lee, formerly a student of Cuddesdon College, and subsequently a Curate in the Diocese of Oxford;[1] and to the Rev. T. W. Perry, then Curate of Addington, in the same Diocese. He also quoted from the *Churchman's Diary*, of which Mr. Chamberlain was the reputed editor.

"I shall now," continued Mr. Golightly, "proceed to set before the reader a series of extracts from the above-named publications, and to furnish him with a few facts, to show the introduction into the Diocese, actual or attempted, of the following peculiarities of the Romish system, viz., Auricular Confession, Altar Crosses and Crucifixes, Processions and Processional Crosses and Banners, Stone Altars, the Romish Wafer, Mixing Water with the Wine at the Eucharist, Elevation of the Elements, Bowing to the Elements, the Priest Crossing Himself, Unction of the Sick, Prayers for the Dead, Masses for the Dead, Romish Vestments, Romish Ornaments, Sisterhoods. I shall conclude with a few remarks upon Cuddesdon College and the Lavington Case, with especial reference to the position of the Bishop of this Diocese."[2]

---

[1] Since then a Bishop of the secret Order of Corporate Reunion.
[2] *Facts and Documents*. By a Senior Clergyman of the Diocese, p. 11. London: Wertheim, Mackintosh & Co. 1859.

In proof of the existence of Auricular Confession in the Diocese, Mr. Golightly quoted from the *Churchman's Diary*, and referred to the Confessional revelations which had just been made public at Boyne Hill, in the Diocese, and to the Rev. W. Gresley's book, *The Ordinance of Confession*, whose author was at the time Vicar of Boyne Hill. As to the use of Crucifixes, he merely relied on the *Directorium*, without mentioning any instances in which they were in use in the Diocese; but as to Altar Crosses, he said :—"The Bishop of Oxford removed an Altar Cross from the shelf of the Communion Table in Cuddesdon College Chapel; but he defended the use of Altar Crosses, when attached to the east wall of the Church, to the Churchwardens of Holywell Parish, and in a speech (January 8, 1859) at the consecration of Addington Church, near Winslow. He objects, however, to Crucifixes."[1] As to Processions, Processional Crosses, and Banners, after citing the *Directorium*, he added :—"A Procession with Processional Crosses took place at the anniversary of Cuddesdon College in 1855, and was so strongly objected to by some of the clergy, that the Bishop promised that it should not occur again."[2] Yet on January 8th, that very year, his lordship had taken part in a procession at the consecration of Addington Church, near Winslow, in which a Banner was carried, and also a Processional Cross, by the Curate, the Rev. T. W. Perry, one of Mr. Purchas' assistants in bringing out his *Directorium*. The Bishop had consecrated, in 1848, three Cemetery Chapels at Oxford, with illegal Stone Altars, and he was reminded that in addition there were, at that moment, Stone Altars at St. Thomas', Oxford; Wolvercote, Littlemore, St. John's, Sandford, Radley, and Binsey, all in his Diocese. For the charge of using Wafers and the Mixed Chalice, Mr. Golightly quoted the *Directorium*, and as to Elevation of the Elements, he mentioned that it had been practised by the Rev. F. G. Lee, at Kennington Church, near Oxford. For the rest of the charges, viz., Bowing to the Elements, the Priest Crossing Himself, Anointing of the Sick, Prayers and

---

[1] *Facts and Documents*, p. 12.
[2] *Ibid.* p. 13.

Masses for the Dead, Romish Vestments and Ornaments, he quoted only the *Directorium*. Mr. Golightly had a strong case, but it would have been much stronger if he could have proved that the Romanising books he had cited were actually in use in the Diocese. He concluded by giving a list of 125 Members of Oxford University who had seceded to the Church of Rome, including eighty-six clergymen.

I dare say that some of my readers may think these were comparatively small things, when compared with what we see around us to-day; but I may remind them of what the Ritualistic *Church Review* said about them six years later:—"The Protestant is quite right in recognising the simplest attempt at Ritual as the 'thin edge of the wedge.' It is so. . . . It is only the child who is not terrified when the first creeping driblet of water and the few light bubbles announce the advance of the tide; and the Protestant is but a child who does not recognise the danger of the trifling symptoms which are slowly and surely contracting the space of ground upon which he stands."[1] Mr. Golightly recognised the danger, and, to his honour be it recorded, he did his best to protect the Church by raising a warning cry, though he had to pay the penalty of the scoffs and abuse of the men whose unworthy conduct he exposed. But, after all, sensible men know very well that ridicule is not argument.

No sooner was Mr. Golightly's pamphlet published than a great outcry arose in what may now be termed the Ritualistic camp, and great wrath in the Palace of the Bishop of Oxford, whose special failing was that he did not sufficiently curb the extravagances of men who often went further than himself in a wrong direction. Dr. Wilberforce always disliked the man, whether he was a Protestant or a Romaniser, who was the cause of a row. His anger at Mr. Golightly's audacity scarcely knew any bounds. The *Saturday Review* was indecently insulting. "If anybody," it said, "is wanted to do a job extremely dirty and offensive, such as signing a protest complaining of a sermon, or denouncing a brother clergyman, Mr. Golightly is the man for it."

[1] *Church Review*, June 24, 1865, p. 587.

As to the charge against the Bishop of taking part in a procession at Addington, in which a Banner and Processional Cross were carried, the Rev. J. W. Burgon (afterwards Dean of Chichester) gave the following explanation:—"Had the Reverend author of the pamphlet, instead of alarming himself and the Diocese, respectfully asked his lordship how it came to pass that he did not insist on the removal of such a toy [as the Processional Cross] before proceeding with the consecration, he would doubtless have received the same reply which the present writer received when he asked the same question :—'There was no Bishop's procession: and I did not see the toy till it was too late to act; or it was just what I would have done. *In* Church I actually did so, as to the paraphernalia of the Celebration.'"[1] The Bishop's own direct explanation of what took place was given two months later, in reply to an address from seventy-eight of his Protestant clergy :— "The only 'Procession' there," said the Bishop, "was the walking round the new ground to be added to the churchyard, as appointed in the Consecration Service in use in every Diocese in England, and the reading or chanting of the appointed Psalm. The temporary Curate, a stranger to our Diocese and its usages, carried in his hand a Wand, to which he had fastened a small metal Cross. This he did without my knowledge, or that of his Patron; and, as soon as I had the opportunity of speaking to him, at my desire he laid it aside."[2] And so there was a Processional Cross after all; but the Bishop certainly cleared himself from any responsibility or blame for what had taken place. Yet in the very same document in which he completely cleared himself, as to this instance, he actually defended the custom assailed. In their Address to the Bishop the Protestant clergy of the Diocese had said :—"At the Anniversary of Cuddesdon College, and at the consecration or reopening of several Churches, it is reported, and we believe truly, that there have been Processions of Clergymen in Surplices, *with Banners and Crosses*, and chanting Hymns and Psalms:

---

[1] *Guardian*, February 23, 1859, p. 166.
[2] *Address to the Bishop of Oxford of the Rev. E. A. Litton and Other Clergymen of the Diocese*, p. 9. No printer's name or publisher's.

all bearing a close resemblance in many respects to the Romish Processions."¹ The Bishop, in his reply, quoted this statement in full, did not deny that Crosses and Banners were so carried; *defended* what had taken place, and added :—"*I see no objection to such a devout and orderly walking to Church,* . . . and I therefore cannot censure or forbid it."²

The Bishop acknowledged that he had consecrated Cemetery Chapels at Oxford with Stone Altars, but it was without his knowledge, and that subsequently he had used his influence and succeeded in having placed in their room movable tables with wooden legs, but with "stone tops." When such stone slabs had been erected elsewhere in the Diocese, he did not "think it wise to move in the matter," in order to their removal, so long as no "superstitious use" was made of them; indeed, he "saw no objection to their retention."³ Dr. Wilberforce acknowledged that Churchmen in the Diocese did "suffer much from the attempts made *by a few, mostly inexperienced young men*,⁴ to introduce amongst us unusual ornaments or Ritual observances"—so that the Bishop had to acknowledge after all that there *was* just cause for anxiety. In concluding his reply to the Protestant clergy of his Diocese, his lordship censured them for what they had done, declared that the controversy had been "wantonly stirred up," and added the request :—"If at any time any point in my conduct of the Diocese causes you scruple or alarm, that you will tell me privately of your difficulty, instead of flying to inflammatory appeals."⁵ But, unfortunately for his plea, Mr. Golightly *had* told the Bishop "privately," some time before he appealed to the public, what had "caused him scruple and alarm" in the Bishop's conduct at Cuddesdon and throughout the Diocese, and had got *nothing* from him for his pains. In matters of this kind

---

¹ *Address to the Bishop of Oxford*, p. 1.
² *Ibid.* pp. 8, 9.
³ *Ibid.* pp. 12, 13.
⁴ This is exactly what the Bishops now say of the Romanisers; they are but "few," and "inexperienced young men." But where they are now the rank and file will be thirty years hence, if not checked.
⁵ *Address to the Bishop of Oxford*, pp. 15, 16.

public appeals are alone likely to make the Bishops do their duty. If High Church Bishops can only succeed in gagging the Protestants, so as to stifle their *public* protests against Popery in the Church of England, the cause of the Reformation will not long survive in her fold.

To the Bishop's reply a weighty rejoinder was published by the Rev. J. Tucker, B.D., Vicar of West Hendred, Berks, and formerly Fellow of Corpus Christi College, Oxford. Mr. Tucker was one of the oldest clergymen in the Diocese, and his reply was able, learned, and convincing. At the close he addressed the Bishop in words of great power and justice:—

"And now, my lord," he said, "in conclusion, I must make my very serious appeal to your lordship, in the hope that it may not be in vain. I am not writing in the heat, and under the impulse of youth, for I am advancing in years; nor am I conscious of any feeling of bitterness towards yourself or any individual; I have well thought over and calmly deliberated, not only upon what I have now written, but on every step that I have taken in conjunction with those with whom I am associated. It is my conviction, resting, as I believe, on plain matters of fact, that views are being propagated and are spreading throughout our Church, subversive of that pure faith restored by our forefathers, and tending to gradually bring us back into all the corruptions and superstitions of Rome; and under this conviction, I consider myself bound by the most solemn obligations to do what I can in my day, in my humble and narrow sphere, to expose and resist these encroachments, and to uphold God's pure truth.

"I have consequently heartily and readily joined with others of my brethren in the Ministry in remonstrating with the Archdeacons and Rural Deans on their statements and assertions, and in addressing your lordship on the state of things. While others, the majority of the clergy in the Diocese, have also addressed your lordship, they have spoken only of their confidence and attachment to your person, and admiration of your great activity and zeal, and have made general and vague declarations of their disbelief of any danger: *but they have not brought forward one single fact, nor questioned one single assertion of facts made by us.* We, on our part have, in both the *Remonstrance* and *Address*, dealt with *facts, and facts alone;* and, whilst we have most carefully avoided everything that could be construed into disrespect to your lordship, or that could cause unnecessary irritation in the breast of any one, we have asked your lordship to discourage and suppress, so far as you can, certain things which we specify as leading to Popery.

"Your lordship in your reply has refused every one of our requests; *you have conceded nothing;* one thing you admit the existence of, and you admit that it is unlawful; but, instead of promising to exercise your own influence and authority as a Ruler in the Church for its removal, you say to us, 'you have the same power of removing them as I have.' Thus you give your countenance to those who promote what our Reformers condemned, and discountenance those who seek for nothing but what our Protestant fathers upheld. As regards human judgment, let the Church, her Bishops, Clergy, and Laity, judge between your lordship and us. Vital truth is at stake; and it concerns not this Diocese only, nor the Clergy alone, but the whole Church of England, Clergy, and Laity, at home and abroad, to see that the Truth is preserved. . . .

"I respectfully entreat your lordship to abstain in future from casting reflections on any body of your Clergy, however small, who under a sense of duty express to your lordship their honest and deliberate convictions. It cannot tend to uphold either your own character or ours, nor to promote peace. While respect is justly due from Presbyters to their Bishop, they have a right to look to be treated with respect by him."[1]

The address of the three Archdeacons and twenty-four Rural Deans to which Mr. Tucker here refers, was dated February 23rd. It asserted that the statements contained in *Facts and Documents* were, from their "own knowledge of the Diocese," nothing less than "unjustifiable misrepresentations." They denied that the Bishop had "ever sanctioned any peculiarities of the Romish system." They condemned Mr. Purchas' *Directorium Anglicanum* as "a very unwise and mischievous publication"; but they took good care not to term it, as it deserved, a disloyal and thoroughly Popish production. They declared themselves to be "loyal and affectionate sons" of the Church of England, opposed to the introduction of any peculiarities of the Romish system; and, in conclusion, they solemnly affirmed that the statements of Mr. Golightly were "presumptuous and unfounded calumnies against your lordship

---

[1] *A Letter to the Lord Bishop of Oxford.* By the Rev. J. Tucker, B.D., 2nd edition, pp. 15–17. London: James Nisbet & Co. 1859.

in the Diocese."[1] But, as Mr. Tucker so forcibly pointed out, they had "not brought forward one single fact, nor questioned one single assertion of facts" brought forward on the Protestant side. It was all assertion, and *no proof!* But it pleased the Bishop immensely. His reply was all gushing gratitude, though he could scarcely have forgotten that the testimony in his favour was entirely from men who held their offices as Archdeacons and Rural Deans solely and entirely to his nomination, and at his pleasure. He thanked God that his Diocese was *not* "the centre of a Romanising Movement," though it was manifest to the world that the Movement was born in Oxford, and still drew its main inspiration from its University.

In reply to the Address of the Archdeacons and Rural Deans, a Remonstrance was signed by eighty-four Protestant clergymen of the Diocese. In this document they appealed to a series of *facts*, which they enumerated, of a distinctly Romanising character, and challenged those whom they addressed to deny, if they could, their accuracy; and "*to specify, one by one*, what are the statements which they feel bound solemnly to declare are 'unjustifiable misrepresentations,' and 'presumptuous and unfounded calumnies'"[2] in the pamphlet, *Facts and Documents*. My readers will, no doubt, be very much surprised to hear that the Archdeacons and Rural Deans never accepted this challenge, and that they had not the courtesy even to formally acknowledge its receipt. But one of the Rural Deans, to whom the Protestant Remonstrance was addressed, the Rev. Henry Bull, published a reply on his own account, and not as the delegated representative of the others. Mr. Bull declared that their Address to the Bishop was mainly intended as a vote of confidence in him personally. "But the Remonstrants," wrote Mr. Bull, "on the other hand, maintain that there was *no* misrepresentation; and in order to establish their case, challenge us to disprove certain facts stated by the Senior Clergyman. *We do not deny, we never thought of denying them;* but we say the

---

[1] *An Impartial Account of the Recent Agitation in the Diocese of Oxford*, pp. 5, 6. London: Edward Thompson. 1859.
[2] *Ibid.* p. 12.

inference drawn from these facts is unjust; and I must remark that even *facts*, when pleaded to a wrong issue, are virtual *misrepresentations*.[1] So that, after all, Mr. Golightly had but told the truth, so far as *facts* were concerned. And the facts certainly justified the Protestant agitation which arose when they became known to the public.

Mr. Bull's pamphlet was replied to by the Rev. W. H. Freemantle, Rector of Claydon, and himself a Rural Dean in the Diocese. He was subsequently greatly revered and loved as Dean of Ripon. He claimed that those who signed the Remonstrance had no lack of personal affection and respect for their Bishop, but, he added :—

"Public observation has been aroused. Mr. Gresley's book upon the Confessional—his appointment, and Mr. West's to Boyne Hill—Mr. Ridley's Tract upon the Eucharist, at Reading—Cuddesdon College—Holywell stone altar, and the painted chancel—the proceedings at the reopening of Cuddington, Finmere, North Moreton, and Addington Churches—the stone tables at Wantage, and the Oxford Cemeteries—the Sisters of Mercy—these and other subjects which have from time to time been discussed in the newspapers, have turned every eye upon our poor Diocese. . . .

"Why am I to be dubbed a Low Churchman, because I have the Ten Commandments and the Lord's Prayer over my wooden Communion Table; and my neighbour styled a good Churchman, because he has three steps up to his altar, with its super-altar, candlesticks, and stone cross *in relief* upon the east wall? I deprecate this distinction—because I claim to have the law on my side, and I think my neighbour has exceeded it. Let us be true to one another. If we old-fashioned Churchmen, with our wooden tables and whitewashed walls and unadorned chancels, are robbers of churches and blasphemers of holy things, the law is open, and any one may implead us. But if we are found to be quite as earnest and zealous as others in maintaining the decency and spirituality of public worship, and quite as successful in securing the attendance of the people, and in attaching them to the Church of our fathers, and in converting sinners to Christ, then let us not be ridiculed, or

---

[1] *Some Remarks upon the Remonstrance Addressed to the Archdeacons and Rural Deans.* A Letter to the Rev. W. R. Freemantle. By the Rev. Henry Bull, Rural Dean, p. 5. Oxford: Parker. 1859.

stamped with opprobrious names, or branded as Puritans and Dissenters."[1]

The next event in the agitation which arose out of Mr. Golightly's pamphlet, was an address of confidence in the Bishop, signed by the large number of 495 clergymen in the Diocese. If truth and justice always go with the largest number, then, undoubtedly, on this occasion, the Protestants were in the wrong, and those they attacked were in the right. But it is not always so. This Address was very brief, but because of its importance I give it here in full:—

"We, the undersigned Clergy of the Diocese of Oxford, beg permission, under the present circumstances of the Diocese, to approach your lordship with expressions of sincere respect and affection.

"We have been much surprised and distressed at the wide distribution around us of a pamphlet entitled *Facts and Documents Showing the Alarming State of the Diocese of Oxford*, by 'A Senior Clergyman of the Diocese'; which, although in itself wholly unworthy the attention of any reasoning mind, is yet calculated to encourage the heart-burnings of those who are ignorant and under the power of their prejudices.

"We conceive ourselves to be, from our position, the best able to judge of the truth or falsehood of the affirmations made in the pamphlet to which we refer, and we utterly deny that either in public or in those private communications which in all courtesy and kindness you are at all times ready to encourage in your Clergy, you have ever given countenance to practices which might tend to Popery, and we affirm that it has constantly been your aim to encourage true Protestantism, and the religion of the Bible, as set forth and explained in the formularies of our Church.

"We desire to express to your lordship our hearty concurrence in the Address presented to you, with the signature of our Archdeacons and Rural Deans.

"And we thank your lordship for your able and most satisfactory answer given to that Address."[2]

In order to understand the real value of this Address, it is necessary to study the following note, which was attached

[1] *Reasons for Signing the Remonstrance.* By the Rev. W. R. Freemantle, M.A., Rector of Claydon, and Rural Dean, pp. 14-16. London: Nisbet & Co. 1859.
[2] *An Impartial Account*, p. 14.

to it, explaining that portion of the third paragraph which follows "we affirm that":—"The Clergy whose signatures are marked with an asterisk consider the latter part of the third clause to be indistinct, and would prefer that it should stand thus—'Your lordship's aim has always been to encourage a sincere attachment to the distinctive teaching of the Reformed Church of England, as proved by Holy Scripture, and embodied in her authorised formularies.'"[1] The passage which these clergymen would "prefer" to leave out was as follows:—"It has constantly been your aim to encourage true *Protestantism*, and the religion of the Bible, as set forth and explained in the formularies of our Church." That is, they would "prefer" to leave out "Protestantism," and place the Church before the Bible, in order of precedence. No fewer than 212, out of the 495 who signed the Address, had attached to their names the asterisk which indicated their preference for the alteration. This fact alone is a clear and unmistakable proof of the extent to which anti-Protestantism had spread in the Diocese of Oxford, and more than justified Mr. Golightly in placing on the title-page of his pamphlet the words "Alarming State of the Diocese of Oxford." I have, further, looked through the list of names of those who signed this Address, and find in it a large number of those who subsequently were well known as amongst the most advanced Romanisers in the Church of England.

Later on in the year an Address from about 4000 laity of the Diocese of Oxford, including 3 Members of Parliament, 23 Magistrates, and 179 Churchwardens, was presented to the Bishop, in which it was stated:—"We assure your lordship that there exists in the minds of the best friends of our Church a growing mistrust, in consequence of the Romanising tendency of many of the innovations introduced by certain of the clergy into the practices and Ritual of its services;" and expressing a hope that the Bishop would exercise the powers he possessed "to arrest the progress of these objectionable innovations, to allay the fears which we entertain, and to suppress all such causes for further apprehension."

[1] *An Impartial Account*, p. 14 *note*.

Since 1859 Church affairs, from a Protestant point of view, have gone from bad to worse in the Diocese of Oxford. Some slight attempts were made to reform Cuddesdon College for a time, but they were soon dropped; and now the state of things therein is in so unsatisfactory a condition that it may be safely asserted that there is no Institution in the country which has turned out such a large proportion of Romanising and law-breaking clergy as Cuddesdon College, which, by its statutes, is placed under the sole control of the Bishop of Oxford for the time being, and who must therefore be held primarily responsible for what takes place within its walls.

CHAPTER XIV

The St. George's in the East Riots—The Rev. Bryan King—The Rev. Hugh Allen—The attitude of the Bishop of London—The Rector resigns—Church of England Protection Society—Formation of the English Church Union—Its early delight in Ecclesiastical Prosecutions—Opposes Prayer Book Revision "at present"—Dr. Littledale advocates "Catholic Revision"—He is "bowed down" with grief, shame, and indignation—Expulsion of Protestant clergymen aimed at—Preaching in Theatres "a profane and degrading practice"—The Union attempts to prosecute Evangelical clergymen—The Union praises the Bishop of Salisbury for prosecuting Dr. Williams—The Union demands the prosecution and deprivation of the Evangelical Bishop Waldegrave—The E.C.U. demands a cheap and easy way to prosecute Archbishops, Bishops, and clergy—Tries to prosecute foreign Protestant Pastors — The *Church Review* says the Union was established to "enforce the law"—It declares that "to silence the teacher of heresy is the plain duty of the Church's Governors"—Dr. Pusey prosecutes Professor Jowett—Pusey says that "prosecution is not persecution"—The *Church Review* praises prosecutors as men of "moral courage"—The President of the E.C.U. promises obedience to the Courts of Judicature.

IN the year 1859 the Parish Church of St. George's in the East, London, was the scene of prolonged rioting. Its Rector, the Rev. Bryan King, had been appointed to the living in 1842. He was an enthusiastic supporter of the Oxford Movement, and was well known as a very obstinate and self-willed man, as even his warmest friends admit. He lacked tact and a conciliatory spirit, and consequently did not rally many friends around him in his new parish, of no fewer than 45,000 souls, mostly of the very poor, and largely of the criminal class. Mr. King soon made alterations in the Church services, in a High Church direction, which were very distasteful to the majority of those who attended church. At length he even went so far as to introduce the use of the Romish Vestments at Holy Communion. He attached great importance to Ritual, as we learn from a pamphlet which he published in 1860. Referring therein to his introduction of these Vestments in 1857, he remarked:—"I cannot indeed see any reason why I was to be blamed for acting in this instance as I did. These Eucharistic Vestments of the Church are being used in from fifty to sixty Churches in England, and their adoption is being extended in other Churches, I believe, almost every month. I am sure that we shall never succeed in teaching our flocks, and especially the poorer members of them, the deep doctrine of the Holy Eucharist, and the place which that Sacrament holds in the economy of Christian grace as the one act of Worship and Sacrifice offered by the Church to Almighty God, without the aid of such external adjuncts of Ritual."[1] As a matter of fact, Mr. King found that the Ritual he adopted did not attract the poorer members of his parish to his Church at all. The attendance grew less and less, while opposition continued to increase. At the same time Mr. King's remarks may serve to show us how the modern Ritualists teach their doctrine to the eye by Ritual, as well as to the ear, from the pulpit. In fighting the Ritual, therefore, we are fighting the doctrine which it is intended to symbolise and teach.

In the month of December 1858 the office of Lecturer in the Parish Church of St. George's in the East fell vacant. The appointment was in the hands of the Vestry of the parish, who elected the Rev. Hugh Allen to the post. Now Mr. Allen was an out-and-out Protestant, and therefore a stern foe to the Ritualism of Mr. Bryan King. In alarm that gentleman appealed to the Bishop of London (Dr. Tait) to refuse to Mr. Allen that licence without which he could not officiate as Lecturer; but the appeal was in vain. Mr. Allen was licensed on May 17, 1859. On the following Sunday afternoon, the Rector being absent from home, Mr. Allen entered the Church at 3.40 P.M., and insisted on saying the Litany and lecturing, instead of the usual service at 4 P.M., conducted by the Rector or one of his Curates. To this course the Rector at once

[1] *Sacrilege and Its Encouragement.* By Bryan King, M.A., Rector of St. George's in the East 2nd edition, p. 12. London: Masters. 1860.

raised an objection, and the difficulty was settled, after an appeal to the Court of Queen's Bench, by an arrangement by which Mr. Allen was allowed to hold his service at 2.15 P.M. each Sunday, to be followed by the Rector's service at 4 P.M., the arrangement to take effect from Sunday, June 29th. On Sunday, June 5th, unseemly disturbances took place in the Parish Church at both the afternoon and evening services; but on and after June 29th peace was restored for a while. Rioting, however, broke out again on August 14th, and was continued, Sunday after Sunday, with occasional intervals, until the following March, when by order of the Bishop all the Ritualistic ornaments of the Church, which had been the primary cause of the disturbances, were swept away while the Rector was abroad on a twelve months' holiday. Soon after an arrangement was made by which Mr. Bryan King exchanged livings with a country clergyman, and then the St. George's in the East Riots came to an end.

In one sense the Protestant opposition had succeeded, but in reality it had been a disastrous failure. The conduct of the mobs in Church had been disgraceful in the extreme. Hassocks were thrown about, irreverent whistling, joking, and singing were heard, stamping of feet, assaults were made on the clergy, and orange-peel and bread and butter were thrown at the Communion Table. The mob was largely composed of some of the lowest ruffians of that low neighbourhood, and these, caring for neither Protestantism nor Puseyism, nor anything else, used the occasion for their own purposes. The result of all this was that a great spirit of sympathy for the attacked party arose, not merely in East London, but throughout the length and breadth of the land, and the conduct of the rioters was sternly condemned by the respectable Protestants. In the height of the disturbances the Bishop of London, who certainly had no sympathy with Ritualism, and sternly disapproved of the Rector's conduct, wrote to the senior Churchwarden: —"No language can be too strong to express the abhorrence with which all persons of any true Christian feeling must regard such outrages, if they really take place, as is not denied. It is the grossest self-deceit to suppose that they can be justified by any provocation which the Rector's choral service or usual habiliments may have given."[1] But, on the other hand, in the House of Lords, the Bishop said:—"If the Rector of that parish would do what he ought to have done months ago, and say, 'I am unable to manage this parish, I beg the Bishop of the Diocese to manage it for me,' all the mischief might be put an end to."[2]

An important event in the history of the Romeward Movement took place on May 12, 1859, when the "Church of England Protection Society" was formed, which in the following year adopted the now well-known title of "The English Church Union." Amongst the more noteworthy members of the Union whose names appear in its first Annual Report are, Lord Richard Cavendish, Sir Stephen R. Glynne (of Hawarden Castle), Archdeacon Denison, and the Revs. W. J. E. Bennett, R. Rhodes Bristow (now known as Canon Rhodes Bristow), T. T. Carter (of Clewer), J. C. Chambers (editor of the *Priest in Absolution*), John Keble, Bryan King, Hon. and Rev. Robert Liddell, F. G. Lee (now known as Bishop of the O.C.R.), T. W. Mossman (afterwards Bishop of the O.C.R.), J. M. Neale, T. W. Perry, Alfred Poole, R. W. Randall (now Dean of Chichester), J. R. Woodford (afterwards Bishop of Ely), and the Hon. Colin Lindsay, first President of the Union, who afterwards became a Roman Catholic. In the first year of its existence, the Church of England Protection Society issued a Tract on *Remedies at Law Against Disturbers of Divine Service*, with a view, no doubt, to the St. George's in the East Riots, which were proceeding at the time, and on November 24th it sent a deputation to the Bishop of London, to ask him to use his influence with the Churchwardens, to compel them to put down the disturbances. The Bishop received them with great courtesy, told them that the Churchwardens were, he believed, anxious to do their duty in this respect, and then—says the report of the proceedings in the *Union*—"proceeded to urge upon the deputation the duty of the Church of England Protection Society endeavouring to

---

[1] *Life of Archbishop Tait*, vol. i. p. 238.   [2] *Ibid.* p. 246.

persuade the Rector to meet the feelings of the people, and to abate some of the practices objected to as the most likely way of quelling the disorders."[1] The members of the deputation do not appear to have promised to use their influence in this salutary manner; they would, no doubt, have preferred to encourage the Rector in his Romanising practices. That is what the Society actually did, for we are told, in its first annual report, that after the interview with the Bishop, "it offered to assist Mr. Bryan King with such means as it possessed of obtaining for his guidance the best legal advice."[2]

In view of an expected motion in the House of Lords by Lord Ebury in favour of Prayer Book Revision on Protestant lines, the Society circulated for signature a Petition to both Houses of Parliament on the subject. Its purport will be gathered from its opening sentences:—" Your Petitioners are sincerely attached to the Book of Common Prayer, and entirely disapprove of any changes therein *at the present time*. That your Petitioners believe it to be the true exposition of God's Holy Word, and that to alter it, *as proposed*, would be to make it contrary to God's Word."[3] This, be it remarked, was not a Petition against the *principle* of Prayer Book Revision. It was simply inexpedient *for them* that it should take place "at the present time," when it would certainly not have been conducted on Ritualistic lines; and therefore they naturally objected to it "as proposed" by that valiant champion of Protestantism, Lord Ebury. And here I would impress upon my readers the fact that the Ritualists are by no means opponents of Prayer Book Revision; on the contrary, many of their leaders are in favour of it. One of their most prominent and learned champions, the late Rev. Dr. Littledale, who was one of the leading members of the Council of the English Church Union, published in 1867 a pamphlet in favour of Prayer Book Revision:—

"The Rubrics," said Dr. Littledale, "at the end of the Communion Office are *in sore need of revision*. The first three should

---

[1] *Union*, December 30, 1859, p. 823.
[2] *First Annual Report of the English Church Union*, p. 22.
[3] *History of the English Church Union*. By the Rev. G. Bayfield Roberts, p. 16. London: Church Printing Co. 1895.

be totally expunged. They have worked incalculable mischief. . . . So of the two following Rubrics. . . . So of the Rubric enjoining the reverent consumption of the elements."[1]

"The Confirmation Office needs two alterations. The restoration of Chrism and the sign of the Cross."[2]

"I now come to the subject of primary importance, compared with which all that has gone before is light. I mean the Communion Office. It is impossible for any English Liturgical scholar to behold it in its present condition, and to compare it with *the glorious rite of Sarum,* or even with Edward VI.'s First Book, *without being bowed down with shame, grief, and indignation at the enormous wrong-doing which was perpetrated,* and the apathy with which it has been so long regarded. . . . There is no Christian doctrine more prominent in the Primitive Liturgies and the Early Fathers than that of the *Eucharistic Sacrifice,* and its intimate union with the Offering on Calvary. *There is none more studiously obscured by the English formularies,* and albeit theologians know that it is still there, though hidden, yet ordinary readers may well fail to discover it. Our plain duty to souls, to ourselves, and to those branches of the Church which, in this *more happy than we* [he means, of course, the Roman and Eastern Churches], have preserved the doctrine intact, is to bring it once more into due prominence. *First, then, the word 'Altar' needs to be restored.* It is quite right to retain the word *Table* occasionally, in order to prevent the idea of Communion being thrown into the shade, but the other is the earlier, more universal, and more appropriate term. Next, *the liberty of removing the Holy Table,* now practically abrogated, *should be formally withdrawn,* and the position of the priest should be defined *so as to prevent* the present most unseemly and irreverent use of *celebrating at the North End.* . . . Next, it ought to be provided that the accustomed Ornaments, to wit, a *Cross* or *Crucifix,* and not less than *two Lights,* shall stand upon the Altar at the time of celebration, and that the Priest shall be properly vested in Alb and Chasuble, &c."[3]

Now I need hardly remark that if Prayer Book Revision on these lines were carried out, it would make it morally impossible for any Protestant Minister to officiate in the Church of England. And that is, I believe, just what, in their heart of hearts, the Ritualists desire above all things —the expulsion of Protestant clergymen, not directly, but

[1] *Catholic Revision.* By Richard F. Littledale, LL.D., pp. 26, 27. London: Palmer. 1867.
[2] *Ibid.* p. 28.   [3] *Ibid.* pp. 21, 22.

by a side wind. And if Parliament does not refuse the present demand of High Churchmen to hand over the government of the Church to the clergy who compose her Convocations, with a merely nominal control by the Legislature, Prayer Book Revision on these Romanising lines may, ere long, become an alarming fact.

There was another subject of interest which occupied the attention of the E.C.U. during the first year of its existence. For some time previously Sunday Services for the People had been held in Exeter Hall, and Theatres, at which many eminent Church of England Clergymen and Nonconformist Ministers had preached the Gospel to immense congregations, and with the most blessed results. But these services were an abomination in the eyes of the Ritualists of the day. Referring to the Vicar of St. Michael's, Burleigh Street, in whose parish Exeter Hall is situated, the *Union* said:—" Mr. Edouart might as well shut up his Church and take a holiday so long as this monster conventicle at Exeter Hall is braying away in his ears, with Dr. Tait's connivance."[1] This Vicar did all that lay in his power to stop the Exeter Hall Services, though they in no way interfered with the attendance at his own Church. He appealed to the Bishop, who told him that he would take the responsibility from off his shoulders, and so, after a vain struggle, the Vicar gave up the contest, and withdrew his active opposition, under protest. But when he dropped the case, the new English Church Union took it up, at least so far as it related to Theatres, and endeavoured to settle the question by a prosecution of the clergymen who dared to preach the Gospel in such places. First of all, they obtained a legal opinion from Dr. Phillimore, and after that they set about the task of finding a man qualified and willing to act as an aggrieved prosecutor. But all their efforts in this direction were in vain. They discovered that the only man who could act as prosecutor was the Vicar, and he was unwilling to act. So in grief and with much wailing, the English Church Union had to give up the case, and afterwards relate what they had done to their disappointed

[1] *Union*, July 23, 1858, p. 476.

subscribers, in their annual report. And this is what the Committee of the Union said:—

"Your Committee have next to report that the attention of the Society has been directed to the *great scandal* which has been given by certain clergymen of the Church of England, consorting with Dissenting preachers, in the use of Theatres for public worship, in London and elsewhere.

"An opinion upon the legality of such proceedings has been obtained from Dr. Phillimore, by the Society, and published in the newspapers; but the difficulty of 'promoting the office of Judge' in the Ecclesiastical Courts against offenders is very great; and, indeed, it cannot be promoted at all except at the instance of the Incumbent of the parish in which the Theatre is situated. It does not, therefore, appear to your Committee that there is any hope of putting down *this profane and degrading practice* by an appeal to the law."[1]

The Union might easily have abstained from such a display of narrow-minded bigotry as was exhibited by terming the preaching of the Gospel in Theatres "a great scandal," and even a "profane and degrading practice." But the most important thing to notice in connection with this case, is the startling fact that, in the very first year of its existence, the English Church Union endeavoured to get up an ecclesiastical prosecution of *Evangelical* clergy, for an alleged breach of the law. And when we remember how, a few years since, this self-same Union denounced the wickedness of ecclesiastical prosecutions, *when their friends were the defendants*, and literally howled with rage, and even appealed to the sympathies of the public with whining tears, it makes one feel an utter contempt for such inconsistent conduct. The position of the E.C.U. with respect to prosecutions seems to be well expressed in the words of the big and cowardly schoolboy:—"I may hit you; but you musn't hit me!"

And here I may be permitted to mention a few facts proving the great admiration of the English Church Union for Ecclesiastical Prosecutions in its early days. In February 1860 the celebrated *Essays and Reviews* appeared, containing seven Essays written respectively by Frederick Temple, D.D., now Archbishop of Canterbury; Rowland Williams,

[1] *First Annual Report of the English Church Union*, pp. 23, 24.

D.D.; Baden Powell, M.A.; Henry B. Wilson, B.D.; Mark Pattison, B.D.; Rev. Benjamin Jowett, M.A.; and C. W. Goodwin, M.A. A letter was written, signed by all the Bishops in England and Ireland, expressing disapprobation of certain opinions attributed to the writers, and in July 1864, the book was condemned by both Houses of Convocation. But, meanwhile, the High Church Bishop of Salisbury (Dr. W. K. Hamilton) decided to prosecute separately one of the Essayists, the Rev. Dr. Rowland Williams, who was Vicar of Broad Chalke, in the Diocese of Salisbury. The Ritualistic party hailed the prosecution with the utmost delight, nor were Evangelical Churchmen behindhand in their approval. Canon Liddon says that "Bishop Hamilton's action in instituting the suit against Dr. Williams was warmly supported by Pusey, who was at first as sanguine about its results as he was convinced of its necessity."[1] The English Church Union hailed the prosecution with unbounded delight. In their second annual report, in 1861, the Council of the Union referred to the institution of a suit by the Bishop of Salisbury against Dr. Williams in the Ecclesiastical Court of Arches:—

"A suit, after the most mature deliberation, has been commenced by the Bishop of Salisbury. *The Council commend him and his sacred cause to the prayers and good offices of the Union*, though experience of the Ecclesiastical Courts, as now constituted, in these our unhappy intestine wars, proves that the issue must be doubtful."[2]

The charges against Dr. Williams were of a most serious character, involving doctrines of great importance, yet in the opinion of the E.C.U., in 1861, the existing Ecclesiastical Courts were capable of giving judgment on them. At that time it was thought by the Union that to prosecute all clerical offenders against the Church's laws was the bounden duty of every Bishop. The *Church Review* was then the property of the E.C.U., and was edited by its secretary. Commenting on the prosecution of Dr. Williams, it asked:—

"How can a Bishop be ready, as he is under so solemn a vow to be, to 'banish and drive away all erroneous and strange doctrine,

---

[1] *Life of Dr. Pusey*, vol. iv. p. 43.
[2] *Second Annual Report of the English Church Union*, p. 15.

contrary to God's Word,' if, when one of his clergy writes and publishes an infidel work, he will not use *the means which the law provides for making an example of him* to his diocese and to the Church?"[1]

In the following year the E.C.U. demanded that the Evangelical Bishop of Carlisle (as well as Bishop Colenso) should be compelled to retract his Protestant opinion as to Baptismal Regeneration, or be prosecuted:—

"We call upon all our fellow-Churchmen," said the *Church Review*, "who take an interest in the maintenance of the Catholic faith, to unite in this our remonstrance, and to join with us in the demand that the heretical bishops [*i.e.* Waldegrave and Colenso] shall be called to account; and unless they formally retract the wicked errors promulgated by them, *put upon their trial*. If we be asked to point out the tribunal before which they are to be arraigned, we answer, according to the latest precedents in the law books, before the Archbishop, who, *virtute officii*, possesses jurisdiction over the Bishops of his province. In the case of the Bishop of Carlisle this would probably be held sufficient; but if not, or in the case of the Bishop of Natal (the English Ecclesiastical law not being in force in the Cape Colony), let proceedings be instituted under the old Canon Law . . . The tribunal so constituted has power, not only to inquire into the accusation, but if the Bishop arraigned before it be found guilty, to visit his offence with *canonical punishment, extending to deprivation, and even to deposition and degradation.*"[2]

If the English Church Union could at that time, by an Ecclesiastical prosecution, have secured the deprivation, deposition, and degradation of the Evangelical Bishop Waldegrave, it would, I doubt not, have shouted aloud for joy. Their hatred of the Evangelical party, and their desire to expel them from the Church of England, comes out very clearly in the leading article I have just quoted from the official organ of the Union. If they had succeeded, the Union would, I doubt not, have been as much addicted to prosecuting Protestants as the Church Association afterwards became in prosecuting Ritualistic lawbreakers. The great difference between these two societies

[1] *Church Review*, September 1861, p. 166.
[2] *Ibid.* May 17, 1862, p. 301.

is that the E.C.U. *failed*, while the Church Association *succeeded* in proving their opponents to be law-breakers. And although we have, in recent years, occasionally heard assurances from certain Ritualists that they have no wish or desire to expel Evangelicals from the Church, I, for one, am not disposed to place any confidence in such assurances. Give but the English Church Union the *power*, and within ten years there would not be a Protestant clergyman of Evangelical views left within the Church of England, and then we should soon have a Church willing, anxious, and ready to fraternise with the Pope, and submit once more to Papal supremacy.

There was one thing which troubled the English Church Union very much. Ecclesiastical prosecutions of clergy were very cumbersome, costly, and prolonged, and therefore, at its ordinary meeting, held in the offices on April 7, 1862, the President (the Hon. Colin Lindsay) in the chair, a resolution was carried demanding that prosecutions, not only of priests, but even of Archbishops and Bishops, should be facilitated—so anxious were they to put down all their opponents by the strong arm of the law! The resolution was as follows:—

"That, whilst *facilitating the bringing to trial of priests for heresy and breaches of Church discipline* and morality, there should be a mode of procedure laid down for dealing with *Archbishops and Bishops*, if they should offend against the law."[1]

The Great Exhibition, held in 1862, brought to our shores a large number of foreign Protestant pastors. Several of them were invited by Evangelical clergymen to officiate in their churches. The English Church Union was greatly alarmed when it heard the news, and at once took energetic action, and at its annual meeting in June the Council reported:—"The Council have drawn the Bishop of London's attention to the subject, with the view of inducing him to exert his authority, as his lordship's lamented predecessor, Bishop Blomfield, did in 1851; *and have also submitted a case for the opinion of eminent counsel, in order to determine upon the best mode of enforcing the*

[1] *Church Review*, April 12, 1862, p. 229.

law."[1] In quoting this it must not be supposed that I object to the E.C.U., or anybody else, "enforcing the law." Evangelical Churchmen are not afraid of the law, and are quite willing to obey it. Of course, the *Church Review* applauded the action of the Council. One might almost think, in reading the following comments of that newspaper, that he was reading the present official organ of the Church Association :—

"It is not the fault of the English Church Union that the Unordained Foreign 'Protestant Pastors' are allowed to persist in setting both the law of the Church and the law of the land at defiance, by officiating in chapels of the Church of England in this metropolis. True to the obligations of an Association established for the purpose of defending and maintaining unimpaired the discipline as well as the doctrine of the Church of England, *her Council have earnestly endeavoured to enforce the law* which requires that no one shall presume to officiate ministerially in any of the places of worship of the Church who is not in her Holy Orders, and thereby duly qualified for the sacred charge. But as they with whom, after all, the duty rests of giving practical effect to the requirements of the law refuse to act in the case, the Council are unable, without embarking in an expensive and probably protracted course of litigation, to do more than they have done in pursuance of that object."[2]

It will be observed that in "endeavouring to enforce the law," the E.C.U. is described as "true to the obligations" with which it commenced its career. Unfortunately for the Union, there seems to be no law left in 1900 for *it* to enforce. The law is on the side of Protestant Churchmen. In this same year the Rev. D. I. Heath, Vicar of Brading, Isle of Wight, was condemned by the Judicial Committee of Privy Council for teaching certain Broad Church doctrines contrary to the teaching of the Church of England, and it confirmed the sentence of deprivation of his living passed upon him by the Court below. And this is the way in which the English Church Union, through its official organ, hailed with great satisfaction the judgment of the now hated "State" Court. This is what it said :—" This, then,

[1] *Third Annual Report of the English Church Union,* p. 15.
[2] *Church Review,* July 26, 1862, p. 459.

is substantially the judgment of the Privy Council in the case in question. And one who has been proved guilty of such an anomaly and scandal, and refuses to revoke his errors, is *justly sentenced to deprivation*. Let us hope it will act as a salutary warning."[1] One of the strongest defences of suppressing lawlessness in the Church by the strong arm of the law, was published by the English Church Union, in its official organ, early in 1863. It is well worth reading. The article was headed "Prosecutions for Heresy," and in reply to those who objected to prosecutions it said:—

"Now, to all this ribald nonsense we simply reply that a tainted sheep is removed from the flock, not for his punishment—save as that punishment may be the means of recovery to health—but that the rest of the flock may not be infected. *To silence the teacher of heresy is the plain duty of the Church's governors.* Whether that silence shall be only for a definite time, or for life, or until the offender has purged himself of his wrong-doing, ought to depend upon the particulars of each offence. But the object of the *temporary punishment* of an heretical priest must be always considered to be, first, the protection of the flock entrusted to his charge from his pernicious influence; and, next, his own correction, with a view to a recantation of his error, and his submission to her judgment who has authority 'in controversies of faith.' If any one is so unmindful of his Ordination vows as to write against the faith to which they have solemnly committed him, *he can only be dealt with by the action of the law. It is the only means by which he can be set right.* And right he must be set, or he will make others go wrong. How can the man who is himself in doubt teach others the truth? And if he have disqualified himself from discharging the prophet's office, why should he take the prophet's pay? ... The Church's revenues are for the teaching of the Church's faith. Let those who do not hold that faith be restrained from the sacrilege of appropriating funds which have been provided to teach and maintain it."[2]

Dr. Pusey formed one of "*three* aggrieved" ones, who, in 1863, prosecuted for heresy Professor Jowett, late Master of Balliol College, Oxford, but with the result that the case against Professor Jowett was dismissed by the Oxford Chancellor's Court. Dr. Pusey found it necessary, before the case was heard, to write to the *Times*, of February 19,

[1] *Church Review*, June 14, 1862, p. 362.
[2] *Ibid.* January 31, 1863, p. 113.

1863, a defence of Ecclesiastical Prosecutions, in which he said :—"*Prosecution is not persecution.* It would be an evil day for England when it should be recognised that to *appeal to the majesty of the law* is to contravene truth and justice." The *Church Review* was delighted with Pusey's letter, and burst forth in praise of prosecutors. It said :—

"None better than Dr. Pusey know the difference between prosecution and persecution. *There is something noble in the learned Professor's vindication of the majesty of law.* Evil day, indeed, will it be for England when it shall be deemed an act of cruelty to afford a man accused of wrong the opportunity of purging himself from that accusation by the solemn process of a legal inquiry. *Dark will be the gloom which obscures the horizon of England's Church when there shall not be to be found among her sons any who will have the moral courage to bring before the Courts to which they may be amenable those who are engaged in poisoning the streams of religious knowledge at their very fountain head.*" [1]

In 1864 the English Church Union unanimously passed a resolution to start a fund to assist in prosecuting Bishop Colenso.[2] At its annual meeting the same year the President of the E.C.U. actually declared that it was the duty of the Union to obey the decisions of the Law Courts. He said :—"With respect to discipline the same argument applies. That which has been laid down in the Canon Law, and has been received and acted upon in the Church, *especially in her Courts of Judicature*, we are, I think, clearly bound to 'defend and maintain unimpaired.'"[3] I do not think the present President of the English Church Union would make such a declaration now.

It will thus be seen that in its early years the English Church Union paraded itself before the public as the great maintainer of law and order in the Church. And so—to do it credit—it continued, until it found that law and order were against its sacerdotal and Romanising claims. From that time it has slowly adopted the principles of rebellion against every law and order in the Church opposed to its preposterous claims, and has, in practice, approved of

[1] *Church Review*, February 21, 1863, p. 183.
[2] *Ibid.* March 19, 1864, p. 285.
[3] *Ibid.* June 18, 1864, p. 603.

every clergyman of the Ritualistic party being a Pope to himself, and the embodiment of ecclesiastical anarchy.[1]

The English Church Union has been the best friend to the Church of Rome seen in England since the Reformation. It has, indeed, in only too many instances, been the Preparatory School for Rome. In how many it is impossible for me to say. But I have discovered that the 78 clergymen in the Church of England, mentioned in the Appendix on the next page, were members of the English Church Union when they seceded to Rome. I challenge the Ritualists to produce a list of those who have seceded to Rome direct from the ranks of the Church Association. I do not think they could find even one.

Here for the present I must close, reserving for a future occasion my general comments on the Romeward Movement, and what ought to be the Evangelical policy towards it. We can learn many things even from our opponents, and it may be well if the Evangelical party were to learn from them the wisdom of paying more attention to the outward organisation of the Church. Those, on the other hand, who value some of the Romanising changes introduced by the Ritualists, would do well to remember that it is possible to pay too heavily for even good things. To secure musical services, and histrionic performances, by a sacrifice of our Christian liberty to priestly bondage, is at best a poor bargain.

[1] Further information on the attitude of the E.C.U. towards Ecclesiastical Prosecutions may be found in the pamphlet, *Ecclesiastical Prosecutions, Originated and Advocated by the English Church Union*. By Walter Walsh, pp. 8. London: Church Association, 141 Buckingham Street, W.C.

APPENDIX

A List of Clerical Members of the English Church Union who have Seceded to Rome.

Akers, Rev. George
Andrews, Rev. Septimus
Angus, Rev. George
Barlow, Rev. T. W.
Barnes, Rev. A. S.
Barnes, Rev. Thomas
Bennett, Rev. Morden
Boothby, Rev. Herbert
Briggs, Rev. H. C.
Bromage, Rev. R. R.
Camm, Rev. J. Brooke
Camm, Rev. R. P.
Cane, Rev. V. C. B.
Chase, Rev. C. H.
Clarke, Rev. A. G.
Conder, Rev. R. F. R.
Cooke, Rev. W. A.
Corrance, Rev. H. C.
Darlington, Rev. Joseph
Davis, Rev. T.
Donaldson, Rev. A. M.
Duthie, Rev. C. J.
Duthoit, Rev. W.
Egerton, Rev. J.
Eskrigge, Rev. J.
Farman, Rev. S.
Fawkes, Rev. A.
Filmer, Rev. J. H.
Fletcher, Rev. Philip
Foster, Rev. C. G.
Fownes, Rev. J. E. C.
Godley, Rev. R. J. D.
Gorman, Rev. G. T.
Greene, Rev. Joseph J.
Grindle, Rev. E. S.
Grisewood, Rev. H.
Hardy, Rev. H. J.
Hickman, Rev. H.
Hoare, Rev. J. W. D.
Hodson, Rev. C. E.
Hope, Rev. Douglas
Hunnybun, Rev. W. M.
Jackson, Rev. Edmund
Kennard, Rev. C.
King, Rev. Owen C.
Lord, Rev. F. B.
Lyall, Rev. W.
Madan, Rev. J. R.
Mather, Rev. F. H. V.
Maturin, Rev. B. W.
Milton, Rev. A. T.
Newdegate, Rev. A.
North, Rev. H. W.
Osborne, Rev. Lord T. Godolphin
Paine, Rev. A. H.
Parker, Rev. H. M.
Phillipps-Treby, Rev. E. M.
Powell, Rev. A. H.
Rivington, Rev. Luke
Russell, Rev. H. P.
Sankey, Rev. R. B.
Sharpe, Rev. A. B.
Shipley, Rev. Orby
Sperling, Rev. J. H.
Sproston, Rev. S.
Stanley, Rev. the Hon. A. G.
Tatlock, Rev. W.
Tatum, Rev. G. B.
Theed, Rev. E. A.
Tydd, Rev. T. H.
Walls, Rev. C. J.
Watson, Rev. E. J.
Wedgwood, Rev. R.
Westall, Rev. A. St. L.
White, Rev. J. B.
Wilson, Rev. H. L.
Wood, Rev. R. S.
Wyndham, Rev. F. M.

INDEX

ACTON, Cardinal, startling letter to, 196, 197
Adapted Roman books, quotations from, 242-244
—— Newman's opinion of, 241
—— Bishop Hamilton on, 241
—— Bishop Wilberforce, on, 242
—— Bishop Blomfield on, 245
—— Dr. Hook says they "will make men infidels," 242
Alderson, Baron, 307
Allies, Rev. T. W., 239
—— pays "a sacred debt to the Roman Church," 305
—— writes in defence of a Church he "thoroughly hated," 304
—— exercises a "laudable subtlety," 305
—— claims to hold Roman doctrine, 307
—— his interview with the Pope, 308
—— and Bishop Wilberforce, 304-308
—— extracts from his *Journal in France*, 305, 306
Altars, condemned by the Judicial Committee of Privy Council, 264, 359
—— Bishop Gilbert on, 291
Apostolic succession, accepted by Froude, Keble, Palmer, and Newman, 9
Argyll, Duke of, on Protestant unity, 23
Arnold, Rev. Dr. Thomas, his *Principles of Church Reform*, 26-28
—— on the rights of laymen, 26
—— on *Tract X.*, 44
—— on *Tract XC.*, 154
Ashley, Lord, and the Jerusalem Bishopric, 202-205, 210.
Association of Friends of the Church, 33-37
—— its real objects, 34, 35
Association for the promotion of the Unity of Christendom, The, 349-357
—— its founders' traitorous and secret message to the Pope, 356
Auricular Confession, Pusey's Protestant notes on, 133-135

Auricular Confession, Pusey afraid to practise, 132
—— Pusey goes to, for first time, 133
—— Bishop Blomfield denounces a preacher of, 271
—— and Clerical Retreats, 282, 283
—— Episcopal inquiry into, at St. Saviour's, Leeds, 321-325
—— wives and, 321
—— questioning women on the Seventh Commandment defended, 324, 325, 378, 379
—— a Plymouth inquiry concerning, 337, 338
—— Puseyite identical with Roman, 351
—— charges against the Rev. Alfred Poole as to, 374-380

BAGOT, Bishop, on the *Tracts for the Times*, 107, 108, 222, 223
—— and the Oxford Martyrs Memorial, 112, 119
—— on *Tract XC.*, 166-168, 222.
—— on the proposal to prosecute Pusey, 233
Barnabo, Cardinal, De Lisle's startling revelations to, 352-354
—— reply from De Lisle, 354
Barnes v. *Shore*, 273-276
Bateman, Mr. James, and Theological Colleges, 388, 389
Bath Judgment, The, 344-346
—— protest against, 348
Beckett, Rev. H. F., on the Confessions of wives, 323
Belaney v. *Totton*, 234
Bellasis, Mr. Serjeant, 139
Bennett, Rev. W. J. E., 317-320
—— the Bishop of London and the, 317-320
Bickersteth, Rev. E., on the *Library of the Fathers*, 90
Bird, Bishop, replies to Protestant protests, 237
Blachford, Lord, on Cranmer, 111, 217
Blackburn, Protest against Puseyism from, 237

INDEX

Black Gown in the Pulpit, The, declared to be legal, 248
—— at Exeter, 268, 269
Blomfield, Bishop, prosecutes the Rev. F. Oakeley, 141-143
—— censures *Tract XC.*, 179
—— on "Adapted" Roman books, 245
—— denounces a preacher of Auricular Confession, 271
—— the Romanising party severely censured by, 316, 317
Bloxam, Rev. J. R., 186
—— his traitorous and secret negotiations with De Lisle, 186-191
—— "a living and moving secret," 187
Bolton, Protest against Puseyism from, 237
Bowden, Mr. J. W., 25, 89
Boyle, Dean, on the effect of Pusey's Confessional work, 280
Brawling in Church, case of *Burder* v. *Langley*, 235, 236
Breeks v. *Woolfrey*, 125-127
Bricknell, Rev. W. S., his *Judgment of the Bishops upon Tractarian Theology* cited, 178, 179
Brighton Protestant Defence Committee, 23
Bristol Church Union, The, 326-330
—— a "Statement of Principles" of, 328, 329
—— opposed by Pusey and Keble, 328, 330
Bull, Rev. Henry, 400, 401
Bunsen, Baron, on Hampden's election, 80, 81
—— and Pastor Spörlein, 117, 118
—— and the Jerusalem Bishopric, 201-204, 211
Burder v. *Langley*, 235, 236
Burgon, Dean, 396
Butler, Dean, on Clerical Retreats, 282, 283

CAMBRIDGE, Holy Sepulchre Church, restoration of, 251-253
—— judgment in case of, 252, 253
—— Camden Society, denounced by Dr. Close, 254
Camoys, Lord, on the Puseyite Movement, 234
Candlesticks and Candles, judgment of Judicial Committee on, 359
Cardwell's *Doctrinal Annals*, 42
Church, Dean, on the Evangelical Movement, 4
—— on the Reformers, 111

Church, Dean, on the contest for the Poetry Professorship, 215
Church Unions, 326
Church and State, views of the early Tractarians on, 24-26
Clerical Retreats, 282, 283
Close, Rev. Dr., on *The Restoration of Churches is the Restoration of Popery*, 254, 255
Collette, Mr. Charles Hastings, on Newman's ordination as a Roman Catholic priest, 261, 262
Coloured Cloths on Communion Table, judgment of Judicial Committee on, 359
Confession (see "Auricular Confession")
Copleston, Bishop, censures *Tract XC.*, 179
Corporate Reunion with Rome, 115-117, 159-164
—— Pusey on the basis of, 144, 145
—— secret negotiations with Romanists for, 184-200
Cowley Fathers, The, on priests as peacemakers, 10
Credence Tables, 252, 253, 359
Cross, The, on the Communion Table, 288, 289
—— judgment of Bishop Phillpotts, 288
—— Mr. B. Whitehead on the law as to, 289
Crosses, judgment of Judicial Committee on, 360
Cuddesdon Theological College, 389-392, 394, 396, 404

DALGAIRNS, Mr. J. D., 160, 257
De Lisle, Mr. Ambrose Phillipps, on *Tract IV.*, 43
—— on *Tract XC.*, 165, 166
—— becomes a secret emissary to Oxford, 185
—— Newman opens his heart to, 185
—— promises to bring some foreign Theologians to Oxford, 186
—— his secret negotiations with the Oxford leaders, 184-200
—— his first visit to Oxford, 187
—— letter to Cardinal Barnabo, 352-354
Denison, Archdeacon, 330
—— Bishop Spencer's correspondence with, 341-342
—— the Rev. Joseph Ditcher prosecutes, 342-346
Ditcher v. *Denison*, 342-346
Dodsworth, Rev. William, exposure of Pusey's Confessional practice by, 309, 310, 313

INDEX

Dominic, Father, his narrative of Newman's reception into the Church of Rome, 257, 258
Dublin Review, 115, 136
—— on Froude's *Remains*, 20, 104

EAST GRINSTEAD Convent, 363-374
Egerton v. *All of Rode*, 129, 130
Elphinstone v. *Purchas*, 289
Embroidered Lace on Communion Table, judgment of Judicial Committee on, 359
English Churchman, The, started by the Puseyites, 238
—— recommends the prosecution of Evangelicals, 246, 247
—— denounces public praying in an unconsecrated place, 271, 272
—— wishes to reduce the distance to Rome, 289
English Church Union, The, 408-420
—— the first founders of, 408
—— and Prayer Book Revision, 409
—— and services in theatres, 411, 412
—— attempt to prosecute Evangelical clergy by, 411, 412
—— and *Essays and Reviews*, 412, 413
—— praises the prosecution of the Rev. Dr. Rowland Williams, 413
—— wants to prosecute Archbishops and Bishops, 415
—— demands the prosecution of the Evangelical Bishop of Carlisle, 414
—— obedience to the Courts promised by the President of, 418
—— list of Clerical Seceders to Rome from the ranks of, 420
Episcopal Veto, The, denounced by Bishop Phillpotts, 77
—— judgments of Justices Hill and Wightman on, 385, 386
Evangelical Churchmen and the Puritans, 3
—— the real descendants of the Protestant Reformers, 2
—— Puseyite anxiety to expel, 246-248
Evangelical Movement, The, Canon Liddon on, 3
—— Mr. Gladstone on, 4
—— Mr. H. O. Wakeman on, 4
—— Dean Church on, 4
—— Lord Shaftesbury on, 5
—— Earl of Selborne on, 5
—— Rev. W. H. B. Proby on, 5
—— Mr. Lecky on, 6, 7
—— not a supplement to the Oxford Movement, 7-10
—— Its spiritual and philanthropic blessings, 3-7

Exeter Surplice Riots, 268, 269

FABER, Rev. F. W., his *Sights and Thoughts in Foreign Churches*, 218-220
—— how he deceived the public, 218
Faber, Rev. G. Stanley, 102, 181, 224
Fasting, Pusey's *Tract* on, 42
—— *Homily* on, 42
Fathers, The, Pusey's quotations from, 234
—— Tractarians and, 90, 91, 133
Faussett, Rev. Dr., on *The Revival of Popery*, 99, 100
—— denounces Dr. Pusey's sermon on the Eucharist, 227
Freeland v. *Neale*, 291, 292
Freemantle, Dean, 401
Froude, Rev. R. H., 109
—— on Apostolic Succession, 9
—— on Tradition and the Bible, 11
—— on Church and State, 24, 25
—— Extracts from his *Remains*, 96, 97, 98
—— Newman on the opinions of, 92
—— Dr. Hook on his *Remains*, 106, 107
Fust, Sir Herbert Jenner, Judgment in the Oakeley Case, 142, 143
—— Judgment in *Breeks* v. *Woolfrey*, 126
—— Judgment in *Faulkener* v. *Litchfield*, 252, 253
—— Judgment in *Barnes* v. *Shore*, 275, 276
—— Judgment in *Freeland* v. *Neale*, 291
—— Judgment in *Gorham* v. *Bishop of Exeter*, 294

GARBETT, Rev. James, The, contest for the Poetry Professorship at Oxford by, 212-217
—— attempt to prosecute for heresy, 250
Gilbert, Bishop, and Sackville College, 290-292
—— and St Margaret's, East Grinstead, 365, 366
Girdlestone, Rev. C., 37
Gladstone, Mr. W. E., on Evangelical Churchmanship, 4
—— describes the services at Margaret Chapel, 140
—— and St. Saviour's, Leeds, 287
Golightly, Rev. C. P., exposes the Romanisers, 181, 182
—— and the Lavington case, 385, 386
—— and Cuddesdon College, 389-392
—— on the Alarming State of the Diocese of Oxford, 393-404

Golightly v. *the Bishop of Chichester*, 385-386
Goode, Dean, 11, 91, 220-223, 301
Gorham Case, The, 292-303
—— Judgment of Sir H. Jenner Fust in, 294
—— Judgment of the Judicial Committee of Privy Council in, 295-297
—— Clerical Declaration in support of judgment in, 336
Griffiths, Rev. John, 154, 156

HADLEIGH, Tractarian Conference at, 29-31
—— Newman's report of, 31
Hamilton, Bishop, on Pusey's "Adapted" Roman books, 241
Hampden, Rev. Dr. R. D., the case of the, 46-85
—— appointed Regius Professor of Divinity, 50
—— Lord Melbourne on opposition to, 51, 63
—— Dean Stanley on opposition to, 54
—— his Letter to the Archbishop of Canterbury, 64
—— appointed Bishop of Hereford, 67
—— protest of thirteen Bishops, 67
—— reply of the Prime Minister, 68
—— Archdeacon Hare's reply to the critics of, 69, 70
—— Pusey and Keble try to prosecute, 72-77
—— Election of, as Bishop of Hereford, 77-79, 82, 83
—— protest at Bow Church, 80
—— addresses of sympathy with, 83, 84
Hare, Archdeacon, 69, 70
Hawker, Rev. John, 275
Hawkins, Rev. Dr., 55, 56, 84, 231, 232
Heath, Rev. D. I., 416
Homilies, The, on Prayer for the Dead, 126
Homily on Fasting, 42
Hook, Rev. Dr., on the *Tracts for the Times* and Froude's *Remains*, 106, 107
—— subscribes to the Jerusalem Bishopric Fund, 206
—— the Romanisers denounced by the, 207, 250, 322
—— thinks Pusey under Jesuit influence, 268
—— charges Pusey with Jesuitism, 285
—— refuses to join the Yorkshire Church Union, 330
Hope-Scott, Mr. James R., 169, 238, 260
—— opposition of, to the Jerusalem Bishopric, 205, 206

ISLINGTON Clergy and High Church principles, 101

JELF, Rev. William Edward, on Confession, 281
Jelf, Rev. Dr. W. J., 159
Jerusalem Bishopric, The, 201-212
—— Dr. Hook supports, 206-208
—— Mr. Gladstone supports, 211
—— Pusey's bitter opposition to, 209, 210
—— Lord Ashley and, 202-205, 210
—— Newman's protest against, 211, 212
Jesuitism, Pusey charged with, by Hook, 268, 285
Jowett, Professor, prosecuted by Dr. Pusey, 417, 418
Judicial Committee of Privy Council, The, Archbishop Tait on, 331
—— Judgment of, in *Liddell* v. *Westerton*, 253, 264, 359, 360
—— Judgment of, in *Burder* v. *Langley*, 236
—— Judgment of, in *Gorham* v. *the Bishop of Exeter*, 295-297
—— Judgment of, in *Barnes* v. *Shore*, 276
—— Lord John Russell on, 332
—— Judgment in *Ditcher* v. *Denison*, 346
—— Judgment in *Martin* v. *Mackonochie*, 361

KEBLE, Rev. John, author of the Oxford Movement, 12
—— his sermon on *National Apostasy*, 22
—— tries to prosecute Dr. Hampden, 72-77
—— on the Reformers, 111
—— on *Catholic Subscription*, 172-176

LANGLEY, Rev. W. H., suspended for Brawling in his own Church, 235, 236
Lavington Case, The, 381-387
Lay Address to the Queen, 332-334
—— Royal action on the, 334
—— to the Archbishop of Canterbury, 335
Lecky, Mr., on the Evangelical Movement, 6, 7
Leeds, St. Saviour's, 262-264, 284-287
—— the Rev. Richard Ward and, 285, 286
—— Hook terms it "a semi-Papal colony," 286
—— traitorous resolution by clergymen at, 321

Leeds, St. Saviour's, Confessional inquiry at, 321-325
—— scandalous *Statement* by the clergy of, 323-325
—— secessions to Rome from, 325
Library of the Fathers, 90, 133
Lichfield Theological College, 388
Liddell v. *Westerton*, 253, 264, 357-361
Liddell, Dean, 53
Liddon, Canon, on the Evangelical Movement, 3, 7
—— and Cuddesdon Theological College, 391, 392
Littledale, Rev. Dr., on the Protestant and Catholic Religions, 8
—— on Prayer Book revision, 409, 410
Lushington, Dr., 307, 343, 358
Lyne, Mr. Francis, 44

MACLAGAN, Archbishop, on Episcopal prosecutions, 143
Macmullen, Rev. R. G., 65, 66
—— secedes to Rome, 284, 285, 287
Mai, Cardinal, 193, 195
Manning, Archdeacon, on the real tendency of Puseyism, 286
Marriott, Rev. Charles, demands the prosecution of Rev. J. Garbett, 250, 305
—— on Clerical Retreats, 282
Marshall, Nathaniel, D.D., his *Penitential Discipline of the Primitive Church*, 281
Martin v. *Mackonochie*, 361
Maskell, Rev. W., letters on Pusey's Confessional practice, 309-312
Maurice, Rev. Peter, on *Popery in Oxford*, 101, 102
Metropolitan Church Union, 326, 327
Monk, Bishop, censures *Tract XC.*, 178
Moresby Faculty Case, The, 130, 131
Mozley, Rev. J. B., 34, 89, 114, 238, 239
—— his *Review of the Baptismal Controversy*, 303
Mozley, Rev. Thomas, 54, 63, 91, 110
Musgrave, Bishop, censures *Tract XC.*, 178

NEALE, Rev. J. M., and Sackville College, 290-292
—— the Rev. John Scobell's charges against the, 363-374
—— sly and cowardly Confessional practice of the, 363-374
—— Bishop Gilbert's stern censure of the, 365, 366

Neale, Rev. J. M., sad condition of young lady penitent of the, 371, 372
Newman, Mr. F. W., 15, 16, 24, 55
Newman, Rev. J. H., was he ever an Evangelical? 13
—— on Scripture, tradition, and private judgment, 10, 11, 14
—— on Rome as Babylon and Antichrist, 14, 15
—— on the First Prayer Book of Edward VI., 16
—— on the essence of sectarian doctrine, 9
—— *Lectures on Popular Protestantism* quoted, 11
—— on the need for a second Reformation, 16
—— his secret interview with Wiseman at Rome, 18-21
—— its effect upon Wiseman, 19, 20
—— on Church and State, 25
—— on subscription to the Thirty-Nine Articles, 47, 48
—— his *Elucidations of Dr. Hampden's Statements*, 53-57
—— on the worship of images, 104
—— and *Tract XC.* 147-168
—— withdraws his censures of the Church of Rome, 168, 169
—— "not to be trusted," 239
—— his secession to Rome, 256-258
—— his visit to Rome, 259-262
—— when was he ordained a Roman Catholic priest? 259-262

OAKELEY, Rev. Frederick, 138-146
—— at Margaret Chapel, 138-141
—— on the work he did there, 138, 139
—— claims the right to hold all Roman doctrine, 140, 142
—— prosecution and deprivation of, 141-145
—— on his idea of a loyal Churchman's work, 146
—— his secession to Rome, 146
Oxford, Alarming state of the Diocese of, 393-404
Oxford Martyrs' Memorial, 109-113
—— Pusey objects to it as "unkind to the Church of Rome," 110
Oxford Movement, The, its founders not sound Protestants, 12
—— was it born in Oxford or Rome? 22
—— the Rev. William Palmer's narrative of its birth, 29
Oxford Protestant Magazine, 111, 112
Overton, Canon, 89

INDEX

Overton, Canon, on the difference between Evangelical Churchmen and Puritans, 3

PALMER, Rev. William (of Magdalen College) anathematises Protestantism, 183
Palmer, Rev. William (of Worcester College), 19
—— his *Narrative of Events* quoted, 240, 241
Papal Aggression, the, 314-317, 332, 333
Parker Society, the, 224, 225
Percival, Hon. and Rev. A. P., 9, 32
—— defends the *Tracts for the Times*, 171, 172
Phillpotts, Bishop, denounces the Episcopal Veto, 77
—— censures *Tract XC.*, 178
—— orders the use of the surplice in the pulpit, 248
—— withdraws his order, 248
—— and the Exeter Surplice Riots, 269, 270
—— prosecutes the Rev. W. G. Parks Smith, 288, 299
—— and the Gorham Case, 292-303
—— threatens to excommunicate the Archbishop of Canterbury, 300
—— Goode's reply to, 301
Piers, Rev. Octavius, prosecuted for "publicly praying in an unconsecrated place," 271, 272
Pius IX., his opinion of Dr. Pusey and his work, 245, 308
—— secret and traitorous message from founders of A.P.U.C. to, 356
Poetry Professorship at Oxford, The, contest for, 212-217
—— Pusey's indiscreet interference with, 214, 215
Pollen, Rev. J. H., 321
Poole, Rev. Alfred, the Confessional case against the, 374-380
Pope, the, Oxford Tractarians wish to be "in active communion" with, 187
Prayer Book revision, 138, 409
—— Dr. Littledale advocates, 409, 410
Prayers for the Dead, 125-131
Proby, Rev. W. H. B., on the Evangelical Movement, 5
Protestantism, anathematised by Rev. W. Palmer, 183
Purchas, Rev. John, 387, 388
Puritans, The, difference between and Evangelical Churchmen, 3
Pusey, Rev. Dr., 40, 41, 42
—— joins the Oxford Movement, 41

Pusey, Rev. Dr., tries to prosecute Dr. Hampden, 72-77
—— his early Protestantism, 87, 88
—— founds a Theological Society, 88, 89
—— his pamphlet on *Tendencies to Romanism*, 119-125
—— his Protestant notes on Auricular Confession, 133-135
—— on the basis of Union with Rome, 144, 145
—— his double dealing about Purgatory and Invocation of Saints, 145
—— his sermon on *The Holy Eucharist a Comfort to the Penitent*, 226-234
—— suspended by the University of Oxford, 230
—— rejects Transubstantiation, 228
—— his veracity challenged, 230-232
—— challenges a prosecution, 233
—— Bishop Bagot says it was not "a straightforward proceeding," 233
—— his quotations from the Fathers, 234
—— his "Adapted" Roman books, 241-245
—— extracts from these books, 242-244
—— Pope Pius IX.'s opinion of, 245, 308
—— thinks God is "drawing" Newman to Rome, 256
—— his remarkable correspondence with Bishop Wilberforce, 265-268
—— his sermon on *Entire Absolution of the Penitent*, 277-279
—— Dean Boyle on the effect of Pusey's Confessional work, 280
—— Dr. Hook says that he is under Jesuit influence, 268
—— Hook charges him with Jesuitism, 285
—— will do everything for Roman Catholics, 287
—— exposure by Allies, Dodsworth, and Maskell of the Confessional practices of, 309-313
—— Bishop Wilberforce inhibits, 314
—— Professor Jowett prosecuted by, 417, 418
—— in praise of ecclesiastical prosecutions, 418

RANDALL, Dean R. W., and the Lavington Case, 381-387
Reformation, The, and Justification by Faith, 1, 2
Reformers, Dean Church on, 111
—— Lord Blachford on, 111
—— Rev. Thomas Mozley on, 110

INDEX

Reformers, The, Keble on, 111
Reserve in Communicating Religious Knowledge, 34, 132
—— Extracts from, 213
—— Bishop Wilberforce on, 216, 217
Restoration of Churches, The, Dr. Close on, 254, 255
Rickards, Rev. S., 35
Rivington, Rev. Luke, 48
Robinson Wright v. *Tugwell*, 248
Romeward Movement, The, Newman's subtle plan for promoting it, 115–117
—— secret negotiations with Romanists to promote the, 184–200, 352–357
Rose, Rev. H. J., 148
Russell, Lord John, on the Hampden Case, 67–69
—— the Oxford Movement distrusted by, 314
—— the Durham Letter by, 315
Russell, Rev. J. F., 88

SACKVILLE COLLEGE, East Grinstead, 290–292
Salisbury (Bishop of) v. *Williams*, 413
Scobell, Rev. John, case of, against the Rev. J. M. Neale, 363–374
Secret negotiations with Romanists, 184–201, 352–357
Selborne, Earl of, on the Evangelical Movement, 5
—— on the Fathers, 91
Seventh Commandment, The, questioning women on, defended by Puseyites, 324, 325, 378, 379
Shaftesbury, Earl of, on the Evangelical Movement, 5
Shore, Rev. James, case of the, 273–276
Shrewsbury, Lord, 195
Smith, Rev. W. G. Parks, prosecuted by Bishop Phillpotts, 288, 289
Society of the Holy Cross, its secret birth, 349
Solicitors' Journal, on Prayers for the Dead, 128
Spörlein, Pastor, scandalous and traitorous advice to, 117, 118
St. Barnabas', Pimlico, 340
St. George's in the East, Riots and Disturbances at, 405–409
St. Margaret's, East Grinstead, 363–374
Starkey, Rev. Samuel, prosecution of, for "publicly praying in an unconsecrated place," 271, 272
Startling and Treacherous Proposal, A, 187–194
—— particulars sent to Rome, 192–196
Stone Altars, condemned as illegal, 252, 253, 359

Stone Altars, in the Diocese of Oxford, 394, 397, 401
Stuart, Rev. Edward, says we are not to "go direct to God," 10
—— refuses to obey his Bishop, 361, 362
Sumner, Archbishop, on Non-Episcopal Orders, 23
Sumner, Bishop, suspicious application to, 281, 282
Surplice in the Pulpit, The, Bishop Phillpotts orders its use, 248
—— withdraws his order, 248
—— disturbances at Exeter, 268, 269
Symons, Rev. Dr., Dr. Pusey's opposition to, 249
—— Dr. Hook refuses to vote against, 250
—— failure of the attack on, 250

Tablet, The, on Newman's ordination as a priest, 260
Tait, Archbishop, on *Tract XC.*, 154
—— on the Judicial Committee of Privy Council, 331
—— a Declaration in favour of the Gorham Judgment signed by, 336
—— and the Rev. Alfred Poole's Case, 374–380
Taylor, Rev. Rowland (Martyr), 30
Theological College, A, founded by Dr. Pusey, 88, 89
Theological Colleges, 388–392
Thirty-Nine Articles, The, Newman on subscription to the, 47, 48
—— Keble on *Catholic Subscription* to, 172–176
Tracts for the Times, 24, 31, 34, 35, 38, 135, 167, 171, 172
—— names of the writers of the, 40
—— extracts from, 137–139
—— Mr. John Adolphus, Q.C., on, 44
—— Dr. Hook on, 106
—— Bishop Bagot on, 107, 108
Tract XC., 147–168
—— list of pamphlets on, 147–149, *note*
—— Newman's object in writing, 149
—— extracts from, 150–152
—— Romanists delighted at the publication of, 152
—— letter of the Four Tutors on, 152, 153
—— Dr. Arnold on, 154
—— resolution of the Heads of Houses on, 155
—— how their decision was arrived at, 156
—— Roman Catholic comment on, 164–166
—— Bishop Bagot and, 166–168, 222

Tract XC., Pusey's defence of, 176, 177
—— Manning's opinion of, 177
—— Episcopal condemnations of, 178, 179
Tucker, Rev. J., 398, 399

WAKEMAN, Mr. H. O. on the Evangelical Movement, 4, 8
Ward, Rev. Richard, and St. Saviour's, Leeds, 285, 286
Ward, Mr. Wilfrid, 159, 188
Ward, Rev. W. G., The, 182, 248
—— the treasonable letter of, to the *Univers*, 160-164
—— defends *Tract XC.*, 170, 171
—— double dealing in the Church of England by, 199
—— on deception, 220
—— list of pamphlets on the case of, 248, 249, *note*
Wells Theological College, 388
West v. *Shuttleworth*, 127
White, Rev. Blanco, his early warning to Newman, 16
Wilberforce, Bishop Samuel, and the Hampden case, 55-57, 65, 72-77
—— on the perils from Puseyism, 239, 240
—— and the Rev. T. W. Allies, 304-308

Wilberforce, Bishop Samuel, on Pusey's "Adapted" Roman books, 242
—— his remarkable correspondence with Pusey, 265-268
—— Dr. Pusey inhibited by, 314
—— and Cuddesdon Theological College, 389-392
—— and the State of the Diocese of Oxford, 393-404
Williams, Rev. Isaac, 29
—— his contest for the Poetry Professorship at Oxford, 212-217
—— extracts from his *Reserve in Communicating Religious Knowledge*, 213
Wiseman, Cardinal, his secret interview with Newman and Froude in Rome, 18-21, 261
—— its powerful effect on his after life, 19, 20
—— on Froude's *Remains*, 20, 104
—— on *Tract XC.*, 165
—— visits the Tractarian leaders at Oxford, 191, 192
—— secret negotiations with the Romanisers by, 191
Wright, Rev. Dr. William, 387

YORKSHIRE CHURCH UNION, The, Hook refuses to join, 330

THE END